Herb Gardening For Dummies®

Cheat Sheet

Low-Growing Herbs for Small Places

Do you have a small space, some nook where you can create a garden of low-growing herbs? You probably want plants that are small and don't spread like wildfire. Each of the following herbs is small (none taller than 10 inches), and they all have pretty flowers:

- **Corsican mint** *(Mentha requienii):* Tiny pale purple flowers in summer.
- **Dittany of Crete** *(Ocimum dictamnus):* Small flowers with large, pink bracts.
- **Feverfew** *(Tanacetum parthenium):* 'Golden Moss' is a dwarf cultivar.
- **Lavender cotton** *(Santolina chamaecyparissus* var. *nana):* The smallest of the santolinas, with bright yellow flowers.
- **Roman chamomile** *(Chamaemelum nobile):* Small, yellow and white, daisy-like flowers.
- **Saffron** *(Crocus sativus):* Lilac flowers in autumn.
- **Thyme** *(Thymus* spp.*):* Look for red-flowering thyme, *T. serpyllum* var. *coccineus,* and *T. serpyllum* 'Rainbow Falls.' They have colorful flowers *and* foliage.
- **Violet** *(Viola* spp.*):* Try purple, yellow, and white Johnny-jump up, *V. tricolor,* or Labrador violet, *V. labradorica,* which has purple-tinged leaves and lavender-blue blooms.
- **Wall germander** *(Teucrium chamedrys):* Purple-pink blossoms.
- **Yarrow** *(Achillea* spp.*):* Choose among woolly yarrow, *A. tomentosa* 'Primrose Beauty', which has pale yellow blossoms; Greek yarrow, *A. ageratifolia,* with white flowers and silver foliage; and Siberian yarrow, *A. siberica*, with its gray leaves and white flowers.

Dangerous Herbs

Here are some of the more common herbs to be wary of, including a couple that can "worke eternal sleepe."

- **Aconite** *(Aconitum napellus):* This herb, also known as monkshood and wolfsbane, deserves a skull-and-crossbones; it's highly poisonous.
- **Aloe** *(Aloe barbadensis):* Juice from these stems is great for minor burns, but never use it internally.
- **Comfrey** *(Symphytum officinale):* Laboratory research indicates that comfrey, even in low concentrations, is carcinogenic in rats.
- **Deadly nightshade** *(Atropa belladonna):* In folklore, a favorite ingredient of witches' brews. The common name says it all.
- **Foxglove** *(Digitalis purpurea):* The source of a powerful heart medication, floxglove can cause convulsions and even death if used improperly.
- **Hellebore:** Both American false hellebore *(Veratrum viride)* and black hellebore *(Helleborus niger)* are dangerous characters; they are major-league skin irritants and can be fatal if ingested.
- **Hemlock** *(Contium maculatum):* Think nausea, paralysis, and death.
- **Pokeweed** *(Phytolacca* spp.): All parts of mature plants, including their pretty purple berries, are toxic.
- **Wormwood** *(Artemisia absinthium):* Absinthe (as a drink) has been banned worldwide.

For Dummies™: Bestselling Book Series for Beginners

Herb Gardening For Dummies®

Cheat Sheet

Scents and Sensibility: Herbs for Fragrance

The term "fragrant herbs" may be redundant, for we can't think of a scentless herb. But there are fragrances and there are fragrances. Some gardeners love the scent of rosemary, for example, and others are less enthralled. Here are herbs whose leaves and/or flowers keep us olfactorily ahhhing and ohhhing.

- **Bee balm** (*Monarda didyma*)
- **Calamint** (*Calamintha nepeta*)
- **Catmint** (*Nepeta faassenii*)
- **Curry plant** (*Helichrysum italicum*)
- **Garlic chives** (*Allium tuberosum*)
- **Lavender cotton** (*Santolina chamaecyparissus*)
- **Lemon balm** (*Melissa officinalis*)
- **Patchouli** (*Pogostemon cablin*)
- **Rose** (*Rosa spp.*)
- **Southernwood** (*Artemisia abrotanum*)

The Herbal First-Aid Kit: Plants to Make You Feel Better

We're not suggesting you toss your traditional first-aid kit, but why not supplement it by creating a small garden stocked with plants that heal? These herbs belong in any backyard pharmacy.

- **Aloe** (*Aloe vera*): For burns
- **Chamomile** (*Matricaria recutita, Chamaemelum nobile*): To relax
- **Calendula** (*Calendula officinalis*): For cuts and scrapes
- **Feverfew** (*Chrysanthemum parthenium*): For migraines
- **Garlic** (*Allium sativum*): To protect the heart
- **Ginger** (*Zingiver officinale*): For motion sickness
- **Lavender** (*Lavandula spp*): For stress
- **Lemon balm** (*Melissa officinalis*): For fever
- **Mint** (*Mentha spp*): For digestion, upset stomach
- **Valerian** (*Valeriana officinalis*): For pain

Tea Time: Ten Herbs for Brewing

If you're growing herbs, it's only proper that your cup of tea be herbal, either herbs alone or tea brewed with herbs. Here are the first ten herbs we'd put in our tea garden:

- **Anise hyssop** (*Agastache foeniculum*)
- **Bee balm** (*Monarda didyma*)
- **Catnip** (*Nepeta cataria*)
- **Chamomile** (*Chamaemelum nobile* and *Matricaria recutita*)
- **Costmary** (*Chrysanthemum balsamita*)
- **Geranium** (*Pelargonium* spp.)
- **Lemon balm** (*Melissa officinalis*)
- **Lemon verbena** (*Aloysia triphylla*)
- **Mint** (*Mentha piperita* and *Mentha* 'Hillary's Sweet Lemon')
- **Sweet cicely** (*Myrrhis odorata*)

The IDG Books Worldwide logo is a registered trademark under exclusive license to IDG Books Worldwide, Inc., from International Data Group, Inc. The ...For Dummies logo and For Dummies are trademarks of IDG Books Worldwide, Inc. All other trademarks are the property of their respective owners.

For Dummies™: Bestselling Book Series for Beginners

Herb Gardening FOR DUMMIES®

by Karan Davis Cutler and Kathleen Fisher

&

the Editors of the
National Gardening Association

IDG Books Worldwide, Inc.
An International Data Group Company

Foster City, CA ◆ Chicago, IL ◆ Indianapolis, IN ◆ New York, NY

Herb Gardening For Dummies®

Published by
IDG Books Worldwide, Inc.
An International Data Group Company
919 E. Hillsdale Blvd.
Suite 400
Foster City, CA 94404
www.idgbooks.com (IDG Books Worldwide Web site)
www.dummies.com (Dummies Press Web site)

Library of Congress Catalog Card No.: 99–67175

ISBN: 0-7645-5200-7

Printed in the United States of America

10 9 8 7 6 5 4 3 2 1

1B/RS/QR/QQ/IN

Distributed in the United States by IDG Books Worldwide, Inc.

Distributed by CDG Books Canada Inc. for Canada; by Transworld Publishers Limited in the United Kingdom; by IDG Norge Books for Norway; by IDG Sweden Books for Sweden; by IDG Books Australia Publishing Corporation Pty. Ltd. for Australia and New Zealand; by TransQuest Publishers Pte Ltd. for Singapore, Malaysia, Thailand, Indonesia, and Hong Kong; by Gotop Information Inc. for Taiwan; by ICG Muse, Inc. for Japan; by Intersoft for South Africa; by Eyrolles for France; by International Thomson Publishing for Germany, Austria and Switzerland; by Distribuidora Cuspide for Argentina; by LR International for Brazil; by Galileo Libros for Chile; by Ediciones ZETA S.C.R. Ltda. for Peru; by WS Computer Publishing Corporation, Inc., for the Philippines; by Contemporanea de Ediciones for Venezuela; by Express Computer Distributors for the Caribbean and West Indies; by Micronesia Media Distributor, Inc. for Micronesia; by Chips Computadoras S.A. de C.V. for Mexico; by Editorial Norma de Panama S.A. for Panama; by American Bookshops for Finland.

For general information on IDG Books Worldwide's books in the U.S., please call our Consumer Customer Service department at 800-762-2974. For reseller information, including discounts and premium sales, please call our Reseller Customer Service department at 800-434-3422.

For information on where to purchase IDG Books Worldwide's books outside the U.S., please contact our International Sales department at 317-596-5530 or fax 317-572-4002.

For consumer information on foreign language translations, please contact our Customer Service department at 1-800-434-3422, fax 317-572-4002, or e-mail rights@idgbooks.com.

For information on licensing foreign or domestic rights, please phone +1-650-653-7098.

For sales inquiries and special prices for bulk quantities, please contact our Sales department at 800-762-2974 or write to the address above.

For information on using IDG Books Worldwide's books in the classroom or for ordering examination copies, please contact our Educational Sales department at 800-434-2086 or fax 317-572-4005.

For press review copies, author interviews, or other publicity information, please contact our Public Relations department at 650-653-7000 or fax 650-653-7500.

For authorization to photocopy items for corporate, personal, or educational use, please contact Copyright Clearance Center, 222 Rosewood Drive, Danvers, MA 01923, or fax 978-750-4470.

About the Authors

Karan Davis Cutler: A former magazine editor and newspaper columnist, Karan Davis Cutler is the author of seven other garden books. She publishes regularly in horticultural magazines and is an eight-time winner of the Quill & Trowel Award from the Garden Writers Association of America.

Kathleen Fisher: Kathleen Fisher is former editor of *The American Gardener,* published by the American Horticultural Society. A longtime newspaper reporter, she is now working on her fourth gardening book as a free-lance writer and editor.

National Gardening Association: The National Gardening Association is the largest member-based, nonprofit organization of home gardeners in the United States. Founded in 1972 (as "Gardens for All") to spearhead the community garden movement, today's NGA is best known for its bimonthly publication, *National Gardening* magazine. Reporting on all aspects of home gardening, each issue is read by some half-million gardeners worldwide.

For more information about the National Gardening Association or its magazine, write to 180 Flynn Ave., Burlington, VT 05401, USA. Send e-mail to nga@garden.org, or visit the Web site at www.garden.org.

ABOUT IDG BOOKS WORLDWIDE

Welcome to the world of IDG Books Worldwide.

IDG Books Worldwide, Inc., is a subsidiary of International Data Group, the world's largest publisher of computer-related information and the leading global provider of information services on information technology. IDG was founded more than 30 years ago by Patrick J. McGovern and now employs more than 9,000 people worldwide. IDG publishes more than 290 computer publications in over 75 countries. More than 90 million people read one or more IDG publications each month.

Launched in 1990, IDG Books Worldwide is today the #1 publisher of best-selling computer books in the United States. We are proud to have received eight awards from the Computer Press Association in recognition of editorial excellence and three from Computer Currents' First Annual Readers' Choice Awards. Our best-selling ...*For Dummies*® series has more than 50 million copies in print with translations in 31 languages. IDG Books Worldwide, through a joint venture with IDG's Hi-Tech Beijing, became the first U.S. publisher to publish a computer book in the People's Republic of China. In record time, IDG Books Worldwide has become the first choice for millions of readers around the world who want to learn how to better manage their businesses.

Our mission is simple: Every one of our books is designed to bring extra value and skill-building instructions to the reader. Our books are written by experts who understand and care about our readers. The knowledge base of our editorial staff comes from years of experience in publishing, education, and journalism — experience we use to produce books to carry us into the new millennium. In short, we care about books, so we attract the best people. We devote special attention to details such as audience, interior design, use of icons, and illustrations. And because we use an efficient process of authoring, editing, and desktop publishing our books electronically, we can spend more time ensuring superior content and less time on the technicalities of making books.

You can count on our commitment to deliver high-quality books at competitive prices on topics you want to read about. At IDG Books Worldwide, we continue in the IDG tradition of delivering quality for more than 30 years. You'll find no better book on a subject than one from IDG Books Worldwide.

John Kilcullen
Chairman and CEO
IDG Books Worldwide, Inc.

Steven Berkowitz
President and Publisher
IDG Books Worldwide, Inc.

Eighth Annual Computer Press Awards ≥1992

Ninth Annual Computer Press Awards ≥1993

Tenth Annual Computer Press Awards ≥1994

Eleventh Annual Computer Press Awards ≥1995

Dedication

To my mother and father, loving parents who were the first to point me down the garden path. — Karan

To my late parents: Herb (of course), who taught me the importance of compost and the joys of fresh-picked tomatoes; and Ruby, who made sure I always had plenty of books and forgave me when I scribbled on them with my crayons. — Kathleen

Authors' Acknowledgments

We've depended greatly on the kindness of many (herb-growing) strangers — and friends. For specific help, we are especially indebted to Gwen Barclay; Hank Becker, Agricultural Research Service; Kathy Bond Borie, National Gardening Association; Rosalind Creasy; Barbara Ellis; David Ellis, American Horticultural Society; Donald M. Maynard, University of Florida; Patsy Jamieson; Susan Romanoff, Gardener's Supply; and Holly Shimizu, Lewis Ginter Botanical Garden. We'd also like to express our gratitude to IDG Books senior project editor Tim Gallan for putting up with not one but two strong-minded gardeners; and to copy editor Patricia Yuu Pan for her perceptive comments and queries.

Publisher's Acknowledgments

We're proud of this book; please register your comments through our IDG Books Worldwide Online Registration Form located at http://my2cents.dummies.com.

Some of the people who helped bring this book to market include the following:

Acquisitions, Editorial, and Media Development

Senior Project Editor: Tim Gallan

Acquisitions Editor: Holly McGuire

Copy Editor: Patricia Yuu Pan

Technical Editor: Holly Shimizu

Editorial Coordinator: Jill Alexander

Editorial Manager: Pam Mourouzis

Editorial Assistant: Carol Strickland

Production

Project Coordinator: E. Shawn Aylsworth

Layout and Graphics: Amy Adrian, Barry Offringa, Tracy Oliver, Jill Piscitelli, Brent Savage, Michael A. Sullivan, Brian Torwelle, Dan Whetstine, Erin Zeltner

Proofreaders: Laura Albert, Marianne Santy, Corey Bowen, Ethel M. Winslow

Indexer: Anne Leach

Special Help
Amanda Foxworth, Joan Friedman

Cover Photography
PhotoBotanic by Saxon Holt

General and Administrative

IDG Books Worldwide, Inc.: John Kilcullen, CEO; Steven Berkowitz, President and Publisher

IDG Books Technology Publishing Group: Richard Swadley, Senior Vice President and Publisher; Walter Bruce III, Vice President and Associate Publisher; Joseph Wikert, Associate Publisher; Mary Bednarek, Branded Product Development Director; Mary Corder, Editorial Director; Barry Pruett, Publishing Manager; Michelle Baxter, Publishing Manager

IDG Books Consumer Publishing Group: Roland Elgey, Senior Vice President and Publisher; Kathleen A. Welton, Vice President and Publisher; Kevin Thornton, Acquisitions Manager; Kristin A. Cocks, Editorial Director

IDG Books Internet Publishing Group: Brenda McLaughlin, Senior Vice President and Publisher; Diane Graves Steele, Vice President and Associate Publisher; Sofia Marchant, Online Marketing Manager

IDG Books Production for Dummies Press: Debbie Stailey, Associate Director of Production; Cindy L. Phipps, Manager of Project Coordination, Production Proofreading, and Indexing; Tony Augsburger, Manager of Prepress, Reprints, and Systems; Laura Carpenter, Production Control Manager; Shelley Lea, Supervisor of Graphics and Design; Debbie J. Gates, Production Systems Specialist; Robert Springer, Supervisor of Proofreading; Kathie Schutte, Production Supervisor

Dummies Packaging and Book Design: Patty Page, Manager, Promotions Marketing

◆

The publisher would like to give special thanks to Patrick J. McGovern, without whom this book would not have been possible.

◆

Contents at a Glance

Cartoons at a Glance

By Rich Tennant

page 31

page 59

page 7

page 105

page 329

page 207

page 289

Fax: 978-546-7747

E-mail: richtennant@the5thwave.com

World Wide Web: www.the5thwave.com

Table of Contents

Introduction

*T*he introduction is most unread section of any book. And we know that you'll do just fine if you never read this one. You'll still be able to produce a 10-foot row of Italian parsley from seed and keep bee balm coming up every spring. You'll be able to grow enough basil to provide all your neighbors with pesto, and you'll learn how to dry lemon verbena so you can brew a cup of tea in winter, long after the garden season has ended. You'll know what to do if leafminers attack your lovage. Or rather, *when* leafminers attack your lovage, since it's almost inevitable that they will. And you'll discover how to improve your soil and which garden tools are *really* necessary.

Since this introduction is optional, we'll make it as short as we can. After all, you've already decided you want to grow herbs. We don't have to convince you to take that first step, but permit us to applaud your good sense. To paraphrase a chapter title from *Gardening For Dummies,* growing things makes life better. That goes two times double for growing herbs, plants that make our lives more beautiful, more tasty, more fragrant, more comfortable, and more healthy. And more interesting.

About 25 years ago, we also took that first step and began growing herbs. Here's why:

- ✔ **Double the pleasure.** Perhaps more than any other group of plants, herbs are equally ornamental and practical, beautiful and useful. Most are lovely as garden plants — there's no better blue flower than borage's, no more fascinating foliage than santolina's. And then herbs have second lives to offer the gardeners who grow them — as flavorings, bouquets, scents, medicinals, beauty aids, dyes, repellents, and more.

- ✔ **Freshness.** If you've substituted dried herbs for fresh, you know there's a real difference between leaves plucked from the garden and what's in the bottles on your spice rack. The produce sections of supermarkets continue to get better and better, but it's still unusual to find more than a half-dozen culinary herbs. Fresh herbs are available to most of you only if you grow them yourselves.

- ✔ **Safety.** As a group, herbs are less likely to have been sprayed with pesticides than vegetables or fruits, because they're more resistant to diseases and insects. All the same, growing your own cilantro and horehound is the best way to ensure that they haven't been treated with toxic chemicals and are safe to handle — to use in the kitchen or to add to the medicine chest.

✔ **Choice.** Go to a local nursery and you won't find pennyroyal (to ward off mosquitoes) or lady's bedstraw (to make a sleep pillow). Those herbs and scores of others, especially those used in medicines and crafts, simply aren't sold as live plants. Even culinary herbs can be hard to locate, especially unusual cultivars. Plants of 'Crispa' spearmint, which has round curled leaves, and 'Lockwood' rosemary, a trailing type that is perfect in a window box, won't be on the shelves of your garden center. For anything out of the ordinary, you're going to have to order seeds by mail and grow them yourself.

✔ **The lure of lore.** Growing herbs not only makes you familiar with the culture of specific plants, it introduces you to the huge and sometimes downright wacky world of herb lore (for example, horseradish to treat worms in children, marjoram to fortify the nerves, sage to make women fertile). Most remedies should be taken with a grain of salt — and a good number shouldn't be taken at all! But what fun to know that parsley grows better for a wicked gardener than a virtuous one. That's something you'll want to point out to an overconfident friend who is raising an especially fine crop.

✔ **Comrades of the spade.** As much as we love growing herbs, we think the best thing about starting an herb garden is that it inevitably leads you to other gardeners. They're a wonderful bunch, welcoming, generous, and enthusiastic. In 1735, the Englishman Peter Collinson wrote a to Virginian with whom he exchanged seeds and plants: "I think there is no Greater pleasure than to be Communicative and oblige others . . . Wee Brothers of the Spade find it very necessary to share. . . ." Wee Sisters do, too.

How to Use This Book

We've crammed much of what we know about growing herbs between these yellow covers. Each chapter was written primarily for beginners, readers who have never owned a spade and don't know the difference between an annual and a perennial. At the same time, we hope that what we have to say also will interest intermediate, even experienced gardeners. Growing herbs is a huge subject — there are hundreds and hundreds of books on the topic — and there's always something new to learn. No one, including us, knows it all.

Just as you don't have to read this introduction, you don't have to read every word of *Herb Gardening For Dummies* — or read Chapter 4 before you read Chapter 5. We've tried to begin at the beginning — or at least where we think it may be most helpful for a novice herb gardener to start — but you're free to skip around. Go straight to topics that you want to know about, or want to know more about. If you're interested only in culinary herbs, we won't be put out if you ignore the instructions for herbal soaps.

At the same time, we're pretty sure that once you catch the herb bug, you'll want to know more about everything. You'll want to remember that dill's scientific name is *Anethum graveolens,* and that it's a member of the carrot family, and even that it once was prescribed as a cure for hiccups. You'll certainly want to know when to sow its seeds (which are so slow to sprout that tradition has it they travel to the Devil and back seven times before they germinate), and what kind of soil is needed to produce healthy plants.

We're even confident that once you've grown parsley, you'll want to know about growing and using lemongrass, wormwood, and dozens of other herbs. So in whatever order you read this book, we hope that eventually you'll read it all, and that we've provided enough advice and encouragement to get your herb garden off to a great start. We hope, too, that growing herbs will lead you to vegetables, fruits, flowers, shrubs, vines, and trees. Remember, growing things makes life better.

We give you some tips on herbal remedies — how herbs can be used to treat some medical conditions. Note, however, that the information in this book is not intended to replace expert medical advice or treatment. Please be sure to see a professional health-care provider before beginning any health program.

How This Book Is Organized

This book has seven logically organized parts, and each part contains related chapters.

Part I: Herb Basics

Before you start pulling packets off a seed rack or loading a flat with young plants, you need to know what you're buying. Part I covers the nitty-gritty of how and where herbs grow, how they were used in the past, and how we use them today.

Part II: Down to Earth

Where you grow herbs is every bit as important as how you grow herbs. This part deals with locale, beginning with the whole of North America and ending in your yard. We also demystify soil, so you'll know what you're digging in and how to make it better.

Part III: The Best-Laid Plans

One of the first — and most creative — steps in growing herbs is deciding how to make them part of your home landscape. Whether yours is a two-acre plot or a two-foot rooftop planter, you need to plan. Follow our suggestions and designs verbatim, modify them to fit your needs, or come up with your own ideas.

Part IV: An Encyclopedia of Herbs

Part IV is an alphabetic encyclopedia of more than 65 herbs, agrimony to yarrow. It's the biggest and most important section of the book, the place where you'll find specific information about how to plant, grow, preserve, and use herbs.

Part V: Weed 'Em and Reap

Time to get down and dirty. This part contains the basic advice and special tricks that guarantee you can turn a tiny basil seed into a lush, healthy plant. It explains how to harvest your herbs, how to propagate new plants, and how to get ready for next year. Put on your garden duds: It's time to turn your thumb green!

Part VI: Cut and Dried: Handling the Herbal Bounty

You're ready for the payoff — your harvest. In Part VI, we reveal everything you need to know about using and preserving the herbs you've grown. Whether you want to make herb vinegar or a potpourri, to brew a medicinal tea or weave an herbal wreath, the information to get you started is in this section.

Part VII: The Part of Tens

No dinner is complete without dessert, and no ...*For Dummies* book is complete without its part of tens. Our lists answer the most-asked questions about herbs and presents our recommendations for filling a garden shed.

Icons Used in This Book

Warns you of potential trouble — be it herbs that are dangerous to you or things that are dangerous to your herbs.

Shows ways you can make your garden Earth-friendly.

Flags special techniques and shortcuts that make gardening easier, now or later.

Points out how to avoid common mistakes.

Helps you sound like a seasoned gardener.

Designates folk beliefs about herbs — which may or may not be true.

Part I
Herb Basics

The 5th Wave   By Rich Tennant

"I used to get fewer instructions when I looked after these people's children."

In this part . . .

Want to grow herbs, eh? The range of herb gardeners is enormous, from Saturday-night-only cooks content to grow one basil plant to spice up their frozen pizza to devotees who tend row after row of medicinal plants and believe that the common cold and nearly every other ailment under the sun can be cured by drinking vats of lemon verbena tea. We suspect you'll end up somewhere in the middle of these extremes, as we have. The problem with something new, as always, is where to begin?

In Part I, we open the door to the fascinating, sometimes zany realm of herbs. You'll get a handle on what makes an herb an herb — we provide the general rules and leave picking plants for your garden up to you. There's a bit of botany (answers to those "Where did it come from" questions), plus some thoughts about what's both safe and sensible to grow in an herb garden.

And we want you to know that growing herbs is a bit of fun. For instance, did you know that you should drink horehound tea, hot from the fire, if you are poisoned by your stepmother? And if you place a sprig of rosemary under your bed, "Thou shalt be delivered of all evil dreams."

Chapter 1

For Meate and Medicine: How We Use Herbs

*G*ardeners love kindred souls, and when it comes to herbs, there are plenty of kindred souls, now and in the past. Today, when it seems that a synthetic form of everything is available, the interest in growing and using herbs remains keen. Herbnet.com, one of the hundreds of Web sites that focus on the subject, receives more than 10 million hits every month. (A *hit,* in case your interest in herbs is greater than your interest in computers, is an electronic visit by someone using a computer.)

This chapter is a potpourri of herb information — our effort to introduce you to the subject, especially some of its historical and entertaining aspects. First, though, there is the prickly question of how to pronounce the word "herb." If you want to sound exceeeeeedingly British, it's *h*erb, with the "h" sounded; if you believe the American Revolution was a fine thing, it's "erb." No "h."

As for the importance of the subject, more than a few herbs deserve a place on everyone's plants-that-changed-the-world list. Meadowsweet *(Filipendula ulmaria),* from which acetylsalicylic acid, or aspirin, was derived in 1899, would come near the top of that enumeration. Other candidates? Quinine *(Cinchona* spp.), the original drug to cure malaria; opium poppy *(Papaver somniferum),* the world's most important painkiller; foxglove *(Digitalis lanata),* one of the first heart medicines; and hemp *(Cannabis sativa),* which has kept people tied up in knots — or when smoked, has freed them from time and space. And coca *(Erythroxylum coca),* the plant responsible for Coke, Pepsi, and the nickel return on aluminum cans.

We've only begun to discover the power of plants to enrich and improve our lives. Many more species will be added to the plants-that-changed-the-world list if we are wise enough to protect them and their habitats.

What Makes an Herb an Herb?

If it's true that in the beginning was the word, we need to start with the word "herb." It's not simple to tell you what an herb is, as every encyclopedia, dictionary, and garden book has a definition to promote. Many experts define an herb as an *herbaceous plant* (a plant that forms a soft, tender stem rather than a woody stem), but that definition leaves out many plants, including rosemary, a charter member of the culinary herb hall of fame. And it would include plants like daffodils, which aren't on anyone's herb list.

Herbs are also defined as "useful plants," but hundreds of plants are useful, such as corn and oats, that few of us would call herbs. Others define herbs as "plants grown for medicinal qualities and for seasoning foods," but that definition leaves out dye plants, plants used in rituals, and for making cosmetics, crafts, and more.

The Herb Society of America follows the "big-tent" philosophy and defines herbs as plants valued for their "flavor, fragrance, medicinal and healthful qualities, economic and industrial uses, pesticidal properties, and coloring materials." If it's good enough for the HSA, it's good enough for us — and broad enough. So if you've planted something that tastes or smells good (or bad), cures what ails you, or can be used in some way, feel free to call it an herb. You won't get an argument from us.

As for this book, we focus on some of the most common and popular herbs for their flavor, their medicinal qualities, and for other purposes. Most of the names will be familiar, even if you haven't sown a single seed.

Culinary herbs

The best-known herbs today are those that we use in the kitchen to flavor and color food and drink. If that weren't enough, many are good for you, too. According to the U.S. Department of Agriculture, a teaspoon of dill seed contains 32 mg calcium; a teaspoon of ground basil contains 6 mg magnesium. The healthful-herb champ is the chili pepper: One teaspoon of chili powder contains potassium sodium, ascorbic acid (vitamin C), niacin, and vitamin A. If you substitute chili powder for your multivitamin, we recommend taking each teaspoon with a gallon of milk (to offset the heat of the chili).

Spice is another name for a culinary herb. Purists use the word "herb" when they refer to plants grown for their leaves and stems; spice plants are those cultivated for their flowers, seeds, bark, wood, resin, and roots. You also may come across the word *potherb.* That's an old term that refers to vegetables and herbs used in salads, soups, and stews.

Medicinal herbs

Plants and medicines have been partners as far back as history reaches, although different cultures have had different approaches to herbal remedies. Many Eastern cultures, for example, traditionally view illness as a sign of cosmic disharmony; herbal cures are calculated to restore balance, to create peace between the opposing principles of *yin* and *yang,* rather than treat specific problems.

The European herbal medicine tradition has been less holistic, although there have been comprehensive approaches. The ancient Greeks, for example, viewed life in terms of four universal elements: earth, air, fire, and water; and the four bodily *humors:* sanguine, phlegmatic, choleric, and melancholic (hot, cold, moist, and dry, respectively). "Hot" and "dry" herbs were prescribed for "cold" and "moist" ailments, and vice versa. Astronomy, too, has played a role in herbal medicine, and old herbals are filled with references to herbs "owned by Venus" or "under the dominion of the moon."

Whether their approach was systematic or eclectic, people have prescribed herbs for every condition known to humankind: boils and burns, coughs and constipation, drunkenness and dog bites, fevers and fits, giddiness and gout, heartaches and hiccups, impotence and indigestion, nightmares and nerves, snoring and sneezing, worms and wounds.

Even if you're skeptical about the power of fennel to cure "every kind of poison in a man's body" — the claim in one 13th-century herbal — there's no question that plants are rich with substances that can ease and cure diseases, even prevent them. Early physicians called herbs *simples,* meaning that each herb was a simple, or single, medicine, not a compound. In fact, most herbs contain more than one chemical compound — nearly 1,500 have been isolated to date.

Herbs for other purposes

In addition to their ties to the pantry and medicine chest, herbs have an ancient connection to rites and myths. The lotus *(Nelumbo nucifera)* was sacred to Isis, the Egyptian goddess of fertility; white roses *(Rosa damascena)* and madonna lilies *(Lilium candidum)* represent the Virgin Mary; Greek athletes were awarded wreaths of bay *(Laurus nobilis)*. In Chapter 13, we introduce some of the other ways herbs are used, such as to dye, to create wreaths and bouquets, and to make perfumes, cosmetics, bug repellants, cleaning compounds, and more.

The woolly leaved mullein (shown in Figure 1-1), has been prescribed for scores of ailments — everything from toothaches, coughs, and "fluxes of the body" to warts, colic, and "stiff sinews."

Figure 1-1:
Woolly
leaved
mullein.

Mullein is a good example of the "other purposes" an herb can have. For example, people first coated mullein stalks with suet or pitch and used them as torches more than 2,000 years ago. Mullein has been used in sorcery to light midnight covens (and to guard against witches). American colonists made dyes from its roots and flowers, and stuffed its leaves in their mattresses (and in their shoes to keep their feet warm). Children have turned its leaves into doll blankets, and adults (and more than a few adolescents) have smoked them in place of tobacco.

Women once rubbed mullein leaves on their cheeks, a homegrown substitute for rouge. Mullein decoctions were used to kill worms in livestock, and its honey-scented flowers have flavored drinks and perfumed rooms. Plants were also used as weather predictors: If the blooms cluster at the top of the stalk, a late winter with heavy snow is certain. Flowers thrown into the hearth fire protect a house against storms.

What's a Wort? Plant Names

Plant names are one of the special pleasures of gardening. Who wouldn't want to grow a marmalade bush, maybe next to a bread-tree and just down from a chocolate vine? Herbs, among the first plants to be cultivated, have some of the most evocative common names: starflower, little faces, midsummer men, church steeples, lad's love, bible-leaf, maiden's ruin, horseheal, queen of the meadow, love parsley, Greek hay, fairy clock, stinking rose, coughwort. The list goes on and on. . . .

And what's a *wort?* It's an archaic word for "plant." You see it attached to other words, usually nouns that tell something about what people believed the plant did or how it looked. Lungwort cured lung ailments, spiderwort healed the bites of spiders, and feverwort brought down fevers. Bellwort has bell-shaped flowers, ragwort has ragged foliage, and we don't have to tell you how spoonwort's leaves are shaped. When it comes to herbs, Romeo, there's plenty in a name.

Being common

The problem with common names is that the same name is often used for more than one plant. Starflower, for example, is one name for borage, but it's also the informal name for a native California wildflower and 60 of its cousins, for a group of more than 150 different perennials that grow from *corms,* a bulblike underground stem, and for a clan of 70 evergreen shrubs from Australia. And don't confuse starflower with starwort, which is one name for our native fall-blooming aster. (You guessed it — the shape of the aster flower reminded people of stars.)

What's more, a plant may have many common names. The future King of England is Charles Phillip Arthur George, but that's a numerical nothing compared with southernwood. It's a shrublike perennial that repels flies, fleas, and moths (and once was prescribed as a cure for pimples, worms, baldness, cramps, convulsions, and as "an antidote against all poisons"). When called, southernwood also answers to lad's love, boy's love, old-man, old man's tree, mugwort, sagebrush, and wormwood.

The common names of herbs are great fun, and each has a story — even the ubiquitous dandelion. Its name comes from both Latin *(dens leonis)* and French *(dent de lion).* Each alludes to the plant's serrated leaves, which supposedly resemble the teeth in a lion's mouth — giving rise to another common name for the plant, lion's tooth. But there's more. The dandelion is called earth nail in China, because of its long root. In France, the dandelion is known as *pissenlit,* which highlights its diuretic effect. Tradition holds that anyone who even picks dandelions will wet the bed. Hence, another common

English name for the dandelion, pissabed. Other names? Blowball and pull-ball, after its fluffy seed head; and priest's crown and monk's head, allusions to the flower head after its seeds have blown away.

Being scientific

Over the centuries, a string of prominent scientists has tried to clear up all the cognomen confusion, but it took Swedish naturalist Carolus Linnaeus (1707-1778) to get everyone using the same system to group and name plants. Achieving agreement wasn't easy, especially as some conservatives were scandalized by Linnaeus's views on plant sexuality, but the general rules were established in 1753. (Linnaeus exacted his revenge by naming several noxious weeds after his critics.)

Although the *scientific names* (also referred to as *Latin names, botanical names,* and *Latin binomials*) of plants sometimes change as scientists make new discoveries about plants, the two-word (or *binomial*) system is always the rule. This section shows you how *nomenclature,* or scientific naming, works.

Every plant has at least two names: a *genus name* (a genus is a collection of similar plants, a *genera* is more than one genus), and a *species name*, a descriptive name for a distinct group within the genus. (The word species is both singular and plural; there's no such thing as *specie,* unless you're talking money.) For example, the genus name for all the violetlike plants that grow in the wild — there are more than 500 — is *Viola.* The common violet is one type, or species, of *Viola;* its species name is *odorata.* So the common violet's scientific name is *Viola odorata.* When written, scientific names are set in italics or underlined, and the genus name is capitalized.

Think you don't need the scientific name? Depending on where you live (or when), *Viola odorata* may not be called violet but little faces, sweet violet, garden violet, and English violet — not to be confused with *Viola tricolor,* which is also known as violet in some parts of the world, but also as pansy, battlefield flower, bird's-eye, Johnny-jump-up, lady's-delight, heartsease, none-so-pretty . . . whew! You get the idea.

Scientific names may look and sound foreign to you, but they are descriptive and often provide clues about a plant: *Odorata* means "sweet" or "fragrant," so any plant with a form of odorata in its species name — such as sweet woodruff, *Galium odoratum* — is fragrant.

Different plants can have the same species name — there's *Althaea officinalis, Borago officinalis, Rosmarinus officinalis, Saponaria officinalis, Valeriana officinalis,* and *Verbena officinalis,* to name only a few. Once you become familiar with some of these terms (*officinalis* means "has medicinal uses"), you'll know something about the herb just from its name.

In addition to their genus and species names, many herbs have a third, *cultivar* name (the word derives from "cultivated variety"). The cultivar name is not italicized or underlined but is capitalized and placed in single quotation marks (for example, *Viola odorata* 'Royal Robe'). A *cultivar* is a plant produced not by Mother Nature but by plant breeders and gardeners *in cultivation*. The plant should be different from or better than the species and other cultivars. 'Royal Robe', for the record, has gorgeous deep violet blooms and flowers in spring and again in autumn.

You often see the word *variety* used interchangeably with *cultivar.* In fact, the two are different things: A cultivar is intentionally bred or selected, whereas a variety is a naturally occurring form that is different from the species. Varieties are designated by the abbreviation "var." For example, rosemary, which has blue flowers, is *Rosmarinus officinalis;* the naturally occurring white-flowered rosemary is *Rosmarinus officinalis* var. *albiflorus.*

We admit that all these distinctions are pretty picky, and that scientific names are a mouthful. Pronouncing them doesn't come easy. We'll let you in on two secrets: First, plant names are horticultural Latin, not classical Latin. And second, no one really knows how the Romans sounded when they spoke. Whether you pronounce *Petroselinum* (the botanical name for parsley) Petroh-seh-LINE-um or Petroh-seh-LEEN-um isn't all that important. Knowing exactly what plant you're seeing or buying *is* all that important.

Remembering scientific names doesn't come easy, either. Don't despair. The longer you garden, the more names you'll recognize and remember.

Sage . . . Is Said to Render Men Immortal

As the saying goes, "Never let the facts get in the way of a good story." Herbs come bearing as many stories as they do names — and many of the tales have nothing to do with the facts. But they're wonderful fun, evocative connections with people and events in other places and other times. Knowing about them makes growing and using herbs a richer experience.

Absolutely every herb is laden with reputed associations and powers. Yarrow, for example, has been cultivated for at least 5,000 years. Most plant-name scholars believe it gets its genus name *Achillea* from Achilles, the warrior hero of *The Iliad*. Achilles, according to one version of the Greek myth, used yarrow during the Trojan War to treat the wounds of Telephus, the son of Hercules. (This myth also leads to the plant's common names, such as bloodwort, soldier's woundwort, staunchgrass, and knight's milfoil.)

Yarrow is also associated with seeing into the future. According to British folklore, a woman could discover who her husband would be if she picked yarrow leaves in a churchyard and recited this verse:

> *Yarrow, sweet yarrow, the first that I have found,*
>
> *In the name of sweet Jesus I pluck thee from the ground;*
>
> *As Joseph loved Mary, and took her for his dear,*
>
> *So in a dream this night, my love will appear.*

Other examples of the folklore surrounding herbs? Here are just a few:

- ✔ Sorrel turns red in autumn (and its leaves turn toward graveyards) in honor of the blood spilled by Irish soldiers more than 1,000 years ago.

- ✔ Prometheus used a fennel stalk as the torch when he stole fire from the gods and brought it to earth.

- ✔ Diana, goddess of the hunt, was so enraged that one of her nymphs didn't come to her defense that she turned her into the violet.

- ✔ Rosemary, according to Christian legends, never grows taller than six feet, which was Christ's height.

- ✔ In a Peruvian legend, the nasturtium sprang up from a sack of gold ripped from the hands of thieving Spaniards by the god of the mountains.

- ✔ Garlic sprang from Satan's left footprint when he left the Garden of Eden.

- ✔ The white rose was born of Venus's tears, crying over the slain Adonis. Red roses are the result of Cupid's spilling a cup of wine.

Virtues of delight

If the legends and tales about herbs are numerous, their reputed *virtues,* or powers, are super-numerous — and often supernatural. Herbs can protect against devils and witches, predict the future, make people fall in love, take away sadness, and instill bravery. Herbs can also bring good luck, as anyone who finds a four-leaf clover knows.

Take a look at these other "virtuous" examples:

- ✔ Placing rosemary leaves under your pillow prevents nightmares.

- ✔ To see ghosts, wear lavender.

- ✔ Pick wild chervil and you'll break your mother's heart.

- ✔ A sprig of bay protects against being struck by lightning.

> ✔ Sniffing basil breeds scorpions in the brain.
>
> ✔ A hedge of rue keeps out witches, but rue left at the church will curse a marriage.

Read All About It

The best sources of herb folklore and traditional cures are *herbals,* books containing descriptions and uses of plants. The oldest surviving herbals date back 2,000 years. Most were written by physicians (but also by astrologers and alchemists) and combined botany, natural history, horticulture, cooking, medicine, myth, magic — and mistakes. These are some of the names you'll encounter when reading about herbs:

- ✔ **Dioscorides.** The Greek physician (1st century A.D.) whose writing *(De Materia Medica)* was influential into the 1700s.

- ✔ **Galen.** The 2nd-century Greek physician who codified existing medical knowledge and popularized the theory of humors.

- ✔ **William Turner.** The 16th-century author of the first "scientific" English herbal, *New Herball.*

- ✔ **John Gerard.** Herbalist-gardener author of the most famous and important of all herbals, *Herball or General Historie of Plants* (1597).

- ✔ **John Parkinson.** English gardener and author of the enormous *Theatrum Botanicum* (1640), which describes more than 4,000 plants.

- ✔ **Nicholas Culpeper.** An English astrologer-physician and author of the influential *English Physician,* an early version of home medical reference that has been a strong seller ever since it was published in 1652.

You don't need to live near the British Museum or the Vatican to have access to ancient herbals, as most have been reprinted in inexpensive editions available at bookstores or libraries. You must take that proverbial grain of salt when you delve into their pages. These are the texts, after all, that include illustrated descriptions of the fanciful goose tree. (John Gerard was among those who insisted it was real: "I have seene with mine eies, and handled with mine hands.")

In case you haven't seen one with your "eies," the goose tree is covered with shells in which, Gerard wrote, "are contained little living creatures." If the creatures fell into water, they became birds, "bigger than a Mallard, and lesser than a Goose." If all this weren't zany enough, 16th-century clerics argued over whether or not tree geese were fowl or vegetable, which affected whether or not they could be eaten during Lent, a period of penance and fasting for some Christians.

Sign in, please

You can't read about herbs without running into a reference to the *Doctrine of Signatures.* It was a theory popularized in the 16th century by a Swiss alchemist, physician, and herbalist who wrote under the name Paracelsus. (See the accompanying figure.) The Doctrine of Signatures claimed that plants had *signatures,* or visible qualities, that indicated which ailments they could cure.

Because lettuce contained a milky sap, for example, it was recommended for mothers who were having problems nursing their babies. Herbs with heart-shaped leaves were prescribed for heart ailments (including those that were romantic in nature). Garlic, which has a hollow stem, was said to cure obstructions of the windpipe, and hanging mosses were believed to be antidotes to baldness. Herbs with spotted leaves were prescribed for lung diseases, while those with thorns were recommended for removing splinters. Herbs with yellow flowers were remedies for jaundice. Presumably, herbs with multi-colored leaves or flowers can cure aging surfers still addicted to Hawaiian shirts.

Chapter 2

Herbs 101

· ·

In This Chapter

▶ Understanding the basics of botany

▶ Exploring plant sex

▶ Knowing about invasive and toxic herbs

▶ Finding out about endangered herbs and wildcrafting

· ·

*W*e're going to cover a little science in this chapter. This isn't a return to school, though, and we aren't defining terms and describing processes just to show off. Everything has a practical application in the garden. If you purchase an herb described as "prostrate," you need to know that it crawls along the ground and and isn't a good choice for the back of the border.

And one other point. The information in this chapter applies to all plants, not just herbs. Once you start growing herbs and discover what fun gardening is, you're going to start planting flowers, vegetables, and fruits. These basics also will be helpful then, we promise.

Herb Talk

The first thing to keep in mind is that herbs have different life cycles. You need to know that herbs can be:

✔ **Annuals.** These plants burn their candle at both ends: They germinate, flower, set seeds, and die in one growing season. No matter where you live, you have to plant basil, borage, calendula, summer savory, and other annuals every year.

✔ **Biennials.** Biennials live for two growing seasons — germinating and forming leaves in the first year, then flowering, setting seeds, and dying in the second. Some biennial herbs, such as parsley, are usually treated as if they were annuals and harvested in their first year. Biennials grown for their flowers or seeds, such as angelica and caraway, need a second season in your garden.

✔ **Perennials.** Perennials, such as anise hyssop, mint, monarda, and sweet woodruff, are plants that live for at least three seasons. Horseradish and a few others will probably outlive you.

Perennials are either *herbaceous* — plants such as lovage, whose stems and leaves die back in winter, then resprout from the roots in spring — or *woody.* All woody plants, including shrubs, vines, and trees, are perennial. However, if a gardener tells you she grows perennials, she invariably means the herbaceous kind.

Just because a plant is a perennial doesn't mean that you can stick it in your garden and forget it. Some "tender" perennials, such as bay, can't stand prolonged freezing temperatures; leave them outdoors in autumn and in spring you'll have a bare spot where they once grew. In contrast, *hardy perennials,* tough guys like comfrey and barberry, will be there in spring. USDA Hardiness Zone ratings are an attempt to give gardeners a fair idea of how much cold a plant can tolerate without dying. See Chapter 3 for more information about hardiness zones.

Don't try to memorize all this now — just keep in mind that all herbs don't grow the same way in all locations. Herbs that are hardy in southern Texas may not survive in northern Montana. Knowing the difference between a tender and a hardy perennial can save you from some expensive and time-consuming mistakes. End of lesson.

Herb Anatomy

With herb anatomy, we explore leaves, stems, and flowers. When you have all three — and a little luck — you also have a living plant.

The root of the matter

Forgetting about the bottom half of a plant is easy. Out of sight, out of mind. Yet roots are as important as the plant parts you see aboveground. Roots anchor the plant in the soil. They take in water and minerals through osmosis, store them, and push them up to the herb's aboveground anatomy.

Most herbs have either fibrous roots or a taproot:

✔ **Fibrous roots** are fine and highly branched; herbs with fibrous roots are more susceptible to droughts because these roots grow closer to the soil surface. Plants with fibrous roots are easier to transplant and divide.

✔ **Taproots** are long and tapering with a few small side roots, or hairs. Usually thick and fleshy, taproots store moisture and stretch deep into the soil. Plants with taproots can withstand temporary droughts but are less easy to transplant and cannot be divided.

Stem dandy

Stems not only hold up the leaves and flowers, they carry water and nutrients to them from the roots. Only a few herbs — flax is one — are grown primarily for their stems, although the stems of many species are used in cooking and medicines.

When gardening books, including this one, tell you to cut below or above a *node*, they're referring to the places along a stem where leaves are attached. The clear spaces between nodes are called *internodes;* without enough light the internodes stretch more than usual, producing tall, spindly plants that gardeners term *leggy.*

Leaf it be

The leaf, as science teachers like to say, is like a factory. This part of the plant captures light, and through the process called *photosynthesis* uses the solar energy to produce food. Anyone with an herb garden ends up being keen about leaves, as many of the most popular herbs have only small flowers. Herb gardens can be beautiful, nevertheless, because leaves come in all sorts of sizes, colors, textures, and shapes. (See Chapter 6 for more on this topic.)

Each leaf variation (and there are scores) has its own name, but you can grow bee balm successfully for 50 years without knowing that its leaves are "simple, usually serrate," or have great luck with geraniums without calling their leaves "alternate, palmate or pinnate, simple or compound, usually lobed."

We won't pretend that we remember the difference between mucronate and aristate leaf tips, but we can tell you that knowing some common terms will help you make sense of entries in plant encyclopedias. You'll also be better able to identify herbs whose labels you've lost and understand other gardeners' descriptions. Following are a few of the most general leaf terms — ones that you will encounter so often that you'll want to remember them:

- ✔ **Deciduous.** Plants with leaves that die in winter and are replaced by new leaves in spring.

- ✔ **Evergreen.** An everyday term for plants that retain leaves throughout the year.

- ✔ **Simple.** A single leaf, like mint's. (See Figure 2-1.)

- ✔ **Compound.** A leaf that is made of several leaves, or *leaflets,* like those of chervil, which is also shown in Figure 2-1.

- ✔ **Blade.** The flat part of the leaf.

- ✔ **Margin.** The leaf's edge.

- ✔ **Lobed.** A leaf, like most geraniums', that has deep cuts.

✓ **Serration.** Leaf margins that are jagged, like most mints'. (A leaf without serration, such as that of orrisroot, has *entire* margins.)

Figure 2-1:
Simple and
compound
leaves.

How the stems and leaves are put together on a plant accounts for its *growth habit*. Knowing an herb's growth habit is necessary if you're to pick the right plant for the location you have in mind. If you're looking for herbs to cover that steep, unmowable strip on one side of your backyard, look for the words *mat-forming, prostrate, cushion-forming, groundcover,* and *mound-forming*.

Erect plants grow upward. Some shoot straight up, rigidly vertical and often with few side stems, like bee balm. Others with more branched stems tend to sprawl. *Climbing* (or *scandent*) plants want to grow even farther upward.

Sex and the Single Herb

Flowers qualify for plain brown wrappers because they are all about *sex*. Botanists may call flowers "modified shoots," but the rest of us know that most are wanton characters who use their good looks to advertise their sole purpose in life: reproduction.

A last note on flowers. You're going to come across the word *bract* (that's botany talk for the modified leaves that circle the base of a blossom). In most flowers, they are small, green or brown, and pretty nondescript. In a few plants, such as bee balm, they are large, colorful, and look like flower petals.

Shaping up

The ancient Greeks were talking about atoms when they wrote about "the symmetry of their shapes and sizes and positions and order," but they could have been describing the wonderful shapes, sizes, and arrangements of flowers. You'd guess that a *single,* or *solitary,* is one flower on one stalk, but flowers also come in *clusters,* or *inflorescences.* In fact, most herbs produce flower clusters rather than singles.

Gardeners describe flowers both in terms of the individual blooms and the way those blooms are arranged. Knowing the basic terms for these inflorescences (see the accompanying figure) helps you to choose the flower shape you want. And when other gardeners start talking blossoms, it won't be all Greek to you.

✔ **Composite.** A daisylike flower, such as the sunflower, that looks like a single but actually consists of a center made up of scores of tiny, tightly packed disc flowers surrounded by a ring of ray flowers (rays are the flower parts we pick off while reciting, "He loves me, He loves me not.").

✔ **Panicle.** An open, loosely branched cluster of flowers on a branched stem. Southernwood and sweet woodruff have panicled flowers.

✔ **Raceme.** A cluster of flowers attached to a single, upright stem with short, individual stalks, such as those of sage and comfrey.

✔ **Spike.** An upright stem of flowers like those of agrimony and hyssop, which have little or no stalk and attach directly or almost directly to the stem.

✔ **Umbel.** An umbrellalike structure, with each flower stalk emerging from the same place at the top of the stem. Dill and lovage have umbel inflorescences (see the figure).

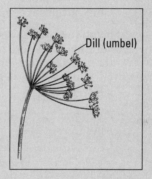

Dill (umbel)

The birds and the bees

Flowers — they have sex on the brain. Their function on earth, at least from their point of view, is to produce the next generation. To do that, the pollen on the male *stamen* has to get to the *pistil,* the female part of a blossom. The trip is quick if the plant has *perfect flowers,* blooms that contain both male and female parts (horticultural housemates, so to speak).

Plants with *imperfect flowers* have blossoms that are either male or female. Some imperfect plants have both male and female flowers on the same plant (called *monoecious,* which means "one house"); some have male flowers on one plant and female flowers on another *(dioecious,* or "two houses"). Here's where the birds and the bees (and other insects and the wind) come in: They are essential for getting pollen from one flower to another.

To produce seeds or fruits, *fertilization* or *pollination* has to occur. These are the possibilities:

- ✔ If a plant with perfect flowers, such as nasturtium, keeps to itself, it's known as *self-pollination.*

- ✔ *Cross-pollination* occurs when the pollen from a flower on one plant fertilizes a flower on another plant.

Plants with imperfect flowers must cross-pollinate, but many perfect flowers also cross-pollinate — it's Mother Nature's way of keeping plants genetically vigorous and healthy.

Why is all this important to you?

- ✔ If you want plants to produce flowers and fruits and are planting a dioecious species, you need both a male and female plant.

- ✔ If you're using row covers to protect plants from pests or the cold and your herbs require cross-pollinating, you must remove the covers so that bees and other pollen-carrying insects can reach the flowers. Keep your pepper plants under wraps and you'll be buying chilies, not stringing your own.

- ✔ If you want to harvest seeds from your garden to plant next year, you want the seeds to *come true,* to produce plants exactly like those they came from. Many plants cross-breed with their cousins (different cultivars or varieties of the same species) as well as their siblings. If they do — as do sunflowers — the seeds they produce may provide some surprises.

The good news is that you don't have many pollination worries when you grow herbs. Most have perfect flowers and either self- or cross-pollinate with ease.

One last bit of sex talk. Many of the herbs you grow will be *species* — plants straight from Mother Nature.

Now enters the *hybrid.* Usually developed in cultivation, in someone's garden or laboratory, a hybrid is the product of crossing two distinctly different species, varieties, or cultivars. A cross between two different species should contain an × before the species name, such as *Mentha* × *piperita,* which is the scientific way of saying peppermint.

The actual crossing and recrossing and cross crossing and double crossing gets complicated, and it doesn't take long before the identity of grandparents and parents is lost. Therefore, many hybrid cultivars are given just genus and cultivar names. *Pelargonium* 'Lady Plymouth', for example, is a eucalyptus-scented geranium with lavender-pink flowers and white-margined leaves. (Despite being a Lady, she has no idea who her father was.)

Producing hybrid seeds and plants is time-consuming and an expensive business, so hybrids tend to cost a little more. Remember: Seeds from hybrid herbs don't come true. The parent plant may have pink flowers, but the children may be redheads.

Caution: Invasive Herbs Ahead

Although we're card-carrying, unrepentant herb appreciators, we need to tell you that all herbs aren't created equal, or equally nice, as you'll find out if you choose *invasive herbs* as companions for your genteel basil and ladylike rosemary. As the term suggests, an invasive plant is a botanical Attila the Hun. Draw a line in the sand and these bullies hop over it. When a garden seed catalog says a plant is "carefree," "vigorous," and "grows anywhere," be prepared for something that can scale a telephone pole faster than you can get rid of a telephone solicitor.

Rue the day

Climbing and clambering plants are especially notorious for exterminating everything in their path. There's a good reason why kudzu *(Pueraria lobata),* which the Chinese use to treat alcoholism, is known as "the vine that ate the South." It's shown in Figure 2-2. English ivy *(Hedera helix)* and wild grape *(Vitis* spp.) are two more vigorous vines that are used medicinally — ivy for controlling skin problems, grape as a diuretic — but both may be prescriptions for trouble in your garden.

Figure 2-2:
Stay away
from kudzu.

The seed stops here

You can usually dig or pull invasive herbs that multiply by seeds more successfully than you can perennial climbers and crawlers. Just don't give the seeds time to get the upper hand.

Lay down a thick layer of mulch to discourage seeds from sprouting and to smother young plants. Pouring boiling water on seedlings is a lethal treatment, and you can kill some plants by repeatedly cutting off their tops.

Tilling is supposed to bury seeds, blocking the light they need to sprout. Not so! Churning the soil usually brings more seeds to the surface — where they will sprout — than it buries.

If you do nothing else, stop invasive plants from reseeding by picking their flowers as soon as they wilt. This tedious activity is known as *deadheading*. Get into the proper mood by wearing a tie-dyed shirt and playing a Jerry Garcia CD.

Most non-vining herbs make congenial neighbors for the other occupants of your garden, but not all. Turn your back on spearmint, and it will overwhelm the lettuce and lay siege to the parsley. For the record, English herbalist John Gerard observed that a mint root "creepeth aslope in the ground . . . and now and then in sundry places it buddeth out afresh." If he meant that you will quickly have enough mint to make a julep for everyone at the Kentucky Derby, Gerard was right on the money.

Set out a tidy clump of garlic chives, famous for its pungent flavor and power to ward off disease, and you'll discover that even two or three unpicked flower heads will give birth to hundreds of new plants. Come spring, your well-tended garden will look like scruffy lawn. Hoe down the grasslike stalks and they reappear, as dependable as the swallows that arrive each year at the San Juan Capistrano mission.

Invasive is as invasive does

Once an invasive takes hold in your yard, you might feel that a nationwide alert should go out; but, like politics, all gardening is local. Sweet marjoram is a weed in southern California, but it must be grown as an annual in areas where the mercury goes below 35°F. English ivy is a steroid case in the Southeast, but it must be pampered to survive in northern Vermont.

While the master list of universally incorrigible herbs is short, a list for your region may be much longer. To avoid catastrophe — years of swearing at yourself for planting that ~#@*! thing — find out which herbs may turn traitor. If you yearn to make a concoction that calls for an unabashed bully, don't plant more of it. Do the world a favor and harvest some from a friend's lawn or help a native plant society tidy up a park. Remember, you can make spring tonics and harvest greens without introducing dandelions to your garden. Consult other gardeners, local nurseries, and the local extension service about invasives. And if your neighbor brings you kudzu seedlings, find a nice way to say, "In a pig's eye."

Underground travelers

Some herbs, such as mint, travel by sending out rootlike stems, or *rhizomes*, that scoot just under the soil surface, sprouting new plants as they go. Scratching mint off your plant list won't make your garden an invasive-free zone, however. Other herbs overrun their neighbors by scattering seeds that sprout in the most awful conditions — such as the spaces between your patio stones — and without any help from you. Toss 100 basil seeds on the ground and you'll be buying, not making, pesto. But let one dandelion flower go to seed and you'll have enough plants to make wine for the Bowery Boys.

Be prepared to arm yourself as an "herban" guerilla if you plant any of the following:

- ✔ **Artemisia** *(Artemisia* spp.*)*. Gardening books advise dividing this herb to create more. But artemisia, famous for thriving in poor soil, multiplies so rapidly on its own that you'll need a calculator to add them up.

- ✔ **Comfrey** *(Symphytum officinale)*. Notice that *Symphytum* has the same root as the word sympathy. Trust us, you'll get neither sympathy nor comfort from comfrey when your plants multiply.

- ✔ **Costmary** *(Chrysanthemum balsamita)*. Costmary leaves traditionally were used as bookmarks, thus the herb's other common name, Bible leaf. The plant is rarely found in the wild, but in the garden it increases fast enough to supply bookmarks for the Library of Congress.

- ✔ **Fennel** *(Foeniculum vulgare)*. The seeds taste like anise, its leaves like dill. But watch out! Fennel has invaded farm fields in California and Virginia, where it is now officially *herbus non grata.*

- ✔ **German, or annual, chamomile** *(Matricaria recutita)*. This herb self-sows almost anywhere. In Boulder, Colorado, where Celestial Seasonings teas get poked into those little bags, chamomile sprouts in sidewalk cracks, a pleasant alternative to crab grass.

- ✔ **Herb-Robert** *(Geranium robertianum)*. Long associated with snakes, this plant slithers through the garden with ease, popping up where you least expect — or want — it.

- ✔ **Horseradish** *(Armoracia rusticana)*. You are likely to leave behind a few bits of root when you dig horseradish, and every bit will turn into a new plant. Once you have it, you have it.

Solitary confinement

No self-respecting herb garden is complete without spearmint or yarrow, but pulling, digging, or tilling these ground-spreaders may mean more plants, not fewer. To keep them from crowding out the carrots and zinnias, grow them in containers, either aboveground or sunk in the garden. For containers that you plan to bury (which should be at least 18 inches deep) cut away the bottom, and then set it so its lip is 2 inches *above* the soil surface.

- ✔ **St. John's wort** (*Hypericum perforatum*). St. John's wort is an herbal mood-lifter with a reputation for getting wildly out of hand in the garden. Keep an eye on it, or you could end up depressed.

- ✔ **Tansy** (*Tanacetum vulgare*). Tansy can repel flies, ants, and other insects, and it can be a pest in its own right.

- ✔ **Violet** (*Viola odorata*). Shrinking violets? Don't believe it. One day you have a demure clump of violets, the next week there are enough plants to open a flower shop.

- ✔ **Yarrow** (*Achillea* spp.). Multiplying without help may be okay for a plant that reputedly heals bruises, burns, wounds, and sores; conditions oily hair; *and* looks great in dried arrangements.

Danger Ahead

Herbs have been associated with curses every bit as long as they have been associated with cures. The 16th-century English poet Edmund Spenser wrote of the power of herbs, pointing out that they could "worke eternal sleepe."

If you have small children — or big children or even no children — you need to be aware that a good number of herbs are toxic. Their effects range from irritating skin to causing death. When Socrates drank hemlock, he wasn't kidding around.

Here are some of the more common herbs to be wary of, including a couple that can "worke eternal sleepe."

- ✔ **Aconite** (*Aconitum napellus*). This herb, also known as monkshood and wolfsbane, deserves a skull-and-crossbones; it's highly poisonous.

- ✔ **Aloe** (*Aloe barbadensis*). Juice from these stems is great for minor burns, but never use it internally:

- ✔ **Wormwood** (*Artemisia absinthium*). Absinthe, as a drink, has been banned worldwide.

- ✔ **Deadly nightshade** *(Atropa belladonna)*. In folklore, this is a favorite ingredient of witches' brews. The common name says it all.

- ✔ **Hemlock** *(Contium maculatum)*. Think nausea, paralysis, and death.

- ✔ **Foxglove** *(Digitalis purpurea)*. The source of a powerful heart medication, floxglove can cause convulsions and even death if used improperly. It's shown in Figure 2-3.

- ✔ **Pokeweed** *(Phytolacca* spp. *)*. All parts of mature plants, including their pretty purple berries, are toxic.

- ✔ **Comfrey** *(Symphytum officinale)*. Laboratory research indicates comfrey, even in low concentrations, is carcinogenic in rats.

- ✔ **Hellebore.** Both American false hellebore *(Veratrum viride)* and black hellebore *(Helleborus niger)* are dangerous characters; they are major-league skin irritants and can be fatal if ingested.

Figure 2-3:
Danger!
Foxglove.

With herbs, it's downright stupid to imbibe first and ask questions later. Don't put any herb in your mouth without knowing what it is and what it does. If your skin is unusually sensitive, don't going rolling around in your herb garden. Above all, clearly label any dangerous herbs, and fence them to protect those who can't read.

The Wild Ones

Wildcrafting is the term for gathering herbs and other plants from the outdoors. This activity is so popular that many species are being threatened by overcollection. Irresponsible collectors who take plants for profit are only part of the problem. The other part is that familiar feeling that we all have when we see a stand of goldenseal or bloodroot: "Oh, it won't matter if I take just a few." Of course everyone else has the same feeling, so multiply "take a few" by 100 or 1,000 collectors and you see the problem.

Know the score before you go wildcrafting. Some herbs — dandelion and plantain *(Plantago major)* are preeminent examples — can be collected without a second thought about survival of the species. Other plants are problematic. Native orchids and lilies now grow in such small numbers that they should never be disturbed. Overcollection threatens goldenseal, *(Hydrastis canadensis)*, ginseng *(Panax quinquefolius)*, and several species of *Echinacaea*, our native coneflowers. And that's only a partial list.

Here are some other rules of the plant-collecting road:

✔ **Get permission to harvest** (most public lands have regulations that you must follow when collecting plant material). Collect plants away from trails and roads. Be careful, too, that you don't damage the environment.

✔ **Be sure you're collecting what you think you're collecting.** Hemlock is highly toxic and looks like a half-dozen other benign herbs. You need an expert by your side or an illustrated handbook of native plants.

✔ **Collect only from large, healthy stands of plants.**

✔ **Never dig more than 5 percent (5 in 100) of any stand of plants.**

✔ **Collect seeds and avoid digging.** You can grow nearly all herbs from seeds, so rather than dig entire plants, collect their seeds. (Collect a bit from several plants, leaving behind at least three-fourths of the seeds.)

✔ **Don't harvest more than you can replant, sow, or use.**

Nearly all threatened herbs are available for sale from nurseries. Make sure the firm you patronize *propagates* its plants — grows them from seeds or cuttings — rather than digs them in the wild and puts them in pots. Seeds also are available for most endangered herbs.

Part II
Down to Earth

In this part . . .

Ground Zero is the focus of Part II; all the things you need to know so that you try growing cilantro and rosemary under the 200-year-old oak that grows in your backyard. We'll fill you in on regional peculiarities, hardiness zones, and the garden conditions that herbs require. And then we'll go underground to look at soil, show you how to evaluate the soil in your new garden site, and explain how you can improve on what Mother Nature gave you.

Chapter 3

Home Ground

- -

In This Chapter

▶ Understanding your climate and weather

▶ Getting to know plant regions and zones

▶ Looking at origins: natives and exotics

▶ Finding the best spot for your garden

- -

*L*ocation, location, location — words as important to gardeners as to real-estate agents looking for a quick sale. Gardeners in Honolulu never fear having a frost, while gardeners in Barrow, Alaska, can expect less than a week of frost-free days each year. It's a big country out there — and where you live affects what herbs you can grow, how you grow them, when you grow them, and how successful you're likely to be.

In addition to looking at the big picture — factors such as climate and topography — this chapter can help you assess your property and make sensible decisions about where your herbs can grow best. Now isn't the time for choosing between a kidney-shaped border crammed with medicinals or a four-square bed of kitchen herbs — it's time for the basics.

Weather to Be or Not to Be

Trust us, weather *will* be, and it will have much to do with your growing herbs successfully. You don't have to be a seasoned gardener to know that the backyards of Minneapolis, Minnesota, aren't filled with 50-foot coconut palms and lush banana trees — tropical plants can't survive winter in the far north. But do you know that sugar maples and birch trees won't survive in San Diego, Miami, or Houston? Heat limits what you can grow just as much as cold does.

Most of us are pretty casual about the words *climate* and *weather,* but the experts tell us they're not the same thing. Climate refers to prevailing, or average, conditions. Weather is what's happening right now in your backyard. New Hampshire has a cold climate, but the weather today in Nashua may be hot and humid.

Several factors influence your garden's climate:

- ✔ Latitude and elevation
- ✔ Lay of the land
- ✔ Direction that the wind blows

In general, the farther north of the equator you live, the colder and longer winter will be and the shorter your growing season. The latitude for Dallas is about 10 degrees south of Boston's. On average, gardeners in Dallas have almost 60 days more each year to garden than people in Boston do. That may not sound like much, but 60 days is long enough to produce enough dillweed to make gravlax (which is where all salmon could end their days if they can't make it back upstream).

But latitude is only part of the story. The higher up you live, the colder it will be in both winter and summer, and the shorter the growing season. The informal rule is that every 300 feet of elevation means 10 garden days lost. In fall and spring, those who live at low elevations get rain while those of you perched in the clouds are getting snow. These differences can occur only a few miles apart. It can be raining in Burlington, Vermont, but snowing like crazy in Stowe, a ski resort only 35 miles away.

Far north, head-in-the-clouds gardeners may have brief garden seasons, but most have the advantage of a winter-long snow cover. Snow is a great plant mulch, making it possible for some perennial herbs to survive in conditions far colder than they can without snow to protect them.

As a rule, winds in the United States blow west to east. Mountain ranges can block the wind currents that push our weather (or send it in unexpected directions). Live on the west side of the Cascade mountains, for example, and you'll get all the rain you need and then some. Move to the other side of that range, where rain is as rare as a dog that comes when it's called, and you'll need extra watering cans in your toolshed.

Large bodies of water also affect weather, typically by moderating it. If you're lucky enough to have an oceanfront address or live on the shore of a good-sized lake, your garden season probably will be two or three weeks longer than that of someone who lives a couple of hundred miles inland. And while your daytime temperatures in spring may be cooler, your chance of having nighttime frosts is reduced. Even small lakes can have these effects, but to a lesser degree.

The Grass Is Always Greener

Wishing for rain is pretty normal for Salt Lake City gardeners, and gardeners in Durango, Colorado, might be willing to trade their souls and 100 shares of

Amazon.com for just two more weeks of frost-free days. Even if someone else's region doesn't look better to you, it certainly looks different.

Fortunately for North American gardeners, some scientists study climate zones full time. One result of their work is the U.S. Department of Agriculture's Hardiness Zone Map. Check it out in Figure 3-1.

Developed to help gardeners account more precisely for regional differences, the zone map divides North America into 11 zones based on a range of average annual minimum temperatures. Zone 1 is the coldest (below –50°F) and Zone 11 the warmest (above 40°F). In 1990, the USDA revised the map by dividing each zone into two subzones (the *a* subzone is, on average, 5°F colder than he *b* subzone). Check out the Web site for the U.S. National Arboretum at www.ars-grin.gov/ars/Beltsville/na for a full-color version of the map.

How low do you go?

Garden authors cite zone ratings when they write about perennial plants. (You don't have to worry about hardiness zones with annuals, because they live only for one growing season.) You also see zone ratings given for perennials at nurseries and in plant catalogs. For example, rosemary usually is designated as a Zone 8 plant, which means you can grow it in your garden 12 months a year in Zones 8 and warmer, but it's unlikely to survive in Zones 7 and lower. If you want to keep your rosemary alive, you'll have to bring it inside in winter.

TIP

Strictly by the numbers

We know that our weather memories are notoriously bad, and we suspect yours are too. To a gardener, every dry summer seems like the driest ever, every early frost the earliest ever. Although climate and weather records are available for the major cities throughout North America, National Weather Service data may not exist for your location. Your Cooperative Extension Service or local airport may have some records, but the best weather records are those that you keep.

One of the most useful garden tools is a weather diary, a daily record of high and low temperatures and precipitation in *your* garden. You'll need several years of records before you can draw conclusions — for example, that the last frost of spring almost always comes in the second week May. But keeping records will make you weather-savvy, and being weather-savvy means making fewer mistakes in the garden.

If you ignore our advice about keeping a weather diary and still want to know how much rain fell last year, or when the first frost came, log on to the National Weather Service (www.nws.noaa.gov). For long-time climate records and trends, see if a nearby library has a copy of *Climates of the United States*. Scientists at the National Oceanic and Atmospheric Administration (NOAA) compiled this two-volume gold mine of facts from every state.

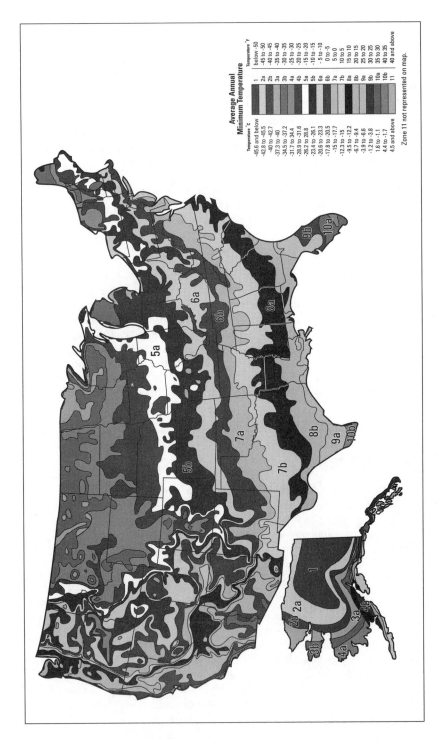

Figure 3-1: USDA plant hardiness zones for the United States. The map shows the extreme low teperatures that you can expect in an average winter.

We say rosemary is "usually is designated" Zone 8 because books, catalogs, and plant tags may differ on the zone ratings of individual plants. That difference of opinion is one reason why buying locally grown perennial herbs is a good idea — you know they'll be hardy.

But minimum temperatures are only part of the story.

How long can you go?

Except for gardeners living where the mercury never dips below freezing, most of us have a *growing season* — the time between the last and first frosts — that is far shorter than 365 days. As you might expect, gardeners who live in the North or at high elevations have the fewest days for growing herbs. The garden season in Fairbanks, Alaska, for example, is only 88 days long, while gardeners in Tampa, Florida, have more than 300 days to cultivate and gather herbs.

The last- and first-frost dates aren't guaranteed. Those dates are based on 50 percent probability, which means there is a 50 percent chance that frost will come *after* the spring date and *before* the autumn date. Put another way, if you set out basil seedlings on the frost-free date of March 19 in Birmingham, Alabama, you have a 50 percent chance that they'll be killed by a late frost.

When the dogwood flowers appear

Long before the NOAA (National Oceanic and Atmospheric Administration) became our weather guru, gardeners relied on natural signals, or *phenological signs*, to know when to plant and harvest. The term *phenology* comes from the Greek word *phaino*, meaning "to show or appear;" phenological signs are recurring events in the life cycles of plants and animals.

Natural signs adjust for variations in day length, temperature, rainfall, and more, which make them more reliable predictors than a single indicator like an average frost-free date. The first blooms of the pink lady slipper, which appear a week after the black flies arrive and just as the volunteer apple trees flower, are Karan's most trustworthy sign that all danger of frost has passed, and it's safe to set out basil and other tender herbs.

A worldwide phenological network of gardeners and scientists exists, but the best phenological data are those you collect in your garden, your microclimate. Record any natural event you like: the date that the bluebirds return; the first appearance of fireflies or mosquitoes; the first chamomile flowers. After you have several years of observations, the correlations jump out.

By the way, "When the dogwood flowers appear, / Frost will not again be here."

The length of your garden season affects how well some herbs will do for you — and how you should grow them. Even if your weather seems as hot as Hades, you may not be able to produce mature plants if you have a season shorter than 100 days. Most large-leaf basils, for example, take about three months to reach full size. If your growing season is very short, you should start seeds indoors. Even warm-weather gardeners may want to begin indoors: It gives anyone a head start.

How hot do you get?

The average temperatures during your growing season also influence your herb garden. You have only 119 days between the first and last frosts, if you live in Green Bay, Wisconsin, but your mean, or average, temperature in July and August is a relatively balmy 70°F. In contrast, gardeners in San Francisco have at least 307 growing days (in fact, they only have a killing frost one year out of 10), but in July and August the mean temperature is about 60°F. Many herbs don't grow in temperatures lower than 50°F (as the mercury rises, growth rates rise). Chile peppers have plenty of time to turn red in the "City by the Bay," but they may not have enough heat.

Lots and lots of heat, however, can be too much for some herbs to handle. Many plants like cool conditions, since lower temperatures make it easier to *respire,* the botanical version of breathing. Respiration rates double for every additional 16°F, so prolonged high heat means your cilantro has to pant. (In the Southeast, heat partners up with humidity, creating ideal conditions for many plant diseases to strike.) If you live in an area where every day is a scorcher, check with local gardeners about herbs that don't grow well for them.

Don't despair if you feel that all of this information seems to be getting way too complicated. Keep in mind that most of us live in a *temperate climate* — a climate that has distinct seasons and average temperatures above 60°F in summer and gets at least 30 inches of precipitation each year. That means that in summer, we can grow most herbs outdoors — in our gardens and on our decks, patios, or rooftops.

Who Grows There?

The study of what naturally grows in what region is called *plant geography.* North America's plant geography is amazingly diverse. Scientists have identi-fied more than a dozen different *floristic* (from *flora,* or plant) *regions.* There is everything from the arctic tundra of Alaska and northern Canada, with its grasses, lichens, and sedges, to the hot, arid deserts of the Southwest and the steamy tropical conditions of southern Florida and Hawaii. Plants in gar-dens there wilt at the very thought of frost.

Your address, please

Many herbs, such as members of the onion family, are native to more than one region, but here is a short list of herbal home addresses.

- ✔ **Africa.** *Aloe vera* (aloe), *Artemisia afra* (wild wormwood), *Coffea arabica* (coffee), *Gloriosa superba* (glory lily), *Ocimum* spp. (basil), *Pelargonium* spp. (scented geraniums), *Ricinus communis* (castor bean)

- ✔ **Australasia.** *Colocasia esculenta* (taro), *Eucalyptus* spp., *Melaleuca alternifolia* (tea tree), *Pandanus odoratissiums* (screw pine)

- ✔ **China.** *Artemisia annua* (sweet Annie), *Cinnamomum camphora* (camphor), *Ginkgo biloba*, *Panax ginseng*

- ✔ **Europe.** *Artemisia absinthium* (wormwood), *Borago officinalis* (borage), *Calendula officinalis* (pot marigold), *Chamaemelum nobile* (Roman chamomile), *Crocus sativus* (saffron), *Digitalis* spp. (foxglove), *Foeniculum vulgare* (fennel), *Humulus lupulus* (hops), *Laurus nobilis* (bay), *Lavandula* spp. (lavender), *Mentha* spp. (mint), *Origanum* spp. (oregano), *Petroselinum crispum* (parsley*)*, *Rosmarinus* spp. (rosemary), *Salvia officinalis* (sage), *Silybum marianum* (milk thistle), *Thymus* spp. (thyme), *Valeriana officinalis* (valerian)

- ✔ **Indian Subcontinent.** *Allium sativum* (garlic), Berberis spp. (barberry), *Cinnamomum zeylanicum* (cinnamon), *Elettaria cardamomum* (cardamom), *Piper nigrum* (pepper)

- ✔ **Middle East.** *Allium* spp. (onion, garlic), *Anethum graveolens* (dill), *Brassica* spp. (mustard), *Cannabis sativa* (hemp), *Carum carvi* (caraway), *Coriandum sativum* (coriander), *Cuminum cyminum* (cumin), *Papaver somniferum* (opium poppy), *Rosa damascena* (damask rose), *Trigonelia foenum-graecum* (fenugreek)

- ✔ **North America.** *Capsicum* spp. (chile peppers), *Echinacea* spp. (coneflower), *Eschscholzia californica* (California poppy), *Hamamelis virginiana* (witch hazel), *Helianthus* spp. (sunflower), *Hydrastis canadensis* (goldenseal), *Monarda* spp. (bee balm), *Panax quinquefolius* (American ginseng), *Passiflora* spp. (passion flower), *Sassafras albidum* (sassafras)

- ✔ **South and Central America.** *Capsium* spp. (chile peppers), *Cephaelis ipecacuanha* (ipecac), *Erhthroxylum coca* (coca), *Pimenta dioica* (allspice), *Tropaeolum* spp. (nasturtium), *Vanilla planiflolia* (vanilla)

- ✔ **Southeast Asia.** *Myristica fragrans* (nutmeg, mace), *Syzygium aromaticum* (clove)

Natives or *indigenous plants* are those that grew in North America before people from other parts of the world arrived on the continent. In contrast, *exotic species* (also called *exotics, non-natives,* and *introduced plants)* are floral immigrants, species brought to a location from other continents or regions. Which plants are here on green cards may surprise you. Dandelions are as common as flies at a picnic, but the dandelion isn't a native plant. It came to New England with the first settlers, who used its leaves in the stewpot and its roots to treat liver diseases. Like the colonists, it liked it here and made itself at home, or *naturalized.* Chicory, another familiar roadside flower, is also an exotic.

Flora who?

Flora, of flora and fauna fame, was a Roman fertility deity, the goddess of springtime flowering plants and "all that flourishes." Ancient Romans celebrated the festival of Floralia (April 28-May 1) into the 4th century. A licentious event, it featured obscene art, unclothed women, and casual sex.

In Greece, Flora was known as Chloris and was the consort of Zephyrus, the West Wind, who filled her garden with flowers.

For the record, Faunus was the Roman god of animals, the fields, and shepherds. In Greece, he answered to the name Pan, a pipe-playing fun-lover, half man and half goat. Mysterious and scary sounds in the night were attributed to him, hence the word *panic*.

Some exotics have become *invasive,* which means they have made themselves too much at home: They are crowding out important and desirable native plants, changing the natural ecological balance on which other living things depend, and making general pests of themselves. (For more on invasives, see Chapter 2.)

However, most exotics are welcome guests — and among them are some of our most popular herbs. (See the sidebar, Your address, please.) Knowing who comes from where is fun for its own sake, but the geographical origin of an herb also tells much about the garden conditions that will best suit its *cultural needs* (what a plant needs to succeed in cultivation, such as highly acid soil or great amounts of water). Herbs from hot, arid regions are used to sandy soil and prepared for drought. Planting them in heavy soil and watering them frequently is a prescription for disaster.

Don't worry too much if the herbs you want to grow come from the Himalayas and you live on the prairie, or if they come from the tropics of Africa and you're gardening in northern Idaho. Herbs don't have to be natives to do well in your garden — they just have to be able to cope with the conditions in your garden. The good news is that most herbs are remarkably flexible: They survive — even thrive — in conditions as broad as the proverbial barn door.

If Life Were Fair

In a perfect world, we would all have Garden of Eden conditions. Put another way, each of us would have a sunny, sheltered, well-drained, southwest-facing plot with organically rich loam and plenty of rainfall. But life isn't fair, something you learned if you couldn't find a date for your junior prom. Don't waste time railing about your setting, or *microclimate.* Instead, get to know it, especially its peculiarities, anything that makes it different from your *macroclimate,* the prevailing conditions of your region.

As you look at your site, begin with the big picture. Are you located in the bottom of a small valley — which often means cold nighttime temperatures? Or are you located on a north-facing slope — where your plants will receive less direct sun? Then located look more closely. Does the wind come roaring through one part your property? Is there an area that stays wet for three days after it rains?

At the same time you're assessing your site, remember that an herb garden has a few requirements of its own. We've reduced the must-have list to the bare essentials, starting with sun.

Let the sunshine in

Light is *the* most critical consideration when locating any garden — it's the one element that you, the gardener, can't supply. Most herbs are devoted sunbathers. To them, sun is as essential as a fast food is to a teenager. At a minimum — and it really is a minimum — herbs need six hours of full sun daily (*full sun* is unobstructed sunlight). Eight hours of full sun is better than six. (Herbs labeled "full sun" do best if they have an entire day of unobstructed sunlight.)

Not only do sun-starved gardens warm slowly in the spring and cool quickly in fall, but their residents tend to be spindly, weak, and tall, and susceptible to diseases. In most regions, the best location for herbs is a southern exposure. In hot areas, you may need to site your garden so that it receives some protection from the afternoon sun. (If the choice is between morning and afternoon sun, choose morning sun, which will warm things up early in the day yet give plants relief during the hot afternoon hours.)

If you're reading this in the middle of winter, don't forget that deciduous trees cast shadows, as do shrubs, fences, buildings, and other vertical structures. Midsummer is the best time to measure what's shading what — trees are in full leaf and the sun (in the Northern Hemisphere) is high in the sky. (See Figure 3-2.)

Finally, if you're planting in rows, run them from east to west, and plant tall herbs or vines on the north side of the garden. Both these techniques help plants get the best possible sun exposure and keep taller plants from shading their smaller neighbors.

Figure 3-2:
Take note of where deciduous trees cast shadows in midsummer.

Shady characters

A few herbs — angelica, chervil, ginger, sweet woodruff, and violet come to mind — actually prefer a semi-shady site. Others, and the list is longer than you might expect, do moderately well in partial shade.

If your garden doesn't get full sun, try some of these herbs:

- Bee balm
- Betony
- Catnip
- Chamomile
- Chives
- Cilantro
- Comfrey
- Costmary

- Dill
- Fennel
- Feverfew
- Horseradish
- Lemon balm
- Lovage
- Mint
- Mustard

- Pennyroyal
- Tansy
- Tarragon
- Valerian
- Watercress
- Wormwood

When the wind blows

Thomas Hill, who wrote the first how-to garden book in English in 1577 (*The Gardener's Labyrinth*) was quick to point out that both gardens and their gardeners need fresh air: "Evil aire . . . doth not only annoy and currupt the plants . . . but choke and dul the spirits of men."

To keep your herbs — and yourself — from being annoyed, corrupted, choked, or dulled, keep your garden away from low spots, where air can pool. (See Figure 3-3.) Cold air is heavier than warm air; that's why low areas are susceptible to frost. Pick a mountain town with "Hollow" in its name, and you've probably picked a place that holds some kind of record for a late spring frost.

Figure 3-3:
Cold air
likes to
settle in
low-lying
areas.

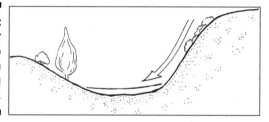

Poor air circulation also provides the stagnant conditions plant diseases love, especially in humid climates. Do everything you can to ensure good air circulation. If you must fence your garden to ward off wildlife, four legged or two, don't make it a solid wall that will keep your herbs from getting the fresh air they need.

At the same time, if your property is near the ocean — or regularly in the path of fierce winds — your herbs may need protection. Any garden site that regularly gets winds in the 15-mph range needs a *windbreak,* or wind barrier.

Anything that obstructs wind does more than keep your herbs from being tattered and torn, or toppling over — it also safeguards the soil from erosion and helps keep it from drying out. If it's cold, wind can annihilate a row of young basil plants in a matter of hours (or, if you're lucky, just slow their growth for weeks to come). In contrast, hot winds *desiccate,* or dehydrate, plants, and that, too, can be lethal.

If the wind that roars through your garden is constant, you'll probably want a permanent windbreak, such as trees, shrubs, vines, fences, and walls. Temporary barriers can tame winds that come and go — mostly in early spring, for example. You can choose from dozens of possibilities, including floating row covers (secured), wire cages wrapped with plastic, cloches, and more.

Before you erect a permanent barrier, make absolutely sure you know the direction of the prevailing winds. Put your windbreak on the wrong side and you could have cold winds pooling on your angelica and rosemary. By the way, you don't have to build the Great Wall of China. Semi-open structures do a better job than solid ones (plus they don't blow over in gales).

Living windbreaks are one of the most attractive solutions, but they're also like kids' appetites: They get bigger and bigger. Plant them — especially trees — at a distance (from your garden) of four times their mature height from your garden.

Water, water everywhere

You only have to watch the news to know that some regions get *lots* more rain than others. If it doesn't rain at your house during the growing season, you'll have to water. It's a simple as that. (For instructions on when and how, skip to Chapter 10.)

But if it does rain, especially if it rains often and long, make sure you don't pick the wettest spot on your property to grow herbs. Does a river run through it? Is the turf spongy? These are dead giveaways, Mother Nature's way of saying, "Not a good idea."

Waterlogged ground is air-poor, and your herbs' roots need air, as well as moisture. A large number of common herbs not only don't like wet ground, they prefer moderately arid conditions. Putting a garden where "watriness shall exceed," as Thomas Hill put it, is a prescription for disappointment.

TIP

Put a damper on it

Some herbs are willing to put up with ground that tends to stay damp — not soppy wet, or heavy, or packed. The soil should be rich in organic matter and drain well — but retain a bit more moisture than catnip or sage like.

- Bee balm
- Borage
- Cardamom
- Chervil
- Dill
- Elecampane

- Ginger
- Horseradish
- Lemon verbena
- Marsh mallow
- Sorrel
- Valerian

You can do one of two tests to measure your soil's *porosity* — how fast or slow it drains.

- ✔ **If you suspect your soil drains poorly,** dig a hole 1 foot deep and 1 foot square, and fill it with water. Refill it 24 hours later, and then keep track of how quickly the water drains. If the hole doesn't empty in 12 hours, drainage is poor.

- ✔ **If you suspect your soil drains too rapidly,** water your garden area thoroughly — at least to a depth of 6 inches. After 48 hours, check the soil. If the top 6 inches are dry, your soil dries faster than it should to support most plants.

You can do a number of things to your soil to make it drain better or retain water better. (Those details are in Chapters 4 and 7.) Raised beds, which you find out about in Chapter 4, are one solution for moderately wet spots. But if the ground is excessively wet, it may require draining. Think backhoe, drainage tiles, dry wells, money. Then think about putting the garden somewhere else.

Are We There Yet?

Creating a garden is hard work. It takes time and energy. But a garden is made in soil, not stone. If in three years — or even one year — you decide that your first choice about where to grow herbs was a mistake, then you're allowed do-overs, a horticultural mulligan. Most gardeners have a section of unusually healthy turf where herbs or vegetables or flowers once tried to grow.

Carefully consider the placement of your herb garden. Anticipating every problem is impossible, but here are a few last-minute thoughts about where to grow herbs:

Situate your garden plot

- ✔ **Near, but off, the beaten path.** You want family and friends to walk near your herbs but not on them.

- ✔ **Close to a water supply.** Being near a faucet will keep you from having to buy a 1,000-foot hose.

- ✔ **Away from the street and other sources of possible contamination.** Contaminated soil is commonplace alongside roads and driveways and surrounding buildings, so avoid gardening in these locations if you can. If you must use a problematic site, have your soil tested for its lead content. (Lead contamination comes from leaching paint and paint chips, and from years of auto exhausts when lead-based gasoline was the norm.) Your county health department can point you to a lab in your area that can test for different contaminates.

Remember, you're going to eat some of these plants.

✔ **Away from buildings.** Houses and garages cast giant shadows and are famous for the lousy soil that builders use as backfill around foundations.

✔ **Close to your tools and supplies.** If you want to work on your biceps, however, place your garden far away from the toolshed.

✔ **In clear view.** We get pleasure in just looking at our gardens. You will too.

Chapter 4

There's No Place Like Loam

In This Chapter

▶ Taking a close-up look at soil

▶ Understanding soil texture and structure

▶ Investigating what's living underground

▶ Evaluating and improving your garden soil

Some gardeners are downright contentious about the word *soil,* insisting that it's not the same thing as *dirt.* Soil, they insist, is the stuff in the your garden; it's what you grow plants in. Dirt is what you wash off your hands or sweep under the rug.

Soil. Dirt. Even "planting medium." It's the place roots call home. Soil anchors plants to the earth and supplies the oxygen, water, and nutrients that they need to live. Call it what you want. The gardener's secret is never to treat soil like dirt.

Looking Down Under

Hydroponically inclined gardeners grow herbs in water. Herbs also can live in artificial soil, but your backyard isn't filled with water or artificial soil. You have the real thing — most likely a *mineral,* or *inorganic,* soil, made primarily from rock that has weathered for millions of years. According to soil scientists, there are at least 15,000 variations of the real thing, each with its own *profile,* a description based on a vertical cross-section at least 5 feet deep.

A soil profile reveals distinct layers, or *horizons.* The thickness and composition of each depends of where you live, but most soils have at least two distinct horizons lying above the bedrock — topsoil and subsoil.

✔ **Topsoil horizon.** The uppermost layer that most gardeners call *topsoil* is the region that houses the roots of most herbs. This is the place where organic life and matter are most abundant, and where nutrients break down. Plants need healthy topsoil, the deeper the better — fortunately, you can improve topsoil.

✔ **Subsoil horizon.** Lying below your topsoil is the *subsoil,* or accumulation, horizon. Fine particles and other substances leached downward collect in this layer (or layers), but it contains little organic matter and is difficult to modify or improve. The roots of very large plants, such as shrubs and trees, sometimes extend into the subsoil.

Herbs grow differently in different soils, It's no accident that garden adages about soil abound, including, "Good soil makes good gardeners." If growing plants is new to you, repeat after us: Good soil does make good gardeners. And good gardens.

What's Good Soil?

Good garden soil, according to the professionals, consists of 25 percent air and 25 percent water, at least 5 percent organic matter, and 45 percent mineral particles. Your soil's mix — how much air, water, and organic matter it contains, and the kinds of soil particles in it — affects how well your herbs grow. Savvy gardeners keep improving that mix. It doesn't matter how long you've been growing herbs and other plants: Garden soil is always a work in progress.

Air to breathe and water to drink

The percentages in the preceding paragraph are correct — half of healthy soil consists of air and water! In fact, plant roots don't grow in the soil particles themselves, they grow in the spaces between the tiny particles — the same passageways through which oxygen, water, dissolved nutrients, and soil organisms travel.

Take a look at how air and water affect the quality of your soil:

✔ **Air.** Plants absorb the oxygen they need through their roots. A few plant species thrive in ground so wet that it contains almost no air. That may be okay for watercress, but not for most herbs or many macro- and microorganisms that live in your soil.

✔ **Water.** Soil may be 25 percent water, but most plants are 90 percent water! (Now you know why plant leaves become limp during a drought.) Roots not only suck up water, they take in the food that plants need for healthy growth. In a drought, your herbs get hungry, as well as thirsty.

If too much water is in the soil, your plants can suffocate — and so can the other living organisms that dwell underground and keep your soil healthy.

It's a jungle down there

Imagine that "soil" is the mystery word in a game of 20 questions, and you're asked, "Animal, vegetable, or mineral?" Your answer should be, "All three." You find out about the mineral part elsewhere in this chapter, but here's the animal and vegetable part.

You probably know about the merits of earthworms, but did you know that an uncountable number of other beneficial organisms, plant and animal, also dwell in your soil? We won't attempt to supply a directory of what's down there, except to say that there are billions and billions of residents, most of them too small to see. In the soil, good things come in small packages.

The macroorganisms (everything from voles, worms, and grubs to nematodes and plant roots) are world-class soil-openers, aerating it as they move. They do the initial breaking down of organic matter in the soil by digesting leaves, roots, stems, and each other. Then the microorganisms (protozoa, bacteria, fungi, viruses, and more) go to work on the residue their larger neighbors leave behind. Most of these organisms live in the top 8 inches of soil, right where your herbs' roots are growing. They moderate soil chemistry, transforming nutrients into forms plants can use, and improve soil structure by increasing its moisture-holding capacity while also helping it to drain better. In a nutshell, they make soils rich, healthy, and easy to work, or friable.

As the worm turns

Charles Darwin called earthworms the "intestines of the soil;" farmers call them "Mother Nature's plows." Earthworms feed on organic matter, depositing their castings, or excrement, as they burrow through the soil. Scientists estimate that a 1-acre garden with organically rich soil contains about 1 million worms; their castings are rich in nitrogen, phosphorus, and potassium, the three foods plants most need.

The equation is simple: Lots of worms equals good soil. In spring, dig a cubic foot of soil and count: Five worms is okay, 10 is excellent. And if, in the digging, you happen to cut a worm in half, the answer is, "Yes. Earthworms grow new heads if no more than the first 6 or 7 body rings are lost."

Do you have just a few worms in your soil? Add organic matter, and they will come.

Earthworms and other organisms keep the soil healthy. They power the underground decay cycle. Your job is to keep *them* healthy by regularly supplying the organic matter that they need. Organic matter can be anything from grass clippings, potato peelings, and tree leaves to animal manure, cocoa hulls, and compost (the Rolls Royce of organic matter). You can dig it into the soil or spread it on the soil's surface. Chapters 7 and 10 explain how to best to handle and add organic matter to your garden; soil fertility is covered in Chapter 7.

Eventually, the organic matter in your soil chemically changes into *humus* — it's horticultural gold. If a gardener had visited the garden of Eden, Czech playwright Karel Ĉapek wrote in 1931, he would have ignored Eve and exclaimed, "Good Lord, what humus!"

Rock on

Particles, or *separates,* of large rocks make up between 95 percent and 97 percent of the *solid* portion of mineral soils (the rest is organic matter). Soil scientists classify soil separates by their size, beginning with boulders, any rock that measures about 10 inches across. That may sound small to you if you thought a boulder was something big enough to sunbathe on. But those of us with official boulders in our gardens refer to them as "those #%*!! rocks."

We hope boulders, stones, pebbles, and gravel are scant in your garden, leaving you free to focus on the small end of the soil-separates scale — sand, silt, and clay. Almost all soils contain a mix of all three. (See Figure 4-1.)

How much you have of each of the following determines your soil's *texture:*

- ✔ **Sand.** Sand particles, which can be fine or coarse, are the largest of the three, measuring from 2 mm to 0.5 mm across. You can see them clearly without magnification. Gardeners with sandy soil, which feels gritty, often call it *light soil* because it is easy to cultivate whether wet or dry.

    Because sand particles are larger and irregular, they don't cling together closely. As a result, sandy soil drains quickly — water reaches 12 inches deep in 24 hours. Quick drainage also makes sandy soil less fertile than other soils because the nutrients leach out as quickly as the water does.

- ✔ **Silt.** You'll need a microscope to see silt particles (0.5 to 0.002 mm), but you can recognize them by touch: Dry, silty soil feels smooth, like flour or talcum powder. Most silt particles have an irregular shape as sand particles do, but are thinly coated with clay.

    Water tends to run off silty soil, but once it penetrates the surface, silt retains moisture and nutrients better than sand does. (Water reaches 8 inches in 24 hours).

✔ **Clay.** Clay particles measure less than 0.002 mm across. Because of their size and makeup, clay particles stick together — and feel sticky when wet. Clay soils retain nutrients, but they also retain moisture so well (water reaches only 4 inches deep in 24 hours) that plants may not get the oxygen they need.

Clay soil, which may be tinged red, gray, or blue, stays wet and cold in spring. Because clay is harder to dig when wet or dry, it is often referred to as *heavy soil*.

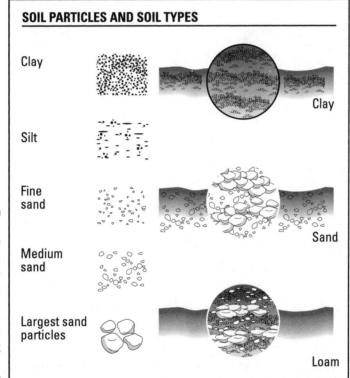

SOIL PARTICLES AND SOIL TYPES

Clay

Clay

Silt

Fine
sand

Sand

Medium
sand

Largest sand
particles

Loam

Figure 4-1:
The size of
the mineral
particle
determines
the soil tex-
ture. Loam
is the ideal
soil for most
plants.

Your garden soil won't be all sand or all clay, however, but a mix. If that mix is 40 percent sand, 40 percent silt, and 20 percent clay, you have *loam,* the ideal soil for gardening.

A feel for texture

Most gardens — including ours and probably yours — don't come with loam. Luckily, loam isn't required for growing herbs. But you still need to know your soil's texture, its relative percentages of sand, silt, and clay.

One way to get an idea of your soil's texture is to take a handful of damp dirt from your garden plot and squeeze it. If it forms a sticky ball, you have clay or heavy soil; if it won't form a ball, you'll be working sandy, or light, soil. Loam is in the middle: It forms a ball when squeezed, but the ball crumbles when dropped. (See Figure 4-2.)

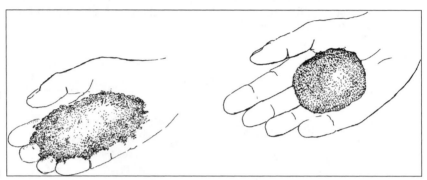

Figure 4-2:
Take the
squeeze-soil
test.

Texture triangle

To take exact measurement of your soil's texture — one based on the way that particles settle out in a liquid environment — you need a large, straight-sided glass jar with a screw-on lid, dishwasher detergent, water, and the U.S. Department of Agriculture's (USDA's) Textural Triangle (shown in Figure 4-3).

Test the texture (Try saying *that* three times fast!):

1. **Dig straight down and collect about 1 cup of soil from the top few inches of your garden.**

2. **Air dry and pulverize the soil; remove any stones.**

3. **Place the soil in the jar, add 1 teaspoon of detergent, and fill two-thirds full with water.**

4. **Screw on the lid, shake vigorously, and let the jar sit overnight.**

   By morning the soil will have settled, and you'll see the layers clearly: Sand on the bottom, silt in the middle, clay (which may look more like muddy water than a solid layer) above the silt, and clear water on top. (See Figure 4-4.)

5. **Measure the three soil layers and determine the percentage of each soil type.**

   For example, if your sample contains 1 inch sand, 1 inch silt, and 3 inches of clay, the total is 5. To find the percentages, divide the total into each measurement and multiply by 100: $1 \div 5 \times 100$; $1 \div 5 \times 100$; and

$3 \div 5 \times 100$. That works out to 20 percent sand, 20 percent silt, and 60 percent clay. With 60 percent clay, you can guess that your soil is "heavy," but to know precisely what kind of soil you're starting with, use the texture triangle, which is shown in Figure 4-3.

To find your soil's texture, locate the percentage of each particle type, and follow the inward line (parallel to the side adjacent in a counter-clockwise direction). The point where the three lines intersect indicates soil's texture classification.

Determining your soil's texture class on the USDA triangle not only gives it a name — such as sandy clay, silt loam, or loamy sand — it tells you how well your soil can retain moisture and nutrients, and what herbs will grow best. If your site is sandy loam, for example, it's ready-made for thyme and other Mediterranean natives. Herbs that need more moisture such as chervil and marsh mallow, need extra watering if you grow them in sandy loam.

Soil texture is literally writ in stone. Trying to change your soil's texture by dumping truckloads of clay or by adding 2 tons of sand is both impractical and unproductive. (One estimate is that it would take 5 tons of sand to *modestly and temporarily* alter a 1,000-square-foot garden with clay soil.) But you can make your soil better. The secret's not in the sauce, it's in the structure.

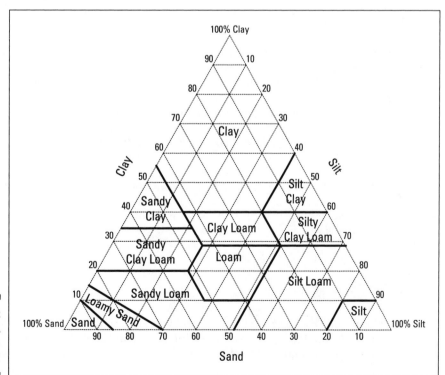

Figure 4-3:
The USDA texture triangle.

Figure 4-4:
As the soil
settles, you
can see its
components.

*Water

*Clay

*Silt

*Sand

A sense of structure

When gardeners discuss soil *structure,* they're talking about how well or poorly the soil particles cling, or *aggregate,* together. Sand, as the squeeze test shows, is like a dysfunctional family: It hardly binds together at all. In contrast, clay particles clamp together so tightly that it's hard to separate them, like newlyweds.

Soils that fall between these extremes are referred to as being *friable* or as having *good tilth.* Their particles aggregate enough to hold moisture and nutrients, but they also drain well, so that plants don't drown.

Friable soil has spaces, or pores, between its particles (as we mention in the section "What's Good Soil?" that space accounts for half of any healthy soil's volume). Water and nutrients, as well as roots and other below-ground life, move through the spaces.

You can't change your soil's texture, but you can improve its structure. Begin by not making things worse. Don't do anything that compacts your soil, such as walking back and forth across it or driving equipment across it, especially when it's wet.

R$_x$ for Soils

How can you make your soil better? We give you two words: organic matter. Organic matter is a cure-all. It improves soil structure, helping sandy soils to retain water and clay soils to drain. It opens soils, making them easier to till, and improves their nutrient content. It feeds the billions of soil organisms and even helps modify soil pH (more on that subject in the section titled, "P.S. . . . pH" in this chapter).

Compost is the crème-de-la-crème of organic matter (see Chapter 7 for compost-making directions), but everything you add to your soil helps, from carrot tops to cow dung. Fresh matter decomposes more quickly than dry materials (but also robs plants of needed nitrogen); chopped matter decomposes more quickly than materials that haven't been shredded. Organic matter that you dig into the soil breaks down more quickly than matter you spread on the soil's surface. Last, organic matter decomposes more quickly in warm soil than in cold.

At a minimum, you need to add 1 inch of chopped or fine organic matter or 4 inches of bulky matter to your garden each year. Two or four times that amount is better. Don't be stingy. It's hard to imagine a garden with too much organic matter.

Chapters 7 and 10 give fuller details on the special merits (and drawbacks) of different organic materials. Organic matter really is a magic bullet for improving your soil. Please trust us on this one, and follow this advice.

- ✔ **Sandy soils.** Sandy soil is the natural home of many herbs, but if your conditions are more conducive to building castles than growing sweet woodruff, you need to make some changes in your soil. The solution is easy. Add organic matter. Add more organic matter. Add still more organic matter.

  Sandy soils warm quickly, so organic matter will break down faster. That means you'll need large quantities of organic matter. The material should be a mixture of things that break down rapidly, such as grass clippings and composted manure, and things that take their time to decompose, such as straw.

- ✔ **Clay soils.** To open clay soils or other soils that have become compacted, dig in rough organic matter, such as half-decomposed compost, shredded bark, and roughly chopped leaves. Then dig in more organic matter, "et cetera, et cetera, et cetera," as the King in "The King and I" likes to say.

  If your soil texture is primarily clay, take extra care not to cultivate it when it's wet, and do not add sand. (For more concrete details, see the sidebar titled, "Can the sand" in this chapter.)

- ✔ **Wet soils.** Soils that stay too wet — and usually contain more than their fair share of clay particles — are also candidates for organic matter. Pour it on, and dig it in.

Can the sand

You may hear or read that you should add sand to clay soil to make it drain better. It's commonplace advice. Today, though, soil scientists say in no uncertain terms: "Don't do it." If you combine the right amount of clay and sand, what you may get is a cementlike mix. So just say no to sand. Instead, add organic matter, which not only improves drainage but supplies nutrients to the soil at the same time.

A Bed Above the Others

If you have a large property, finding a better location for your garden is the easiest solution if the site you've picked drains poorly. If moving the garden isn't possible or practical, and generous amounts of organic matter don't do the trick, you may want to drain, regrade, or ditch the area. Those are substantial and expensive undertakings, jobs you may not be able to do yourself. Before you phone a landscaper or back hoe operator, consider creating a raised-bed garden.

Raised beds — slightly elevated garden plots — are ideal for growing herbs. Despite being in vogue, raised beds aren't anything new. (Listen to Brother Walahfrid Strabo describe his 9th-century garden patch: "That it should not be washed away, / We faced it with planks and raised it in oblong beds / A little above the level ground.")

Raised beds ensure excellent drainage, warm more quickly in spring (which lengthens your growing season), and they require less bending, making cultivating and harvesting easier on your back. Last, they're easy to maintain and attractive.

Six inches is a good height for an herb bed (an inch or two lower in hot, dry climates where the soil dries out quickly); they can be any shape, but rectangular beds are the most practical. You want to be sure you can reach the center of a bed from either side as you garden. (Compacted soil is the problem you're correcting, so make sure your beds are sized and shaped so you never walk on them.) Kneel down and stretch out your arm. That distance doubled, and then minus 4 inches is as wide as your bed should be.

After you figure out the size of the bed, you need to decide if you want it to be freestanding or permanent:

> ✔ **Freestanding, or mounded, beds** are easy to build — use a rake or hoe to pull up soil from the surrounding area to create an elevated bed —

and they're easy to modify, resize, or eliminate. They also erode easily, which means you'll have to keep mounding up the sides to keep water and nutrients from running off the bed.

A freestanding bed is a good first step if you're not sure raised beds are for you.

✔ **Permanent beds** — wood- or stone-sided beds — take more time to build and are more expensive; once built, they're more difficult to modify or remove. But they are largely erosion-proof, and can add a decorative element to your landscape.

Wood beams, timbers, flagstones, bricks, and concrete blocks are among the building materials that are used to frame a raised bed. (Treat wood with a nontoxic preservative to resist decay.) Bury the frame about 3 inches in the soil to discourage weeds that spread underground and to provide extra support for the sides. Dig the soil in the bed to a depth of at least 8 inches (do this before you build the frame). Next, spread a thick layer of rough organic matter over the surface, and then add soil that has been heavily amended with still more organic matter to within 2 inches of the top of the frame.

If you must purchase topsoil, be aware that it usually contains little organic matter and few nutrients, so be sure to mix it with compost or some other organic matter (50:50 ratio).

P.S. . . . pH

Your soil's *pH* (potential hydrogen) is a measurement of acidity or alkalinity. The actual measure is of the number of hydrogen and hydroxyl ions, but all you need to know is that most herbs do fine in neutral or near-neutral soils, with a pH of pretty much anything from 6.0 to 7.5. Neutral is 7.0 on the 1.0-to-14.0 pH scale; soil that measures below 7 is acidic, or *sour,* whereas soils above 7 are alkaline, or *sweet.*

If your soil is strongly acidic (below 5.0) or highly alkaline (above 9.0), your herbs will rebel, or die on the spot. That's because soils at the extremes of the pH scale tie up mineral nutrients, making them unavailable to your plants (or the elements become too available, which can be toxic). Moreover, soil organisms also like neutral or near-neutral soil. There are no pH extremists among them, so keeping them alive and working requires your keeping the soil's pH in rein.

You can test the pH of anything organic. Once people got a pH meter and probe in their hands, there was no stopping them, so we now know that lime juice registers 1.8, near the bottom of the pH scale; ammonia is 11.5 (for the record, devil's food cake is 7.5).

Remember that gardening is always local: Your soil's pH may be different from your region's, even your next-door neighbor's.

If you're adding herbs in an established garden where a variety of plants are doing fine, don't worry about testing for pH. But if yours is a new plot, it's a good to check out its pH level. You can do this yourself — soil-testing kits from the simple to the complex are sold at garden centers and by mail-order suppliers (instructions will be included in the kit).

We're dedicated do-it-yourselfers, but we recommend having an initial pH test done by the professionals, either through your local Extension Office or a private laboratory. A professional test will be more accurate than one you do, it can be expanded to test for nutrient deficiencies in your soil, and it will include specific recommendations for remedying any problems or imbalances in your soil.

Small pH problems — only slightly too acid, for example — can be handled by adding organic matter generously and regularly to your soil. Peat moss and composted sawdust lower the pH; wood ashes raise pH.

If your soil needs a major-league pH adjustment, by a point or more on the pH scale, these are the general guidelines.

✔ **Soil that is too acidic.** Calcitic limestone, or calcium carbonate, is the standard material used to sweeten garden soils. Fall is the best time to lime soil. The general rule is 6 pounds of lime per 100 square feet to raise the pH by one point. The amount of lime needed is affected by your soil's texture and by its initial pH number. Sandy soils need less lime, heavy clay soils more. Very acid soils need more lime to raise the pH one point than moderately acid soils do.

In other words, one size doesn't fit all. It's another reason we suggest having professionals test your soil, to take advantage of the specific recommendations they'll supply with your test results.

✔ **Soil that is too alkaline.** Soils that are too sweet are normally treated with elemental sulfur. Again, there is no hard-and-fast rule about amounts — both the soil texture and the degree of alkalinity will affect how much sulfur you should add. The general recommendation is 1 pound of sulfur to lower the pH one point per 100 square feet, but the bag of sulfur should carry more specific application numbers.

Few soils are wildly acid or alkaline, so if you're working without specific recommendations from soil experts, go slow and start small when adjusting pH. It's better to change pH gradually rather than making the entire correction with one application. Soil, remember, is a work in progress.

Part III
The Best-Laid Plans

In this part . . .

Too many gardeners think "plant" first. They get home with several flats of annuals and perennials and maybe a shrub or two, and then they decide where they're going to put them. We, too, have commited this sin and we won't be able to stop you completely!

But by thinking first about design — such as the size and shape of planting beds and how they flow together with your home, garage, sheds, fences, and other elements — you'll create a more pleasing canvas on which to display and use your herbs.

If you can't decide where to start, we have some sample designs to stimulate your thought processes. Copy them exactly or use them as a starting point. And if you have a small yard or none at all, we show you how to grow herbs in containers on a patio, balcony or deck, or even indoors.

Chapter 5

Designing Your Herb Garden

. . . .

. . . .

*Y*ou may think that you need one special place for your herbs, that you must corral them off in a corner of your landscape as if they were frisky colts or youngsters who don't play nicely with other children.

This is the unfortunate fallout from herbs' colorful history, during which they have been rounded up in beds like wheels or laid out like Persian carpets. Impressive as these designs can be, the notion that this is the highest, best, and only way to grow herbs keeps them from being used as creatively as they can be.

Sure, you can shape your herb garden like a 16th-century lover's knot or Elvis's guitar. But a more important consideration than the configuration of your beds is the condition of your soil and exposure to sun (good) and wind (bad). A site near the house is often convenient, but it may be too soggy or shady for Mediterranean culinary herbs, which achieve optimum health by sprawling in the sun for hours, unlike the rest of us. You can find out all about those considerations in Chapters 3 and 4.

If you're already an avid gardener, you may not have room for a special herb bed. Not to worry! As you discover more of their charming ways, you'll find that herbs mingle merrily with existing plantings, accentuating their colors or clothing their bare feet. Most herbs are so amenable to growing in pots that you can play musical plants, trying the rosemary in the perennial border for its visual pizzazz, then scooting the pot close to the barbecue for smoking bluefish, and finally whisking it inside when winter winds begin to blow.

Before you make that trip to the nursery or dig your first hole, ask the most important question of all: Why am I growing herbs in the first place?

What's Your Pleasure?

The usual definition of herbs assumes that you want to use them in some practical way. Will you harvest oregano, dill, and rosemary daily to season gourmet meals? In that case, you want them just seconds away from your chopping block, right outside the kitchen door. A raised bed or flagstone area may be in order, because you want to be able to snip your chives or pull your parsley without getting on your knees in the mud.

Are you going to be whipping up tinctures and tisanes for a good night's sleep or to cure a headache? In that case, you might harvest the entire herb crop once a year to dry for the months ahead. No need to plant your echinacea or valerian next to the back stoop, but you'll still want your herb patch where you can reach it with the garden hose.

But maybe all this talk of crops and harvests smacks too much of menial labor. Instead of being like Ma Joad toiling in the fields, *Grapes-of-Wrath* style, you picture yourself as Greta Garbo pining, "I vant to be alone." If so, your garden needs to be a retreat, a place where you can escape workaday cares and wallow in pure pleasure. Hey, buddy, do herbs have a deal for you! Textures, scents, colors — herbs have 'em. Put your herbs in the nether reaches of your property (or at least as nether as your personal patch of earth allows) and screen them from prying eyes with conifers or vine-clad trellises.

Perhaps you're a more cerebral than sensuous sort. If you want to astound your friends with discourses on Dioscorides, or the mythical link between sweet marjoram and Aphrodite, you'll also want a historically appropriate place to grow your herbs, perhaps tying them in an elaborate knot or laying them out in monasterian squares.

No time or energy to create a herbal Taj Mahal in the back forty? All you need is a sprig of sage for the Thanksgiving turkey or enough mint for a single julep on Derby day? That's okay, too. Herbs are famously agreeable to being tucked in among other pretty plants or keeping a low profile in out-of-the-way corners.

Formal design, tux optional

Many of you may have formed your impressions of herb-garden design through woodcuts of medieval monasteries. These images usually show large walled gardens with raised, rectangular beds. Everything growing in them had a use: The monks raised the "purely" ornamental flowers for decorating the altar.

Meanwhile, outside the monastery walls, Europeans with an excess of time or money were taking the opposite tack by creating knot gardens, probably the most impractical garden design ever devised. Intended to be admired from upper stories, knot gardens required boxwood or various herbs to be planted in squares, circles, triangles, fleurs-de-lis, and loop-de-loops, and then meticulously pruned so they seemed to be growing over and under each other. Those swirls might contain the equivalent of a healthy, 20-foot row of rosemary, but a gardener couldn't gather much more than a leaf or two from such an arrangement without spoiling its appearance.

The tradition of geometric designs for kitchen gardens came to American shores in the 1600s, and was eventually translated in Pennsylvania by no-nonsense German settlers. Theirs was the so-called foursquare garden: four perfectly square blocks separated by two-foot walkways. These gardeners eventually modified the look with more beds and rectangles, but still with nary a hint of a curved line.

Formal design is first and foremost geometric, with straight paths and symmetric plant placements. Some plants are more formal than others as well, forming tidy mounds with not a leaf out of place, and these are obvious choices for a traditional herb garden. Statuary and heavy urns containing topiary also look at home in a formal garden.

Informal designs, the laid-back look

It was the stiff-upper-lip English, ironically, who gave us the relaxed cottage garden tradition, in which plants grown for household use were mingled in a seemingly haphazard fashion, usually in a small front yard. Favorite herbs include flowery calendula, chive, monarda (bee balm), artemisias, and damask roses, alongside fragrant lilacs, lily of the valley, mock orange, and dame's rocket.

But in fact, the "bones" underlying these cottage gardens were often as geometric as those of the monasteries. What made these gardens seem informal was the lavishness with which plants were crammed together, often climbing up the side of the dwelling and 'round the door, and flopping onto the walkway so that hard surfaces seemed softer.

Today, the trend in American gardens is toward a more natural look in garden design. Beds and paths are shaped with flowing curves, emulating those you would see in a woodland or meadow or on a hillside. Garden ornaments, too, may look as though they were left casually behind — wooden wheelbarrows, antique tools, or perhaps a thatched birdhouse.

Design Basics

Beginning gardeners invariably think first about flower color, and the more boisterous the better. Some never tire of the unrelenting yellow of marigolds or the magenta of petunias. But usually, like a Lothario ready to settle down, a seasoned gardener begins to look beyond superficial flashiness to more lasting qualities: foliage color and texture, the shape of the entire plant, and fragrance. In all of these attributes, herbs are champs.

Before you go on to plant selection, though, you need to understand some of the "hard" stuff.

Dem garden bones

Winter is the best time to see if your garden has structure, or what the experts call its *bones*. Even after annual herbs have given up the ghost and most of the perennial herbs are hibernating below ground, your eye should be able to discern rhythmic horizontal lines in your paths and the edges of your beds. You should see strong vertical lines — perhaps with the bonus of a snow-shrouded garden ornament, such as a statue.

Creating edges, paths, and other hardscapes

Landscape designers use the word *hardscape* for the permanent, nonliving parts of your garden design. That includes natural elements, such as boulders, as well as all the things made of rock, concrete, wood, or plastic.

You can edge your herb bed with one of the shrubby or low-growing herbs popular for that purpose (read more about them in the section titled "Developing good habits" in this chapter), but most gardeners find it easier to employ non-living materials: landscape timbers, stone, or bricks. You might use bricks to create a wheel-shaped herb bed, dividing it into "pie slices" with additional bricks, or lay square stones for a checkerboard herb bed, next to or even within a patio.

Any landscape needs paths, both for visual reasons — to create a sense of movement and boundaries — and practical reasons — to help you get from one area to another without walking on your mint and oregano. Herb garden designs often have intersecting paths with an ornament placed in the center. If you widen the path, you create a terrace, giving you room to kneel or stoop when you want to harvest a sprig of mint for tea, or cilantro for sauces, or sweet Annie for a dried bouquet. Or use it as a place where you can place a bench to kick back and relax.

Garden ornaments

Because herb gardens are both historic and homey, they cry out for decoration. You don't have to spend a lot of money. Browse roadside shops and check out auctions and estate sales for recycled, weather-beaten treasures. Or make your own scarecrow with last year's fashions! Here are just a few of the ornaments often associated with herb gardens:

- ✔ Birdhouses and feeders
- ✔ Birdbaths
- ✔ Old wagon wheels
- ✔ Old well pumps
- ✔ Small fountains

- ✔ Stone urns
- ✔ Sundials
- ✔ Whirligigs
- ✔ Wood gates
- ✔ Wood wheelbarrow

In a formal herb garden, your paths probably will be straight. In a cottage or mixed garden, you can give them sinuous curves, perhaps winding under an arched trellis of passion flower (*Passiflora* spp.) or hop *(Humulus lupulus)*. Paths can be covered with turf, gravel or other small stones, bark mulch or flagstone, or dotted with stepping stones. But the material of choice for herb gardens is aged brick, which seems to speak of the plants' history. Permanent and solid, its texture is as perfect a foil for feathery leaves as its mellow reds or yellows are for herbs' many shades of green.

Choose rue for blue

When it comes to flowers, the best-known culinary and medicinal herbs are somewhat limited. Basil, parsley, and mint all have tiny and relatively colorless flowers that, while capable of driving bees into passionate frenzies, should be removed if you want to keep the fresh flavor of the herb or avoid lessening its health-giving components.

Many herbs have a preponderance of blue, purple, and pink flowers so that those of us who are partial to this combination can reap huge satisfaction by combining thyme, chive, oregano, rosemary, sage, with perhaps a border of lavender.

Bee balm, or monarda, gives you intense deep pink ('Marshall's Delight') and red ('Cambridge Scarlet'). You can add yellow to the palette with elecampane, evening primrose *(Oenothera biennis)*, goldenrod *(Solidago* spp.), St. John's-wort *(Hypericum perforatum)*, and tansy. Calendula takes you into sunny oranges.

You will create a more lasting tapestry of color, however, by collecting herbs with an eye to their foliage.

✔ **Gray, white, and silver.** Herbs are famous for pale foliage that helps tone down or blend bright colors that might otherwise clash. Choose from catmint, curry plant, lamb's ear *(Stachys byzantina),* virtually any lavender, sage, santolina, or woolly thyme. Among the artemisias, in addition to southernwood and wormwood, look for *Artemisia alba* 'Canescens'. Or how about one of the gray-green dianthus cultivars, such as 'Miss Sinkins'?

✔ **Purple and red.** You can bring deep burgundy red into the garden if you plant perilla, purple sage ('Purpurea'), or the basil cultivars 'Rubin' and 'Osmin'. Orange mint gets its name from its smell, but its leaves have a subtle purple color.

✔ **Yellow.** Just look for some form of *aureum,* the Latin word for "gold," in a species or cultivar name. You can buy golden feverfew, golden pot mar-joram, golden oregano, golden hop, golden sage, golden thyme, or golden valerian.

✔ **Blue.** Color is often in the eye of the beholder, but to most, rue has the bluest foliage among herbs, especially the cultivar plant called 'Jackman's Blue'.

✔ **Bronze.** Like rue, bronze fennel is in a color class by itself with its dis-tinctive, shimmery, reddish brown foliage.

✔ **Variegation.** You don't want to overdo *variegated* leaves — those that are tinged with white, yellow, pink, or some combination — if you don't want your garden looking like a three-ring circus. But a few variegated plants scattered here and there are a lively counterpoint to solid green. Tri-colored sage, which has swirls of pink and white on the usual green, and variegated catmint (*Calamintha grandiflora* 'Variegata') are among the most popular variegated herbs. You'll also find subtle colors among the pelargoniums, or scented geraniums. Look for 'Fair Ellen', 'Chocolate Mint', and 'Skies of Italy'.

Fuzzy, frilly, shiny, lacy

As you grow and study herbs, you'll notice that the texture of their leaves is even more varied than their color. Deciding which plants contrast most strik-ingly when planted next to each other is one of the endless pleasures of herb gardening. For fuzziness, Nature hasn't invented anything more pet-able than lamb's ear, an ornamental perennial. Its herbal cousin, betony, has greener but still hairy leaves (and contains tannins that can soothe a sore throat or cure diarrhea). A scented geranium, or pelargonium, collection is a menagerie of tactile thrills: velvety, sandpapery, or crinkly. Here are some of the herbal tex-tures you can stroke or stare at:

- ✔ **Fernlike.** Leaves that are divided or toothed like fern leaves are include chamomile, chervil, feverfew, parsley, and tansy. Those of valerian are deeply divided, too, but the effect is quite different on this five-footer.

- ✔ **Feathery.** Dill, fennel, southernwood, wormwood, and yarrow are among the herbs with leaves so finely divided as to approach hairlike. Anise has fine leaves at the top of the plant, while those near its base are more parsleylike.

- ✔ **Smooth 'n' shiny.** The slick, glossy leaves of bay, eucalyptus (*Eucalyptus* spp.), myrtle, and laurel add light to a garden.

- ✔ **Tiny leaves.** When you visit a well-stocked herb nursery, you may think the thyme breeders are having a contest to see who can produce the dinkiest leaves. Ground-huggers such as 'Minus' thyme have the smallest — pinpoints that that would do pointillist painter Georges Seurat proud.

- ✔ **Prickly.** What's the point? Spiny leaves will give your domain a bit of drama. Try cardoon or its relative globe artichoke *(Cynara scolymys)*, liver-rejuvenating milk thistle, or a thicket of the prickle-surfeited eglantine rose.

- ✔ **Rough.** Running your finger across a sunflower leaf will send shivers down your spine, but for true grit, grow sage. Rub a leaf over your teeth to clean them after dinner — it's good for your gums, too!

- ✔ **Succulent.** These plants have their own botanical category because of the way their thick, fleshy leaves store water. Aloe is the most common herb among them. Purslane *(Portulaca oleracea)*, a nutritious weed that is rich in anti-aging anti-oxidants, looks a bit like a jade plant that's been stomped on.

- ✔ **Pleated.** The leaves of lady's mantle and nasturtium are round and puckery, while those of silver sage *(Salvia argentea)* add white fuzz to the garden mix.

Developing good habits

You may not be able to distinguish the sandpapery look of sage leaves or the satiny sheen of basil from a distance. But your eye will enjoy the differing overall shape of plants, which is often referred to as *habit*.

Some groundcover plants, such as strawberries, crawl flat along the ground like a World War II private on the front lines, while others, like mullein, soar skyward like Gulf War rockets. Other herbs form perfectly rounded humps or sprawl lazily. Still others are climbers, such as passion flower (*Passiflora* spp.) and hop (*Humulus lupulus*).

In an informal garden, you can add to visual interest by combining as many shapes as possible. Repeating a shape gives rhythm to your design. In a *border* (a planting area that backs to a wall or fence), put tall plants toward the back; in a *bed* (a planting area exposed on all sides), set tall plants in the center. Floppy plants work best along the edges, while groundcovers will blanket bare earth between other herbs. (Make sure that taller neighbors don't steal all their sun.)

In a formal garden, where plants are traditionally the same height, you may want them to have similar habits, as well.

- **Tall spires.** Angelica, black cohosh *(Cimicifuga racemosa),* evening primrose, Joe-pye weed *(Eupatorium* spp.), mullein, pokeweed *(Phytolacca americana)* and other vertical herbs have an air of stateliness and drama. These plants command attention, so use them sparingly. Mullein also has a basal rosette (a circle of foliage near the stem) of big felty leaves, so you'll get a habit and texture bonus.

- **Big 'n' bushy.** Lovage, marsh mallow, meadowsweet *(Filipendula ulmaria),* and Jerusalem artichoke look less like the Washington Monument and more like the Capitol Building. Tall, yes, but also gobbling up lots of ground. (They won't raise your taxes, however.)

- **Grasslike.** The fanlike foliage of orrisroot, like that of all irises, is handsome long after the flowers are gone. For a similar grasslike shape, lusty lemongrass and chipper chives are the long and short of it, respectively.

- **Monster leaves.** Grow cardoon or castor bean *(Ricinus communis)* for pure mass. Castor bean is a tropical plant that reaches 10 feet in a single year, with palm-shaped leaves more than a foot wide. Oil from its seeds is pressed to make the old-fashioned laxative, castor oil. The seeds are highly poisonous, though, and other parts of the plant can give people with sensitive skin a rash.

- **Mound.** Some herbs form such perfect mounds that you want to reach down and pet them like a sleeping cat. These make good edging plants, or you can use them for contrast with floppy or spiky plants. Good mounders include chamomile, feverfew, many lavenders, and some of the artemisia clan such as 'Silver Mound' and 'Powis Castle'.

- **Groundcovers.** Creepy crawly herbs, such as sweet woodruff, will cover ground and suppress weeds between other plants. An herb-gardener's trick is to tuck chamomile and the low-growing thymes between stepping stones, where they release their fragrance when you step on them.

- **Hanging.** Herbs with limp stems look lush dangling from a hanging basket or draped across the side of a raised bed or window box. A few good candidates are borage, catmint, lemon balm, and other mints, rosemary, thyme, nasturtium, oregano (especially dittany of Crete, *Origanum dictamnus),* and some scented geraniums, or pelargoniums.

✔ **Vines.** Use climbing herbs such as hop, honeysuckle (*Lonicera* spp.), Carolina jasmine *(Gelsenium sempervirens),* climbing nasturtium, or passionflower on a trellis for privacy or to give other herbs a windbreak.

Aroma wasn't built in a day

Look up the word "fragrance" in a thesaurus, and what do you see? A list of herbs, from ambrosia to vanilla. In fact, fragrance so characterizes herbs that coming up with a list of herbs that *don't* smell wonderful might be the easiest way to deal with this category. Nonetheless, we plunge daringly ahead, suggesting a few of our favorites. Crush a few leaves of the following plants and see if you agree:

✔ **Pelargoniums.** Also known as scented geraniums, these olfactory superstars deserve billing above the title, as they say in the marquee biz. You can choose from scents such as rose, apricot, almond, mint, cinnamon, nutmeg, chocolate mint, coconut, eucalyptus, lemon, orange, camphor, pine, strawberry, and apple.

✔ **Mints.** If geraniums get the gold medal, mint and thyme tie for silver. There are mints that smell of apple laced with menthol, or lime, chocolate, banana, ginger, grapefruit, orange, and more.

✔ **Thymes**. Go for straight for lemon thyme, which actually does smell like citrus. Then try orange, caraway, lavender, mint, and nutmeg. There's even a thyme that smells like oregano.

✔ **Lavenders**. The discerning nose will find some varieties sweeter and others more medicinal. English lavender *(Lavandula angustifolia)* has the clean scent of lingerie drawers and lace handkerchiefs, while French lavender *(L. stoechas)* smells more like something used for treating sports injuries and battling bugs.

✔ **Catmint.** Said not to attract cats the way catnip does, *Nepeta mussinii* also has a stronger and more appealing scent for the human nose. Some compare it to mint jelly; we think it has undertones of pine or cedar.

✔ **Curry.** *Helichrysum italicum* lets you marvel at how Nature stuffed the aroma of curry, an East Indian concoction made of up of as many as 20 different herbs and spices, into a single plant. Ironically, curry is not a culinary herb, but the silvery 12- to 18-inch plants make a great edging, and you can pluck the leaves for potpourri.

Themes and Variations

An herb garden is its own theme, but you can specialize by choosing only herbs from the Bible, herbs used by Native Americans, herbs for teas, or herbs for dyes. Or you can tuck herbs into other specialized gardens, such as rock gardens, vegetable gardens, or even water gardens.

Rock gardens

Many of our most popular culinary herbs are native to the Mediterranean, where summers are warm and dry, winters are mild, and soil is poor and rocky. These plants are happy when snuggled against a warm rock, which retains heat at night but keeps roots cool by day. If you have a rock wall or retaining wall, you may be able to plant herbs in some of its crevices. Or perhaps you'll decide to give herbs a rock home of their own.

An alternative is to create a *scree* bed, in which you use coarse gravel to mimic a sunny hillside. Build it either on a natural incline or create a slope with large rocks and a mix of gravel and well-draining soil. The scree bed should be at least a foot deep. When planting the herbs, remove any potting soil from their roots. Then mulch the herbs with gravel and water generously for the first few weeks. Before long, the plants will take care of themselves.

The best herbs for planting in the crevices in rock walls are small plants that cling, creep, or droop. Good candidates include

- **Corsican mint** *(Mentha requienii)*
- **Creeping rosemary** *(Rosmarinus prostratus)*
- **Creeping sage** *(Salvia reptans)*
- **Creeping thyme** *(Thymus praecox* subsp. *articus,* 'Minus', 'Elfin')
- **Dwarf artemisia** *(Artemisia pontica, A. stellerina* 'Silver Brocade')
- **Dwarf lavender** *(Lavandula angustifolia,* 'Jean Davis', 'Rosea')
- **Feverfew** *(Tanacetum parthenium* 'Aureum', 'Golden Moss', 'Golden Ball', 'White Stars')
- **Oregano** *(Origanum vulgare* 'Compacta', 'Aureum Crispum')
- **Pinks** *(Dianthus gratianopolitanus* 'Tiny Rubies'; *D. chinensis)*
- **Santolina** *(Santolina chamaecyparissus* 'Nana')
- **Violets** *(Viola* spp.)

Under the big topiary

Topiary is the ancient art of clipping woody plants into shapes: spirals, pompons, wreaths, geometric patterns, even giraffes and cowboy boots. Most topiaries are appropriate only in formal gardens, although whimsical topiaries have a place in informal gardens. Topiaries are often grown in containers and make an especially nice feature as the centerpiece where paths intersect.

Topiary plants need to have small, dense leaves and to grow back rapidly after shearing (which makes them bushy). Among herbs, the most popular choices are bay, rosemary, and myrtle *(Myrtus communis)*.

You may be able to create some simple topiaries, shapes such as cones, by working freehand, but you will find the job easier if you buy a wire frame or shape your own with chicken wire. After fitting the frame over the plant (or beside it,

if you are creating a wreath or working with a vine), tie the plant's new, pliable stems to the frame with green twist ties or other soft material. Check frequently as your plant grows to make sure the old ties aren't too tight; retie them if necessary. After the plant covers its frame, you need to give the plant frequent haircuts.

A specialized topiary that is easy to create with woody plants is called a *standard* — sort of a botanical lollipop with a single stem and a round head. Herbs that will work for standards include curry plant, lavender, lemon verbena, sage, and santolina.

To make a standard, remove the plant's lower limbs (usually about one-half to two-thirds of the way up the stem), then pinch back new growth on the rest of the plant to encourage bushiness. When the foliage at the top of the plant is large and dense enough, clip it into a ball shape.

Gone fishin'

If you already have a water garden, you may want to take advantage of it to grow some herbs. The following plants need standing water to flourish but don't need a big pond. These herbs are restrained enough to grow in a plastic-lined whiskey barrel or similar-sized container.

BEWARE

✔ **Lotus** *(Nelumbo* spp.*)*. Asians cook and pickle both the roots and seeds of the lotus, and drink rice wine through its stem. For a smaller pond, look for the American lotus, *Nelumbo lutea,* sometimes called "pond nuts." It has yellow flowers and grows 2½ to 5 feet tall.

✔ **Sweet flag** *(Acorus calamus)*. Native Americans chewed the root of this iris for toothaches and boiled the root to treat burns (the Food and Drug Administration banned it as medicine after studies linked it to cancer). Look for the variegated form, and grow it for its striking, white-bordered foliage.

✔ **Water chestnut** *(Trapa natans)*. This floating annual is the source of those crunchy white vegetables you get in Asian dishes. The plant is an annual with white flowers; the "nuts" are inside spiny black pods.

✔ **Watercress** *(Nasturtium officinale)*. One of the few water plants that loves running water, watercress is happy alongside a stream or waterfall and yields peppery leaves for salads or sandwiches.

Herb gardeners often spend a good deal of time trying to make their soil drain better. (See Chapter 4 for details on soil drainage.) Fortunately, some herbs are happy in damp soil. Just remember that there is a difference between damp and soppy. These plants need plenty of moisture but won't put up with having their feet in standing water

✔ **Black cohosh** *(Cimicifuga racemosa)*. This native perennial grows more than 6 feet tall and bears long, off-white flower clusters. You'll find its roots in capsules for symptoms of menopause.

✔ **Elderberry** *(Sambucus nigra)*. You may be familiar with elderberry wine, which is made from berries of this shrub. It has white, flat-topped flowers, and its leaves are used to treat the flu.

✔ **Horsetail** *(Equisetum* spp.). This grasslike perennial contains silica and can be used to scrub and polish metal. Grow it in a container or it will romp all over your garden.

✔ **Male fern** *(Dryopteris filix-mas)*. The ancient Greeks used the fronds of this 3- to 4-foot fern to expel worms. He's a good looking guy, too.

✔ **Marsh mallow** *(Althaea officinalis)*. A 6-foot perennial with pale lilac flowers like those of a hibiscus, marsh mallow has roots known for their power to sooth sore throats.

✔ **Swamp sunflower** *(Helianthus angustifolia)*. This moisture-loving perennial has 3-inch wide flowers similar to those of other wild sunflowers and grows 7 feet tall. Its nuts are not only rich in vitamin E but contain substances that relieve pain and inflammation.

✔ **Water mint** *(Mentha aquatica)*. This herbs smells like its landlubber kin. It will spread like them, too, if you don't keep it contained.

✔ **Willow** *(Salix* spp.). The white willow, whose bark is used as a painkiller, is too big for most gardens. Choose rosegold pussy willow *(S. gracilistyla)* or the black catkin willow *(S. melanostachys)*. Both have interesting catkins but stay under 10 feet tall.

The Pretty Magnificent Seven

Well, *we* think these designs are pretty magnificent and had fun with them in our own gardens. But feel free. Make the designs bigger or smaller, rounder or squarer. Mix 'em or match 'em. Put medicinals in the Shakespeare beds or bee herbs in the culinary stair steps. We're here to encourage and inspire, not to make home visits to see if you stayed between the lines.

Raising 'em right, a beginner's garden

Our first herb gardens were variations on the design shown in Figure 5-1. You can give yours a new cast of characters every year. The sage will get too big; transplant it and use the space for more parsley. If the dianthus rebels against your hot summers, experiment with licorice plant.

Build this garden at least knee-high with landscape timbers. If you place a board atop one edge (this is optional) you can sit and admire your lavender. Or let plants along both sides spill over the edges. Located just outside the kitchen door, this garden gives you quick access when tarragon chicken is on the menu.

Flying high, a garden for bees and butterflies

If you enjoy watching butterflies float and bees industriously wallowing in pollen, consider planting a garden of their favorite herbs. (Check out Figure 5-2.) The flowers of nearly every herb attract bees, which means that if you react severely to stings, you should lop off flower buds ruthlessly *before* they can open.

Figure 5-1:
This simple raised bed allows flexibility in plant choices and easy access to frequently harvested herbs.

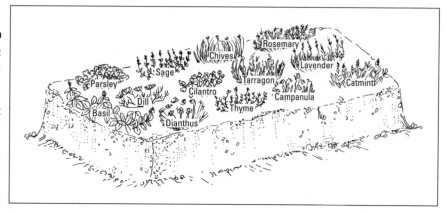

Since most people enjoy butterflies even more than bees — their lugubrious gliding and floating make a nice counterpoint to the frenzied vibrations of the honey-producers — we've created a garden that also includes a few of their favorite plants, as well as plants that supply food for their larvae. (As with second marriages, attracting butterflies is a case of "love me, love my children.")

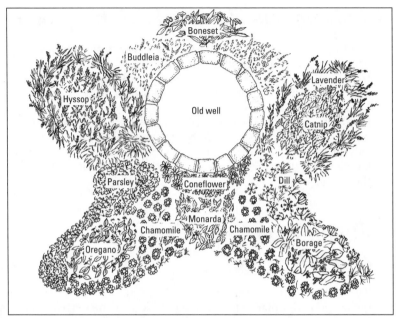

Figure 5-2:
Most herbs attract bees, and some are the favorite foods of butterfly larvae.

Our butterfly site is an old well that needed gussying up to keep it from looking like a wart on the landscape. This central feature could just as well (forgive the pun) be an old tree stump or a rock too big to move. The garden butts up again the edge of a deck, so viewers can look down on it.

We also added a trio of *skeps*, straw or wicker beehives that are available in various sizes where you find garden decorations. If you have only a tree stump or small rock, one skep will do nicely. (Prolong the life of a skep by bringing it indoors for the winter and during prolonged periods of rain.)

The butterfly shape may be *way* too cute for a lot of gardeners, but if children are frequent visitors to the garden, cute is in order. At the butterfly's nether end, we've included a little puddle pub. Some male butterflies congregate in mud puddles, because during mating season they need the sodium and other minerals that leach from the soil. Here, poorly draining soil, otherwise cursed by gardeners, is ideal. (You'll need to make mud with the garden hose on days that it doesn't rain.) To one side of this area, set out a shallow dish of water for butterflies that don't patronize mudbaths, such as hackberries, commas, and questionmarks. (Yes, these are butterflies, but don't expect to attract any semicolons.)

Although you should normally harvest herbs on a sunny day, you might want to break that rule if you create a bee garden, or if you find that your herbs attract unruly throngs of them. If you collect herbs on an overcast day, the bees will be more laid back.

Bee and butterfly garden: More about the plants

Butterfly bush. Our garden includes this shrub, *Buddleia davidii*, to provide height behind the well — and because you can't be a self-respecting butterfly gardener without it. It smells just like the bees' honey, too! Cultivars range from pink ('Pink Delight') to magenta and pale blue, to the dark purple 'Black Knight'. Be careful, though, since butterfly bush can self-sow shamelessly in some climates.

Butterfly weed. Most butterfly gardens also include pink-flowered milkweed *(Asclepias syriaca)* or orange butterfly weed *(A. tuberosa),* an environmentally important group of plants because they're the only ones on which monarch butterflies lay their eggs.

Monarchs undergo metamorphosis in a *chrysalis* (a *cocoon* is the protective covering for a moth caterpillar) that appears to have a necklace of 24-carat gold. Another name for butterfly weed is *pleurisy root.* Native Americans used it to treat respiratory ailments, but the root is toxic in high doses, so don't make it part of your herbal medicine chest.

If you don't have a well or similar feature, you could plant the tall boneset in the center and plant 2-foot-tall butterfly weed on the outside. If you grow milkweed, plant it in the center, because it grows to 6 feet.

Boneset. All members of the *Eupatorium* genus attract butterflies. The best known is probably towering Joe-Pye weed *(E. purpureum)* the purple-headed 7-footer named after an 18th-century snake-oil salesman who traveled the country promoting Native American culture and medicine.

For something only half as tall, use white-flowered boneset *(E. perfoliaturm).* Its common name had nothing to do with setting bones, but refers to the infectious disease dengue, called "bone break fever" because victims feel as though their bones are being broken. While 19th-century doctors used boneset frequently to induce sweating and vomiting, it's another herb you'll want to leave to the bees and butterflies.

Will's way, a Shakespearean conceit

Conceit has other meanings than "uppity." It can mean an elaborate metaphor, an extended comparison like those that gave Shakespeare so much pleasure. Or it can mean a fanciful idea, the likes of which herb gardeners are quite fond. We're kind of uppity about our Shakespearean garden design (shown in Figure 5-3), created for those who might picture themselves strolling along their garden path with an old college chum, quoting lines from Ophelia's death scene, or perusing sonnets at dusk. Shakespeare's plays and poems are full of more plants than anyone could cram into a single garden, so the list of substitutions is limited only to the time you have to spend hunkered down with "The Greatest Works of."

Figure 5-3:
Many public gardens have a Shakespearean corner where you can get more ideas for this literary theme.

For this place to read or meditate, all the plants flower in restful shades of blue and pink, and the design is formal, which is less distracting than the random patterns of an informal garden.

Because bay and rosemary are both handsome, aromatic plants but are not cold hardy in most of the country, we imagine them growing in ornate containers in four corners, so they can easily be brought inside to overwinter.

If you see a Shakespearean area in a botanic garden or grand private landscape, it will often have a bust of Will as a focal point. But ours is a homey retreat, not a library, and let's face it, the man is extremely dead. To bring life and music to this haven, how about a place for avian friends to splash? To stick to the theme, you can dub it your Bard Bath.

Shakespeare garden: More about the plants

Honeysuckle. Europeans once used common honeysuckle (or more poetically, woodbine, *Lonicera periclymenum*) to treat infected skin. Don't confuse it with Japanese honeysuckle *(L. japonica),* an out-of-control weed in much of the country. Common honeysuckle is just as fragrant, but its flowers are more often tinged with red.

We picture honeysuckle clambering over an *arbor,* a support made of three sections of simple latticework (available at lumberyards and large garden stores) on two sides and another across the top. Locate the arbor against a fence or hedge, or you can create a back for this bower with additional pieces of lattice.

Chamomile bench. Herbal benches planted with low-growing plants such as chamomile are an appealing idea — until it rains. Here's a simple solution: two planters of chamomile flanking a seating area made from planks. This way, you can sit on the fragrant herb when the weather is dry, or drag your fingers through the pungent foliage when it's not.

Rose. *Rosa eglanteria,* the sweet briar, or eglantine rose, is the "official" rose of Shakespeare. Its single pink flowers appear only in spring. Forget flowers. The leaves of this shrub waft the scent of green apples on a breeze, especially after a rain. But sweet briar isn't happy until it's 6 feet tall and almost as wide. You can find some hybrids of old-fashioned musk roses *(R. moschata)* — such as apricot-colored 'Felicia'— that are slightly smaller.

Dianthus. If your site is right — full sun and soil that drains well and is near-neutral — you can try growing one of these romantic and usually fragrant annuals and perennials. Rand Lee, long-time chairman of the American Dianthus Society, says that the cheddar pink *(D. gratianopolitanus)* is his favorite for the front of a border. They're intensely fragrant and have gray-green leaves.

Bayberry. Lists of Shakespearean plants often include the common myrtle, *Myrtus communis.* We suggest substituting bayberries, cold-hardy native plants from the same family. In the North, use *Myrica pensylvanica,* which grows from 5 to 12 feet high and spreads equally wide. In the South, choose the evergreen bayberry, *M. cerifera,* which grows even bigger. You can prune it or choose from many compact cultivars that will give you privacy without swallowing your whole property — and thrill you with its bayberry candle scent when you brush against it. (Zone 7 gardeners are on the borderline and can generally grow either of these species.)

Something's cooking, a culinary garden

If you love to cook, grow your herbs where you can snatch a handful easily in all kinds of weather. We've designed our culinary herb garden (shown in Figure 5-4) for a house with steps that descend from the kitchen door toward the west, giving most of the garden a warm, sunny exposure. This hot site, combined with the overhang from the house, may mean watering more often (the overhang will block much of your rain).

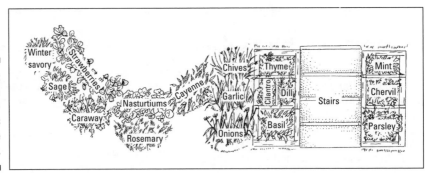

Figure 5-4:
This garden puts cooking herbs right outside your door.

To either side of the stairs, we've built stair-step raised beds for this cook's most frequently used herbs. Like automobile mileage, yours may differ. The raised bed to the right of the stairs gets a bit less sun, so here's where we've planted the more shade-tolerant mints, parsley, and chervil.

The garden ornament that inspired the U-shaped bed was an old metal washtub on which we mounted a whirligig of a washerwoman. (In some parts of the country, whirligigs get about as much respect as pink flamingos. Check your own neighborhood taste-makers for prevailing attitudes — then feel free to ignore them.)

We've used the tub as a place to sink a pot of rosemary, which can be lifted out and brought inside during the winter. Because the tub is so large, we had room to tuck other herbs around the edges, and we chose nasturtiums to add bright colors to the garden.

Patio pleasures, a garden for the senses

Herbs are some of the most sensuous plants ever created, but gardeners don't always situate them where all their amenities can be savored. Because most of them don't release their delectable fragrances into the air by themselves, as lilacs or rugosa roses do, and must be crushed or at least brushed against, we urge you to plant them where you can finger them or even dance on them.

The area to the north of the patio shown in Figure 5-5 is shady and damp, providing ideal conditions to grow tall valerian and sweet woodruff as a groundcover.

Fragrant, feathery-foliaged fennel (say that fast 20 times) and the fragrant double soapwort cultivar 'Rosea Plena' are containerized (both species are invasive in a friendly climate), and next to our chaise we have a wrought-iron shelf for herbs that we like to caress: scented geraniums are a great choice. So are rosemary, thyme, lemon balm, or lavender.

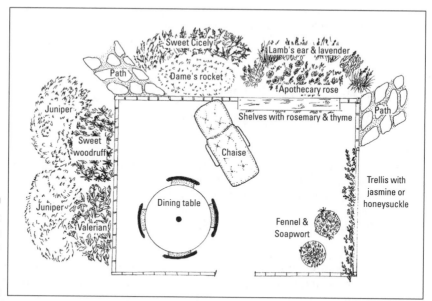

Figure 5-5:
This patio is full of herbs to smell and touch.

Patio gardens: More about the plants

Lamb's ear. If you're an herbal purist, you will grow betony, or *Stachys officinalis,* at the base of your apothecary rose. You can use betony to make a tea that may cure a headache or sore throat. But no garden for the senses is complete without lamb's ear, betony's second cousin. It likes full sun, makes a fine edging plant, and its fuzzy gray leaves are endless fun to pet. It self-sows unless you get a non-flowering cultivar, such as 'Silver Carpet'. Both stachys tolerate a little shade, and will be perfectly happy on the north side of your big rose.

Dame's rocket. Also called sweet rocket and dame's violet, *Hesperis matronalis* will perfume an entire garden when it produces its magenta (occasionally white or lavender) flowers in early summer. This plant lives only a couple of years, but self-sows eagerly. Europeans use the new leaves of dames rocket to spice up salads and because they're rich in vitamin C.

Carolina jasmine. A southeastern native, *Gelsenium sempervirens* is an evergreen vine with fragrant yellow flowers that open in early spring. Herbalists use it for facial pain, but it's extremely poisonous; gardeners in areas where the average minimum temperature is zero (Zone 7) and south should plant it for its scent and year-round screening. Gardeners in colder regions can plant woodbine, a honeysuckle we also recommend for the Shakespeare garden.

Juniper. The common juniper, *Juniperus communis,* is the plant whose berries are used medicinally and to flavor gin. If you just want a pretty, low hedge, you can plant golden yellow 'Depressa Aurea'. For privacy, choose three or four 'Hibernica', plants that grow 15 feet high but only a foot wide. If you expand your search to Chinese juniper, *J. chinensis,* you can still have pungent foliage and find shrubs that grow both relatively tall and broad. 'Sea Green', which grows 6 feet high and across, is a good choice.

We've also designed this patio to give you some privacy, with a trellis to the north and an evergreen shrub to south, so neighbors can't catch you as you wallow around in the thyme or rub leaves of lamb's ear over your face.

Tied up in knots, a garden for teas and medicines

If you look at drawings of old knot gardens, you can see that they weren't intended for growing herbs for harvest so much as for showing off the wealth (or leisure time) of their owners. Often, the areas between the "knot" were not filled with plants but pebbles or turf, or earth that was colored with crushed minerals. A *closed knot* had no paths between blocks to allow access for picking the herbs.

But even if you have both space and time to spare, you may want to put it to a more productive purpose that impressing the neighbors with your pruning skills. So in the interest of efficiency, we've produced an intensively planted but relatively simple knot design (shown in Figure 5-6) that will allow you an ample variety of herbs useful for medicine and tea. The traditional knot in the center, based on an equilateral triangle, is a *triquetra* (also known as a *shamrock design*). By surrounding it with an outer edging, we've provided divisions for six additional herbs.

The center figure of this knot design is triquetrous — based on a triangle with three acute angles.

The germander of an idea

Germander *(Teucrium chamaedrys)* has fallen by the wayside. At some point in history, people thought it could treat almost every ailment under the sun — quaint things like dropsy, quinsy, melancholy, and palsy, which sound like four of Peter Rabbit's siblings. It was a long-standing favorite remedy for gout.

But mostly, germander was so popular for making knot gardens that some people called it poor man's box, since not every Elizabethan could afford boxwood. (Gardeners have been clipping various forms of common boxwood, *Buxus sempervirens,* into hedges and edges for about 6,000 years.) With a knot garden or without, you can enjoy its chivelike aroma in potpourri, wreaths, and similar crafts.

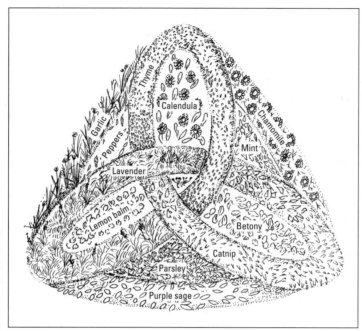

Figure 5-6:
This knot design is easier than it looks.

Consider how much you will be cutting any of these herbs before you plant, since some sections are bigger than others. (And if you harvest too much of a knot, you'll "untie" it!) Although knot garden plants are usually low-growing, we're breaking the rules by allowing taller plants, such as anise and fennel, in the center. Because this area is the hardest to reach, you might want to use the space for an herb that you won't be consuming — you may not harvest your own echinacea root, for instance, since the capsules for cold prevention are so readily available. Or you can follow another tradition and plunk an ornament, such as a sun dial, in the center.

Keep the whole design to 5 feet across or less if you want to have any hope of reaching plants near the center without treading on the bed.

Because you want your herbs to knit together quickly, plant them — annuals in particular — close together. You can make your plants appear to grow under and over each other by pruning one plant on the underside of its growth and pulling the long top growth over the adjacent plant — exactly like a person combing what hair he has left over a bald spot.

The next list contains good candidates for tying a knot. If, like most of us, you find knots too quaint and time-consuming, use several of these plants along the edge of a less contrived herb bed to give added punch to the picture you've painted:

Tying a triquetra knot

Try your hand at creating the knot garden shown in the accompanying figure. Choose a sunny, level site that can be seen from above, even if the vantage point is only as high as a low porch or deck — a second-story window is even better.

1. **Remove all turf grass and weeds, and generously amend the soil with organic matter.**

   For details on amending soil, see Chapter 8.

2. **Using stakes and string, draw the outline of the equilateral triangle that serves as the basis for the triquetra.**

   A carpentry device called a *combination square* can help you figure the three 45-degree angles, but if you know how big you want your design to be (say 4 feet on a side), just triple this measurement to get a total length for your string (in this case, 12 feet). Then have a friend help you move the pegs around.

   To check an angle, measure an equal distance from each peg — 1 foot, say — and mark the string at this point. If you connect those two points, the distance between them will also be 1 foot, and you have a 45 degree angle

3. **Draw the inside arcs.**

   Tie a string to the peg, and with a stick tied to the other end, pull the string taut as you draw the arc in the earth. Mark the arc with ground limestone or flour.

4. **Make the outside arcs freehand, again using limestone or flour.**

If you give the arc less curve, the garden will require fewer plants. Just remember to make the midpoint of each curve at a similar distance from the rest of your design, as indicated by the arrows.

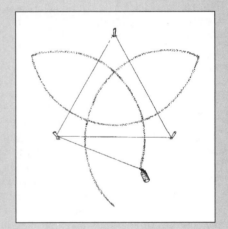

✔ **Boxwood** (*Buxus sempervirens* 'Suffruticosa', 'Vardar Valley', 'Newport Blue')

✔ **Bush basil** (*Ocimum basilicum minimum*, 'Purple Bush', 'Green Globe', 'Green Bouquet')

✔ **Dwarf sage** (*Salvia officinalis*)

✔ **Hyssop** (*Hyssopus officinalis*, 'Pink Sprite')

✔ **Lavender** (*Lavandula angustifolia*, 'Hidcote', 'Jean Davis', 'Lady'; 'Munstead')

✔ **Santolina** (*Santolina chamaecyparissus*, 'Nana'; *S. virens*)

   ✔ **Southernwood** *(Artemisia abrotanum; A. camphorata)*

   ✔ **Winter savory** *(Satureia montana)*

Fine friends: A mixed garden

Mixing herbs with vegetables, or herbs with flowers isn't a radical technique. English cottage gardeners were doing it centuries ago. Today, the most upscale "lifestyle" magazines show tidy country gardens filled with edibles and cutting flowers, surrounded by gravel paths and protected from predators by fences that mix the rustic (saplings with the bark still attached) and the necessary (chicken wire to keep out predators).

The garden in Figure 5-7 combines the stylish, the practical, and the historical. You can choose your own styles of fencing, from collector's English wattle to recycler's chainlink. White picket is never passé. The four beds are a rectangular version of the old German four-square garden. The ground around them should be easy to care for, perhaps just a mower's width of turf. A thick layer of mulch or gravel is better still.

Figure 5-7:
Herbs and vegetables are famously good chums.

The beds are raised and edged with board or landscape timber, making the garden easier to weed and harvest. More important, raised beds provide better drainage. In arranging these plants, we had two important considerations:

✔ **Boon companions.** We suggest placing the plants based on some version of what is called *companion planting*, which holds that some plants fare better or worse, depending on who their neighbors are. (A concept we all can relate to.)

The scientific jury is still out on a lot of these relationships, but we do know that *diversity* — growing a variety of plants rather than tending a *monoculture* of a single species — is healthier whether you're trying to grow food crops or restore a rain forest. Basil, which may repel the tomato hornworm, has long been paired with tomatoes, and fragrant yarrow may scare away insects that plague the squash family. Southernwood supposedly strikes terror into flea beetles, a scourge of eggplant.

✔ **Let a swag be their umbrella.** You can also use plants to create microclimates for others. (See Chapter 3 for more about microclimates.) Some companion plants may work their magic simply because they shade the roots of their chums. You can create even more shade with tall plants, such as the tansy and berry bushes we've planted on the west side, or a tall *swag* of pole beans or other climbers, which we've put on the south side of the garden.

A *swag* is a rope that hangs in a curve between two poles (you may be familiar with the term as it relates to window drapes). In gardens, you can make a swag with a vine, such as English ivy. In Figure 5-7, we've hung a length of netting for pole beans to climb on. A row of giant sunflowers is another popular and cheery approach to creating shade in the garden.

Chapter 6

Of Herbal Bondage: Ideas for Limited Space

*H*erbs adapt so well to containers that you can grow an impressive collection even if you have nowhere to garden but on a balcony or in a window box. Most annual herbs can thrive in pots for their brief span on earth, and many perennials also cotton to these cozy confines.

Even if you have a sprawling estate, you should consider containerizing some of your herbs — for several good reasons. If you have heavy clay soil, pots can give herbs better drainage. You can readily move frost-shy plants (like rosemary) and tropicals (like ginger) indoors. If your herbs seem unhappy, you can instantly give them shadier, sunnier, wetter, or drier conditions.

You can grow herbs with different soil and water needs next to each other if they're in pots. And if you simply don't like the way your herbs are arranged, you can create new combinations in minutes, rather than hours, weeks, or months. By setting potted herbs on pedestals, stairs, concrete blocks, or old milk crates, you can bring them closer to your nose for sniffing, to your fingers for stroking, and to your pruners for harvesting.

Container culture requires some new tricks but also offers fun and new opportunities.

Containers: Choosing and Using

If you buy pots at a garden center, you have two basic choices: clay (which is also called *terra cotta*) or plastic. Clay looks natural and earthy and blends with any decor. Because the material is porous, it "breathes," so herbs growing in clay pots are less likely to get waterlogged. In fact, remember to give a clay pot a good soak before you first plant in it, or the clay will suck the moisture from the soil like a sponge. (Containers made from *hypertufa,* which is a mixture of cement, peat, and perlite, have most of the advantages of terra cotta.)

On the down side, clay is heavier than plastic. And, if you should drop a clay container — while wrestling a potted 'Meyer' lemon onto the sunporch in fall, for instance, or if the soil in your potted thyme freezes in February — it will break.

Plastic pots are no longer synonymous with tacky. You can find a range of inoffensive colors, including some that look a lot like terra cotta. Plastic weighs less than clay, so moving herb pots is easier. Plastic isn't porous, so any plants growing in plastic pots need watering less often. This factor isn't necessarily an advantage, though, because herbs need excellent aeration. Fairly new to the market are plastic pots that have a reservoir on the bottom, which improves drainage yet supplies water when the soil dries out.

Before you plunk down hard-earned cash for new containers, take a look around. You begin seeing potential plant containers when you open your mind to the possibilities. Check out the attic, flea markets, and curbsides. Herbs, in particular, look wonderful in anything that spells "old." Just make sure the container has drainage holes or use your find as an outer container for a more homely pot.

As a general rule, you should use a pot that's only a little larger than your plant's *root ball* (that's the volume of the roots, and it won't really look like a ball). Plants that have long roots, such as parsley, need deep pots. Plants that grow from rhizomes (see Chapter 2), such as ginger, spread horizontally and need shallower pots (sometimes called *azalea pots*).

Cleanliness is next to . . .

To avoid spreading soil diseases, always plant herbs in clean containers. Wash previously used pots with dish detergent, and then dip them in a 10 percent bleach-water solution (1 part bleach, 9 parts water). Rinse the containers and then let them dry completely before using.

For single plants of most culinary herbs, you need a pot from 8 to 10 inches in diameter. A pot 18 inches in diameter can hold as many as three or four plants. Pots, unlike garden beds, restrict root growth. A too-small pot is like a too-small shoe: It will cramp your herb's style. A too-large pot, on the other hand, holds extra water that your plant won't use. Just as in an overstocked refrigerator, the excess can turn ugly and even make your plant sick.

A pot that actually holds plants is a *growing pot.* An outer, decorative container is a *cachepot;* you can slip a plain-Jane plastic growing pot into a cachepot for instant pizzazz.

Growing pots

Use your imagination when choosing a growing pot. The following list is incomplete, but it shows that you can use almost anything to grow herbs. Just make sure the pot is the right size (not too small, not too large) and has drainage holes in the bottom.

- ✔ **Old coffee cans or tins from olive oil or other foods.** Imported brands have the most panache.

- ✔ **Tin cookie and popcorn containers.** Those without lids are almost free at flea markets. You can easily punch holes in the bottom of these tin containers, but they will rust out eventually.

- ✔ **Pottery, such as cookie jars.** These are more expensive than tins but longer lasting. Make drainage holes with an electric drill quipped with a masonry bit. (Practice first on that chipped casserole dish from your ex-mother-in-law.)

- ✔ **Flue tiles.** Used to line chimneys, these rectangular clay tubes can be cut to lengths of 12 or 18 inches to make instant raised beds for individual herbs.

- ✔ **Children's toys, such as sand buckets and trucks.** Metal toys look more charming but are now valuable collector's items. Plastic can be quirky.

- ✔ **Work boots.** Like baby shoes, these boots obtain their appeal from the creases of hard wear. If they come from a beloved foot, even better.

- ✔ **Watering cans.** Glossy garden magazines with "Country" in the title show these cans sprouting herbs and other plants. Pretty nifty, but the spout and handle take up extra room if your space is tight.

- ✔ **Seashells.** Unless you beachcomb in more exotic places than we do, you won't often pick up conches and other shells roomy enough for anything bigger than a seedling. Fortunately, such natural treasures often become yard sale bargains when the neighbors' kids head for college.

- ✔ **Hollow logs.** These items rarely last longer than a season (and drainage is a problem), but if it's the rustic look you seek, the price is right.

✔ **Old galvanized metal buckets and tubs.** A few dents and dings only give these metal objects more personality, and they last virtually forever.

✔ **Whiskey barrels.** These oak containers are probably used for plants more than they're used for bourbon. Rugged, handsome, and big enough for small trees, they rot eventually. Extend their lives by placing them on bricks and lining them with an old trash bag — but remember to include enough holes for drainage.

Cachepots

If that black nursery pot is exactly the right size, leave the rosemary plant in it and hide the plastic in one of the growing pots suggested in the preceding list or in one of the following. Use sphagnum moss to obscure the top of the growing pot.

Consider these decorative containers:

✔ **Wood crates and boxes.** Herbs look down-home and funky arranged in recycled wooden containers, such as fruit crates, packing crates, or antique tool boxes. Lengthen their lives by giving them a coat of polyurethane.

✔ **Baskets.** Every garage sale has a surfeit of old baskets in endless shapes and sizes. You can employ deeper baskets as a surround for larger herbs or group small pots in a shallower one.

✔ **Wheelbarrows.** Often serving as centerpieces in herb gardens, these small vehicles can do double duty as planters or plant holders.

✔ **Window boxes.** You can put your herbs right in your window box (see Figure 6-1), of course, but their roots won't get tangled if you leave them in separate pots. That planting approach also makes it easier to pull out spent herbs and replace them with new ones.

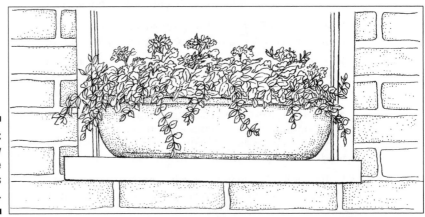

Figure 6-1:
Window boxes are great places for herbs.

Containers: Care and Feeding

When you grow herbs in pots and other containers, you need to handle the essentials — soil, water, and fertilizer — a bit differently than how you would if you were growing the same plants in the ground.

The unreal dirt

Potting soil is a lot like pesto: Such a simple affair with so few basic ingredients, yet all gardeners have their favorite recipe.

Today, almost everyone starts with a soilless mix, whether straight from the bag, amended slightly, or homemade from raw ingredients. *Never* use soil straight from the garden for growing plants in containers. Garden soil quickly becomes hard and compacted, and it invariably contains weed seeds or disease organisms.

The easiest approach to filling containers with a healthy planting medium is to buy a bagged, high-quality potting mix. Many brands are on the market, but nearly all commercial products contain peat, perlite, composted bark, and some nutrients and are astonishingly lightweight when you pick them up. A proper potting mix is also light-colored when dry. Avoid mixes that are heavy and dark in the bag: The manufacturer may have cheated and sacked up plain old dirt mixed with a little peat or perlite.

To be absolutely sure of what your mix contains, make your own. The ingredients listed below are among the common constituents. Some serve to help hold water, and others enable water to drain out.

To help hold water, add:

- ✔ **Sphagnum peat.** Partly decomposed organic material harvested from ancient bogs in Canada and the United States, peat is difficult to wet initially but then helps bind other ingredients together. Peat is also acidic and contains no nutrients. Because peat makes a soil acidic, add about 3 tablespoons of limestone for each gallon of peat-based potting mix.

- ✔ **Coir.** Coir is residue from coconut shells. Because coir is a renewable resource, it is becoming popular as a substitute for peat.

- ✔ **Leaf mold and compost.** Some people just can't resist the idea of mixing in a dab of organic material from their own back yards. Better to look for these as commercial products, but if you use your own, you need to sterilize them in a 180°F oven for 1 hour.

To help water drain, add:

- ✔ **Perlite.** These tiny white pellets come from crushed volcanic rock (obsidian) that has been heated.

- ✔ **Vermiculite.** These silvery flakes, even smaller than perlite pellets, are derived from expanding mica. Vermiculite is great for starting seeds, but it compacts more quickly than perlite in long-term plantings.

- ✔ **Sand.** Sand was once a standard ingredient in most potting soils, but experts now debate whether or not sand belongs in a container. Sand makes your pot much heavier. Consider it only for small containers, or if you need to weigh down a container that is top-heavy. Use coarse builder's sand, not the stuff in your kids' sandbox.

Mixing it up

A basic, soilless potting mix consists of one part each of peat, vermiculite, and perlite with a little limestone thrown in. This mix contains almost no nutrients, so you must feed your plants regularly during the growing season.

For succulents, such as aloe (an essential herb for your kitchen windowsills, where you can grab a stem for treating minor burns), try a slightly lighter soil — one part peat to two each of vermiculite and perlite. A tropical plant like ginger, on the other hand, likes a more humus-rich soil, perhaps two parts peat to one each of vermiculite and perlite.

A final reminder: Potting soil is like bath water. You need to toss it after it's been used (in this case, at the end of the growing season). If you're raising annual herbs, recycle the contents of your containers. As long as the plant wasn't diseased, add it and the soil mix to the compost pile. (If you're growing perennial herbs in containers, repot them, or at least refresh the potting mix they're growing in, every two or three years.)

A no-drainer

It's crucial that your pots have drainage holes. But make sure they don't allow too much drainage so that water gushes out and takes soil with it. To help hold soil in, put a piece of old window screen or a scrap of landscape fabric in the bottom of the pot.

If your pot sits on a wooden deck or any other surface that can stain or rot, place a saucer under the pot to catch runoff water. Many plastic pots come with their own, and most nurseries sell terra-cotta or plastic saucers. Some plastic saucers have ridges that keep the pot raised above any water runoff.

Chuck those shards

Like the urban legend of the alligator in the sewer, some gardening myths refuse to go away.

No matter what you hear to the contrary, do *not* put a layer of broken pieces of crockery, pebbles, or Styrofoam peanuts at the bottom of your container to improve its drainage. You will actually make the drainage worse by giving plants a shallower column of soil and create a place for water to accumulate and rot roots.

An exception is when using cachepots. If you set a growing pot *with* drainage holes inside a cachepot *without* drainage holes, you can become blithely unaware of overwatering and drown your herb in the resulting bathtub. Setting some pebbles on the bottom of the cachepot can lessen this possibility, but you still have to pay attention: Don't let excess water creep up past the bottom of the inside pot. (If you've hidden the inside pot with Spanish or sphagnum moss, peel it back and check occasionally.)

Make sure the saucer is at least as wide as the pot's rim. (And remember that terra-cotta saucers are porous and become damp — they'll ruin wood, carpet, and other surfaces unless you place a nonporous material under them or coat them with polyurethane.)

Beware of plastic hanging baskets that come with attached saucers. The saucers are invariably too small, and water will quickly stream out onto whatever is below. If you can strategically locate your hanging basket over a big planter and you don't mind a bit of splash, it's a nice recycling trick.

Now, the Easy Pot: Putting It All Together

You have a container. You have a bucket of planting medium. You have a plant. Now what?

1. **Lift the herb out of its seed tray or tap it out of its nursery container and examine the roots.**

   If the roots are coiled, badly tangled, or crowded, the plant is *root-bound*. (It's been growing in a too-small container for too long.) Try to loosen and spread the roots before repotting the plant; otherwise, don't disturb the root ball.

2. **Fill the new container with soil to a level that will accommodate the roots.**

   If it's a small plant with long roots, you may need to tip the pot on its side and gently upend it again.

3. **Place the herb in the pot _slightly_ deeper than it was in the original pot.**

4. **Fill in around the plant with potting soil to a level about an inch from the top (less on very small pots.)**

5. **Set the pot in a tray of water for several hours or water it carefully.**

6. **After the soil settles, add more soil to reach a level of 1 inch below the top of the pot and water again.**

   You can also return the pot to the water tray until the soil surface is damp; then let the pot drain until no water runs from the drainage holes.

How dry I am!

Most plants that fail in containers that are placed outdoors do so for lack of water. Heavy spring rains can lure gardeners into complacency. This tendency is especially true with easy-going, low-water plants like herbs. The sun will come up tomorrow, and it will rain a couple times this week, right? Then comes August, a week at the beach, and an adolescent house sitter. . . .

Plan on watering outdoor containers every day from mid- to late summer, more often and for a longer period of time if you live in an arid climate or if the weather is windy. (Gardeners in hot regions also should avoid planting in small containers, which dry out more quickly).

Take a look at these tricks to lessen watering duties:

- ✔ **Mulch.** Mulches (bark or pebbles) will slow evaporation. Because you can't see if the soil is dry, poke under the mulch with your finger to test if it's time to water.

- ✔ **Polymers.** These absorbent crystals swell up like gelatin when wet and then release the water gradually. Follow directions carefully; if you use too much, your herb roots will suffocate in a mass of goo.

- ✔ **Wicks.** You can buy self-watering pots with a built-in wick or make your own wicking system. In _Houseplants For Dummies_ (IDG Books Worldwide, Inc.), author Larry Hodgson recommends making one with a margarine tub filled with water and a wick of yarn or a twist of nylon stocking. Run the wick through the lid of the margarine tub and through your container's drainage hole into the herb's root ball. (Use a chopstick or knitting needle to guide the wick into the drainage hole.)

✔ **Drip systems.** If you have many valuable herbs, you can invest in a drip-irrigation system with timers and little tubes that leak into individual containers.

✔ **Watering wands.** These extension devices attach to a hose for watering hanging baskets. A great tool, but because you can water the basket without lowering it (and without seeing or feeling the soil), using a wand can encourage overwatering.

Fertilizer: A strict diet

Herbs are by and large strict dieters. Like supermodels, they turn soft and vulnerable when overfed. But because most soilless mixes are the equivalent of bread and water (that's *white* bread), you need to give them some chicken and broccoli periodically.

We didn't raise our children on potato chips, and we don't give our container plants junk food either. Give the potted plants the same healthy, organic stuff that you would the herbs in your planting beds: seaweed or fish emulsion. For herbs growing in containers, use half the recommended amount in monthly doses.

The Outdoor Life

To humans contemplating eternal rest, the earth can seem to be a cold, cold bed. But for plants growing in it, the earth is a toasty warm alternative to winter air, which can dip to temperatures well below zero. If you leave your containers of herbs sitting outside in winter, then the plants' roots aren't protected from the cold air.

As a rule, you can leave perennial herbs outdoors in containers all winter if they are hardy to one zone farther north than your home. Gardeners in USDA Zone 6, for example, can leave out most thymes, which are hardy to Zone 5.

You can give your potted herbs some insurance by burying them. In fall, dig holes for the containers of your perennial herbs and tuck them in for their winter sleep under soil and a comforter of leaves. A *cold frame* is handy for this, as is a *nursery bed* — a small tilled garden that you use in spring for starting seeds and in summer for *heeling in*, or temporarily planting, new perennials and other plants.

One warning: If you live in the far North, you may be growing herbs that won't survive even with this coddling. The section titled "Gimme shelter" in this chapter has more on bringing herbs indoors.

TIP

Strawberry jars forever

Strawberry jars, those tall terra-cotta pots with side holes at different levels, are a space-efficient way to grow small herbs such as sweet marjoram, thyme, dwarf geraniums, or bushy basils. But go plant-shopping early: The root ball of each herb you grow needs to be smaller than the hole in your jar.

To make sure water reaches all the plant roots, tap the services of some 2-inch-diameter PVC pipe, a piece about 2 inches shorter than your pot. Attach wire mesh to the bottom of the pipe with wire and drill holes in the pipe, each in a line with one of the holes in the strawberry jar. Fill the pipe with gravel and put more wire mesh on top to keep dirt from clogging it.

Center the pipe upright in your jar and fill the jar with potting soil up to the level of the first holes.

Remove your first herbs from their pots and soak their roots briefly in clean water; cut away any long stringy roots that will be hard to work with. Slide the roots and stem into the hole, angling them slightly downward (if necessary, use a screwdriver to push and guide them) until the plant's *crown* (the place where the stem and roots meet) is even with the edge of the hole.

Add more soil mix, up to the next level of holes, and repeat the process. When you near the top of the jar, center an upright or slightly larger plant — chive, lavender, parsley, and sweet basil are good choices — and fill the jar to about 1 inch of its lip. Water gently and remember to turn the pot frequently so that all the herbs get an equal amount of sun.

The whiskey sour barrel

The half barrel in Figure 6-2 may make you pucker up — not because it's lovable, but because all the herbs in it are lemon-scented or lemon-flavored. The figure also illustrates principles that apply to planting any large container with a group of herbs. For example:

- ✔ Choose plants that require similar cultural conditions — the same amounts of light and water, the same kind of soil.

- ✔ Put a vertical or spiky plant in the center (or at the back if the container will be against a wall). In this case we've used the old-fashioned lemon daylily *(Hemerocallis lilioasphodelus)*. If you prefer something you can use in the kitchen, substitute lemongrass.

- ✔ Save room around the rim for at least one plant that flops becomingly over the side. Lemon thyme *(Thymus × citriodorus)* is usually described as upright, but you can persuade it to droop earthward. Or look for 'Doone Valley', a creeping cultivar with gold variegation.

Figure 6-2:
A tall plant at the center of a barrel planting provides a focal point.

You can grow many other "lemon" plants, including lemon balm, a hardy 2-foot member of the mint family, lemon catnip *(Nepeta cataria* var. *citriodora)*, and even a lemon marigold 'Lemon Gem'. And don't forget that the flower petals of lavender have a distinct lemon flavor.

For you die-hard lemon lovers, here's more:

- ✔ **Lemon geraniums.** Two *Pelargonium* cultivars to look for: 'Frensham Lemon', which is unmistakably citrus, and 'Fingerbowl Lemon', which boasts tiny crinkled leaves.

- ✔ **Lemon bergamot.** *Monarda citriodora* grows 1–2 feet high and has pink-purple flowers. The Hopis used it to flavor game; you can use it for tea.

- ✔ **Lemon basil.** Look for 'Mrs. Burns' or 'Sweet Dani', which won the respected All-America Selection award in 1998.

- ✔ **Lemon trees.** Like lemon verbena, lemon eucalyptus *(Eucalyptus citriodora)* and 'Meyer' lemon trees have to come indoors in winter. Try one or the other in the center of your arrangement, with pots of smaller lemon herbs at its feet.

Hang 'em high

Hanging baskets are another striking way to display herbs — if you have a good place to hang them, as shown in Figure 6-3. While Victorian porches are a great place for hanging ferns (all that cool shade), and smack under the eaves of a house is a great place for baskets of succulents (all that protection from rain), herbs need a sunny home where they can benefit from an occasional shower.

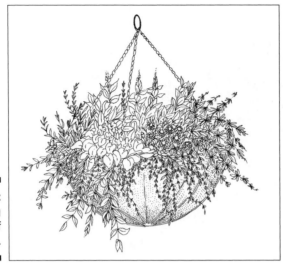

Figure 6-3:
A hanging
basket of
herbs.

An ideal place for hanging baskets is a *pergola,* an arborlike structure that consists of a series of upright supports topped by vertical beams. You can hang baskets not only from the overheads, but on hooks attached to the uprights, as well.

Don't hang your basket so high that you can't reach it for watering, for pinching off dead flowers or stems, or for occasional harvesting. And don't hang it so low that tall friends have to duck under it.

As to the containers themselves, ceramic pots are too heavy to make practical hanging baskets, and terra-cotta pots dry out even faster in the air than they do on the ground. Use either plastic pots or wire baskets lined with sheets of sphagnum moss.

For the residents of your hanging basket, choose herbs that don't grow too tall. Look, especially, for plants that dangle gracefully, things that have words like "creeping" and "prostrate" in their names.

Some good candidates for hanging baskets are

- **Catmint** (*Nepeta* spp.)
- **Creeping savory** *(Satureia repandra)*
- **Creeping thyme** *(Thymus praecox; T. pulegioides,* 'Doone Valley', 'Silver Needle')
- **Curly parsley** *(Petroselinum crispum* 'Triple Curled')
- **Dittany of Crete** *(Origanum dictamnus)*
- **Oregano** (*Origanum vulgare* 'Aureum')

> ✔ **Prostrate rosemary** *(Rosmarinus officinalis* 'Prostratus', 'Lockwood de Forest', 'Huntington Carpet', 'Ken Taylor')
>
> ✔ **Trailing nasturtium** *(Tropaeolum majus* Gleam series)

If plants don't hang down enough initially, you can train woody stems, such as thymes, by tying fishing weights to them.

A Roof Over Their Heads

Several years ago, Kathy asked a nationally known herb expert which herbs grow best indoors. It was a brief chat. "You can't grow herbs indoors," he responded. Later, we learned that he is notoriously cranky on many subjects. We also learned that he wasn't far off the mark.

Don't get us wrong. You *can* grow herbs indoors. In fact, you can grow many beautiful tropical herbs that you can't grow outdoors unless you live just a short swim from Central America. And you can keep others alive, hanging in there for a few weeks of hard winter until you can safely shove them back outside again.

But herbs are not philodendrons or even African violets. In other words, they aren't a snap to grow inside. This section shows you which ones will feel at home in the family room and how to increase your chances of success with some of the more finicky types.

What really works

Of course you can try growing herbs indoors, especially if (like Karan) you live in a climate where the growing season is about as long as a sneeze. You can savor fresh flavors and heavenly scents year-round. Herbs aren't just for Fourth of July cookouts. Rosemary, bay, and bayberry are as closely associated with the Yuletide as mistletoe and Frasier firs.

Indoor gardening isn't harder than outdoor gardening, it's different. As a friend of ours once said, "You have to make that commitment to opening the blinds every morning." Or in the case of herbs, to make sure that the timer has turned on your grow lights. You also have to be vigilant: Herbs that are almost never troubled by insects and diseases in the garden are easy targets when grown indoors.

As a bare-bones essential, you must offer indoor herbs artificial light. And even when you do, many of the plants will balk at confinement, like kids in a classroom. Some herbs are too tall to grow under lights; some have deep tap roots; some require a period of chilling or complete dormancy during the winter months.

How sweet it is!

An unusual tender herb you might want to try in a hanging basket indoors is sweet herb *(Lippia dulcis)*. Garden writer Elvin McDonald says it reminds him of a trailing lantana, "except the blossoms are greenish and conelike." The camphor aroma would seem to contradict its common name, but the leaves are so sweet — 1,000 times sweeter than sugar — you can mince them up for tea time. You can also use the herb to treat colds and colic, as the Aztecs did. Sweet herb likes somewhat moist, rich soil but tolerates average house temperatures.

With other herbs, it's a matter of what we might call quality of life — for both of you. They'll survive, yes. You'll have enough parsley to garnish your lemon chicken but not enough to make tabbouleh. You'll have a sprig of basil to impart some personality to that grocery-store tomato, but pesto? Forget it.

Forget, too, any herbs that you're growing for fruits or seeds, such as fennel or dill. Getting plants *that* far along indoors is impossible without a greenhouse . . . and darn hard even with one!

Gimme shelter

Growing herbs indoors isn't easy, but we also need to say that many perennial herbs *must* come indoors during the cold months in most parts of North America. Leave aloe, bay, ginger, lemon verbena, rosemary, scented geraniums — and many more — outside in December and January, and all you'll have left in spring are a few dead stems and a pot of soil to dump on the compost pile.

Only a handful of herbs appear consistently on everyone's list of indoor favorites. We'd tell you that you can't kill bay, but the instant we do, yours will die. So we'll leave it that bay adapts pretty well to being indoors. We should alert you that if your bay, a symbol of honor, dies, evil may descend on your household. (Well, at least according to folklore.)

Following are a few of the herbs that most gardeners must haul inside when the mercury dips:

✔ **Lemon verbena** can be a good indoor herb, but we warn you: After you've wrestled it inside, your plant will ungraciously drop all its leaves. Don't panic, and don't fertilize. Lemon verbena is *deciduous*, which means it's supposed to lose its leaves in autumn, and it's just going to sit there for a while and look ugly. Let it get a bit dry, and keep an eye open for spider mites and whiteflies. Resume fertilizing and watering in early spring.

- ✔ **Rosemary** is the summer vacation romance that palls when autumn comes around. Without gentle zephyrs and sunlight — and with too much fawning from a well-meaning owner — the death blow is usually root rot from too much water. Use a soil high in perlite, and keep it just barely damp. Barely. It also goes to meet its maker if it gets bone dry.

- ✔ **Scented geraniums**, or pelargoniums, do well inside. Since they are tender perennials, it's come in or else! Indoors, they need plenty of light (who doesn't?), good air circulation, and daytime temperatures around 70°F, 10°F colder at night.

- ✔ **Pineapple sage** *(Salvia elegans)* is another herb that succeeds under a roof — flourishes would be an overstatement. Your plant may even flower (brilliant red), but if it doesn't, you still can use its leaves in drinks.

Many other herbs can survive indoors. Give them plenty of artificial light, and they'll struggle through winter. In their search for sunshine, many plants get leggy and impossibly tall and lean like Ichabod Crane, so prune stem tips frequently to keep them bushy. (Pinching off the ends tells the buds farther down on the branch to start growing.)

Gardeners have moderately good luck with growing these herbs indoors:

- ✔ Artemisia
- ✔ Basil
- ✔ Catnip
- ✔ Chive
- ✔ Curry
- ✔ Costmary
- ✔ Germander
- ✔ Ginger

- ✔ Lemon balm
- ✔ Marjoram
- ✔ Mint
- ✔ Oregano
- ✔ Parsley
- ✔ Rue
- ✔ Santolina
- ✔ Winter savory

Instant herbs

For (almost) instant gratification and no messy soil, try growing sprouts. Cress and mustard are two herbs you can harvest in only a couple of days from sowing. Soak a couple of tablespoons of seeds overnight, rinse well, and then put in a wide-mouthed quart jar with a cheesecloth-and-rubber-band "lid." Lay the jar on its side near an east or west window; rinse the seeds in water twice a day. When you see more leaves than seeds, dig in.

Perpetual Care

So you've picked out a few herbs that you think deserve to share your humble home. Now think of your abode as a bed-and-breakfast and sometime-clinic for plants. Herbs reward you with their pleasant company, but you do need to cater to their appetites and whims. Playing the piano and extra cable channels are entirely at your discretion, however.

Moving day

Psychologists say that for humans, moving to a new home is one of those events, like weddings and births, that is highly stressful, even when happy. The same is true for plants. Moving is a *big* change.

When you take plants from outdoors to indoors, they adapt by producing a different type of foliage: leaves that can make sugars and carbohydrates efficiently in lower light. An abrupt move makes their current "outdoor" leaves turn yellow and drop off or become brown around the edges.

You can ease your herbs' transition by moving them under a tree, an overhang, or a shelter of *shade cloth* (a mesh material available from garden shops or by mail order) for a few days. While the plants are in the transition area, check them carefully for any sign of insects. If you see any, try the pest-management treatments we talk about in the section titled "Buy stock in IPM" in this chapter.

You also need to reduce both fertilizer and water. Less fertilizer slows high-energy top growth (but the roots will keep growing). Drier soil "hardens off" the foliage, preparing it to cope with your home's drier environment. You can help plants adjust to the dry indoor air by enclosing them in a plastic bag for a few days — punch a few holes in the bag so too much humidity doesn't build up.

If you want to start new herb plants indoors — a quick crop of basil, for example — see Chapter 8, which shows you how to sow seeds indoors.

Bright lights, big payoff

In providing light for your indoor plants, the goal is to mimic as closely as possible the light spectrum of the sun. The special bulbs and tubes sold as *grow lights* are supposed to do this, but they don't use electricity as efficiently as fluorescent lights. Gardeners who've tried both swear by fluorescents, which are inexpensive and available at the local hardware store.

For a full range of rays, you need two bulbs: a warm one to provide light from the red end of the sun's spectrum and a cool one to play the blues. Buy a standard workbench fixture that holds two bulbs under a hood so the light is directed down at your plants instead of out into the room. The bulbs should be no farther than 6 inches apart.

Most of these fixtures hang from a chain or cable, which enables you to move them higher or lower. For seedlings and cuttings, the lights should be only a few inches away from the plants. Mature herbs should be about 10 or 12 inches away from the lights. Give your herbs 14 to 16 hours of light a day by plugging the light fixture into an inexpensive timer.

Air of superiority

Good air circulation is also essential to growing herbs indoors, where plants need air movement but not gale-force winds or even a cold draft. To encourage cross-ventilation, keep the door of the room where they're growing open. And don't crowd plants together — space them far enough from their neighbor so their leaves don't touch. If your house or apartment is well-sealed, use a small tabletop fan to get the air moving.

Because the air in most homes is extremely dry, set your containers in trays lined with pebbles and filled with an inch or so of water. The herbs should sit over the water, not in it.

Some may like it hot, but most herbs like it cool, around 68°F during the day. Nighttime temperatures should be 5°–10°F lower. Make sure that the leaves of plants sitting on a windowsill don't touch the glass — if the windowpane freezes, so will the leaves!

Currying flavor

For a handsome house guest with a scent that will drive you wild with desire (for dinner), try cardamom *(Elettaria cardamomum)*. The ground seeds from this member of the ginger family are crucial to Indian cuisine. The white flowers, tinged with violet, are elusive indoors. But the perfume of the 2-foot leaves, which look like thick lances, will have you pining for curry and kebabs.

Eating and drinking

Just as outdoor containers tend to suffer from too little water, indoor plants often get too much. Plants that are growing rapidly use more water, but many perennial herbs go semi-dormant or completely dormant in winter. These plants need much less water than they did in summer.

Watering on a once-a-week schedule may help you remember, but like a good waiter or waitress, you should inquire first if your service is needed. Water most herbs only when the soil surface is dry. Other watering tips:

- ✔ Water less often if your home is cool or if your herbs are growing in plastic pots rather than clay.
- ✔ Water less often if plants seem to be ailing (rapid growth will add to their stress).
- ✔ Don't let your plant sit in a saucer of water.
- ✔ Don't shock plants with cold tap water; water should be tepid — about room temperature.

Observation is key. Some plants are simply thirstier than others. Some, such as basil, even seem to need more water as indoor plants than as outdoor plants.

Use less fertilizer indoors than you would outdoors, because most plants are growing more slowly. If you are using fish or seaweed emulsion, which we recommend, this will be a relief, since they can smell of last week's halibut. Give the plants a monthly shot at one-fourth the recommended dose. (If the smell bothers you, put the plants on a tray and whisk them to a porch or garage at mealtime.)

In sickness and in health

Dry heat, overwatering, and especially the proximity of their neighbors means that when pests strike indoor plants, the damage can spread like a plague. Vigilance is a must.

Although the list of indoor pests is shorter than the list of outdoor foes, some of these foes are extremely difficult to control. Aphids, spider mites, and whiteflies are fond of herbs with succulent foliage and stems; bay and other woody plants are likely homes for scale. Mealybugs are equal opportunity enemies. (For more information about the insects and diseases that attack herbs — and how to combat them — see Chapter 9.)

Integrated pest management, or IPM, is a practice by which you first do every-thing you can to prevent plant problems, then take progressively more dras-tic steps to correct them.

Here's our IPM approach to gardening indoors:

1. **Keep it clean.**

   Remove dry leaves and other debris; use clean containers and potting soil; and clean the surfaces on which plants sit.

2. **Don't crowd plants.**

3. **Don't overfertilize plants.**

   Rapid growth makes plants weak and susceptible to disease and pests.

4. **Isolate anything you bring indoors — cut flowers or new plants — for at least two weeks.**

   Isolate any herbs that become infested.

5. **If plants become badly infested, consider getting rid of them.**

6. **At the first sign of pests, begin spraying the plant frequently with water.**

7. **Dab infested areas with a cotton swab dipped in rubbing alcohol.**

8. **Try spraying with an insecticidal soap.**

9. **Sticky traps will help control flying pests, plus show how heavy the infestation is.**

10. **To smother insects, try a horticultural oil that can be used all year round and on houseplants.**

Part IV

An Encyclopedia of Herbs

The 5th Wave   By Rich Tennant

That's very nice of you, dear. But I really don't think just one beetle in the garden will do much damage.

In this part . . .

We give you comprehensive descriptions of more than 65 herbs. What's more, we tell you what these herbs are used for and how you can grow them.

An Encyclopedia of Herbs

• •

*T*his part of the book is the herbs' coming-out party, except there are more than 65 of them and only one guest — you (and you can dress any way you please). We take you around to each herb and introduce you one by one. After you've sized up each character's appearance, you can decide if the herb is worthy of adorning your garden or if it's something you'll tuck away behind the doghouse.

We also clue you in to some family history (including lookalike plants that you may want to grow or avoid) and some juicy (albeit often ancient) gossip, full of witches and curses and advice to the lovelorn. We note what each herb does to pull its weight in modern society and what it can do for you, from the stewpot to the first-aid kit. (Ancient medicinal uses rarely translate to modern scientific validity.)

With all budding relationships being reciprocal, you need to know what you can do to keep the herbs healthy and happy. So we pass along any quirks the herbs may have regarding soil, sun, and starting seeds.

Agrimony (Agrimonia eupatoria)

Agrimony, a member of the rose family and native to the British Isles, sometimes fails to show up in herbal hit parades. But who can resist a plant that smells like apricots and wants to follow you everywhere you go? Philanthropos, an ancient name for this herb, is thought to refer to its seeds' inclination to cling passionately to the pants or fur of every passerby. Other common names include church steeples — for its spires of little yellow flowers — but also cockeburr, cocklebur, cockburr, and, for a little variety, sticklewort.

*Agrimonia
eupatoria*

Another explanation for the "philanthropic" nickname was that agrimony received credit for a boatload of spiritual and health benefits. The Anglo-Saxons plucked the herb for snakebites and warts. In the Middle Ages you might have put it under your pillow for a sound night's snooze. The Chinese have used it for a millennium to control bleeding and as a tonic for the digestive system and liver.

Agrimony does contain tannins, which are good for diarrhea, and mucilage that can take the scratch out of a sore throat in a gargle and soften skin in the bath. Or you can just enjoy the fruity-scented leaves in a tea or as a garnish for fruit dishes.

Description

Agrimony leaves may be prettier than the flowers on this 3- to 5-foot-tall perennial: Heavily toothed with prominent veins, similar to a raspberry leaf, the leaves are deep green and a bit hairy. Each leaf is divided into six or eight pairs of leaflets and a terminal leaf, with tinier leaves in between. The effect is eye-pleasingly complex. In fact, the plant's genus name comes from a Greek word, *argemone,* meaning "healing for the eyes." The Greeks meant this medicinally, but we think it works aesthetically, as well.

Beginning about midsummer and continuing for a couple months, produces spikes of ⅜-inch, five-petalled, apricot-scented yellow flowers. The blossoms face out and up as though glued around the spike. When the flowers drop off, they leave a three-part calyx that develops into that friendly little bur.

Despite the nice foliage — which is slightly fragrant — you may want to put this herb in an out-of-the-way place where pets and people won't brush against it.

How to grow

Cold hardy through USDA Zone 6, agrimony is happy in ordinary, well-drained soil, is unparticular about pH, and is among the few herbs that prefer a bit of shade. Its seeds can be hard to germinate, even though the plant readily seeds itself where you may not want it. Sow seeds outside in early spring and thin to 8 inches, or start with a division.

Cultivars and related plants

In some herb books you may come across the name, hemp agrimony (*Eupatorium cannabinum*). Five-feet tall with fuzzy pink flowers, it's not related to *Agrimonia eupatoria,* but to the joe-pye weed that is popular as a butterfly-garden plant. Hemp agrimony is toxic to the liver (so just let the swallowtails sip from its blossoms).

Angelica (Angelica archangelica)

The botanical name of this giant member of the parsley family (sometimes called wild parsnip) practically conjures up choirs of cherubim and seraphim. In fact, angelica was once deemed so holy it was thought to be the only herb that witches never used. If Inquisitors came knocking, you could prove your innocence merely by showing them that angelica grew in your garden.

Legend has it that during the days of bubonic plague, an angel came to a monk in a dream and suggested this herb as a cure. The results aren't known, but the celestial name stuck. Angelica does have some antibacterial properties. Native Americans used a Plains species for both internal and external ills. To remember its most common culinary use, think of "angel" as a term of endearment — this is one sweet plant.

Cooks candy angelica and use it to decorate cakes and other desserts. You can steam the stems and eat them like asparagus, or cook it with rhubarb to offset that vegetable's tart flavor. Angelica is used commercially to flavor alcoholic beverages, including gin, vermouth, Benedictine, and Chartreuse.

Angelica contains *furocoumarins*, which can make people highly sensitive to sunlight, and there is some evidence that it contains carcinogens, so limit your consumption. Fresh roots are poisonous, so be sure to dry them thoroughly.

Description

Even if you don't harvest angelica, you might want to cultivate the herb for its statuesque form. The plant grows up to 6 feet tall — 4 feet across — and has shiny 2- to 3-foot leaves. Each toothed leaf is divided into thirds, which again divide into thirds, and the leafstalk has a puffy base that looks like a starched collar. The thick ribbed stems are usually tinged purple.

Softball-sized, off-white starburst flowers open early to mid-summer, usually in the plant's second year. The seedheads that follow are even more dramatic, clusters within clusters; the ribbed seeds are ¼-inch long with papery wings. All parts of angelica are musky smelling.

How to grow

Angelica is one of the few herbs that can thrive in the dank and dark — and the cold (it's hardy through Zone 3). This plant likes its soil deeply dug, loamy, acidic, and very moist (but still aerated). It likes sun or shade but not heat. You succeed best if you live north of Zone 7.

Angelica self-seeds freely, but seeds need light to sprout and can take up to a month to germinate. Just tamp the seeds into the soil; once your plants emerge, thin the seedlings to 2 feet in all directions.

Angelica is a biennial-like plant that dies after it goes to seed in its second season. (To keep the plant growing longer than two years, snip off all flower heads as soon as they fade.) Harvest leaves from the stem the first fall, and roots the next spring or second fall. Roots rot quickly once seeds have ripened. And, remember to always dry the root.

Cultivars and related plants

The Chinese use the roots of Chinese angelica, *A. polymorpha* var. *sinensis*, which they call *dong quai*, to cure all types of "women's problems." Ornamental gardeners put another Asian angelica, *A. gigas*, at the back of their perennial border to enjoy its 3-to-4-inch reddish purple flowers and their purple stems. This species does best where humidity is low and nights cool. American angelica, *A. atropurpurea*, is a native of the central United States and has dark purple stems and white flowers.

Don't try to collect angelica in the wild. It looks all too much like the lethal water hemlock, *Cicuta maculata*, which also grows in wet places.

Kitchen crystal

To crystallize, or candy, angelica, have ready a syrup made by simmering equal parts water and sugar (1 cup each) until the sugar disappears. Use tender angelica stems cut in the plant's second spring. Blanch the stems in boiling water for two minutes, peel, and slice them into 2-inch pieces. Simmer the pieces in the syrup for 20 minutes, cool, and store stems and syrup in a covered container in the refrigerator for three or four days. Reheat syrup and stems, remove stems from any remaining syrup and cool them on a rack.

Anise *(Pimpinella anisum)*

Anise is native to the Mediterranean and Egypt, where it was first used some 1,500 years ago. To quell indigestion, the Romans baked it in after-dinner cakes called mustaceum. In Biblical times, citizens used this herb — along with mint and cumin — to pay taxes, and in the 14th century, King Edward I levied a tax on anise to help pay for the London Bridge.

Pimpinella anisum

A member of the carrot family, anise tastes like licorice. In fact, licorice candy is likely to be flavored with anise, which is easier to grow and safer to consume than true licorice. Several cultures use anise in liqueurs — the Greeks in their famous *ouzo,* the French in the strong aperitif called *pastis.* Anisette is flavored with fennel, coriander, and anise.

Dogs love its scent, and anise has been used to mark trails for foxhounds and scent hares for greyhounds. Mice like it, too. If you're out of cheese, try smearing your traps with anise oil.

Use fresh anise leaves in salads, soups, and stocks, or as a garnish. Bake the tasty seeds in breads, cookies, or cakes; stew them with apples and pears; or steam them with cabbages, onions, carrots, or turnips. Anise is a good breath freshener, used commercially in toothpaste and mouthwash.

Description

A lank and floppy 2-foot annual, anise begins life with round, toothed leaves; but on a mature plant, the leaves are feathery and ferny. The mid-summer flowers are airy, flat, yellowish-white clusters about 2 inches across, followed by tiny gray-brown ribbed fruits shaped like commas.

How to grow

Anise can be a bit touchy in the garden. It won't set seed in climates with fewer than 120 frost-free days. Anise needs full sun but also rebels against heat and humidity. For the best results, the soil should be light and fast-draining, of average fertility. Give your plants shelter from wind and don't make anise compete with weeds or other plants.

A long taproot makes anise hard to transplant, so start it outdoors once the soil and air have warmed. Sow seeds ¼ to ½ inch deep, and thin seedlings to 8 inches apart. (Close spacing enables plants to support each other.) If you live in a cold climate, try starting seeds in peat pots. In the Deep South, sow anise seeds in fall.

Cultivars and related plants

While common anise is a star in Southeast Asian cuisine, the Chinese may use one of their native evergreen trees, star anise *(Illicium verum)* to get an anise flavor. An ingredient in five-spice powder, this magnolia relative bears star-shaped brown fruits. In addition to indigestion, the Chinese use star anise to treat hernias, rheumatism, and back pain.

Anise hyssop (Agastache foeniculum)

Anise hyssop is from a clan of aromatic perennials native to arid parts of the United States, Mexico, and Asia. All produce spikes covered with whorls of tubular, two-lipped flowers, similar to other members of the mint family. But unlike other mints, Agastache species are happy in a drought.

Agastache foeniculum

There is not a wealth of ancient lore or alleged medical wonders surrounding this herb. It just does its modest bit to bring long-lasting texture and color to the garden or to lend a minty-anise flavor to foods or honey. The flower spikes dry well for arrangements and wreaths, and the scent is worthy of your potpourri.

Description

Anise hyssop has relatively tiny flowers of a somewhat faded lavender. But the flowers are so tightly packed on the spike that the overall effect is fuzzy, like a mauve bottle brush. When several 2-foot plants are blooming on their many stems in late summer, it's a refreshing sight, especially as they're usually swaying to the ministrations of butterflies and bees. The toothed leaves look similar to those of lemon balm and some other mints, but smell like anise when crushed.

How to grow

Anise hyssop, which is cold hardy through Zone 4, is happy in dry, relatively poor, slightly alkaline soil and full sun (shade makes them floppy). Plants are easy to start from seed and will bloom in their first year. You may or may not be please by their tendency to reseed.

Cultivars and related plants

Almost any *Agastache* is worth having in your herb garden, butterfly garden, or perennial bed — and especially if yours is a dry climate. Most cultivars have pinkish purple flowers, although some bloom in white, blue, or orange; our favorite is 'Tutti-Frutti', which is the color of raspberry sherbet. All anise hyssops have aromatic leaves, and those with bigger flowers are humming-bird magnets.

Anise hyssop is easily confused with hyssop (described elsewhere in this chapter), which also has tubular flowers but is semi-evergreen and more camphor-scented.

Basil (Ocimum basilicum)

We're going to stick our necks out and say that if you already grow or use one fresh herb, it's likely to be basil. This herb is such a nice, friendly plant — sort of peppery and sort of sweet. Who would connect it with scorpions, madness, and evil?

Ocimum basilicum

Yet there is more than one tale of scorpions found in the brains of people too fond of smelling basil (according to one account from a physician aptly named Hilarius). Basil was said to breed "venomous beasts" if tossed on a pile of horse manure. One reputed source of its name was "basilisk," a creature whose look would literally kill. The Greeks and Romans thought it symbolized insanity and anger, and passed down to the French a belief in cursing while sowing its seeds. *Semer le basilic,* the French idiom for ranting, translates literally as "sowing the basil."

On the flip side, Italian women put a pot of basil outside to give the thumbs-up to a suitor; Indians consider it sacred to Hindu gods; and Haitian shopkeepers sprinkle it about to ensure a good cash flow.

In today's kitchens, basil goes far beyond pesto. It's great in almost any pasta topping. Snip leaves into soups, stir fries, marinades, or over meat on the grill. Add the flowers to salads. The purple-leafed cultivars lend color (as well as taste, of course) to vinegars.

Description

The most commonly grown type, sweet basil, grows 1 to 2 feet tall, 1 foot wide, and has bright green, oval, somewhat puckery leaves with serrated margins. The flowers are spikes of small, white tubular flowers, sometimes tinged with pink or purple, especially in the purple-leafed cultivars.

How to grow

Give basil plenty of sun and moderately rich, well-aerated soil that also retains moisture. Plants wilt easily in drought, so mulch your basil and water it when rain is scant. You can sow seeds in your garden — it germinates easily — but we always start ours indoors, 4 to 6 weeks before the last frost date.

Space plants about 1 foot apart. Basil is pretty enough to plant among your flowers, which will help protect the herb from wind. Just as on the table, basil is a fine companion for tomatoes in the vegetable patch, since it's reputed to repel tomato hornworms.

As soon as plants are 6 inches tall, begin pinching off stem tips and tops that are threatening to bloom; the pinching encourages more branching and leaf growth.

Cultivars and related plants

Basil comes in well over 30 varieties. For quantities of the sweet-tasting type, you can choose big-leafed selections such as 'Mammoth', 'Large Leaf', or 'Genovese'. 'Green Ruffles' has deeply cut, ornamental foliage. To bring burgundy foliage to the garden, try 'Dark Opal', 'Osmin', 'Red Rubin', or 'Purple Ruffles'. The little round buns of 'Spicy Globe', 'Green Globe", or 'Piccolo Verde Fino' basil make an interesting edge for the herb bed or will echo topiary in a formal garden. For the kitchen, experiment with subtle variations in flavor, such as lemon, lime, and cinnamon basils. 'Siam Queen', which won an AAS (All-America Selection) award, and other Thai basils complement Thai and Vietnamese cuisine.

Bay (Laurus nobilis)

Even the gods suffered the agonies of unrequited love. Take the case of Apollo, god of medicine, and Daphne, foxy nymph: Boy meets girl. Girl loathes boy. To hide her from this stalker, Daphne's father, Peneus, turns her into a laurel (bay) tree. Apollo vows to worship the evergreen ever more, and uses wreaths of its leaves to crown champions in all pursuits, from triumphant generals to spelling-bee champions.

*Laurus
nobilis*

In addition to being the official herbal headgear of champs, bay has been credited with protective powers — against lightning and thunder, and general evil and mayhem. If nothing else, if you crumble it on pantry shelves it may protect them from evil insect pests, thanks to a substance called cineole.

Bay is a must for Creole and Spanish cuisine and mixed spices for steaming shellfish. It's a good addition stews, soups, or bean dishes. Because bay leaves are tough and sharp, they're usually used whole and removed before a dish is served. Use bay in moderation — too much makes food bitter.

Description

Bay is technically a shrub, and in its native Mediterranean home can grow into a 40-foot tree. In the United States, even where it can stay outdoors all year, it's rarely half that size; with the indoor-outdoor treatment most of us have to give it, bay stays at around 5 feet or less.

Bay's narrow oval leaves are leatherlike, glossy, pungent, and pointed at the tips. Mature plants may produce little pale yellow flowers in early summer, followed by dark purple berries.

How to grow

Bay requires good drainage, but doesn't mind fairly poor soil. Give your plant protection from wind and full sun, which can scorch the leaves, and don't let it thirst in a drought. Bay is an ideal container plant, which makes it easy to bring inside in Zones 6 and north, where it can't survive winter. Gardeners in Zone 8 and south can leave it outdoors year round, while those in borderline Zone 7 should sink its pot in the ground and mound soil and mulch around it to keep the roots from freezing.

Bay seeds are notorious for turning moldy. Most gardeners opt for starting with a small, purchased plant. Indoors, bay can tolerate temperatures from 45°F to 80°F, but it needs a sunny window. Keep the soil just barely moist, and don't feed it in winter.

Cultivars and related plants

Few plants offer a better illustration of the need for botanical names than bay, which is also widely known as laurel. Among trees and shrubs with similar names are the mountain laurel, cherry laurel, laurel oak, laurel poplar, laurel willow, laurelwood, bat willow, bar star, and bayberry — and each of these plants is known by still other common names.

Bee balm (Monarda didyma)

Members of this mint-family genus — all native to North America — go by a slew of common names. "Oswego tea" honors its discovery by early American botanist John Bartram near Oswego, New York, and "liberty tea" recognizes its use by revolutionaries in the wake of the Boston tea party.

Monarda
didyma

You're also likely to see the name bergamot; the scent of monarda leaves is evocative of the bergamot orange, the peel of which is used in Earl Grey tea. And the name bee balm is for the siren song it sings to those fuzzy little pollinators. Hummingbirds love it too.

Many people just call the plant monarda. It's been a popular garden plant in England since it was carried there from Virginia in 1637. "Far too decorative to banish to the kitchen garden or even the herb garden," one British writer observed.

In addition to its charm in the garden, bee balm makes a tangy tea, more citrusy than minty. In cooking, use it with anything that benefits from a touch of citrus — fruit salads, fish, pork, duck, cucumbers.

Description

Like other mints, bee balm has tubular, two-lipped blooms. Those of the species are usually scarlet with red-tinged bracts. All a'whorl atop the stem, the flowers have a raggedly charm, like a red daisy trimmed with pinking shears. You can find natural white forms; and cultivars and hybrids extend bloom colors into pink, lavender, and shades in between. Bee balm grows 2 to 4 feet tall, and the pointed oval leaves have fairly pronounced veins.

How to grow

Bee balm grows naturally along moist stream banks, usually in dappled shade, so not surprisingly, it demands rich, moisture-retentive soil. It does best in Zones 3–7. In the humid South, or when drought-stressed elsewhere, it often becomes disfigured by powdery mildew — not a pleasant prospect when you want a cup of Oswego tea. Watering only at the roots and open spacing will help prevent mildew, but your best protection is to buy mildew-resistant cultivars.

Flowering starts in midsummer and continues for two months if you remove spent blooms. A valuable addition to a butterfly/bee/bird garden, monarda also is a natural for pondside plantings and other damp spots.

Bee balm may self-seed and spreads by underground stems, although at a more leisurely pace than other mints. Clumps die out in the center, so you need to divide it every couple of years. You can start it from seed, but division in spring is easier.

Cultivars and related plants

You can find more than 30 bee balm cultivars and hybrids available, and if your climate isn't conducive to powdery mildew, you can pick whichever shade suits your fancy.

'Croftway Pink' and 'Cambridge Scarlet' are two old forms still widely available. For disease resistance, look for 'Marshall's Delight', a deep pink, or 'Gardenview Scarlet'. 'Adam' (white) and 'Blue Stocking' (violet) do better in heat and drought than most cultivars.

For your lemon-herb garden, look for *M. citriodora,* lemon bergamot. Other *Monarda* species contain more medicinal compounds. *M. punctata* (spotted bee balm, or horsebalm) is high in antiseptic compounds. It has whorls of cream-colored flowers spotted with purple. M. *fistulosa* (wild bergamot) is high in geraniol, which helps prevent tooth decay.

Betony (Stachys officinalis)

If you're already an enthusiastic gardener, you probably know or grow lamb's ears, *Stachys byzantina,* beloved for its fuzzy foliage. Betony, or bishop's wort, is its cousin, and comes with more flamboyant flowers and a history as a cure-all.

*Stachys
officinalis*

Ancient Egyptians believed betony had magical powers, and the Romans listed some four dozen ills it would allay. It would shield you against both evil spirits and bad dreams, at least if you harvested it without using iron and dried it in the shade with the root still attached. It was said that snakes would fight to the death if surrounded by it, and other beasts would search it out when injured.

Betony tea is bland, but the tannins in it are good for diarrhea. Nor will you waste your time gargling a betony infusion for a sore throat. The jury is still out on its reputed power against what herbalist Mrs. Grieve calls "languid nervous headaches," but it contains some chemicals that might do the job.

Description

Another member of the mint family, betony is a 2-foot-tall European perennial. In late spring or early summer it erupts into spikes of small neon violet, tubular blossoms that continue opening until early fall.

The leaves are worthy of attention, too, textured as they are with veins, wrinkles, and oil glands, scalloped and hairy along the edges. The lower leaves are roughly heart-shaped, while those near the top are narrow ovals without any stalks.

How to grow

Hardy in Zones 4–9, betony likes its soil deep, rich, and moist but well draining. If its feet get wet in winter, it will turn up its toes and die. Happy plants spread to form handsome mats that should be divided every two or three years to keep them from flagging (diminishing). Betony prefers full sun but can take some shade, especially in the South.

You can start the species from seed or by division. Plant them at least a foot apart.

Cultivars and related plants

In addition to the popular lamb's-ears, you can grow big betony (*S. macrantha/S. grandiflora*), which is almost identical but as a native of the Caucasus is hardy farther north, through Zone 3. It flowers in several colors: white ('Alba'), pink ('Rosea'), purple-pink ('Superba'), and violet ('Violacea').

Borage (Borago officinalis)

If even a fraction of the reputation that borage has for "making men and women glad and merry" were true, college fraternities would have borage blasts and radio psychotherapists would have to seek new careers. Borage sprigs, a late 17th-century herbalist wrote, "are of known virtue to revive the hypochondriac and cheer the hard student."

Borago officinalis

Borage has been a welcome garden plant in Britain since the 1400s, perhaps because English gardeners knew the popular Latin saying, "I, Borage, bring alwaies courage." That quality was one reason why impatient maidens of yore added borage to the drinks of slow-to-propose suitors.

Or perhaps the popularity of borage is due to the sky-blue color of its blooms and the cool-as-a-cucumber flavor of its leaves and stems. According to ancient sources, it's a good addition to "drinkes that are cordiall" Appropriately, one of its common names is cool-tankard.

Freeze the flowers in ice cubes for your own cool tankard, candy them, or toss them in a salad. If the fuzz doesn't bother you, you can eat the leaves, too, steamed or raw (just be sure to peel the stems). Borage is difficult to dry and impossible to freeze. Use it fresh or preserve it in vinegar. Despite fears that borage may be toxic to the liver, trusted experts assure us it is safe to drink and eat as long as you avoid "chronic consumption."

Description

Borage is an annual that can reach 2 or 3 feet high, but it tends to sprawl in a laid-back mound. Tiny white hairs on the leaves and on the hollow, succulent stems create something of an aura around it, totally in keeping with the star-shaped, heavenly blue flowers that open in humbly drooping clusters. Five long stamens with black anthers heighten the drama.

How to grow

Borage is tough, but be good to it by adding well-rotted manure to your soil. This herb also needs good drainage and doesn't like competing with weeds; mulching helps retain essential moisture.

Add full sun and your plants will repay you by reseeding in perpetuity. Plant your first seeds where you want the borage to grow, since it has a long tap-root and can be hard to transplant. Given borage's floppy nature, you should space plants at least 1½ feet apart, mingled with plants of a similar devil-may-care habit, in a wildflower garden, vegetable patch, or among casually arranged herbs.

Cultivars and related plants

Borage blooms *ought* to be blue, but if you need a white flower in your garden, look for *Borago officinalis* 'Alba'; *B. officinalis* 'Variegata' has green leaves marked with white. If you live in Zone 5 or warmer, you can try another *Borago* species, *B. pygamaeta,* a short-lived perennial that has pale blue flowers.

If you love blue-flowered plants as much as we do — here's where all that scientific botany stuff gets to be fun — get to know borage's extended family, a Who's Who of the cerulean class: forget-me-not *(Myosotis)*, lungwort *(Pulmonaria)*, Virginia bluebells *(Mertensia)*, *Anchusa*, and *Brunnera,* sometimes called perennial forget-me-not.

Burdock (Arctium lappa)

You just know that a plant with nicknames as diverse as beggar's buttons and love leaves (not to mention pig's rhubarb) has got to have a mixed reputation. Burdock, a native of Europe and Asia Minor, is a prickly pest in fields and along roadsides; even Shakespeare, who knew his flora, called upon its image several times to represent woe or annoyance.

Burdock once was considered a first-rate blood purifier and cure for skin diseases. The 17th-century English physician, Nicholas Culpeper, often given to unbridled inclusiveness, credited it with power over everything from "shrinking in the sinews" to rabies. Five hundred years ago, burdock was mashed into wine to treat leprosy. From the Middle Ages to modern-day Asia, it's been used to treat cancer, and it does contain some anti-tumor substances.

The fresh root contains some antibiotics, which may explain burdock's reputation for skin disorders, including dandruff and acne. You can dry the root to make a tea, which, as a diuretic, might lessen PMS symptoms. The herb also has a long-standing reputation as a liver tonic, which is one reason the Japanese (who call the root *gobo*) cook it in soups and stews.

Every part of burdock but the flowers and — of course, the bur — can be eaten fresh or cooked. The root tastes a bit like celery and a bit like potato, faintly sweet, and should be scrubbed or peeled like a potato and used in much the same way. If you're going to eat the stem (which also should be peeled) or leaves, pick them while they're young and fresh.

Description

This biennial, a member of the daisy family, is an attention-getter at 5 feet tall. Burdock is made even more commanding by magenta, thistle-type flower heads and wavy, spade-shaped lower leaves (gray with down on the underside) that can be a foot long. Upper leaves are smaller and more oval. The flowers give way to round fruits bristling with hooks. The taproot, the part most often used, grows as long as 3 feet.

How to grow

Some gardeners may bristle as the thought of deliberately planting a prickly thistle on their home ground, but burdock won't look out of place in a wild-flower area, and will peer protectively over shorter plants from the back of a border.

Most people grow burdock as an annual. You can start it indoors from seed, but the huge taproot doesn't allow it to be confined for long. Give it rich, moisture-retentive, and — most important — deeply dug, loose soil. Some gardeners create a mound for it so it will be easier to harvest. You can dig the root at the end of the growing season, or wait until next spring, when you won't have the prickles to contend with.

Cultivars and related plants

Chalk up another one for using botanical names, since there are a lot of plants with "bur" or "dock" in their common names. Common burdock or lesser burdock (A. minus) often grows just as big as its "great" cousin but has shorter flower stalks and hollow leaf stalks.

Calendula (Calendula officinalis)

Often called pot marigold, calendula was loved by gardeners (and Romantic poets) long before the *Tagetes* now planted at every hamburger franchise ever came on the scene. Calendula was both a clock and a calendar. Linnaeus, the guy who came up with botanical names, wrote that the pot marigold flower was open from 9 a.m. to 3 p.m.(making it appropriate landscaping for modern banks). Its name came from the observation that it was open the first day of each calendar month.

Calendula's traditional uses were as much magical as medicinal. One herbal declared that if the planets were properly aligned, and if the gatherer was sinless and said Our Fathers and Hail Marys (three each), that wearing a calendula blossom would give him a vision of anyone who robbed him. It might also grant visions of fairies and a faithful husband-to-be. Culpeper recommended a plaster of calendula flowers, hog's grease, and turpentine for strengthening the heart.

Calendula tea was prescribed for treating measles (12 flower heads steeped in 1 pint boiling water) as late as 1900 in some parts of England, where it was known as measle-flower.

Today, you can put calendula's antiviral and antifungal properties to work in oils and creams for treating wounds, skin problems, and bug bites. In the kitchen, it's know as the poor person's saffron. Use its petals in paella, polenta, and other dishes that call for that spice — which is kept in the safe at our grocer — and you'll get a similar color, if not taste. Or just toss flowers in a salad to make it sizzle with summer color.

Description

In its natural state, this member of the daisy family calendula is a cheerful yellow-orange daisy, about 18 inches tall with numerous branches. The leaves are aromatic when crushed, and tiny hairs cover the plant all over.

How to grow

Start calendula from fresh seeds in early spring; it germinates better in slightly cool conditions, and in the Deep South can sometimes be sown in fall. Transplant seedlings into full sun or part shade in moderately fertile soil; space plants at least 10 inches apart so they have room to branch and good air circulation, as they're prone to powdery mildew.

Calendula usually starts blooming about six weeks after germination, but it may peter out during the hottest part of the summer. Keep pinching off the flowers for their many potential uses and they'll oblige by making more.

By all means include calendula in the ornamental garden, with other hot colors or, for a vivid contrast, with blues or purples.

Cultivars and related plants

If your favorite use of calendula is looking at it — whether to lighten your heart or to see fairies — you may want to collect some of its many cultivars, which look great planted together. Most of them are double-flowered. There are new ones almost every year, some with a second color on the petal tips or edges, and many with a contrasting center. A few, like the dahlia-lookalike, 'Radio', border on gaudy. Many seeds come in mixes, such as 'Art Shades Mixed' (apricot, orange, and cream) or 'Kablouna Mixed' (tall crested flowers that include gold, orange, and lemon, all with dark centers).

Caraway (Carum carvi)

Grow caraway if you're into billing and cooing. Cultivated for five millennia, this biennial in the carrot family has been deemed capable of keeping both pigeons and lovers from straying. Shakespeare's contemporaries dipped roasted apples in the seeds. Then the Scots, who called caraway salt water jelly, dipped buttered bread in them. English herbalist John Parkinson wrote that such uses would dispel colds or "wind in the body." The Germans still use it to make kummel, a liqueur.

Caraway and cabbage isn't just alliterative. Caraway is great in slaw and a must for sauerkraut and the pork that often accompanies it. Nor did caraway and apples stop with the Elizabethans. Try it in applesauce or apple pie, or a Waldorf-type salad with mayonnaise.

Parkinson wasn't full of hot air, either: You can make a caraway tea to combat flatulence, bloating, and other digestive miseries.

Description

Like its relatives fennel and dill, caraway has delicate, fernlike leaves, which have the same anise scent as the seeds do. Once a plant reaches 18 to 24 inches tall, it produces white, umbrella flowers — usually in the summer of its second year, but occasionally at the end of the first. Then come the famous seeds with five ribs and pointed ends. The long taproot is like parsnip, both in appearance and taste.

How to grow

Sow seeds ½ inch deep in spring (if you live in the South, in fall as well) in loose, fertile soil that retains moisture well. Thin seedlings to 8 inches. Caraway prefers full sun, although a bit of shade is your only hope in hot, rainless, humid summers. If you've given it the right spot and don't collect all its seeds, it may surprise you with a return visit.

You'll have to plant many rows to stock the cabinet for a season of caraway cookery, so if space is limited, make your meager harvest a festive occasion.

Catnip (Nepeta cataria)

Okay, it's our age. We always associate catnip with cartoon cats like Tom, the archenemy of Jerry, or Sylvester, the bane of Tweety Bird, because mouse and bird respectively so often used the herb to make their escapes.

In about two-thirds of domestic cats, and also the big fierce ones like lions, volatile oils contained in catnip leaves induce utter ecstasy. Herbalists of old claimed that the root had a more unpleasant effect on humans, making "the most gentle person fierce and quarrelsome." Folklore also has it that hangmen chewed the root to work up enthusiasm for their job. Fortunately, catnip tea is made from the leaves, not the root, and has yet another result: It makes most people tranquil or sleepy.

In addition to making little stuffed toys for Fluffy or Snowball, you can dry catnip leaves for tea, which may aid digestion as do many other mints. If you like the taste of the fresh leaves, include them in salads, or candy them. And if the smell appeals to you, toss a few in your potpourri. Just don't open the lid while Mitten is on the prowl.

Description

Catnip is a 2- to 3-foot erect, branching perennial with downy gray-green toothed leaves shaped like stretched-out hearts, 1 to 3 inches long. Like other mints, it has square stems and spikes of tiny two-lipped flowers. In this plant, they're white with purple spots, blooming from mid-to late summer. Native to Europe and Asia, catnip has naturalized in parts of the United States, especially the mid-Atlantic.

How to grow

Unlike many mints, catnip likes fairly dry, even sandy soil — good drainage is a must. It will develop its pungent scent best in full sun, although some southern growers urge a little shade. There's a saying that if you plant catnip from seed, the cats won't know it's there. That's because handling the plant is what sends out the "come and get it" signals. Propagation from cuttings or root division is much easier than starting from seed, however. Plants tend to die out after about three years, so if you and your cat are addicted, take some insurance cuttings.

A word to the wise: Keep catnip well away from other valuable plants, since they're likely to get flattened in any feline free-for-all. (Although they may nibble a bit to release more scent, cats don't eat catnip; they roll in it.)

Cultivars and related plants

All members of the *Nepeta* genus are called catmints, and we like having them in the ornamental garden for their blue flowers and gray foliage. The most commonly planted cousins are an 18-inch high hybrid, *N.* x *faassenii* (often called *N. mussinii*) and a cultivar, 'Blue Hills Giant', which gets twice as big. Catmints tend to flop over, so they perform prettily at the edge of a raised bed, in a large container, and in rock gardens.

Chamomile (Matricaria recutita, Chamaemelum nobile)

The story of chamomile is complicated by the fact that there are two of them. The Germans think that a 2-to-3-foot-tall annual from Europe and western Asia *(Matricaria recutita,* or German chamomile*)* is the only true chamomile, and that the other is a weed; the English think that a 9-inch creeping perennial from western Europe and Ireland *(Chamaemelum nobile,* or Roman chamomile) is the only true chamomile, and that the other is a pest.

Chamae-
melum
nobile

Fortunately, this issue has not sparked a major war, since the plants not only look and smell a great deal alike but are also used the same way — to make a relaxing tea. As everyone, from the herbalist Dioscorides to Peter Rabbit's mother, knew well.

Chamomile does contain some sedative chemicals, and many herbalists are convinced it's also good for heartburn. Antiseptic and anti-inflammatory compounds make a chamomile compress or ointment worth trying for rashes and other skin problems. Try an infusion in your bath if you have poison ivy.

Description

Both chamomiles have delicate, threadlike leaves and daisylike flowers with white rays and an endearing, cone-shaped button center. Besides being taller, German chamomile is more upright and produces more flowers per plant. The leaves of Roman chamomile are thicker and flatter, but the acid test is to tear open the *receptacle* — the swelling behind the flower head — and see if it is hollow (German) or solid (Roman). Roman chamomile is hardy through Zone 3.

Most people compare the scent of the chamomile flowers and foliage with apples. The Greeks thought so, since they gave the plant a name meaning "earth-apple" that evolved into chamomile. The Spanish call it "little apple" — *manzanilla* — and use it to flavor a sherry of the same name.

How to grow

You can grow both chamomiles from seed, but the annual German chamomile is the easier to find on seed racks, and the easier to germinate. It prefers light, moisture retentive soil but is forgiving, and tolerates drought and alkaline soil. Sow in spring or fall (if you've collected your own seeds, stratify them; see Chapter 11 for details); thin seedlings to 8 inches. Heat launches the flowering season, and you should be able to get about three good harvests every two weeks.

When conditions are right, German chamomile reseeds into every nook and cranny. Since you won't get more than two or three cups of chamomile tea from a single plant, you'll want to cheer on all the volunteers. And fortunately, having chamomile as a companion is said to make every plant healthier. Set it where ever you can use its cheery face and ferny foliage, but be ready for offspring.

Roman chamomile, hardy through Zone 3, also grows almost anywhere. It doesn't like hot dry weather, though, which is why American gardeners can rarely pull off the English tradition of a chamomile lawn. (Queen Elizabeth has one at Buckingham Palace.) In very hot regions, give plants some after-noon shade; elsewhere, full sun. Start Roman chamomile from seed, cuttings, or division, and space plants about 1 foot apart.

Cultivars and related plants

If your garden conditions are right for Roman chamomile (impossibly mild like the Pacific Northwest), you can grow a variety developed for lawns, 'Treneague', which never flowers. (We love the idea of a flowering lawn, but bees are a disadvantage if you like to go shoeless.) Want more flower rather than less? A double form, 'Flora Plena', was bred for twice the tea.

Breeders tinkering with the German form have put their money on chamomile as medicine; several newer cultivars, such as 'Bodegold', are said to contain more essential oil.

Chervil (Anthriscus cerefolium)

Chervil may be the Rodney Dangerfield of herbs. Even though it's a key ingre-dient in the famous French herb mixture fines herbes, some otherwise ster-ling cookbooks and gardening books swear it's the same thing as sweet Cicely. Which it's not. No respect, or at least, not nearly enough.

Anthriscus cerefolium

People have been growing chervil almost forever. By one account, a basket of its seeds was found in King Tut's tomb. The Romans took it with them as they expanded their empire. Both they and the Greeks cooked it, including the root (which was candied to treat stomachaches), but the Saxons used it raw in soups and salads. Once prescribed to prevent plague and to cure hiccups, chervil's reputation as a blood purifier has made it a traditional spring tonic in central Europe.

Follow the tonic tradition and use chervil with spring vegetables for a subtle anise note. Later in summer, chervil is good with cold soups and salads. Preserve it in spreads such as cream cheese, butter, or sour cream. Eggs are another popular destination for chervil, which is high in protein and contains calcium and magnesium. Herbalists say it may reduce high blood pressure.

Description

Chervil does have a good deal in common with sweet Cicely. Both are members of the carrot family and have white umbrella flowers and somewhat ferny leaves, similar seeds, and an aniselike flavor. But while sweet Cicely is a perennial, chervil is an annual. Growing 1 to 2 feet tall, with thin, branched stems, it has divided leaves that are easily mistaken for parsley's. And like parsley, it comes in both flat-leaf and curly varieties.

How to grow

In hot sun, chervil either goes to seed early or shrivels faster than the Wicked Witch of the West when Dorothy doused her with that bucket of water. Plant it where it will get some summer shade, near a deciduous tree or shrub, or among taller herbs, vegetables, or ornamentals. You can begin harvesting this herb about eight weeks after germination, so can harvest continually if you sow seeds every couple of weeks in spring and again in late summer. Harvest leaves just before the flower clusters open. (Better still, remove flower stems to encourage new foliage.)

Chervil seeds need light to germinate, so just press them into the soil with your hand and keep the soil moist. Once the seeds sprout, thin plants to 10 inches. (Chervil seeds don't age well, so don't keep them over winter.)

Note chervil's delicate nature if you dry it: Expose leaves to high heat and they will be as tasty as yesterday's newspaper.

Cultivars and related plants

Breeders haven't tinkered much with chervil, but you might look for the curly leafed form, 'Crispum'. Cow parsley (*A. sylvestris*) is a perennial hardy through Zone 6 and described politely as a meadow plant that reseeds. Still, someone thought its lacy form worth naming 'Ravenswing' when combined with purple-brown foliage. Use it to give airy grace to a border, but when it reseeds, you'll have to cull the green-foliaged interlopers.

Chicory (Cichorium intybus)

Chicory, the bonnie-blue roadside denizen, has endured an up-and-down reputation. Relished by the Romans and commended by such notable writers and poets as Virgil, Ovid, and Pliny (who mixed it with vinegar and rose oil for headaches), it's long been popular as a coffee substitute or additive. You find chicory coffee mostly in New Orleans and in upscale restaurants, where it's right at home with trendy salad greens radicchio and endive, two relatives. Chicory fans believe that adding the toasted, ground root to regular coffee creates a smoother taste. There is some scientific evidence that chicory is a mild sedative, so chicory-laced coffee also smooths out the coffee drinker.

Cichorium intybus

The azure flowers once hinted at chicory's value as an eyewash, at least in regions where most everyone had blue eyes. Early colonists carried its seeds from their homelands to North America, where it won praise primarily as livestock fodder. In a letter to George Washington, Thomas Jefferson wrote that it was "one of the greatest acquisitions a farmer can have." Today, state road crews sipping real coffee mow it down with nary a thought.

Chicory leaves not only look like a dandelion's (they're in the same family), but have a similar taste and health benefits. (Modern herbalists believe that the herb benefits the liver and may have heart benefits.) But while dandelion leaves are gathered in spring, you should collect chicory's in fall. Most people enjoy the bitter edge of fresh chicory, but if it isn't your cup of tea, cook them in several changes of water. They're too ethereal to freeze or dry.

Description

Chicory, a sunflower cousin, can grow to 5 feet or more from a clump of leaves that look like a dandelion's. As it grows upward, it branches with sparse, smaller leaves, leaving its stem nearly naked. Then, from late summer to early fall, it glows with one-and-a half-inch-wide, true blue flowers. The ray petals have squarish, ragged tips. Many blue flowers glow at dusk, but Linnaeus, the Swedish botanist, included chicory in his flower clock because it closes midday.

How to grow

Succory, an old common name for chicory, stems from Latin for "run under." That's because chicory's taproot can grow 2 feet down and 2 inches across. If you're going to dig its roots, give yourself a break by double digging its bed and throwing in lots of compost. Plant this perennial at the edge of your vegetable or herb plot where it won't be disturbed, perhaps near a trellis that will shade it from summer heat. While it's cold hardy through Zone 3, southern gardeners may struggle to grow it well.

Sow seeds ¼-inch deep in early spring and thin the plants to about a foot apart. Plants usually flower in their second year. Some growers blanch the leaves — covering them with a newspaper or cloth — to reduce their bitterness.

Cultivars and related plants

If you don't want to dig a roadside plant, try 'Biondissima Trieste' or 'Spadona', traditional Italian cutting chicories ready to harvest in 50 days.

Once upon a time, radicchio was what you got if you cut back chicory and let it regrow in cooler weather. Today, you can buy radicchio cultivars, such as 'Red Verona' and 'Early Treviso' that blush prettily from the get-go. Northern gardeners plant them in the spring, while southerners start seeds in summer and harvest them in fall or winter.

Witloof chicory is a relative that produces a tight cone of pale leaves and usually goes by the name of Belgian endive. It's an outdoor-indoor crop (the hybrid 'Witloof Zoom' is a good cultivar.). Sow seed in spring, then lop off the aboveground plant parts after the first frost and dig the roots. Store the roots in damp sand in a cold place for at least one month, then reset upright in moist, organically rich soil. Like mushrooms, endive needs to grow in the dark (with temperatures in the 50s and high humidity). If you don't have a dungeon, cover them with flowerpots in your basement.

Chives (Allium schoenoprasum)

Those who crave chives on their baked potatoes and bagels lop the flowers off, as mercilessly as the Red Queen in Wonderland. But those round, fuzzy, purple-pink heads are one of our favorites for the spring garden. Plant lots and lots of chives, because you'll want plenty of leaves *and* blossoms.

Allium schoeno-prasum

Nicholas Culpeper believed that only a professional "alchymist" could prepare chives safely. Raw leaves, he wrote, emit "vapours to the brain, causing troublesome sleep and spoiling the eyesight." On a more positive note, chives are a folk remedy for whooping cough (take in a bread-and-butter sandwich). Today, some herbalists feel that chives can help lower blood pressure, and even help prevent cancer. If nothing else, they're full of vitamins A and C. And they taste great. Even the flowers are edible.

Use chives fresh. The freezer will turn them to mush, the oven, to crispy brown sprigs. (Commercial chives are freeze-dried.) Culinary possibilities include omelets and other egg dishes, cooked vegetables of all kinds, butter and soft cheeses. Make them a last-minute addition to sauces and soups.

Description

Allium schoenoprasum is a hardy perennial, closely related to onions and garlic. It grows from bulbs in clumps of grasslike, onion-scented hollow leaves, pointed at the tip and usually about a foot tall. In mid-spring, on stems roughly the same height, the plants produce pretty balls of tightly packed lavender blossoms, rather like clover flowers.

How to grow

If ever there were a beginner's herb, chives is it. (Or rather, are it. You'll note that it's always plural, like scissors and pants.) Chives are hardy throughout the United States, can take sun or partial shade, and almost any soil that's not off the chart in pH. As with most plants, organically rich soil and good drainage suits them best.

Chive seeds need temperatures of 75°F or less to sprout, and they take two to three weeks. Like most perennials, they're pretty sleepy the first season — dare only to take a snip or two. A better approach is to buy young plants or bulbs, or find a friend who will dig you a clump or two. Should you get more than one clump (6-10 bulbs each), set them 8 inches apart. And don't let grasslike weeds get near them, or you may not be able to separate the good guys from the bad guys.

Chives are like other grassy plants: Grazing makes them grow. You may hear that you shouldn't harvest all the leaves from a clump at once, but commercial harvesters do — just leave about 3 inches. Clumps need dividing every three or four years, so you'll have plenty to share with friends — or spread them around your own spread.

To bring chives indoors for a short-lived winter crop, dig a small clump (or divide a large one) three or four weeks before your first expected frost. Pot it up but leave it outdoors for a couple of months in a protected location to go dormant (the tops should die back). When you bring it in, the bulbs will think it's spring and send up shoots.

Cultivars and related plants

Although chives seem pretty perfect just the way they are, breeders have given us 'Forescate', which has more intensely rosy flowers, and 'Sterile' (trademarked as Profusion Chives), which has more flowers and is seedless. (As a rule, cultivars easily cross-pollinate, so you can't plant them close together if you want to collect seed and grow the same plant next year.)

Garlic, or Chinese, chives, *Allium tuberosum,* have solid, flatter leaves and star-shaped, sweet-scented white flowers that bloom in late summer or fall; taller than common chives, they can reach 2 feet. Garlic chives can be invasive — every seed the flowers produce seems to sprout. They're good with the same foods as regular chives, but use them with a lighter hand the first time around since they have a zingier, hotter flavor.

Cilantro or coriander (Coriandrum sativum)

Cilantro leads a double life and easily deserves two separate entries. The leaves taste musky and the seeds taste lemony. The leaves have a starring role in Asian and Latin American cookery, whereas the seeds are a key ingredient in Middle Eastern staples, such as curry.

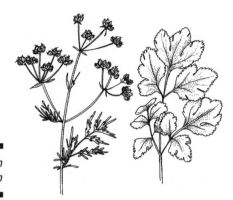

Coriandrum sativum

Cilantro is native to none of these regions, but comes from the Mediterranean. Its seed, known as coriander, has been toted around the world for some 5,000 years. It's appeared in Egyptian tombs, in the Old Testament, and in *The Thousand and One Nights,* where it played the role of an aphrodisiac. Pliny described its medical use for such appalling conditions as spreading sores, diseased testes, carbuncles, and "fluxes of the eyes, too, if women's milk be added."

The green herb, known as cilantro, seems "new" to many Americans who are just discovering ethnic cuisine. Today you can find it next to its kin, parsley, in many groceries, although the flavor is still not universally adored. The ancient Greeks were among its detractors, comparing its aroma to that of a bed bug. Coriander's name stems from *koris,* the Greek word for bug.

A must in dishes like salsa or gazpacho, cilantro also enhances sauces for fish, chicken, lamb, and is good tossed into a green salad. (It adds needed zip if you're trying to cut down on dressing.) Growing your own cilantro also lets you use the root, which offers a crunchy variation on the flavor of the foliage.

Although curry is the destination of much coriander seed, the sweet citrusy tang adds a lively note to otherwise rather tame vegetables, such as cauliflower, potatoes, parsnips, and other root vegetables. Try it in rice and pasta dishes, baked in fruits, or in soups and stews.

Description

Cilantro is an annual herb with divided leaves that make it look very much like flat-leafed parsley (appropriately, Chinese parsley is one of its more common common names). Its bottom leaves are rounded, while those near the top are smaller and ferny. Plants grow to about 20 inches — 8 inches wide — and bear flat clusters of small white or pale purple flowers followed by round, beige fruits.

How to grow

Cilantro wants only what you give all your favorite plants: soil full of organic amendments that drains readily and full sun (or light shade in very hot regions). After spring's last frost date, sow seeds directly in the garden. After they sprout in about two weeks, thin seedlings to 10 inches. If you have the space (and the need), sow successive crops every three weeks into summer. Because cilantro bolts in heat, Southerners usually plant seeds in fall and give their plants afternoon shade.

Cilantro won't ruin the looks of your ornamental bed, but it's no raving beauty. Most people relegate it to the herb or vegetable patch where they can plant as many as they want to consume. Harvest plants for leaves when they're about 6 inches tall.

Cultivars and related plants

If you're growing this herb for foliage rather than seeds, you may be disappointed with the species because it insists on seeding after two months. Look for strains called long-standing or Chinese, or cultivars such as 'Leisure', 'Santo', or 'Slo-Bolt'.

Vietnamese coriander *(Polygonum odoratum)* is an unrelated perennial with the same taste as *Coriandrum sativum,* but to keep it going for next season you need to overwinter it indoors. Southern gardeners may succeed with another unrelated plant, Mexican or Cuban coriander *(Eryngium foetidum).* From Central America, it's related to the spiky ornamentals called sea hollies, and one of its common names is thorny coriander.

Clary (Salvia sclarea)

Before the advent of the Breathalyzer, inebriation was measured more subjectively. Clary sage used to be a substitute for hops in beer, but also served to make intoxicating drinks more bitter and potent, "fit to please drunkards, who thereby, according to their several dispositions, become either dead drunke, or foolish drunke, or madde drunke." Another writer described the effect as "insane exhilaration." The herb was added to Rhine wine along with elder flowers, which changed the flavor to that of muscatel without benefit of muscat grapes.

Clary's common name derives from "clear eye." Its seeds, when wet, ooze a mucilage, and a seed put in the eye was said to extract any foreign matter — at a cost, we would think, of even greater discomfort. Today, clary, or clary sage, has fallen by the way as a mainstream herbal medicine, but perfume-makers continue to use it as a fixative to keep other odors on track, and aromatherapists claim that its scent alone can induce euphoria — that old insane exhilaration.

*Salvia
sclarea*

If you like the smell and taste of clary, use it the same way you do common sage. Some herbalists still use clary to treat for gas and indigestion, so it can't hurt to include the leaves in an after-dinner tea.

Description

Clary is a biennial and resembles common sage and other members of the mint family with its square stems and spikes of two-lipped flowers, which are either pale lavender-blue or white. Even while still in bud in early summer, the flowers are made showy by surrounding bracts of white, lavender, or pink. Growing 2 to 3 feet tall, clary sage bears leaves shaped like elongated hearts, fuzzy, wrinkled, and up to 9 inches long. The aroma is variously described as musky, balsam, fruity, and disgusting.

How to grow

The last thing you want to do for clary sage is fuss over it. Give it average soil with very good drainage and full sun. It tolerates both drought and a wide pH range.

Clary is easy to start from seed, indoors or out. Space seedlings 10 inches apart in the garden. After the first killing frost, cut back the plant tops. Northern gardeners should mulch plants to prevent frost heaving. (It will survive winters through Zone 5.) Plants may self-sow after they bloom in their second year, but collect a few seeds, just in case.

Many people think clary is far prettier than common sage. Set it in the middle of an ornamental bed and its big, textured leaves will turn heads at the same time that its long-lasting flower spikes draws legions of butterflies and bees.

Cultivars and related plants

Turkestan clary *(Salvia sclarea* var. *turkestanica)* is sometimes described as a naturally occurring variety, but it's also sold as a cultivar of clary sage and labeled *S. sclarea* 'Turkestanica'. Its stems are taller and pinker than the species, and its flowers are white specked with pink. You can also choose a white cultivar, 'Alba'.

Another aromatic salvia sometimes used the same ways as clary sage is meadow clary, *S. pratensis*. It typically has violet flowers, although they can be white or pink. Cultivars bloom in rosy-red, deep blue, and dark purple.

Comfrey (Symphytum officinale)

You may know of the 1957 case of Sam Sheppard, the Cleveland physician found guilty of murdering his wife and the inspiration for the film, *The Fugitive*. He steadfastly maintained his innocence, and his claim is, well, a lot like that of comfrey.

For more than 2,000 years, comfrey, or knitbone, had a reputation as a healer of wounds, and broken bones (because its parts were so mucilaginous and sticky). The 17th-century herbalist Nicholas Culpeper claimed that it was so powerful a knitter of broken bones that "if they be boiled with dissevered pieces of flesh in a pot, it will join them together again." It was used internally as well, for a host of ailments.

More recently, we've learned that comfrey contains allantoin, a substance that causes cells to multiply — which should be good in healing wounds and knitting bones. But it also contains pyrrolizidine alkaloids, or PAs, and beginning in the late 1970s, researchers began to connect PA with a disease that causes major blood vessels from the liver to clot.

Ever since, most herbalists advise *never* to use comfrey internally. Anyone with liver problems and pregnant and nursing women shouldn't use it externally, either. Others can use it as a compress or poultice for about any insult to the body's outer covering, from bruises to cuts and scrapes. Many herbalists recommend a comfrey infusion to soothe hemorrhoids.

Description

As with comfrey's safety, opinions are mixed on the eye-appeal of this herb, a kin of borage. Erect and brawny, it rises to at least 4 feet tall and equally wide, is floppy in wind and rain, and bears 10-inch lower leaves covered in itch-producing hairs. The stems have pronounced "wings." Even those left cold by comfrey's charms thaw a bit when it blooms — from late spring to early summer, occasionally much longer. Its forked tassels of bell-shaped flowers in blue-violet, pink, or pale yellow are hard to resist.

How to grow

Consider long where you put comfrey, as it is not only large but made quite permanent by a taproot that can burrow as deep 6 feet. Comfrey doesn't produce many seeds, so most gardeners start it from divisions or root cuttings. With that long root, it needs soil that's loose, deep, and rich with organic matter. Hardy through Zone 3, comfrey can grow in partial shade, but full sun makes the stem stronger and less apt to fall over on blustery days.

Cultivars and related plants

Common comfrey has a red-flowered form, 'Rubrum'. There are 34 other species in this genus, all smaller than common comfrey, and most are hardy through Zone 3. One is Caucasian comfrey *(S. caucasicum),* which has bright blue flowers. Foot-high 'Goldsmith' has leaves edged in gold. Russian comfrey *(S. × uplandicum)* grows 3 to 4 feet tall and has a cultivar with lavender flowers and white-edged leaves, 'Variegatum'.

Costmary (Tanacetum balsamita)

Over time, costmary has been used for a plethora of quaint problems, including "quotidien ague, catarrhs, and rheumes," as well as consumption and vermin. One recipe for a skin ointment called for boiling costmary with a snake's tongue in olive oil, then mixing it with wax, resin, and turpentine.

Tanacetum balsamita

Poor costmary has lost much of its élan since colonial times, and like many of the chrysanthemum clan, it's had to endure a change of name to *Tanacetum* by picky botanists. A native of Asia, its common name comes from the word *costus,* a term meaning "from the orient." Some English gardeners have called it mace, but it's not related to the spice you buy under that name, which comes from the red covering of nutmeg seeds.

Other common names are more telling: Alecost, because it was use to flavor ale, and Bible leaf, because American colonists used it as a place marker in the Good Book. The mary in its name linked it to the Virgin Mary, but its use went beyond symbolism. Churchgoers sniffed or nibbled it to revive themselves during long, dull services.

Some people compare the smell and taste of costmary to wintergreen — minty, cool, and powerful. Use its leaves in cooking as you would other mints, but with a lighter hand. Its camphor scent makes it a pleasant addition to a bath or facial steam.

Description

You may hear arguments about the smell of some herbs, but even the species name advertises costmary's redolent scent. Appropriately, balsam herb was another of its common names.

A perennial, native to Europe and central Asia, costmary grows 3 feet tall, is woody at its base, and forms mats with its rhizomes. Silvery hairs cover the serrated leaves. The leaves at the bottom of the plant are up to a foot long, those toward the top rarely half that. The negligible yellow ray flowers bloom in late summer or early fall, and not at all in partial shade.

How to grow

Costmary is hardy through Zone 4. Buy small plants, or start from divisions, setting them out in spring in the North, early fall in the South. Give costmary plenty of space — 18 inches is a bare minimum. Plants need only average soil as long as it drains well; grow in partial shade or sun. Locate costmary where it can show off its handsome foliage, perhaps among long-blooming annuals.

Cultivars and related plants

Two other herbs, feverfew and tansy, were shuffled into the *Tanacetum* genus along with costmary. You find out more about them elsewhere in this section. All these plants have daisylike flowers and scented foliage. The best known is probably the painted daisy *(T. coccineum)*. Also called pyrethrum (it's the basis of the well-known organic insecticide), it has both single and double forms in red, pink, and white.

Dill (Anethum graveolens)

Dill — its common name comes from a Norse word meaning "to lull to sleep" — is a friend to the digestive system from stem (bad breath) to stern (gas). Across time and cultures, from the Egyptians some 3,000 years ago, to the Chinese 1,000 years ago, and into modern times, dill has come to the rescue as "a gallant expeller of wind" in the words of Nicholas Culpeper.

Another traditional use of dill was in "gripe water," a drink cherished by new fathers whose turn it was to tend the crying baby. (One suspects that the gin added to gripe water was more efficacious than the dill.) Today, of course, most of us know dill for flavoring the pickles that buddy up with burgers and decorate deli platters.

Dill, which is packed with vitamin C, calcium, magnesium, iron, and potassium, is especially good on salmon and is a regular addition to sour cream. Toss it into your food at the last minute, since heat, like drying, steals its zip. The opposite is true of the tangy seeds; simmer them in soups, stews, and sauces to your heart's content.

Description

Dill is an annual from the Black Sea and Mediterranean regions. It looks a lot like its cousin fennel, except that it gets only 2 to 3 feet tall. Plants have a single hollow stalk, and the feathery leaves divide into hair-thin, blue-green leaflets. The tiny yellow flowers appear in 6-inch compound clusters that look like exploding fireworks. That's appropriate, since the pods, filled with ribbed, aromatic seeds, explode readily when ripe.

How to grow

Like the rest of the carrot clan, dill doesn't like to be transplanted. Direct-sow its seeds, just barely covered, as soon as you can work the ground in spring, preferably in full sun and light, in sandy soil of average fertility. When seedlings are about 2 inches tall, thin them to 8 to 10 inches apart. Sow more seed every three or four weeks to keep the dillweed coming.

Protect dill from winds, or stake plants to keep them from snapping. You can cut about one-fifth of a plant's foliage as soon as the leaves are big enough to use. The foliage will brown soon after the plant flowers (in hot weather, dill bolts quickly). Collect seeds as soon as they darken.

Dill is a graceful foil for heavy leafed plants and a friendly companion for cabbage. It's a favorite food for the larvae of the swallowtail butterfly. Plant enough dill so you and butterflies-in-waiting can both have your share.

Cultivars and related plants

For more thrills from dill, pick cultivars bred for special uses. 'Bouquet', a standard cultivar, produces large seeds early in the season. 'Dukat' is slow to bolt so offers more dill foliage, especially where summers are hot. 'Fernleaf', winner of the All-America Selections award, is also slow to bolt. Bushy and only 18 inches tall, it's perfect for a flower bed or container.

Elecampane (Inula helenium)

Both the genus and species names of elecampane come from the same root, which legend links to Helen of Troy. She was supposedly clutching fistfuls of elecampane — rather than a make-up bag for her ship-launching face — when Paris whisked her away from Sparta.

*Inula
helenium*

We don't know which of elecampane's reputed virtues inspired Helen's behavior. Common names such as horseheal attest to its use by veterinarians. But elecampane was most revered for curing respiratory system ailments. "It amendeth the cough . . . ceaseth the hard fetching of breath," gardener Thomas Hill wrote in 1577. The herb was also popular in candy, consumed not so much as a treat, but sucked for asthma symptoms and "when travelling by a river . . . against poisonous exhalations and bad air." Modern research supports some of elecampane's longtime uses for respiratory distress — for asthma, laryngitis, and as an expectorant.

Description

Elecampane is an imposing perennial when it reaches its full 6 feet. Its bright yellow, 3- to 4-inch daisylike flowers have narrow petals, and while few at a time, they keep coming from late spring until frost. The leaves are rough on top with soft fuzz on the underside.

How to grow

Native to Europe and western Asia, elecampane is at home in damp, partly shady places and is hardy through Zone 3. It is most easily propagated from 2-inch pieces of root harvested in the fall of the plant's second year. Each piece of root should have a bud, or eye. Plant the pieces in containers of damp sand and overwinter them in a cool room, about 50°F; set the sprouted roots out in spring (once the danger of frost is passed) in soil that is rich in organic matter, moist, and well-draining.

Space plants at least 2 feet apart. After that, you need do little more than make sure the soil doesn't dry out. Enjoy it in your garden much as you would sunflowers, at the back of an informal border, among wildflowers, or to protect vegetables from sun and wind.

Cultivars and related plants

Inula magnifica can get even taller than elecampane, and most gardeners find it more attractive. The 6-inch flowers have an orange tinge to their central disks and bloom in clusters. Growing to 2 feet or less are swordleaf inula (*I. ensifolia*), Himalayan elecampane (*I. royaleana*), with spidery orange-yellow flowers; and *I. orientalis,* which has fuzzy buds and wavy outer petals.

Fennel (Foeniculum vulgare)

Karan, who is much less tolerant of snakes than Kathy, has considered banishing fennel from her garden. It may ward off evil spirits, but according to the ancients, snakes rub against it to sharpen their eyesight — the better to spot gardeners bearing hoes. On the other hand, it was also reputed to heal snakebites.

This sweet-tangy perennial also was recommended "to helpeth digest the crude qualitie of fish and other viscous meats," and was used in drinks "for those that are grown fat, to abate their unwieldiness and cause them to grow more gaunt and lank."

You can take your pick of explanations for why the Puritans called fennel fruits "meeting' seeds" and chewed them at church: A) to keep them awake; B) to dull their appetites, C) to cover the scent of whiskey. (Note: Recent research shows that fennel may actually stimulate the appetite.)

If anise speaks too loudly of licorice for you, try fennel, which is sweeter and lighter. The stalks and hold up better than leaves in cooked dishes. The seeds are popular in cabbage, sauerkraut, and potatoes. Fennel is still recommended for "crude" or oily fish. Cosmetically, fennel helps soften skin and appears frequently in recipes for skin creams and lotions.

Description

A non-gardening friend visiting Kathy's weekend escape in Virginia was so enchanted by this tropical-looking giant, waving in the wind in an old farm field, that he dug some up to grace his patio. Thread-thin, blue-green foliage on a 6- to 8-foot plant does make an arresting site, although in Virginia, California, and other warm areas, fennel self-seeds and is a pestiferous weed. Like closely related dill, it has tiny yellow flowers in a flat umbrella, followed by the famous ribbed seeds.

How to grow

Fennel is cold-hardy through Zone 5; northern gardeners grow it as an annual. Other than sun and humus-rich soil with good drainage, it needs little attention. Start it from seed where you want it to grow, ideally when the soil is around 60°F, and thin seedlings to at least a foot apart. Like other carrot relatives, fennel may attract some swallowtail larvae, but on a plant this big, there is plenty for everyone.

Cultivars and related plants

Foeniculum vulgare is usually divided into two varieties, var. *dulce* and var. *azoricum,* and the horticultural community is hotly divided about which scientific name to attach to which plant. This may be a rare case where you're better off going with a common name. Grow common or sweet fennel if you want primarily foliage and seeds. If you want to eat fennel bulbs as a vegetable, you want finocchio, or Florence fennel, which is an annual or biennial. The "bulb" is actually the swollen base of the stem. Its leaves can be used in the same way as those of common fennel. The same goes for bronze fennel, *F. vulgare* 'Purpureum', a cultivar of sweet fennel often grown as an ornamental for its bronzy-red foliage.

Fenugreek (Trigonella foenum-graecum)

You have to sink pretty low to adulterate hay, but this is fenugreek's claim to fame. Its species name comes from a term meaning "Greek hay," since its maple flavor and scent were used to disguise mold. Earlier, the Egyptians used fenugreek in the mummification process, and other cultures burned it in religious rites. In the Middle Ages it was used to treat liver and kidney diseases, and in the 19th-century, it was a common ingredient in patent medicines. Today, it pops up as an ingredient in artificial maple flavoring, and it may have a valuable role to play in treating diabetes.

Fenugreek is popular in African, Middle Eastern, and East Indian dishes. Yet cooking with this herb can be a challenge. It walks a fine line between a bitter celerylike flavor and the sweetness of maple. Experiment, a bit at a time, with using the ground seeds to season meats and poultry, and in chutneys, curries, and other stews. You can also sprout the seeds for salads.

Description

Fenugreek is a member of the bean family, but with its three-part leaves it more closely resembles clover. It grows up to 2 feet tall. In midsummer, the plant begins producing fragrant, off-white flowers that can keep reappearing for several months. The seedpods look a lot like a green bean's, but point up instead of drooping down.

How to grow

A Mediterranean native, fenugreek asks only for a sunny spot and well-drained, organically rich soil. Sow seeds in spring after the soil has warmed (in cold, wet soil, seedlings are likely to rot). Thin seedlings to 4 inches apart. Seeds ripen about four months after germination.

Feverfew (Tanacetum parthenium)

This daisy-flowered perennial is a good example of the cyclical whims of fashion. Feverfew once was used to reduce fevers, as its common name suggests; to treat toothaches, vertigo, kidney stones, opium overdoses; and to act as a remedy for those "such as be melancholike, sad, pensive and without speech." The species name *parthenium* stems from the account by the Greek historian Plutarch that the herb had saved the life of a worker who fell from a great height while working on the Parthenon. Over time, however, feverfew's popularity waned until, if it were used at all, it was for problems relating to menstruation and pregnancy.

A few herbalists, such as England's John Parkinson, continued to recommend it for headaches — Nicholas Culpeper espoused a rather unorthodox approach of bruising the leaves and applying them to the crown of the head. Then in the late 1970s, its folk use for migraines was brought to the attention of English researchers, and a series of ever more detailed clinical trials substantiated its effectiveness.

The camphorlike taste of feverfew, while pleasant, is not a flavor you necessarily want in your salad dressing. If you want to try feverfew to prevent migraines, chew three to four of the leaflets daily. Keep in mind that there are no good studies on the effects of long-term use. Feverfew leaves cause mouth sores in a few people, and you shouldn't experiment with them if you're pregnant. The leaves lose their medicinal punch when dried; freeze them instead.

Description

Feverfew, a perennial native to southeast Europe and the Caucasus, looks a bit like chamomile. Both have divided leaves and daisylike flowers, but the leaves of chamomile are extremely narrow and fine, while the individual leaflets of feverfew are rounded, with feathery edges. The central cone of the feverfew flower is flat, while that of chamomile is a raised cone.

Woody at the base, feverfew at first forms a tidy mound, then sprawls when flowers begin blooming. It usually grows to about 2 feet tall and tends to be somewhat short-lived.

How to grow

Feverfew's original habitat is scrubby and rocky, and today it has made itself at home in English hedgerows and along U.S. roadsides and forest margins. In other words, you won't have to baby it in your garden. Give it full sun or partial shade, and ordinary soil that drains readily, and it will be happy. It's hardy through Zone 4.

In mild areas, you can sow feverfew seeds directly in the garden. In the North, start them indoors in March for planting out after the last-frost date. Once you grow feverfew, it's likely to self-seed. If not, you can propagate new plants by division or taking cuttings. Space plants about a foot apart.

Bees dislike feverfew, so don't plant it among vegetables or other plants that need pollinating. The plant is handsome near the front of an ornamental border if you keep it deadheaded.

Cultivars and related plants

Scientists have made great sport of the chrysanthemums, renaming them in spite of public outcry. Those that have been shuffled into *Tanacetum* with feverfew include costmary, tansy, and the painted daisy.

You can buy feverfew cultivars with more golden foliage ('Aureum'), many with double flowers ('Snowball', 'White Pompon', 'White Stars'), and dwarf types suitable for rock gardens or smaller containers ('Golden Moss', 'Santana', and 'Silver Ball').

Flax *(Linum usitatissimum)*

Throughout much of history, flax, or linseed, has been something of a one-man band.

The Egyptians wrapped their mummies in cloth woven of its fibers. Fishnets, bowstrings, sheets, purses, and bandages were just a few of its destinations. "[I]n what production of the Earth are there greater marvels to us than this?" the Roman scholar Pliny asked. It was popular for ship rigging, until the Tudors concluded that *Cannibis sativum* yielded stronger rope. There is no report on whether it got both sails and sailors higher.

A constituent of linoleum, linseed oil is a drying agent in oil paints, varnishes, and inks. The seeds can be used whole or ground into a flour and used in place of eggs as a thickener. Like other mucilaginous herbs, they can soothe the digestive tract and normalize either constipation or diarrhea.

If, like us, you just like its sky-blue flowers, they have lore of their own, offering protection from sorcery. The Bohemians believed that 7-year-olds who danced in a field of flax would become beautiful people. (Perhaps you know a second-grade teacher who could use a flax bouquet.)

Be sure that flax seeds are brown before you use them, since unripe seeds are toxic. Try sprouting the seeds for salads, or sprinkle them on cereal to add a nutty flavor. Crushed seeds are good in bread, and are used in tea to treat constipation, as are other fiber laxatives; follow your cup of linseed tea with a big glass of water.

Description

Flax is a wispy annual, 18 inches tall with an erect stem bearing narrow 1-inch leaves. The stem branches near the top, holding a 5-petal, blue flower at the end of each branch. The flowers are only a ½ inch across but numerous enough to create a star-spangled effect above these graceful plants. Flax begins blooming in mid-summer, and keeps it up for more than two months. Seeds develop in round, brown capsules.

How to grow

Flax can be fussy about soil. It can't be too sandy, too heavy, too rich or too lean, and of course, must drain well. Adding plenty of organic matter to whatever nature gave you should give it what it needs (except sun).

You can start flax from seed in either spring or fall, in warm-weather regions. Weed the bed well, since flax's shallow roots will make cultivation difficult. Thin seedlings to 4 inches apart.

Cultivars and related plants

Linum usitatissimum 'Regina' was bred especially for weavers; 'Omega' is a cultivar grown for its seeds, which contain higher amounts of omega-3 oil, a compound that helps prevent cardiovascular disease. *L. perenne* is a perennial lookalike with uses similar to common flax's. Other flax for the ornamental garden includes the perennials *L. flavum,* with yellow flowers, and *L. narbonense,* with blue flowers; and another annual, *L. grandiflorum,* which has rosy pink flowers.

Garlic (Allium sativum)

Whether you love to cook French, Mexican, or Italian dishes; can't resist a good yarn about gods or monsters; or want to prevent aging or heart disease; you need more garlic in your life.

Allium sativum

Many of the stories surrounding garlic associate it with evil, or at least an evil odor. According to a Mohammedean legend, garlic sprung up where Satan's left foot trod as he left the desecrated Garden of Eden. Wearing it in foot and horse races was said to keep competitors behind you. Garlic breath has been a mark of lower classes. But, hey, it saved Ulysses from being turned into a pig, and we all know we should string some around our necks when vampires are in the neighborhood.

In the past, garlic was used to treat such dread ailments as leprosy, smallpox, and anthrax in cattle. But unlike many herbs, it medicinal reputation may have increased in the scientific age. Among many potential health applications of garlic — one recent book suggests using it to treat 33 conditions, from allergies to yeast infections — the best-documented use is prevention and treatment of cardiovascular disorders, such as high blood pressure, hardening of the arteries, and stroke. It appears to work by preventing blood coagulation.

Description

Some lilies may be too regal to admit it, but garlic is family, along with chives, leeks, onions, and shallots. Garlic is unexciting in the garden in direct proportion to its value when harvested. The useful part — the compound bulb that is divided into cloves — is hidden underground. The gray-green, bladelike leaves are solid and grow 1 to 2 feet tall; the tiny white or pinkish flowers, which pop out of a pointed, papery pouch in rounded clusters, are ho-hum even by allium standards. Many garlics developed for eating don't bloom at all.

How to grow

This underground powerpack needs a deeply worked bed of fluffy, generously amended soil that both retains moisture and drains well. Slightly acid soil is best, as is full sun. Get rid of the weeds before you plant bulbs, since you'll have a hard time separating grass blades from garlic blades.

Don't be tempted to plant supermarket garlic. Buy cloves intended for planting from a garden center or mail-order supplier. Plant them, unpeeled, pointed end up, 2 inches deep and 5 inches apart. Side-dress the rows with compost and mulch to keep weeds at bay; mulch again once the ground is frozen. When growth begins in spring, pull the mulch back. Clip off any flower stalks that appear so that the plant's energy goes to the bulb.

Dig garlic when the plants' leaves begin to turn brown — and don't forget to save the biggest, outer cloves for replanting.

Cultivars and related plants

As with any popular plant, there are a lot of options with garlic (and mail-order companies that sell nothing else). Broadly, they're divided into softnecks and hardnecks. The easiest to grow are the softneck type known as artichoke garlics (try 'California Early', 'California Late', 'Inchelium Red, or 'Mudci').

Many cooks prefer a hardneck type called rocambole, but it doesn't store as well as the softnecks do; good cultivars are 'Purple Rocambole', 'Spanish Roja', 'German Red', and 'Killarney Red'. Elephant garlic is a different species, *A. ampeloprasum,* and is more closely related to the leek. It has larger bulbs and milder flavor than garlic's but doesn't overwinter in the North.

Geranium (Pelargonium spp.)

Scented geraniums, more properly called pelargoniums, are perennial natives of South Africa. They were first introduced to England in 1690, and popularized about a century later in a five-volume publication by a fellow appropriately named Robert Sweet. Once you try a few, you'll be hooked. The first time we sauntered into a well-stocked garden center for just one or two of these scent-sationals, we were lucky to leave with our bank account in the black.

Pelargonium

'Old-Fashioned Rose' smells just like its name, and the lemon-shaded edges and pleating on the leaves of 'Lady Plymouth' are irresistible. And 'Cody's Nutmeg' not only wafts a spicy scent when you stroke its mint-green leaves, but always seems to have a few airy white flowers. And of course, you'll have to get 'Coconut' for a hanging basket. . . .

Description

Every scented geranium is different, and not even subtly so. Some have leaves as big as the palm of your hand, sharply lobed and rough as a two-day beard. Leaves of others aren't much bigger than a quarter, scalloped, and downy as a peach.

Many pelargoniums squat coyly at just about 6 inches, while others shoot up quickly to a couple feet or more, and twice as wide. The differences in their scents *can* be subtle, and even require a certain amount of imagination.

These herbs, like an expensive wine or a symphony, need no excuses for being other than pure sensuous pleasure. Sample and savor, and pass along those that don't live up to your expectations in care of our publisher. . . .

How to grow

Pelargoniums' natural habitat has trained them to expect little in the way of water or fertilizer. Give them light soil amended with organic matter; a monthly diluted feed of organic fertilizer during the growing season; and enough water to keep them from wilting. What they must have is plenty of sun, so don't buy more than your south-facing windows or grow lights can accommodate in winter. Keeping them in pots that fit a bit tight helps restrain their growth.

Don't be afraid to prune pelargoniums back — a little careful cutting will give you a bushier plant. Pelargonium cuttings can root in damp sand year-round, so this is a good way to give yourself some insurance plants or share with friends.

Pelargoniums are hardy only through Zone 10 but do reasonably well indoors in winter. Stems of older plants become woody.

Cultivars and related plants

One of our favorite mail-order sources lists more than 50 scented geraniums. The names often clue you to their scent — but not to their size. If your space is limited, watch for words like "vigorous" and "robust."

A few that have done well for us? *Pelargonium* 'Clorinda,' with a sweet cedar fragrance and bright rose flowers; *P. crispum,* or lemon geranium; *P. crispum* 'Variegatum', a lemon-scented cultivar with cream-and-white leaves; *P.* 'Graveolens', or rose geranium; apple geranium, *P. odoratissimum;* and *P.* 'Royal Oak', which has pink flowers and oaklike leaves that smell like balsam.

Ginger (Zingiber officinale)

Accept no substitutes! When a recipe calls for fresh ginger root, you won't find the same mingling of sweet, spicy, and hot in a bottle. A native of tropical Asia, this herb appeared in Chinese herbals as long as 5,000 years ago. Chinese sailors discovered its most popular medicinal use, preventing seasickness. Cooks of that country sometimes use it with a heavy hand in seafood dishes in the belief that it prevents shellfish poisoning.

The Greeks ate it tucked in bread to help them digest heavy meals, thus paving the way for gingerbread. In the Middle Ages, fair maidens gave the spicy breads to knights preparing for tournaments.

*Zingiber
officinale*

Today ginger is grown commercially in Jamaica, as well as in India, Africa, and China. Fresh ginger is must for stir fries, marinades (especially for salmon and swordfish), and is good in dressings for cold, cooked vegetables. Try it grated on steamed carrots or summer squash. If you need to keep it longer than three weeks, peel and slice it into a bit of sherry, and store in the refrigerator. The sherry will add its own sweet tang to sauces and soups.

Ginger works so well against motion sickness that some cruise ships now make it available for passengers. It also seems to ease symptoms of morning sickness, and most herbalists consider it safe to use in pregnancy if you don't have a history of miscarriage.

Description

You might guess ginger's tropical origins from its narrow, lance-shaped leaves, up to a foot long in a grasslike clump. (It's no relation to the cold-hardy ground cover called wild ginger in the *Asarum* genus.) Compared to other members of the genus, the blooms are rather unexciting green cones with tiny dark red flowers. The leaves and flowers both have a ginger scent, however. You're probably familiar with the knobby mature root, which has a tan skin covering a cream-colored and crunchy interior.

How to grow

You can buy a plant or the root from a nursery, or buy a root (called a *hand* because of the way it branches) from the grocery store. Make sure it's plump and smooth, not dry and wrinkled, and that it has several eyes like those you see on potatoes. You may have better luck with one of the green roots sold in Asian markets.

Whether in the ground or a container, ginger needs loose, organically rich soil, warmth, and humidity. Set the hand two inches deep (about one foot apart, outdoors), keep the soil moist, and feed your plant monthly with compost tea. In eight to ten months, you can harvest the root. Save a plump piece to start your next crop.

Cultivars and related plants

The foliage and flower of *Zingiber officinale* are both fragrant, but if it's aroma you want, try white butterfly ginger *(Hedychium coronarium),* the plant used in Hawaii for leis.

Horehound *(Marrubium vulgare)*

This herb's common name comes from the ancient Greeks, who called it "the seed of Horus" (the Egyptian god of light) and espoused its use for fending off rabies from dog bite. Also used (no doubt disastrously) as a poison antidote, horehound was also recommended for intestinal worms and was soaked in fresh milk to repel flies. Otherwise, horehound has been used with amazing consistency for coughs and colds, recognized as an effective expectorant for more than 2,000 years.

Then in 1989 the U.S. Food and Drug Administration caused a huge flap among herbalists — even the most conservative — by decreeing that while horehound is safe, it doesn't work very well as a cough medicine. Buy or make some horehound candy the next time you're wheezing and hacking, make a tea with its leaves and flowers and put it to the test.

Most people disguise the bitter flavor with sugar or honey, and possibly some lemon. To keep horehound on hand in winter, make a syrup or honey (instructions are in Chapter 13) and keep it in the refrigerator. Don't consume too much, because this herb is also a laxative.

Description

The British once spelled the common name hoarhound, referring to the herb's woolly looking stems and leaves. Its musky fragrance, which disappears with drying, may remind you of an artemisia.

In other respects, this perennial bears many mint family hallmarks, such as square stems and two-lipped flowers. The white blooms, which appear in whorls along the stem in mid to late summer, are followed by capsules containing four barbed seeds. Bushy and up to 2 feet tall, horehound is hardy through Zone 4.

How to grow

If you see a plant described as tolerating a wide range of conditions, look out, because it can take over like neighbors who've heard about your new swimming pool. That's horehound. It grows in poor soil without much extra water, and in sun or partial shade. Plant the seeds with a light covering of soil in spring or fall; thin seedlings to 12 or 18 inches. Don't expect your plants to flower until their second year. You can also start new plants from division, but more likely, you'll need to weed out volunteers.

Cultivars and related plants

No cultivars of this aggressive plant exist, but it does have an even more aggressive distant cousin: black horehound, *Ballota nigra*. You're unlikely to find it for sale or even in gardens due to its "very unpleasant smell." Also called black stinking horehound, even cattle refuse to eat it.

Horseradish (Armoracia rusticana)

Beginning in the Middle Ages, this eastern European member of the mustard family was used widely to cure worms in children and applied as a plaster for "sciatica, gout, joint-ache or hard swellings of the spleen and liver." "It doth wonderfully help them all," Nicholas Culpeper gushed.

Armoracia rusticana

But as a condiment, horseradish was popular only in northern Europe, not the British Isles. As late as the mid-17th century, English herbalist John Parkinson dismissed the herb as too coarse for refined tastes and delicate constitutions. In fact, the "horse" in its name meant "coarse."

The English and French came around, of course. In today's kitchens, horseradish's use is generally limited to slapping on roast beef sandwiches and hot dogs, although spring leaves can be eaten like spinach. Modern herbalists recommend it for blowing open clogged sinuses.

Store harvested roots in a perforated bag in the refrigerator. We like to add a dab in mayonnaise-based salads, such as potato salad, and chicken, tuna, and ham salad for sandwiches. Try a pinch in a cream-based soup, sauce for vegetables, or spreads for bread.

Description

The lower leaves of this perennial, which is hardy through Zone 3, are more than a foot long with wavy edges. As the plant reaches its mature height of 3 feet or more, the leaves become smaller and more lance-shaped. Each tiny white flower, borne in clusters, has four petals. The roots can extend 2 feet into the soil.

How to grow

If you want good-sized roots, make sure your soil is rich with organic matter, deeply dug, and well-draining so that the fleshy taproot can grow without rotting. The root has brittle sideshoots, and any pieces left in the ground are likely to sprout. For that reason, you may want to consider planting it in a container sunk into the ground.

Start horseradish from roots in spring or fall, spaced at least a foot apart in full sun. If your growing season is shorter than 150 days, plant in fall or wait until the second year to harvest the root. Take cuttings from your harvested root and replant them for a new crop.

Cultivars and related plants

If you like Japanese food, you may have noticed the green paste that comes with paper-thin ginger when you order sushi. This is *wasabi*, an even hotter relative of horseradish. You can buy wasabi ready-made, as a powder to be mixed with water, or fresh in Asian groceries.

Hyssop *(Hyssopus officinalis)*

Confusing hyssop with anise hyssop *(Agastache foeniculum)* is easy. Both have spikes of purplish flowers, are members of the mint family, and are irresistible to bees. But there are more differences than similarities. (Hey, we warned you about common names.)

Hyssopus officinalis

Hyssop is a shrubby evergreen that, instead of smelling like tasty anise, smells like something you might use to clean the bathroom floor. The fragrance is pleasant enough but clearly medicinal, although the plant once was used as a potherb. Hyssop was once used to clean holy places; the word hyssop stems from the Greek *azob,* meaning holy herb.

In spite of its medicinal scent and taste, many cooks use hyssop in tomato sauces. It marries especially well with cranberries, other fruits, and stuffing. When you have a cold, try inhaling hyssop in steam, or prepare it as tea or a gargle. For cleaning, add a strong hyssop infusion into a solution for scrubbing down the kitchen or bathroom floor.

Description

A native of Europe and Asia, hyssop grows up to 2 feet tall and 3 wide and bears 6-inch spikes of intense blue-violet flowers from midsummer to early fall. The flowers are not only brighter but also larger than those of anise hyssop, up to a half-inch across with two upper lips and three lower lips. The leaves differ from the typical mint in being smooth and lance-shaped.

How to grow

Hyssop needs plenty of sun to keep it from becoming leggy. Otherwise, it needs only light, well-drained soil, and a bit of deadheading and pruning now and then to stimulate growth and keep it tidy. You can start it from seed, planted a week or two before the first frost date, or from cuttings or root divisions. Attractive to butterflies and hummingbirds as well as bees, it is hardy through Zone 3.

Cultivars and related plants

Need a break from blue? Look for *Hyssopus officinalis* var. *alba* for white flowers, var. *roseus* for pink. There are also strains selected for being more compact in size. A perennial called hedge hyssop (*Gratiola officinalis*) is planted for historical interest, but it should never be used as a home remedy.

Lady's bedstraw (Galium verum)

Once used by both rich and poor for stuffing mattresses, *Galium verum* is sometimes called Our Lady's bedstraw, an allusion to the legend that the Virgin Mary used it to line the manger in Bethlehem. Another name, maid's hair, came from the little yellow flowers that reminded some people of peroxided tresses. The genus name has its root in *gala,* the Greek word for milk, because the herb once was used to curdle milk and give the resulting cheese a yellow tint.

*Galium
verum*

Medicinally, lady's bedstraw is linked to urinary problems, such as kidney stones and bladder infections, although not favored by most modern herbalists. No question about its efficacy as a dye, though: the leaves for yellow and the roots for red.

Description

This delicate perennial lends an airy note to the garden, with thin leaves that climb the stem in whorls, and clusters of tiny yellow flowers from spring to late summer. It averages about 2 ½ feet tall, although it tends to sprawl instead of growing upright, especially in a partly shady location.

How to grow

Start lady's bedstraw in spring, either from seed or by dividing an established clump. Space plants about 18 inches apart. Not particular about soil, the plants do well in sun or partial shade. The plants are hardy through Zone 3. Keep an eye open for slightly invasive behavior.

Cultivars and related plants

You might want to look to the entry for another member of the *Galium* genus, sweet woodruff. A third *Galium*, cleavers *(G. aparine),* is an annual that also answers to the name goosegrass. It has bristly leaves and a long-standing reputation among herbalists for curing skin problems.

Lavender (*Lavandula spp.*)

Is any herb better known for its scent than lavender? From lingerie drawer sachets and expensive soaps to lavender wands and just short of a million aromatherapy products, lavender is a scent most people find clean and refreshing.

A famous story about lavender involves Rene-Maurice Gattefosse, a French perfume chemist who discovered its healing properties in the 1920s when he burned his hand and plunged it into a vat of lavender oil. This successful move is credited with launching aromatherapy.

The Romans thought that the asp — that little Egyptian snake that snuggled up with Cleopatra — lived among lavender plants. But that didn't keep people out of the lavender patch. After all, it was also believed to be an aphrodisiac, good for "the panting and passion of the heart."

We think lavender tastes like perfume and has enough to do without masquerading as food. You can use lavender in virtually any cosmetic or cleaning agent that you want to scent, and of course, in potpourris, sachets, and sleep pillows.

Description

There are at least 25 species of lavenders, not to mention many, many cultivars. As a rule, the plants are small (less than 3 feet), many-branched woody shrubs with gray-green or silvery 2-inch leaves, narrow and lance-shaped. In late spring to midsummer, lavenders produce lovely 6- to 8-inch spikes of tiny, two-lipped purple flowers.

How to grow

Lavenders require full sun and soil that has a neutral or slightly sweet pH, is rich with organic matter, and that drains in minutes. (Some growers believe that sandy, less fertile soil produces plants with more fragrance.) Buy plants not seeds, since you can't count on species coming true, and seeds usually take forever to germinate. Or start from cuttings or by layering.

Space plants 2 to 4 feet apart, depending on the species and how much pruning you want to do. Provide some shelter from wind to protect the flower stalks. Unfortunately, very few lavenders can survive a winter colder than winters in Zone 8.

Lavenders also play myriad roles in an ornamental garden — edging walkways or borders, scattered among other perennials for contrast of form and foliage, or as residents in rock gardens. They are classic companions to roses, helping to hide thorny or bare stems, and send bees into a frenzy.

Cultivars and related plants

English lavender (*Lavandula angustifolia*), the most commonly grown species, is hardy through Zone 5 and offers numerous cultivars, including 'Hidcote', 'Munstead', and 'Twickel Purple', all with purple flowers and growing 18 to 24 inches tall. For pink, choose 'Hidcote Pink' or 'Miss Katherine'; for white 'Nana Alba', a fine dwarf cultivar, only 10 inches tall.

Spike lavender *(L. latifolia)* is a more upright species that is hardy through Zone 6. *L. dentata,* or fringed lavender, has gray-green foliage and dark purple flowers; it's hardy only through Zone 8.

Worth looking for and trying to grow indoors is French lavender *(L. stoechas),* which has extremely narrow leaves. The flowers are not only a vibrant rosy purple, but appear in tight little cylinders topped by a flag of pink petals. A variety, *L. stoechas* var. *pedunculata,* has even more dramatic, elongated blooms.

Lemon balm *(Melissa officinalis)*

So you've spilled hot coffee on your computer's hard drive, discovered that you threw away those records the IRS wants, and received an irate phone call from your teenage son's girlfriend's father (all before noon). . . . Sounds like you could use a cup of the beverage "esteemed of great use in all complaints supposed to proceed from a disordered state of the nervous system." You need some lemon balm.

Three centuries ago, people believed that a morning glass of wine flavored with lemon balm would "renew youth, strengthen the brain, relieve languishing nature and prevent baldness." The Roman scholar Pliny went so far as to suggest that a warrior could stanch a wound merely by tying lemon balm to his sword. Sixteenth-century writer John Gerard reported that beekeepers rubbed it onto their hives to keep the swarm together. (The genus name *Melissa* is Greek for "bee.")

Science has borne out lemon balm's antibacterial and tranquilizing effects, although these are less pronounced that those of other herbs. Today we know the herb, sometimes called just balm, as a soothing tea, a too-eager colonizer in the garden. And by another common name, sweet Melissa, which the Allman Brothers borrowed for their 1972 hit song, *Melissa.*

Use this delicately flavored herb fresh in salads — vegetable, fruit, or meat — or add it at the last minute to foods that benefit from a hint of mint, such as seafood, broccoli, asparagus, rice, or couscous. Lemon balm's combination of relaxing and healing qualities make it a fine addition to bath water and facial washes.

Description

Despite the pretty names, this perennial is a scraggy little herb, usually only about a foot tall. Its leaves are somewhat heart shaped with toothed edges, and make it look like a diminutive nettle. Sporadically through summer it produces the small clusters of yellow or white flowers that bees love so much. Let your fingers check for the signature scent of lemon and mint.

How to grow

It's hard to go wrong with lemon balm. It's happy in any ordinary soil, although your plants will have bigger, plumper leaves if you add generous amounts of organic matter and water during a drought. Cold hardy through Zone 4, this herb needs midday shade in the South. If it gets beat up in hot weather, shear it back to the ground; it will regrow. Balm doesn't spread rampantly like other mints but does self-sow. Remove the spent flowers if you don't want more lemon balm — or more bees.

You can start lemon balm from seed, but it's easier to take stem cuttings or divide an established plant (its shallow roots are thick and matted). Space plants about 18 inches apart.

Cultivars and related plants

If you want a lemon balm you can show off to friends, look for one of the variegated cultivars, such as 'Aurea', or the appropriately named 'All Gold'. (These cultivars need protection from hot sun even more than the species.)

The balm of Gilead, *Cedronella canariensis,* has a balsam rather than a lemon scent. It's appropriate for potpourri but not the teacup. Vietnamese balm (*Elsholtzia ciliata*) combines lemon and floral flavors — it's not our cup of tea, but you might feel differently.

Lemon grass (Cymbopogon citratus)

If you buy an herb book more than 10 years old, it probably won't list lemon grass. That's because a decade ago, you couldn't find a good Thai or Vietnamese restaurant anywhere in North America outside large coastal cities. Lemon grass is a key ingredient in those cuisines, which have the twin virtues of being low-fat and exquisitely spiced. You can chop the stems into soups, sauces, seafood, and poultry, for a lemon taste without the tang of citrus.

Cymbopogon citratus

Lemon grass has medicinal properties, as well. Traditional uses are for inducing sleep (Brazil), for controlling fever (in the Caribbean, where it is called fever grass), and for treating ringworm (India). It does contain a mild sedative and shows power against fungal infections, such as athlete's foot and ringworm, when taken either in tea or applied as a compress. Lemon grass also has insect-repelling properties, so is worth including in homemade bugbanes.

Description

This perennial from India and Sri Lanka forms a clump similar to many of the ornamental grasses popular in today's gardens. Its narrow, blue-green leaves shoot up to 3 feet from the plant's onionlike base and are tough-textured with razor-sharp edges. The late-season flower panicles can add another 2 feet, but only gardeners with subtropical conditions are likely to ever see them. Worry not: It's the hollow stems that are most often used in cooking.

How to grow

Give lemon grass full sun and organically rich, moisture-retentive soil. To get started, beg or buy a division; plant it at the same depth it was growing. (If you're using a container, choose one that is at least 12 inches across.)

In Zone 9 and south, well-watered lemon grass forms a clump 3 feet wide. Yours is unlikely to be that large, but you can still divide clumps to obtain more plants. Divide during the growing season (cut the leaves of the new division down to 3 or 4 inches to reduce stress) or well before the first fall frost to overwinter indoors in pots. Harvest young lemon grass stalks while they're still tender.

We use lemon grass to give height to large containers, and have even used it as a support for delicate annual vines such as nasturtium.

Cultivars and related plants

Another *Cymbopogon,* citronella grass *(C. nardus)* is more famous for its mosquito-repelling properties than lemon grass is. You'll find its essential oil in those familiar yellow patio candles. Oils from members of this genus also are used in perfumery, especially for a synthetic violet scent. The best source of these oils is said to be palmarosa *(C. martinii* var. *motia,* sometimes called geranium, or rosha, grass). The scent, comparable to that of a rose geranium, is worth trying to capture in potpourri or homemade cosmetics.

Lemon verbena *(Aloysia triphylla)*

Why do we struggle to grow this tropical shrub? The nose knows. In the garden it only takes a gentle touch to trigger the release of its lemon-lime scent. In a potpourri, the aroma lasts for months.

Aloysia triphylla

Brought from South America to England in 1784, lemon verbena was once all the rage as a tea in France and Spain, and as a cure for indigestion, flatulence, lethargy, and depression. In Colonial and Civil War America, it was popular in perfumes and the little nosegays called tussie-mussies.

You can use lemon verbena as you would any of the other lemon herbs. The flavor won't fade in cooking and makes a pleasant tea, or add it to marinades and dressings. An infusion of lemon verbena lends a squeaky clean scent to cosmetics or cleaning agents.

Description

Lemon verbena is a deciduous shrub that grows to a dozen feet or more on the Isle of Wight or in Florida but stays under 5 feet in most gardens. Its narrow, lance-shaped leaves appear in whorls along the stem and are a bit hairy. The flowers — tiny lavender tubes — appear in airy spikes but won't make the evening news.

How to grow

Lemon verbena prefers organically rich, well-draining soil that keeps its roots moist but never soggy. Plants rarely produce seed, so start with a purchased plant or stem cutting. Most gardeners grow this herb, hardy only through Zone 9, in a container, moving it outdoors in summer and back inside for winter. Feed plants with diluted fish emulsion while they're actively growing, and be firm about keeping small weak branches pruned off.

In winter, remember the word *deciduous:* Plants drop all their leaves and go dormant, which means no fertilizer and just a dribble of water now and then. Lemon verbena is notorious for attracting whitefly and other pests, so follow our preventive recommendations in Chapters 7 and 10.

Cultivars and related plants

All the members of the verbena family have traditional medical uses, including the *Lippia* species from tropical America and Africa (used by native peoples for stomach upset and cramps, gas and bloating). Mexican oregano

(L. graveolens) can be used like other oreganos in cooking. It's big enough to be used as a hedge in Zone 9 and warmer, but must be brought indoors farther north. Other verbena family members are in a genus of the same name and include vervain *(Verbena officinalis)*, once used by the Druids in religious ceremonies, and recommended by today's herbalists for anxiety and stress.

Lovage (Levisticum officinale)

Lovage is celery to the max — both in stature and flavor. In fact, people who've never tasted unblanched celery and think of that vegetable as all crunch and no flavor are in for a surprise when they try this big, brawny cousin.

Levisticum officinale

Nor can lovage be ignored in the garden, for it grows up to 5 feet tall and 3 feet wide. And you have to like a plant with a common name — it was once called love parsley — derived from being used as an aphrodisiac. It could also be considered something of a deodorant. Travelers used to put it in their shoes to keep their sweaty feet from stinking. Others chewed the seeds to dispel flatulence. Modern herbalists recommend a decoction of the dried root as a cure for bloating.

As a medicinal herb it was never such a giant, although 17th century physician Nicholas Culpeper liked it for agues, quinsy, and pleurisy, and advised, "The leaves bruised and fried with a little hog's lard and laid hot to any blotch or boil will quickly break it." The "old writers," according to British herbalist Maude Grieve, used it for kidney stones and urinary problems; modern studies show that it is an effective diuretic.

In the kitchen, use lovage stems, leaves, and seeds like celery: Chop the raw stems and leaves for salads, steam or lightly sauté the stems for stuffings or stir-fries. But not so much! This herb easily overwhelms other ingredients. Lovage makes an especially happy marriage with tomato. Snip it into spaghetti sauces, or use the hollow stem to sip tomato juice — or a Bloody Mary.

Description

To envision this carrot-family perennial, multiply celery by a factor of two or three. Lovage has the same ribbed, U-shaped stems and the same compound, toothed leaves, dark green and shiny. The root, as might be expected, is stout, up to 6 inches long. The minuscule flowers are in umbels, about 3 inches across, the small seeds are grooved. Plants are hardy through Zone 4.

How to grow

Celery has a reputation for being difficult to grow. Not so lovage. Start it from seed, indoors or out. One plant will be more than enough for the average family. Remember that big root and give it deeply worked soil, preferably with lots of organic matter and a bit acidic. Site it in full sun (a bit of shade is fine in the South) where it can spread out, and top dress it with compost each fall. A floating row cover protects it from aphids and swallowtail caterpillars.

Should you need more lovage, divide the clump in spring. Lovage seeds don't remain viable for long; if you collect your own, sow them in autumn, or store them in the refrigerator until spring. To produce large roots for medicine, hold back on manure (which promotes leaf growth) and keep flowers pinched off.

Cultivars and related plants

Carrot-family plants in the sound-alike genus *Ligusticum* are sometimes called lovage. Scots lovage *(L. scoticum)* has been used like celery and lovage in that country. Osha *(L. porteri)*, which sounds more like a workplace watch-dog federal agency than an herbal medicine, is a Rocky Mountain denizen that Native Americans used to boost the immune system. (Note: Even nurseries that sell the seeds say this plant is a challenge to grow.)

Marjoram, sweet (Origanum majorana)

Oh, what a tangled web! Someone should have held an Herbal Peace Conference, agreeing to call all of the *Origanum* genus either marjoram or oregano. But no such luck. A mishmash of common names prevails. Some species are called marjoram, some oregano, and a few flop back and forth.

*Origanum
majorana*

The best we can do here is to focus on the plant that is always called marjoram, or sweet marjoram. The word "sweet" distinguishes its sweeter, more delicate flavor (in the Middle Ages this herb was used in perfumes and cosmetics) from the robust, pizza-esque tang of other culinary oreganos. It was this marjoram that the Greeks lay on graves to assure sweet dreams for the dead; and because the herb was associated with Aphrodite, the goddess of love, they also used to wreathe the heads of newlyweds.

Marjoram is a staple of Greek and Italian cuisines. German cooks grind the herb into sausage and add it to potato soup. Sweet marjoram is also great with squash, mushrooms, eggplant, and most root vegetables. Its clean, fresh scent makes it worth adding to homemade cleaning agents.

Description

In its native Mediterranean, sweet marjoram is a shrubby, evergreen perennial, growing up to 2½ feet tall. But since it is hardy only through Zone 9, in most of the United States it is treated as an annual. A member of the mint family, sweet marjoram has many branching square stems; its oval leaves are gray-green and fuzzy. Marjoram's most distinguishing characteristic is the knotlike look of its buds before they open — it's also called knotted marjoram. The tiny white, lavender, or pink flowers have round, oily bracts and (if you look *very* closely) a one-lipped calyx with a slit down one side. Plants bloom from early to late summer.

How to grow

You can try starting marjoram from seed, indoors four to six weeks before your last frost date, or sow directly in the ground when that date is past. Many gardeners buy plants, though, because of the name confusion, because cultivars or hybrids won't come true from seed, and because wet conditions make seedlings susceptible to damping-off. Set plants in full sun, about 6 inches apart, in good garden soil amended with plenty of organic matter.

Once established, sweet marjoram grows quickly, although plants may sulk in the humidity and clay soil found in the far South. Begin harvesting in mid-summer to supply your kitchen and to keep your plants shapely and productive. To overwinter marjoram indoors, pot up a division (cut the top back to 2 inches) in the fall, well before the first frost.

Cultivars and related plants

Closest in flavor to sweet marjoram is its hybrid cousin Italian oregano, or hardy sweet marjoram, *Origanum × majoricum*. This evergreen perennial, winter-hardy through Zone 7, grows to about 15 inches. The flowers are like those of common oregano; the leaves are similar to but less fuzzy than marjoram's.

Pot marjoram, or Cretan oregano *(O. onites)*, is another little evergreen shrub, a bit less cold-tolerant than hardy sweet marjoram. Its taste lies somewhere between marjoram and oregano but with a biting edge. Use it with restraint.

Marsh mallow (Althaea officinalis)

No, you won't find any part of this plant in those white bits of fluff that are burnt to a crisp by kids at summer camp. But marsh mallow was a sweet treat (made by boiling the peeled root many times and adding sugar) many great-great grandparents would have recognized.

Consumed at least since the days of the Egyptians, marsh mallow was considered a delicacy by the Romans; in other cultures, it was a food for the poor, who boiled the herb and then fried it with onions and butter.

This desultory history as food is at odds with the marsh mallow's sterling reputation as a medicine (the genus name stems from *altheo,* meaning "to cure"). It is champ when it comes to mucilage — the stuff that swells up when wet — and its ability to soothe the body inside and out has been touted for centuries. The Roman Pliny enthused that whoever consumed a spoonful "shall that day be free from all diseases."

Make a decoction from dried, powdered marsh mallow root to drink for a sore throat, or make a thick gel to treat wounds, burns, or sunburns. For a face and body lotion, combine marsh mallow with rose water and lavender.

Description

Brought from Europe by early American colonists, marsh mallow is a hardy perennial, often growing more than 5 feet tall and covered from stem to stern with tiny hairs. Its velvety leaves are spade-shaped with teeth and several lobes. The flowers are typical of the mallow family (which include rose-of-Sharon, hollyhock, and hibiscus); up to 2 inches across with five notched petals, they are lilac-pink with brighter reddish-purple anthers.

How to grow

With the common names marsh mallow and water mallow, you can guess that this herbs grows in boggy and wet places in the wild. But you get more mucilage from roots if they are growing in soil that drains well but is watered frequently. If you start from seed, plan on not harvesting roots until the third year; if you plant divisions in spring, you can collect some roots in the second fall. Save root pieces with buds (eyes) to replant. Set them 18 inches apart in a sunny location. Marsh mallow is hardy through Zone 3.

Cultivars and related plants

Marsh mallow has escaped to swampy places in the United States, especially salt marshes in the mid-Atlantic and lower New England. However, if you see a mallowlike plant growing in shallow water with white flowers, it's probably common swamp mallow *(Hibiscus moscheutos)*. Up to 8 feet tall, swamp mallow may have red or pink flowers, and there are many showy cultivars. Less ornamental but used medicinally in the same way as marsh mallow is common mallow *(Malva sylvestris)*. It is a native of Europe and Asia and has five-lobed scalloped leaves and 2-inch magenta flowers. Naturalized in the United States, common mallow self-sows readily in the garden.

Milk thistle (Silybum marianum)

A thistle — particularly one whose botanical name looks like "silly bum" — would seem to be the last thing you'd want in your garden, kitchen, or medicine cabinet. All the same, a host of well-respected gardeners adore this annual. Every part of it is edible: young leaves in salads; mature leaves boiled like spinach; shoots peeled and steamed like asparagus ("Surpasses the finest cabbage," one early writer enthused); the root prepared like a parsnip. Even the unopened flower heads were once eaten.

Known as a liver protector since the first century A.D., the active ingredient in milk thistle seeds is silymarin. Modern laboratory and clinical studies have shown silymarin to protect the liver and help it recover from hepatitis, cirrhosis, and even the highly poisonous death's cap mushroom.

If you want to help ensure a healthy liver, buy the readily available capsules. You can certainly try eating parts of the plant, as gourmands of old did. But keep those prickly edges in mind. Wear gloves when stripping the edges off mature foliage before you steam the leaves.

Description

An annual or biennial native of the Mediterranean and southwest Europe, milk thistle shoots up from a basal rosette to 5, even 7, feet, stout and branching to 2 or 3 feet across. The smooth, shiny leaves clasping the stem are scalloped and dramatically veined and marbled with white. (Common names such as Mary's thistle refer to a legend that the white color comes from the milk of the Virgin Mary.) The thistlelike flowers, 2 inches across, are flaming magenta.

How to grow

Milk thistle is one of those plants that grows too easily. It is a noxious weed in warm climates such as in California, and has naturalized in old fields and along roads in the eastern United States. This plant is happy in poor, dry soil (as long as drainage is good) and germinates from seed in one or two weeks.

Connecticut garden writer Fred McGourty grows milk thistle in his famous perennial borders, calling it "pure elegance when planted among the summer phloxes of similar tint." The leaves alone can add some excitement to your herb garden. But he reports that his passion for it has put something of a strain on his marriage, ever since his wife made the mistake of tossing its spent stalks in the compost — 2,000 seedlings germinated there and 2,000 more where the compost was spread. In a wildflower meadow you worry less about stray seedlings — and possibly not at all, since the seeds are a favorite treat for goldfinches.

Cultivars and related plants

Also known as Our Lady's Thistle (and as blessed thistle or holy thistle) is *Cnicus benedictus*. In the Middle Ages this herb was deemed excellent for "old rotten and festering sores." It does have antiseptic properties, and as a bitter herb is sometimes used to stimulate the appetite. (A bitter herb on the tongue gets your gastric juices flowing.)

Two more cousins are yellow-spine thistle, *Cristium ochrocentrum,* which some native American Indians used as a cure for syphilis, and pasture thistle, *Cristium pumilum,* a favorite plant of Henry David Thoreau, who was astonished by the number of bees it attracted.

Mints (Mentha spp.)

We're fairly sure you won't want to grow all the mints. About 20 species exist, but between bees and breeders, you can avail yourself of more than 1,000 hybrids. For beginning herb gardeners, the choice usually comes down to spearmint *(Mentha spicata)* and/or peppermint *(M. × piperita).*

Mentha

Until 300 years ago everyone thought all mints were alike, but liked what they knew. The Pharisees demanded mint (along with anise and cumin) as a tax. In the first century A.D., mint was thought to "stir up the minde and the taste to a greedy desire of meate" and to incite lust. The Greeks rubbed it on their bodies after a night at the baths. Centuries later, European herbalists recommended mint for everything from the "bitings of mad dogs" and "all manner of breakings out on the head" to upset stomachs, tearing eyes, and "nervous crudities."

By that measure, modern medicinal uses of mints are limited. Mints are good for aiding digestion, so don't hesitate to reach for the after-dinner mints. Pliny suggested hanging mint in sickrooms to "reanimate the spirit." Use mint anywhere you want yourself and others to feel clean and refreshed: in a steam tent when you have a cold, or in facial lotions when you're itchy or tired.

Mint is a must for Middle Eastern dishes, such as tabouleh and cucumber raita, and is especially good with carrots. Or try it with fish, beans, and creamed soups. Try adding an infusion of mint instead of water to a brownie or chocolate cake mix. And of course, add it to ice tea on a hot afternoon or to a mint julep as the sun goes down.

Description

Spearmint and peppermint are easier to tell apart by taste than appearance. Peppermint is stronger and has a "bite" to it — hence the "pepper" in its name. Both are perennials, growing between 2 and 3 feet tall. Peppermint leaves tend to be more lance-shaped and less wrinkled; its stem is reddish, and it spreads along the top of the ground. Spearmint is a subway herb, traveling underground. Spearmint may bloom a little earlier in summer than peppermint does, with white flowers rather than the pink or lilac of peppermint blooms. The flowers of both are tiny, bell-shaped, and held in whorls.

How to grow

Some mints don't produce viable seeds, and many of the plants you may want are hybrids — which don't come true from seed. Buy plants or beg some divisions in spring or fall. You can let them run amok as a groundcover — an olfactory rush to walk on — but most of us restrain them in above-ground containers or tiles sunk into a garden bed. Divide mints about every three years, since, like some middle-aged heads, they get bald in the middle.

Set mints just below the soil surface. The best soil is moist, relatively rich, and slightly acid. Keep them from drying out and prune or harvest them regularly for bushier plants and plumper leaves. Hardiness varies, but peppermint and spearmint are hardy through Zone 3.

Cultivars and related plants

Many mints are said to mingle with another flavor — lemon, lime, grapefruit, chocolate, ginger, even banana. They may not always perform as advertised — just another fluke of mints' highly varied nature.

Mentha × *piperita* 'Citrata' (which has orange, lemon, and lime strains) is sometimes called the eau-de-cologne mint because it's an ingredient in perfume. Hardy through Zone 4, it's off-putting in foods but superb in potpourri.

If you have a pond (or just a soggy spot) you might grow water mint *(M. aquatica)*. Hardy through Zone 6, it can grow submerged up to 6 inches. Water mint is rich in menthol, giving it extra punch in medicines and cleaning solutions.

Looking for variegated leaves? Try pineapple mint. A cultivar of apple mint *(M. suaveolens),* you'll find it listed as *A. suaveolens* 'Variegata'. It's highly ornamental and has a wonderful fruity scent, but is hardy only through Zone 7.

For culinary uses, try curly spearmint, *M. spicata* 'Crispa'; it has round, crinkled leaves, a mild taste, and is hardy through Zone 4. Corsican mint *(M. requiennii)* is more strongly flavored.. This groundcover has tiny round leaves, needs protection from hot sun, and is hardy through Zone 7.

Mustard, black (Brassica nigra)

Mustard was born to snuggle with hot dogs. Of course it's not likely that the Romans, the first to pound mustard seeds and soak them in wine, enjoyed red hots at the Coliseum. But the basic mustard sauce recipe — calling for vinegar, honey, and a pinch of spice — has remained pretty much the same through the centuries. Lively Dijon types are made with with black mustard seeds, milder American yellow mustards with yellow or white mustard *(B. hirta),* or a middle-of-the-road brown mustard *(B. juncea).*

Brassica nigra

In the sickroom, a mustard plaster was a time-honored poultice for respiratory ailments. Externally, mustard preparations were used for neuralgia, rheumatism, headaches, aching feet, and even epilepsy. (Because mustard paste alone can feel too hot too quickly, it is traditionally applied on top of paper.) Nicholas Culpeper said mustard seeds would cure laryngitis, mushroom poisoning, bruises, toothache, "the falling of the hair . . . also the crick in the neck."

Sautéed mustard seeds added to rice, potatoes, or other vegetables provide a Middle Eastern punch. Use them crushed or powdered in salad dressings, in rarebits, and other white sauces. The traditional Southern treatment for greens is to steam or cook them with bacon or salt pork and onions, accompanied with cornbread. White mustard greens are good in salads and sandwiches.

Description

Mustards — there are dozens — are leafy annuals, ranging up to 6 feet tall in the case of black mustard (the spiciest and most often grown for its seeds). Most have stout stalks and broad, usually dark green leaves that are frequently puckered or wrinkled and lower leaves that have lobes or teeth. Each of the bright yellow flowers, which appear on tall spikes, has four petals arranged in a cross shape.

How to grow

Mustard greens get hotter or more bitter when the plants are hot and dry. That means they may need some mid-summer shade from taller plants or a vine-covered trellis. Otherwise, give them full sun and soil that is moisture-retentive, well-draining, and slightly acid. Start with seeds outdoors, a couple of weeks before the frost-free date, then thin the plants to 18 inches apart (for black mustard), less for other types. Top-dress with manure or compost, because mustard plants gobble up nitrogen in their brief but enthusiastic growing season.

Because mustards bolt (quickly go to seed) in hot weather, southern gardeners often plant them as a winter crop. Plants mature in about 50 days, so depending on your climate, you can try planting in both spring and summer (for a fall crop). Of course if you're growing mustard for seed, bolting is the goal, rather than a problem.

In either case, don't let the seeds fall on the ground unless you plan to start making mustard for the neighborhood. This is one prolific plant.

Cultivars and related plants

You can find a world of mustards. Asians cook with wrapped mustards, which curl inward to form heads, and mizuna, a mild *Brassica juncea* variety. There are curled mustards with frilly leaves, and green-in-the-snow types that are small, quick-maturing, and hardy. You can buy big-leaf mustards with purple veins or foliage, and the foot-tall, quick-maturing common leaf mustards. If want a mustard for seeds, look for 'Burgonde', 'French Brown', and 'Tilney'. The last is the source of most commercial yellow mustards.

Many *Brassica* species aren't mustard at all, but cabbages, kales, or broccoli.

Nasturtium (Tropaeolum majus)

Slip a few peppery nasturtium leaves in your dinner salad and guests will be wide awake for the main course, even it it's meatloaf. You can use the flowers as well, but their emergency-beacon colors will give away the surprise.

Tropaeolum majus

The nasturtium is a native of Peru; native Andean tribes used the plant to heal wounds and relieve chest congestion. All parts of the plant are antibiotic. But ever since the Spaniards introduced nasturtiums to Europe in the 1500s, their primary use has been to zip up salads and sandwiches. You can feel virtuous about using nasturtiums as salad greens, since they're packed with vitamin C. Try the flowers and leaves to flavor and decorate vinegar. Unopened flower buds pickled in wine are a substitute for capers.

Description

The nasturtium, an annual vine growing to 10 feet, is charming even before it blooms. The leaves look like a tiny water lily pad with wavy edges, each attached to its stem in the middle, like an umbrella. Then, from summer to fall, the show begins with 2-inch spurred flowers, most often in hot orange, yellow, and red. (You can rebel and buy more pastel shades, such as 'Primrose Jewel'.) The species is a climber, but most of the cultivars form bushy mounds, perfect for containers or trailing over a ledge.

How to grow

Sow seeds (which germinate quickly and easily) outdoors in early spring, or in the South, in fall. In the far South nasturtiums grow through winter, then fall apart when heat arrives.

Nasturtiums like full sun and poor to average soil that drains quickly. Don't overdo the fertilizer or you'll have more leaf than flower. Water plants well, and be greedy when pinching off leaves to munch, which will make plants bushier. Plant vining types about a foot apart, mounding types six inches.

The climbers are lightweight enough to hang on thin wires, strings, netting, heavier vines, or woven through shrubs. The mounders are ready-made for containers; give the trailers a hanging basket or window box, wind them between other plants, or plant around steppingstones as a groundcover.

Cultivars and related plants

This genus includes several semihardy or tender vines. Flame flower *(Tropaeolum speciosum),* which likes cool, moist growing conditions, has notched vermilion petals that are arranged like the blades of a ceiling fan, followed by bright blue fruits. *T. tuberosum* has red and orange flowers, while those of *T. tricolorum* are tubelike, red with a maroon edge and yellow petals. These are all hardy through Zone 8. Canary creeper *(T. peregrinum)* gets its name from its sulfur yellow color and fringed petals that look like a cockatoo's topknot. It's hardy only through Zone 9. All of these species have lobed leaves.

Confusingly, the plant with the botanical name *Nasturtium* is watercress, which you find out about in this chapter.

Oregano (Origanum vulgare)

Given the interchangeable use of the names marjoram and oregano (see the entry for *marjoram* earlier in this chapter), there's reason to question which one is being referred to in various "duste olde" herbals. Most experts say the "true" Greek oregano that can make your kitchen smell like a *trattoria* is *O. vulgare* sub. *hirtum.*

Origanum vulgare

What grows wild in the eastern United States is *O. vulgare* sub. *vulgare*. The name may sound doubly vulgar but the plant doesn't smell or taste like much of anything. It doesn't even live up to its name: *Origanum* comes from the Greek word for "bitter herb." But you'll be bitterly disappointed if you plant the wrong oregano.

Oregano, which contains vitamin A and niacin, is associated with the cuisines of many hot, sunny countries — Mexico and those of Central America, Italy, Greece, and Spain. Most famous in tomato sauces, it's often a star at breakfast, in egg dishes, and homemade bread; and it marries splendidly with beans, zucchini, and potatoes.

Like other mints, oregano is reputed to help settle "wambling of the stomacke," as Nicholas Culpeper put it in 1653. Medicinal plant expert Jim Duke includes it among herbs that may stop bacteria that cause body odor, although you may want to use a commercial product before your big job interview.

Description

Greek oregano is a perennial, 2 feet high with round leaves less than an inch long and unexciting whorls of tiny white flowers. Botanists say it can be distinguished from the wild oregano by tiny oil glands or hairs on the leaves, calyxes, and stems. The flowers of wild oregano are usually pink. But out of flower, the most telling characteristic of Greek oregano is the aroma, which herb expert Art Tucker unfortunately compares with creosote. Yum!

How to grow

Always obtain oregano as a plant so you can determine for yourself if it has a pungent odor. Then, just give the plants full sun in average, well-drained soil, spacing them about a foot apart, preferably among other perennial herbs. If volunteer seedlings pop up, pitch them on the compost unless you decide they're as flavorful as the parent. Division is the best way to get new plants, which are hardy through Zone 5.

Cultivars and related plants

Some oreganos (including wild oregano) are worth growing primarily as ornamentals. The purple-pink flowers of *Origanum laevigatum,* which is not quite as hardy as Greek oregano, attract butterflies and are pretty in arrangements, fresh and dried. Its cultivar, 'Herrenhausen', has reddish purple leaves that become even more colorful in fall.

O. vulgare has several mild-flavored variegated cultivars, such as 'Aureum Crispum' and 'Polyphant', which droop handsomely from a hanging basket or window box. *O. vulgare* 'Compactum' is a dwarf, ideal for containers or the rock garden. It has dark green leaves, pink-violet flowers. All of these are hardy through Zone 7.

Dittany of Crete *(O. dictamnus)* is sometimes called hop marjoram because the dangling flowers — soft green liberally painted with pink — look like *hop strobiles.* You may find the leaves too strong-flavored for foods, but try the flowers in tea. It's hardy only through Zone 8.

Cuban oregano *(Plectranthus amboinicus)* has rotund, scalloped, fuzzy leaves. 'Well-Sweep Wedgewood' has white-edged foliage. Neither plant tolerates freezing but each makes an eye-catching houseplant, and you can batter and fry the leaves. See the entry on lemon verbena in this chapter to read about Mexican oregano *(Lippia graveolens),* a tender plant with an oregano flavor.

Parsley (Petroselinum crispum)

Believe it or not, this healthful little herb was once associated with death. The Greeks dedicated it to Persephone, goddess of the underworld, and wove it into funeral wreaths. Morbid superstitions clung to it well into the Middle Ages, when Europeans were careful to plant it only on Good Friday.

On the other hand, John Gerard said that parsley seeds or roots, boiled in ale, would "cast foorth strong venome or poyson." Early in this century, it was a popular means of inducing abortion. Its most well-documented medicinal use as been as a diuretic, and as a remedy for urinary problems.

The Romans munched this member of the carrot family after a feast to sweeten their breath — or perhaps mask exhalations of wine. Remember that the next time you eye the parsley sprig that decorates your dinner entrée.

Parsley — packed with vitamins A and C, plus calcium, iron, and magnesium — deserves better treatment than a neglected garnish. It's one of the key ingredients in Middle Eastern tabouleh and makes an incredible pesto mixed with lemon and walnuts. And of course, parsley is one of the triumvirate (along with thyme and bay leaf) in a bouquet garni. As a diuretic, it might help with menstrual or post-dinner bloating. But pregnant women should avoid more than a nibble now and then because it can stimulate uterine contractions.

Description

Parsley is a biennial usually grown as an annual, about a foot tall and wide, with deep green, divided leaves. The names of the two most common types speak for themselves. The leaves of the more flavorful flat, or Italian, parsley *(Petroselinum crispum* var. *neopolitanum)* look like they could have just come off the ironing board; those of curly parsley *(P. crispum* var. *crispum)* form crinkled little bunches. If you leave the plant in your garden for a second season, it will put up umbrellas of tiny yellow-green flowers.

How to grow

If you have a slightly shady garden, parsley is one of the herbs that will be content. It likes cool weather, and in the South needs a sunscreen; in the North, it prefers full sun. Parsley seeds are so slow to germinate, legend says they go to the devil and back seven times before sprouting. To speed germination, soak the seeds overnight before sowing. You can start seeds indoors in individual peat pots (so you don't disturb the root when you transplant), but most people find it easier to plant seeds directly in the garden in early spring (or in autumn, in mild climates).

Space parsley plants about 8 inches apart in organically rich, slightly acid soil. Parsley is a favorite of swallowtail caterpillars; remove the caterpillars to a faraway plant if you can't bear to sacrifice a few sprigs of this herb. You can start harvesting leaves once the plant is about 8 inches tall. Cut off the outside leaves to stimulate new growth.

Parsley leaves left over-wintered can be bitter, but if you live in Zones 5 or warmer, your plants will survive and provide a second-season crop.

Cultivars and related plants

You can buy cultivars of either form of parsley, some of which have been bred for bigger leaves ('Catalogno'), sweeter flavor ('Sweet Italian'), stronger flavor ('Italian Dark Green'), or heat resistance ('Sherwood'). 'Forest Green' is curled cultivar with stiff stems, a favorite with market gardeners.

Pennyroyal (Mentha pulegium, Hedeoma pulegioides)

Since at least the first century A.D., European pennyroyal *(Mentha pulegium)* has had two claims to fame: repelling insects and inducing abortions. Pliny thought it was a good flea repellent (for dogs and for homes, as a strewing herb), and in honor of this reputation, it earned its species name from *pulex,* the Latin word for flea. One ancient text, however, claims that drowning insects could be revived in ashes of pennyroyal. (Perhaps useful if you had a flea circus.)

Mentha pulegium

And as early as the fourth century B.C., the playwright Aristophanes was making puns in his works that alluded to the plant's birth-control/abortive abilities. Sadly, more than a few desperate women have died ingesting powerful pennyroyal essential oil.

Native Americans used the American species of pennyroyal *(H. pulegioides)* to cure headaches, chills, and upset stomachs. After the Civil War, it was used to induce sweats in fever victims and to promote menstruation.

Pennyroyal is used in some commercial product insect repellants. Try braiding some around your pet's neck or hanging a bag from his collar. Stuff some in Snowball's and Rover's beds — if nothing else, the beds will smell great. You can make an insect repellent for yourself by spritzing on an infusion, or making a lotion (See Chapter 13). If you have trouble with ants in your garden, try growing a plant near their hill.

While the herb and homemade pennyroyal products are safe for most people in small amounts, you should not use them if you're pregnant. No essential oil should ever be taken internally, but ingesting even tiny amounts of pennyroyal oil can cause convulsions, coma, or death.

Description

"It creepeth much upon the ground," with stems up to 2 feet long, and in midsummer produces tiny lavender flowers in small whorls, 6 inches or more above the leaves. European pennyroyal is a perennial with half-inch leaves, while the American species is an annual, less sprawling with leaves up to twice as big.

How to grow

Pennyroyal needs rich, moisture-retentive, well-worked soil in either sun or shade. Start the European perennial from cuttings or divisions. Although hardy through Zone 5, it needs winter mulch north of Zone 7. Plants spread by underground runners. Since it is no beauty (old nicknames include lurk-in-the-ditch), confine it where it can hang over the edge of a raised bed or container, or tuck it between rocks.

Launch the American species from seed; germination is iffy everywhere, so sow generously and then thin plants to 6 inches apart.

Cultivars and related plants

Australian, or Brisbane, pennyroyal *(Mentha satureioides)* is a Down Under relation, a perennial species that has a pungent aroma and is used to improve digestion. Like other pennyroyals, pregnant women should not use it.

Rose (Rosa spp.)

Seeds from the dog rose *(Rosa canina)* were found inside a 2,000-year-old skeleton in England. That suggests that he/she knew what we know: That the hips (or fruits) of this many rose species are especially high in vitamin C. During World War II, Englishmen (and women) used rose hips to help prevent scurvy when the Germans cut off their citrus supply.

Rosa

Hippocrates recommended rose petal oil for problems with the uterus. India's Ayurvedic physicians took advantage of the rose's astringent properties to soothe wounds and inflammations. In the Middle Ages and Renaissance, attar of roses was a cure for depression; today that expensive essential oil is one of aromatherapy's favorite mood lifters. Use rose water in the bathtub, to splash on your face, or mix with any other cosmetics. Like witch hazel, rose water can be soothing to irritated eyes.

You can eat rose hips fresh, but Texas rose expert Liz Druitt warns that some people are allergic to the *achenes* (the hairy seeds inside the hips). Too many achenes can also cause diarrhea. It's better to use the cleaned hips to make tea, syrup, or topping for fruits and yogurt (Druitt suggests flavoring the sauce with orange liqueur, or spices such as ginger and cinnamon). You can make rose hip jelly or use the petals in salads and vinegars.

Description

If you want roses for hips or fragrant petals, look to old species roses and their cultivars. Herbalists are most likely to grow the following:

- ✔ **The apothecary's rose** *(R. gallica* var. *officinalis).* Grown in gardens for at least 400 years, this rose once was a popular tonic and purgative. This shrub rose grows 3 to 5 feet tall and wide, with rough, deep green leaves and dark pink, semi-double flowers in late spring or early summer. It has a nice, rounded shape but may sucker to form a thicket. Zone 4.

- ✔ **The dog rose** *(R. canina).* Native to Europe and cultivated from the early 1700s, this plant grows 8 to 12 feet tall and is smothered in late spring by single pale pink or white flowers, followed by shiny, dark orange hips— the ones you're likely to find in a health food store. Zone 4.

- ✔ **The eglantine rose** *(R. eglanteria).* This relative of the dog rose was cultivated about 200 years longer, and is notable not so much for the single, bright pink spring flowers, but for the foliage, which releases a fruity aroma with every rain. Growing at least 6 feet tall and wide, it has curved prickles that make pruning an uninviting prospect. Zone 4.

- ✔ **Rugosa roses** *(R. rugosa).* Rugosas rebloom throughout the growing season, with a scent redolent of cloves. Each flush gives you more of the dark orange-red hips that earned the species the nickname "tomato rose." The leaves are wrinkled (rugose) and disease-resistant. The rugosas are famous as seaside plants because they tolerate wind and salt. The thorns are small but numerous. Another common name is "hedgehog rose." There are scores of named rugosas, some hardy through Zone 2.

How to grow

Although you can root roses from cuttings in roughly two months in spring or fall, or in about four months from layering during the growing season, most gardeners begin by buying a potted or bare-root plant.

Roses are greedy feeders that need excellent drainage, so don't stint on the soil amendments. In spite of roses' reputation as sun lovers, all of these roses — and especially the dog and eglantine roses — tolerate some shade, particularly during hot afternoons in warm regions. Give them a monthly top-dressing with compost, regular mulching to keep the roots cool, and generous watering during droughts.

Black spot is the most common disease of roses, especially in humid areas. Alliums of all types — garlic, onions, chives, as well as the purely ornamental species — are a traditional companion plant, apparently because they ooze sulfur into the soil. A spray of compost tea or soda spray (see Chapter 10) is another good preventive.

For more information on growing roses, take a look at *Roses For Dummies,* by Lance Walheim and the Editors of the National Gardening Association (IDG Books). Southern gardeners should see *The Organic Rose Garden* by Liz Druitt. Cold-weather gardeners can learn a lot from Robert Osborne's *Hardy Roses.* A good general reference on roses is *Easy Roses for North American Gardens* by Tom Christopher.

Cultivars and related plants

For fragrant petals, try one of the roses long cultivated commercially for perfume: the damask rose *(Rosa damascena),* to 6 feet tall with semi-double, pale pink to white flowers in summer (Zone 4); or the cabbage rose *(R. × centifolia),* to 5 feet tall with fully double, rose-red flowers in summer (Zone 6). For recurrent blooms to produce hips, consider 'Dortmund', a graceful shrub usually trained as a climber, with single, frilly, bright red blossoms; or 'Old Blush', to 5 feet with semi-double, baby pink flowers (Zone 4).

Rosemary (Rosmarinus officinalis)

Even if you know nothing else about the "language of flowers," you've probably heard that "rosemary is for remembrance." This adage includes all types of remembrance, from being faithful in love, loyal in friendship, and honoring the dearly departed to helping meats and wine "remember" their flavor and encouraging our stomachs to remember their appetites and our brains to remember what day it is. Rosemary contains antioxidants that appear to put the brakes on free-radical molecules, which cause Alzheimer's disease and wreak other havoc on aging bodies.

Whether inspired by rosemary's evergreen nature or its long-lasting smell, the herb's link with memory began with Greek students who wore garlands of it in hopes of acing their finals. The herb has been woven into bridal wreaths, burned as incense (both in religious ceremonies and with juniper, to purify the air of sickrooms), and considered "very medicinable for the head" and for "weyknesse of ye brayne." The herb's ashes were used as a toothpowder.

About the only people who haven't loved rosemary were men of the 16th century, who thought (where *do* these ideas get started?) that the herb prospered only in homes where women called the shots. We assume many a fine rosemary specimen bit the dust as a result.

Rosemary's flavor is not a light one. We combine it with substantial winter foods: delectable roasts (especially lamb), squashes, beans, rich stews, heavy soups, creamy sauces, homemade bread. Because the leaves are like tiny spears, chop or crush them before you add them to foods.

In summer, pick a whole branch of rosemary and lay it on your barbecue coals and/or on top of your food, so the flavored smoke permeates it. (You can try this with any herb, but rosemary's tough leaves stand up to it well, and you won't have to worry about the effect being too subtle.)

Description

Rosemary is a tender evergreen shrub from the western Mediterranean, known for its signature aroma (and flavor) that combines pine, mint, and ginger. The needlelike leaves are a shiny bluish-green on top and downy white or gray underneath. From late spring to mid-summer, it compounds its charms by producing little two-lipped flowers, usually ranging from soft lilac to bright blue. A typical plant holds its branches upright and can grow up to 6 feet in warm climates, less than half that where it lives indoors all or part of the year.

How to grow

Rosemary is slow and difficult to start from seed, so buy a plant. (For a named cultivar, you must begin with a plant, or at least a sprig of a plant). More challenges await you. Rosemary's name means "dew of the sea." Native to scrubby hills near the Mediterranean, this herb needs warmth, good drainage, and humidity, a combination rarely found in gardens.

In Zone 8 and warmer, where you can grow rosemary in the ground, give your plant near-neutral soil, only slightly enriched but with excellent drainage. Wet feet mean sure death, but never let plants dry out completely. Rich soil makes its branches flabby and prey to insects and disease. Site it in full sun, or allow it a bit of afternoon shade if your region is extremely hot.

Rosemary has a long root. It doesn't like to be moved and needs a deep container — established plants need a pot at least a foot deep and wide. Use light potting soil that drains well, and feed your plant monthly (spring through midsummer) with compost tea.

Indoors, rosemary will feel abused in dry, overheated air. Give it a sunny window where the air is cool and circulation is good. Keep the soil damp enough that the foliage doesn't wilt, and mist the plant once or twice a week with room-temperature water. Prune off any limp new growth. In spring, harden it off again, just like a seedling, before it goes outdoors.

If you've made it this far, congratulate yourself. Make more rosemary by taking cuttings when new growth has firmed up, or by layering.

Cultivars and related plants

You can choose rosemary cultivars with golden foliage ('Miss Jessup'), variegated foliage ('Aureus'), a stronger pine scent ('Pine'), trailing forms suited to hanging baskets ('Lockwood de Forest', 'Huntington Carpet', 'Benenden

Blue'), and knock-out pink flowers ('Marjorca Pink', 'Roseus', and 'Pinkie'). 'Arp' has grayish foliage and ice-blue to white flowers but is a hit because of its hardiness, possibly into Zone 6 with protection. 'Tuscan Blue' is upright with bright violet-blue flowers; 'Foto Blue' is semiprostrate with dark blue blooms; and 'Primley Blue' and 'Sudbury Blue' are upright cultivars with clear blue flowers.

Rue (Ruta graveolens)

Rue may set you free — if you don't rue the day you planted it. The genus and common names came from the Greek word "reuo," meaning "to set free." It may refer to rue's reputed abilities for healing, or more likely, for breaking the spell of witches. Hearing that it would prevent eyestrain, painters and sculptors of ancient Rome ate vast amounts.

Ruta graveolens

Used to sprinkle holy water, rue became the "herb of grace," symbolizing repentance. Judges brought sprigs of it into courtrooms to ward off "gaol fever" (jail fever) carried by prisoners; and during the plague, thieves who stole from corpses included "vinegar of the four thieves" in a brew devised to prevent contagion.

Today, the word on ingesting rue is: *Don't.* It can cause powerful cramps, hallucinations, and twitching. More commonly, ingestion and even external contact can cause phototoxicity — ultrasensitivity to the sun — leading to severe burns and blisters.

Description

Rue, a member of the citrus family, is an evergreen perennial native to the Balkans and southeast Europe, somewhat woody near the bottom and growing up to 3 feet tall and wide. The divided leaves are both fernlike and slightly succulent; each powdery-coated leaflet has a spoon or club shape.

From late spring until fall, rue bears clusters of bright yellow, five-petaled, half-inch-diameter flowers with a dimpled green center, followed by an ornamental five-lobed seed capsule. Poor rue has been described as emitting "a powerful, disagreeable odour." We would more charitably describe the smell as "interesting."

How to grow

There's a myth that this perennial will thrive if you steal it from a neighbor. We don't recommend that, but if you do commit a little botanical larceny, be sure to wear gloves. Some people react to the herb's touch as they would to poison ivy.

Better than inviting a criminal record, start rue seeds indoors in late winter. Transplant seedlings to a sunny spot with average, well-drained, neutral to slightly alkaline soil, spacing them about 18 inches apart. You can propagate more rue from cuttings or division. Rue is hardy through Zone 4.

Rue was once a staple of knot gardens. Plant it as an edging, or as contrast to greener (or yellower) or bolder-leafed herbs and ornamentals. The long-lasting flowers are stunning with blues and purples, such as those of salvias.

Cultivars and related plants

Despite rue's limited uses, breeders have liked it enough to select strains with even bluer foliage ('Jackman Blue', 'Blue Curl') and variegated foliage ('Harlequin', 'Variegata'). Another species, fringed rue *(Ruta chalapensis)* has larger flowers and tear-dropped shaped leaves; it is hardy through Zone 8

At least two plants have similar common names. Goat's rue *(Galega officinalis),* a member of the pea family has bright green, lance-shaped leaves and purple flowers. It was once fed to cows to increase milk and used to make cheese. Syrian rue *(Peganum harmala),* a perennial hardy through Zone 8, is the source of a red dye used in Persian rugs.

Saffron (Crocus sativus)

Dreaming of raising enough of this expensive flavoring to make tons of paella? Better knock down your house and a couple of neighbors' so you'll have enough room. The "threads" of saffron are the stigmas from the heart of this fall-blooming crocus. Each flower has only three, so it takes some 60,000 blossoms (and a lot of hand-picking) to make a pound of this golden spice.

The Greeks, Chinese, and Egyptians have used saffron as a dye since ancient times. The Romans were wild about its perfume, sprinkling saffron water on theater benches, flinging the leaves about their banquet halls and cramming them into pillows.

*Crocus
sativus*

Culpeper recommended saffron for strengthening the heart and for menstrual depression, but warned that a large dose could lead to drowsiness or, even more alarming, "convulsive laughter, which ended in death." In the 19th and 20th centuries, it was sometimes mixed with brandy to treat measles. Modern studies link its active ingredient, crocetin, to reduced risks of cardiovascular disease. But for most of us, it would be a lot cheaper to invest in a top-of-the-line treadmill.

Description

Most of us know crocus as a harbinger of spring, so we can be a bit disoriented the first time we see one blooming in fall. The saffron crocus, a native primarily of the Mediterranean region, blooms in September and has 2-inch, rich lilac-colored flowers with darker veins and throats. The long bright orange-red stigma may poke out of the blooms when they close at night.

How to grow

Give your crocuses light, gritty soil of average fertility. They prefer full sun, but will bloom with five hours of sun daily. Crocuses grow from *corms* (a modified bulb), and should be planted in spring or early summer. If you can't buy corms until fall, get them into the ground posthaste: They're putting out shoots and are ready to roll. Set the corms 3 to 4 inches deep and 6 inches apart. You can give them a nutritional boost with a little rock phosphate, but put a layer of soil between corm and fertilizer so your corm won't burn. Plants do best in Zones 5 to 8, disliking both cold, wet climates and hot, humid ones.

Plant crocuses where you can gaze down on them, along a path or toward the front of a bed, in your herb garden among creeping thymes, or in the crevices of a rock garden. They're also wonderful in a lawn where grass grows sparsely, such as under the drip line of a tree.

If you collect the stigmas to make bouillabaisse or risotto Milanese, handle them gingerly, dry with utmost care, and keep them in a stoppered glass vial in a cool place.

Cultivars and related plants

You may see plants advertised as autumn crocuses (or meadow saffron) that are really the bulb of another genus, *Colchicum*. These have bigger flowers and are never bothered by pests because they're poisonous — you definitely don't want to munch any part of them. The toxic alkaloid they contain, called colchicine, was once used to treat rheumatism and gout. Modern plant breeders have harnessed colchicine to manipulate the chromosome count of plants, producing triploid flowers with thicker, damage-resistant petals.

Two other herbs are often stand-ins for saffron: calendula, which we describe earlier in this chapter, and safflower *(Carthamus tinctorius)*. Safflower, an annual with yellow-orange thistlelike flowers, has been used so often to adulterate saffron that it's also called bastard saffron. Its flowers give food a more reddish tinge than true saffron.

Sage *(Salvia officinalis)*

We're not old sages, but take our advice: 'Tis a wise and well-seasoned gardener who plants this herb, although not necessarily an immortal one. The genus name *Salvia* comes from the same Latin word as "salvation," and while the Romans and Greeks thought it enhanced memory (like rosemary), it was the Arabs who concluded that it could bestow immortality. This led to aphorisms like "Why should a man die who grows sage in his garden?" As far as we know, there is not a single surviving male or female from that period.

Herbalist John Gerard said sage was good for senses, memory, and sinews, especially "shakey trembling of the members." Later, the French thought it would assuage grief, and in some places sowed graves with its seeds. In 19th-century America, herbalists touted sage tea for squelching sexual desire and hence, venereal disease.

In truth, sage might enhance your sex appeal, but as an antiperspirant. You can try applying an infusion externally or drinking some sage tea (if you can wait, since it's not effective for two hours). Because sage contains both astringents and antiseptics, it's often recommended for oral hygiene (just rub a fresh leaf over tooth and gum), as a mouthwash to prevent gum disease and bad breath, or as a gargle for sore throats.

As for aromatic appeal, the smell of Mom's sage-and-crouton mix says "Thanksgiving" as strongly as balsam and pine needles speak of Christmas. This herb dances with poultry like Rogers with Astaire. Rub it on duck, goose, or turkey before roasting for a light touch, or mix it in a marinade. Toss it on a grill with Cornish game hens. Not too proud to change partners, sage also does wonders for pork and meatloaf. Pair it with any cheesy dish — quiche, toasted sandwiches, macaroni — and snip it into hearty stews, bread dough, or corn muffins.

Description

Sage is a hardy subshrub (woody at the bottom, with softer new growth above) native to the north Mediterranean. Where happy, it will grow 3 feet tall and wide. The elongated oval leaves grow up to 3 inches long, pebbly in appearance and sandpapery to the touch; their hue is grayer in dry climates, greener in humid ones. Sage's late spring racemes of blue-violet flowers would be reward enough for growing this herb.

How to grow

You can start the species from seeds if you're willing to wait several years for your first harvest, but we recommend buying a plant or two.

Give sage full sun and organically rich, slightly acid, well-draining soil. Prune plants regularly to keep them from becoming leggy (you can use stem cuttings to produce new plants). In winter, poor drainage is invariably fatal (with protection, common sage should survive winter as far north as Zone 5). Sages that are 3 or 4 years old are less vigorous, but even one old stalwart plant usually provides more than enough of this strong-flavored herb for a family.

Because of its high oil content, sage can be tricky to preserve. Make sure it's completely dry before you store your harvest.

Cultivars and related plants

If you tire of gray-green leaves you can buy sage cultivars with foliage that is golden, purple, or the popular 'Tricolor' combining green, white, and pinkish purple and said to withstand humidity and heat better than its parent. There are also sages with bigger leaves, shorter stature, and white flowers.

Of some 900 *Salvia* species, at least 899 of them are worth growing, especially if you live in a hot, dry climate and love their range of purple, magenta, and red flowers. Unfortunately, far too many of them are hardy only through Zone 8, at best.

Here are some of the sages with culinary or medicinal uses, or pungent leaves worth growing for the same reason you might grow scented geraniums:

- **Greek sage** *(S. fruticosa)*. Although inferior to common sage, Greek sage is often used in commercial spice products. More upright (to 4 feet) and less spreading, it often has compound, lobed leaves, and blooms earlier and heavier with pink to mauve flowers. Zone 8.

- **Jim, or blue, sage** *(S. clevelandii)*. This California native stays under 2 feet tall with white, blue, or lilac flowers. It has toothed, wrinkled leaves that you can use like common sage. Zone 8.

✔ **Lyreleaf sage** *(S. lyrata)*. Lyreleaf is native to woods in the northern and central United States, and earned the nickname "cancer weed" because of its traditional use as a cancer cure. Two feet tall with violet flowers, its most attractive feature is the dandelion-shaped leaves with maroon markings, sometimes turning solid maroon in dry conditions. Zone 5.

✔ **Painted sage** *(S. viridis)*. One of the few annual (sometimes biennial) salvias, painted sage is native to Europe, Africa, and western Asia. Sometimes confusingly called annual clary, it is grown for lovely purple or pink bracts that are striking in arrangements, both fresh and dry.

✔ **Peruvian sage** *(S. discolor)*. This plant is hardy only through Zone 9 but has great charm in a hanging basket, with woolly white stems and leaves setting off indigo blue flowers.

✔ **Pineapple sage** *(S. elegans)*. The pineapple sage is soft-stemmed with red flowers; its leaves add tropical fruit to the usual sage scent. It can reach 6 feet in Zone 8 and south. 'Scarlet Pineapple' has especially fine blossoms.

✔ **Spanish sage** *(S. lavandulifolia)*. This is similar to common sage except in one regard: Spanish sage has leaves that are smaller and clustered at the bottom of the plant, so the flowers appear on bare stems. Its flavor is described as stronger than that of common sage; in Spain, it's a diabetes treatment. Hardy through Zone 7.

On a final note: Sagebrush is not a sage; it is more closely related to the artemisias, like southernwood and wormwood, and not a bit tasty. Also unrelated is Russian sage *(Perovskia atriplicifolia),* a popular perennial with late-blooming purple flowers. The leaves are fragrant enough to try in potpourri, however.

Santolina *(Santolina chamaecyparissus)*

Santolina, or lavender cotton, has such a knock-out camphor aroma that you wouldn't be tempted to eat it, but would guess it had medicinal uses out the wazoo. But the ancient herbals are strangely silent about this herb, except to note its brief fling with treating bites, dispelling worms, treating skin problems, or discouraging moths. (Try a sprig of santolina or a bag of clippings in your drawers and closets.)

Blame the Elizabethans for dandifying santolina. Noting the pleasing shape of its foliage and its amenity to pruning — "for it will abide to be cut in what forme you think best" — they used it by the cartload to tie up their knot gardens.

Description

A small, evergreen shrub from the Mediterranean, santolina's species name means "dwarf cypress," and the arrangement of its thick, slender leaves might very well remind you of the neighbor's Leyland cypress hedge. Equally descriptive is the common name lavender cotton, the first part of the name capturing its aroma (more medicinal than most lavenders, however) and the second, its soft, silvery white leaves. Plants can grow to 2 feet tall and up to twice as wide. Although many gardeners whack them off, it is crowned with little yellow button flowers from early to mid-summer.

Santolina chamaecy- parissus

How to grow

Santolina germinates somewhat unevenly, so sow more seeds than you think you'll need when the temperature warms to about 40°F, and give them up to a month to sprout. Starting with plants is easier, especially in a knot garden, since they spread slowly.

This herb prefers slightly alkaline soil, but drainage is the crucial factor, since santolina abhors dampness in the soil or the air. Prune in early spring and again after flowering so that plants, which are hardy through Zone 6, maintain their shape and don't become too woody.

Even if you don't have a knot garden, you'll find santolina the perfect edging plant, ideal for creating a low hedge or defining a path. The delicate gray leaves contrast becomingly with almost anything else you might grow

Cultivars and related plants

'Lemon Queen' is a dwarf cultivar with lemon-colored flowers, while 'Pretty Carol', another dwarf, has silver foliage and bright yellow blooms. *Santolina chamaecyparissus* var. *nana* is extremely small, only 6 inches tall.

Rosemary santolina *(S. rosmarinifolia),* looks a lot like rosemary and smells a little like santolina. Its cultivar, 'Primrose Gem', has pale yellow flowers. Hardy through Zone 6.

Savory, summer and winter (Satureja hortensis; S. montana)

With a name like savory, it's got to be good (our apologies to the jelly people). But savory means tasty and well-seasoned, and for a long time this herb was the "big gun" for European cooks. (People from ancient cultures seemed to try herbs for every ache and ailment under the sun before they considered throwing them into the stewpot. But when you have an average life expectancy of 25 as they did, it stands to reason that _haute cuisine_ might take a back seat.)

Satureja hortensis

Because of savory's fragrance, it was widely planted near beehives to flavor honey. (The Romans, who weren't entirely without taste buds, took the opposite tack, and used savory as a flavoring for vinegar.) In 17th-century England, winter savory _(S. Montana)_ was dried and crumbled for breading meat and fish — still a fine idea. Both species were among the first herbs brought to America by the early settlers.

The genus name comes from "satyr," the goatlike woodland deity whose name is synonymous with men who are, well, a bit goatish. But while summer savory was supposed to increase sexual appetite, winter savory was more like a cold shower. Culpeper thought it could even cure deafness, but Dioscorides and Galen were probably more on target when they said it was "heating and drying."

Traditionally used for colds and other respiratory problems, winter savory does have some mild antibacterial and carminative, or gas-squelching, properties, as do many of the culinary herbal superstars. That works out well, since this herb, which combines the tastes of mint and thyme, has a particular affinity for beans of all types — dried beans such as lentils and favas, bean soups, bean salads, and peas.

Description

Both of these mint-family members have needlelike leaves up to 1 inch long, erect stems, and whorls of blossoms summer through fall.

Summer savory, *S. hortensis,* has the more delicate aroma and flavor of the two herbs. It is a rather slumping annual, growing to 18 inches, and has abundant but tiny pale pink flowers that hunker down in the leaf axils. The gray green, downy leaves often turn purple in fall.

Winter savory, *S. montana,* is a semi-evergreen perennial or subshrub, growing only about a foot tall. The white to pale purple flowers, which often have purple spots on their lower lips, bloom on spikes. The leaves are dark green and glossy, and have a more peppery flavor than the annual species.

How to grow

You can start either type of savory from fresh seeds, sown indoors or out. Like most perennials, winter savory is slow to get moving, so we recommend you opt to buy plants. Space either species about a foot apart in well-drained, neutral to slightly acid soil of average fertility. Summer savory wilts quickly in droughts, so be sure its soil is rich in moisture-retaining organic matter.

Summer savory bolts quickly — flowers and sets seeds prematurely — in hot weather. Plant it where you can harvest it regularly while it lasts.

Prune winter savory often to keep it producing tender new foliage. (Winter savory prunes so well it's often used as a formal edging or in knot gardens. It can be short-lived (although hardy through Zone 4), so take cuttings or make divisions during its second or third year so you won't be without plants.

Cultivars and related plants

Look for creeping savory *(S. spicigera),* a prostrate subshrub still sold under the name *S. reptans,* if you have a rock garden or need an herbal ground cover. Creeping savory has white flowers and is hardy through Zone 7.

Once classified in the savory genus are the calamints *(Calamintha* spp.), which are more minty in flavor. Lesser calamint *(C. nepeta)* is an erect perennial that grows 18 inches tall and has toothed green leaves and masses of quarter-inch mauve to pink flowers. Showy calamint *(C. grandiflora)* can reach 2 feet when it produces its 6-inch flower spikes. It has bigger leaves, to 2 inches long, and the hot pink flowers are more than an inch across. Even more of a knockout is 'Variegata', with pale green and white leaves and magenta flowers that never seem to quit. All are hardy through Zone 5.

Sorrel (Rumex spp.)

There are some 200 species in this genus, many of which are called either sorrel or dock — or in one confusing instance, sorrel dock. Oxalic acid gives all of them a slightly sour taste, but the two species most commonly used for cooking are garden sorrel *(Rumex acetosa)* and French sorrel *(R. scutatus)*.

Rumex

In 1720, John Evelyn wrote that "Sorrel sharpens the appetite, assuages heat, cools the liver and strengthens the heart . . . and in the making of sallets imparts a grateful quickness to the rest as supplying the want of oranges and lemons." The nutrition and taste made not only salads, "but men themselves pleasant and agreeable." We suspect that you, too, know someone who could benefit from sorrel.

Sorrel also was used for venereal disease (usually described more circumspectly as "purifying the blood") and for skin ailments, particularly nettle stings. Popular as a laxative, it contains tannins that also prevent diarrhea; because it is rich in vitamin C, sorrel was often used to prevent and treat scurvy. Both species have been called cuckoo's meate and cuckoo's bread, because it was thought that birds ate them in order to have a clearer song. Birds do like to eat sorrel seeds.

The French started the custom of sorrel soup, then added the herb to ragout and other stews. It's also popular in fish sauces and pâté. You can cook the leaves like spinach, or use them fresh in salads. Not only are they high in vitamin C, they contain vitamin A, calcium, phosphate, potassium, and magnesium.

Description

Sorrel forms clumps of lance-shaped, wavy edged leaves that look a bit like spinach. The mid-to-late-summer flowers are whorled densely around spikes and are star-shaped, first greenish and then flushed with purple or rust, followed by dark brown achenes, or fruits. The reddish brown taproot, up to a foot long, is yellow inside. Garden, or common, sorrel has stems up to 3 feet tall from clumps of 5- to 8-inch leaves, whereas French sorrel tends to form mats, 6 to 20 inches tall and twice as wide, with thick, broad leaves only 1 to 2 inches long.

How to grow

Sorrels are easy to start from seed, indoors or out. Space plants 8 inches apart in the garden in deeply dug soil (to accommodate the plants' long taproots) that is rich in organic matter. Sorrels tolerate partial shade but not drought; most plants are not long-lived but are root hardy through Zone 4.

Pinch off flower heads to keep new foliage coming and to prevent self-sowing. (Not only do plants seed generously, their deep taproots can be difficult to dislodge if you decide to say "so long" to sorrel.) Try it in a deep container. We like it as the "top-knot" of a strawberry jar.

Cultivars and related plants

Two garden cultivars of French sorrel, 'Blonde de Lyon' and 'Nobel', have especially succulent leaves and are perfect for salads. A new selection, 'Profusion', is considered seedless, which will keep you from growing sorrel where you don't want it; 'Silver Shield' has gray-green foliage.

Curled, or yellow, dock *(Rumex crispus)* is a giant, as tall as 5 feet tall with wavy, foot-long leaves. While edible, its historic use is for making salves to treat skin problems.

Sheep sorrel *(R. acetosella)* also has tasty leaves and especially attractive seed pods. Naturalized in North American meadows, it has been used for fevers, inflammation, diarrhea, and by Native Americans as a cancer treatment.

Southernwood (Artemisia abrotanum)

It may sound like the national herb of the Confederacy, but southernwood gets its common name from the fact that it's native to southern Europe, unlike its more northerly counterpart, wormwood *(Artemisia absinthium)*. Commonly known as old man — a tip of the hat to its gray foliage — southernwood was also called lad's love and boy's love. Young men put a sprig in a bouquet to symbolize fidelity to their sweetie, and the herb was said to be an aphrodisiac. (Oddly enough, the genus name *Artemisia* alludes to Artemis, the Greek goddess of chastity).

Young men also burned southernwood, mixed the ashes with oil, and rubbed the solution on their chins to stimulate beard growth. (Old men tried it on their pate.) Burning southernwood was a popular activity, since it was also thought to drive away snakes.

The French called the herb *garderobe* — which sounds like a Web address for horticultural duds — because it was a good moth repellent. Remember that bees don't like it either when choosing a spot for it in the garden. Like rue, southernwood was used to protect judges and other respectable people from prisoners' infectious diseases, and like costmary, it was poked in lapels and tussie-mussies to keep church-goers from nodding off.

The medicinal value of artemisias — even for their longtime use against parasites — is hotly debated. Southernwood does have antiseptic properties, so consider mixing it with oatmeal for a facial mask. Most species dry well for potpourri and crafts; semi-woody types like southernwood make good bases for wreaths.

Description

Members of the aster clan, most artemisias have insignificant flowers and are grown for their aromatic, delicate, divided foliage. Southernwood is a woody perennial that grow to 3 to 4 feet and about as wide, with finely divided gray-green leaves up to 2 inches long. You can barely discern individual leaves for all their threadlike lobes, which are gray underneath and somewhat hairy, especially on new growth. The almost invisible late summer flowers are dingy yellow on panicles 4 to 12 inches long.

How to grow

Start southernwood from a plant or a cutting — semihard stems root easily — spacing plants at least 2 feet apart. As long as they have good drainage, artemisias adapt well to any soil. They don't like wet winters or humid summers, but tolerate light shade and drought. Prune southernwood — hardy through Zone 5 with winter protection — in spring to keep it from looking weedy.

Cultivars and related plants

You can read more about other members of this genus just ahead, under the entries for tarragon and wormwood. But wait! There are still more artemisias.

- **Mugwort** (*Artemisia vulgaris*). This artemisia was used in both medicine and food — and was a beer flavoring before hops came along. Said to repel evil and poisons, it was planted along the roads of Rome for weary soldiers to stick in their shoes. The plant is not attractive, however, and tends to be invasive.

- **Seashore artemisia** (*A. stelleriana*). If you need seaside plants, consider *A. stelleriana,* an evergreen East Coast native that forms silver clumps on sand dunes. Usually available as 'Silver Brocade' (a.k.a. 'Boughton Silver'), it grows up to 6 inches tall and is hardy through Zone 4.

✔ **Silvermound** *(A. schmidtiana 'Silver Mound')*. Silvermound forms a silky, sensuous hump. Cold hardy through Zone 4, it often "melts" and loses its form in the South. 'Silverado' is less shapely but holds up to heat. 'Powis Castle' is another clump former, with feathery leaves of silver gray, hardy through Zone 6.

✔ **Sweet Annie** *(Artemisia annua)*. This annual, a staple of dried bouquets and wreaths, can zoom up to 6 feet in a warm summer, and spread 3 feet wide. Mature plants look like a feathery little conifers with their fine, divided green leaves, wider at the bottom than at the top. In summer it's speckled with cluster of tiny yellow flowers. Its warm autumn fragrance will work wonders for any room (we know firsthand that it even over-powers the smell of wet dog fur and high school football uniforms).

✔ **White mugwort** *(A. lactiflora)*. Need a big bruiser for the back of the border? White mugwort *(A. lactiflora)* is your boy. It's named for its flow-ers; the lobed and compound leaves are green, forming a rosette that shoots up stems 4 to 6 feet tall, with 1- to 2-foot feathery panicles of flowers from late summer to fall. Hardy through Zone 5.

✔ **White sage** *(A. ludovicana)*. This plant has silver foliage but differs from other artemisias in that its 2-to-4-inch leaves form daisy-shaped whorls. Deciduous and soft-stemmed (rather than woody), it grows 2 to 4 feet tall; its gray flowers bloom in summer. Because of underground roots, popular cultivars 'Silver King' and 'Silver Queen' often pop up where not wanted. Zone 4.

Since we're sure you're wondering, the sagebrushes that perfumes the hills of our West and turns into the tumbling tumbleweed used to be artemisias, but have now been reclassified by those wacky botanists and are called *Seriphidium*.

Sweet Cicely (Myrrhis odorata)

Talk about an identity crisis. Here's an herb that tastes like licorice and looks like a fern, and found its way into kitchens as anise, great chervil, sweet chervil, cow chervil, sweet bracken, and sweet fern.

Although a roadside weed in England, sweet Cicely also found its way into gardens, as it was admired by garden guru Gertrude Jekyll. "For its beauty," she wrote, it "deserves to be in every garden; it is charming, with its finely cut, pale green leaves and really handsome flowers."

Maude Grieve's *A Modern Herbal* says that sweet Cicely roots were soaked in wine to treat consumption, and an ointment of sweet Cicely was applied to "cure green wounds, stinking ulcers and ease the pain of gout." The roots were said to increase the lust and strength of "old people that are dull and without courage" and served as "a valuable tonic for girls from 15 to 18 years of age." Having some experience in this matter, we find it hard to imagine that anyone ever needed to increase the lust of high-school-age maidens. . . .

Myrrhis odorata

The flavor of sweet Cicely is usually compared to lovage combined with anise. You can cook the root like other root vegetables, and eat the seeds out of hand. (Like anise, they help to freshen your breath.) Add the seeds and/or chopped leaves to fruit salad or stewed fruits or baked goods.

Description

This perennial from Europe looks for all the world like a big, bright green fern. It grows as tall as 4 feet, and its thick stems are hollow and slightly hairy, while the leaves are white and downy underneath. In late spring or early summer, clusters of white flowers appear, similar to flowers of Queen-Anne's lace. Like others in the carrot clan, sweet Cicely has a long taproot.

How to grow

Sweet Cicely thrives in woodland conditions. That means plants not only need some shade but deep, humus-rich, moisture-retentive soil like you might find in a forest. Even then, sweet Cicely is rarely happy in the Deep South, since it can't take the heat.

If you saved your own seeds, refrigerate them for two or three months before sowing or sow them in the fall. Space plants 3 feet apart. Don't let plants dry out, and remove flower heads to prevent self-sowing — sweet Cicely, which is hardy through Zone 3, is a great naturalizer.

Cultivars and related plants

Myrrhis odorata is the only species in its genus, but a genus of plants native to North American woods, *Osmorhiza* spp., is also called sweet Cicely. Like *M. odorata,* these herbs have aromatic, segmented leaves; their flower clusters are white or yellow-green. Native Americans used them to treat respiratory ailments, skin irritations, and indigestion. Their roots were so attractive to livestock that plants were used to lure horses and other animals into pens.

Sweet woodruff (Galium odoratum)

This delicate herb's claim to fame is as the flavoring agent in May wine. The Germans drink the concoction, called *Maibowle,* on May 1 to celebrate the coming of spring. The honey-and-vanilla-scented herb smoothes the rough edges of the immature grapes. The French name translates as musk of the woods, but most people say it smells less musky and more like new-mown hay. The aroma is barely detectable until the foliage dries.

Galium odoratum

Sweet woodruff's fragrance is produced by a chemical called coumarin, which is used in perfumery for its own sake as well as to "fix" other scents. Pharmacists of old used the herb to mask other, less pleasant smells. An ingredient in high-quality snuff, sweet woodruff was also stuffed in mattresses like its cousin, lady's bedstraw.

Once thought to be good for the kidneys and liver, sweet woodruff has been found to cause liver damage in laboratory animals, and large amounts can trigger dizziness and vomiting. You can employ it in a Maibowle, however, by steeping a couple sprigs in white wine for a day or two. (Most people use an inexpensive Rhine wine; it won't improve your best Pouilly-Fuisse one whit.)

Description

If you think of a ruff as a collar (like those big, starched things the Elizabethans wore), you'll remember that this perennial holds its lance-shaped leaves in whorls 1 to 2 inches across, marching up its stem. Creeping along the ground on horizontal stems, sweet woodruff rarely reaches more than 8 or 9 inches tall. From late spring to midsummer it produces clouds of fragrant, white star-shaped flowers.

How to grow

Even nursery professionals have trouble getting sweet woodruff seeds to germinate. If you don't have a friend who will share a few plants with you, we recommend you purchase plants to get started with this herb.

This woodland native wants a bit of shade and humus-rich soil that doesn't dry out. Sweet woodruff spreads on its own, a tough groundcover, hardy through Zone 3. To increase your stand more quickly, divide plants in spring (make sure each division has a piece of the crown with some root attached) or propagate from stem cuttings.

Cultivars and related plants

Lady's bedstraw is a sun-loving cousin to sweet woodruff; goosegrass *(Galium aparine)* is an annual member of the family. Also known as cleavers and sticky Willie, this herb grows to 4 feet has been used in a variety of folk medicines for treating everything from glandular fever and hepatitis to skin inflammations and psoriasis.

Tansy (Tanacetum vulgare)

The name of this herb comes from a Greek word *athanaton,* meaning "without death" or "immortal." Not only do the cut flowers last almost forever, but tansy was said to be "capital for preserving dead bodies from corruption." Laid in coffins, it apparently kept the deceased from attracting flies until the funeral service was over. It was also rubbed into meat to repel flies and other insects.

Tansy was once an ingredient in cakes and puddings eaten at Easter, when it was thought to counteract any ill effects of a Lenten diet. Culpeper recommended tansy for wives who wished to become pregnant: "Let those women that desire children love this herb; it is their best companion, their husbands excepted. . . ."

This herb is now considered far too strong and potentially toxic to be used in home remedies. If you're not pregnant, it's probably safe in small amounts as a seasoning. One popular destination is egg dishes; chopped leaves will add peppery zip to stuffing, salad dressings, and spreads. A little goes a long way.

Description

A perennial native to Europe, tansy has arching stems that form a mound of finely divided, fernlike leaves; plants reach 2 to 3 feet tall, about 18 inches wide. Also called golden buttons for its 4-inch, flat-topped clusters of ½-inch yellow knobs that appear from late summer through fall, tansy looks quite like its cousin feverfew, especially *Tanacetum parthenium* 'Golden Ball'. The entire plant smells of camphor.

How to grow

Talk about immortal! Tansy is one of those herbs that is easier to grow than to control, since it spreads by underground rhizomes. You should have no problem starting it from seed or from divisions from a neighbor who has way too much. Give tansy a home in a naturalized or contained area — plants are unparticular about soil but need good drainage and plenty of sun — where you can enjoy its graceful form and cheerful flowers. One gardener we know grows this tough customer, hardy through Zone 3, as a low hedge between her lawn and drive and disciplines it with her lawn mower.

Cultivars and related plants

If you want to grow tansy for the long-lasting flowers, try a cultivar called 'Goldsticks', which has larger blooms on its long stems that are easy to cut and arrange. If it's pretty foliage you're after, then try one (or all) of these three: *Tanacetum vulgare* var. *crispum*, or curly tansy, a compact cultivar that has larger, light green fernlike leaves; 'Isla Gold', which has near-gold foliage; and 'Silver Lace', with variegated leaves.

Tarragon, French (Artemisia dracunculus var. sativa)

In the 17th century, some people believed tarragon came from flax seeds that had been inserted in a radish or an onion. This was not a sci-fi propagation theory, but probably stemmed from the fact that flavorful French, or culinary, tarragon cannot be reliably propagated from seeds.

Artemisia dracunculus

Tarragon was said to cure bites and stings of mad dogs and "venomous beasts." The Greeks used it for toothaches (nibble a leaf and you'll feel a numbing sensation); and because it was supposed to prevent fatigue, travelers in the Middle Ages put it in their shoes.

Herbalist John Gerard reduced tarragon to an herbal shrug, which he said was "not to be eaten alone in sallades, but joyned with other herbs . . . neither do we know what other use this herbe hath." What other use, indeed? No Hollandaise, Béarnaise, or sauce tartare is complete without this herb, which is also a standard ingredient in the herb mix known as fines herbes and among the most popular herbs for herbal vinegar.

Description

Tarragon, a perennial from central and eastern Europe, doesn't look a thing like most other artemisias, since its 1- to 3-inch, bluish green leaves aren't divided, but look more like blades of grass. It will grow up to 2 feet tall with somewhat lax stems. Tiny yellow-green flowers rarely open and are almost always sterile.

How to grow

Always buy tarragon as a plant, either at a local market where you can do a scratch and sniff, or from a mail-order supplier you trust. Seeds are invariably those of Russian tarragon (*A. dracunculus* var. *dracunculoides);* it grows to 5 feet and has 6-inch pale green leaves that are about as tasty as lawn grass.

One plant will be enough. Give it organically rich, well-worked soil that drains well and full sun (perhaps a little afternoon shade in hot regions. Periodic light pruning is a good idea, as is a loose mulch during the winter months. Divide your plant every two or three years to keep its long fibrous roots from tangling and committing suicide. These fierce roots inspired the plant's name, from the French word *estragon,* meaning "little dragon." Tarragon is hardy through Zone 4.

Cultivars and related plants

Kin to tarragon by taste is the sweet marigold *(Tagetes lucida),* a relative of our garden marigold. Also known as Mexican tarragon, this yellow-flowered herb is upright and slender, with lance-shaped leaves nearly identical to tarragon's. It's hardy only through Zone 8 and is usually grown as an annual, especially by gardeners in the Deep South where high temperatures can keep tarragon plants from doing well.

Thyme *(Thymus spp.)*

The next time you're harvesting thyme for the bouquet garni, pick a sprig to hide under your pillow. It will either A) dispel melancholy or B) prevent nightmares. Maybe both.

There are two explanations for thyme's name as well. It may mean "courage," since it was an invigorating tonic. (During the Crusades, ladies who fancied a particular knight presented him with a scarf embroidered with a sprig of thyme.) More prosaically, the name may stem from a word meaning "to fumigate," as it often was burned to drive off insects and assorted vermin.

Thyme contains a powerful antiseptic, thymol, which was popular for treating wounds until World War I. It is still found in mouthwashes and other commercial products. Europeans use it for respiratory ailments; and it seems to ease the spasms of coughs. Try sipping thyme tea, make a thyme syrup, or make a "tent" with a towel and inhale its steam.

The antiseptic properties make it a good ingredient for a face lotion, and as an antispasmodic it may relieve menstrual cramps or an upset stomach. As John Parkinson noted, "To set down the particular uses whereunto Time is applied, were to weary both the writer and the reader. . . ." Not wishing to weary you, dear reader, we'll add only that most of us know thyme as a friend in the kitchen, where it was first used as a preservative rather than a flavoring.

Description

Botanists estimate there are 350 species of thyme — all evergreen perennials and subshrubs in the mint family — plus scores of subspecies and cultivars. Most cooks grow common or English thyme *(Thymus vulgaris),* although there are several "chemotypes" with different flavors, from the high-thymol 'Narrowleaf French' to others — the flavors of which have been compared with tar.

As a rule, common thyme grows 12 to 18 inches tall, spreading as it ages. The base is woody and the branches upright with gray-green, oval or slightly lance-shaped leaves up to a half inch long. Bees are passionate about the small tubular pink or lilac flowers that cluster in early to mid-summer.

Because of its shrubby shape, common thyme can be used as a low hedge. Other thymes, known collectively as "creeping thymes," make ideal ground covers, are elegant in pots or window boxes, and charming tucked between rocks or stepping stones.

How to grow

Thyme, which is hardy through Zone 4, is so easy to propagate from cuttings or divisions that few gardeners start from seed (although that's easy, too). Space plants 6 to 8 inches apart in light soil that has been enriched with organic matter. Harvesting thyme with abandon will keep new growth coming. Plants get sparse and woody in the center after two or three years, so renew your plants by dividing, layering, or taking cuttings from the old ones.

Cultivars and related plants

Once you get hooked on thymes, you may have to pull out all your other herbs to make room for them. You can choose them for variations in taste, such as lemon thyme *(Thymus × citriodora)* and *T. vulgaris* 'Orange Balsam'. Others smell and taste of caraway *(T. herba-barona)* or lavender *(T. thracicus)*. Herb specialists offer dozens of possibilities, including mint thyme, nutmeg thyme, coconut thyme, and more, and it's here that names get muddled. When you visit a nursery, crush a leaf to smell what you're getting.

A popular creeping thyme is *T. praecox* subsp. *arcticus*. As you might guess from the name, it is more cold-hardy than the species, at least to Zone 4. as 'Elfin', 'Minimus', and 'Minor', cultivars of the creeping species *T. serpyllum,* vie for the honor of dinkiest thyme. Also hardy through Zone 4, they stay under 4 inches tall and have leaves the size of pinheads. (If you plan to cook with creeping thymes — and we don't recommend that you do — plant them so they'll hang over the side of a container; otherwise, harvesting will be murder on your knees and back.)

If it's foliage color you want, you can choose lemon thyme's gold-leafed cultivar, 'Aureus', or silver thyme, *T. vulgaris* 'Argenteus', which lights up an herb bed with its white edged leaf and looks beautiful in a hanging basket. Flowers? Look for *T. serpyllum* var. *coccineus,* commonly known as creeping red thyme, which is loaded with magenta flowers and hardy through Zone 4. Also lovely is the more subtle effect of *T. praecox* subsp. *arcticus* 'Alba' (sometimes called 'White Moss') for the tiny white flowers that cover the bright green leaves. It's hardy through Zone 5. And don't overlook woolly thyme, *T. pseudolanuginosus,* a prostrate species with hairy stems and woolly gray-green leaves that's hardy through Zone 6.

Valerian (Valeriana officinalis)

One of our all-time favorite *Saturday Night Live* skits is the faux commercial for a product that is both a dessert topping and a floor wax. Valerian's smell is a bit like that. Often sold as "garden heliotrope" with catalog copy that extols its sweet scent, its roots and the pills made from them smell exactly like an adolescent's dirty gym socks.

So what does valerian's flower smell like? You got it — sort of like sweet gym socks. True fans compare the aroma to vanilla. Cats are said to like it as much as catnip. It's also irresistible to rats: The Pied Piper of Hamelin allegedly owed his success not to musical prowess but to having tucked sprigs of valerian in his pockets.

Valerian is the valium of the herb world, calming the agitated and helping insomniacs nod off with no "hangover" the next morning. In the 14th century, it was written that you could stop men from fighting by giving them juice of valerian. During World War II, some Londoners reputedly took it to ease their jitters during air raids. It's been used to cure nervous disorders, cramps, and vertigo, to stop seizures, to reduce pain, to treat venomous bites, and to heal wounds. No wonder the herb is also known as all heal.

Valerian extracts are almost never found in home kitchens, but they are used commercially to flavor ice cream, baked goods, condiments, soft drinks, liqueurs, and tobacco. Considering our comments about dirty gym socks, we won't mention product names.

Description

Valerian is a hardy perennial growing to 5 feet tall. The tall stems, produced from a rosette of foliage in the second year, are hollow and grooved, branching with rows of toothed, dark green leaves set along the stems like rungs of a ladder. Both the leaves and stems emit the odd, signature valerian aroma when touched. The herb's tiny white or pink flowers are arranged in flat clusters and appear from mid spring until late summer.

How to grow

It's possible to start valerian from seeds, but because they don't stay viable for long, it's easier to begin with plants spaced 18 inches apart. Valerian, which is hardy through Zone 3, grows best in organically rich, moist, slightly acid soil, either in sun or partial shade. Plants sometimes self-sow, you many want to remove spent blooms. Divide large plants in spring every three years or so to keep them healthy; reset the rhizome divisions if you want to increase the size of your valerian patch.

If you want to harvest valerian roots, do so in their second fall. Their strong scent becomes stronger as the root dries, and valerian tea is bitter. We prefer to admire the plant in the garden and buy stress-reducing valerian capsules when book deadlines loom.

Cultivars and related plants

Don't let the common name garden heliotrope confuse this plant with true heliotrope *(Heliotropium arborescens)*. A 2-foot-tall annual with deep green, puckered leaves, it has deep purple blue flowers that most people think smell like cherry pie.

Red valerian *(Centranthus ruber),* which is also called Jupiter's beard, is a short-lived perennial that grows in dry, chalky soil, most famously on England's white cliffs of Dover. The tubular, spurred flowers are most commonly red, but there are pink and white flowered types as well. Hardy through Zone 5.

Violet (Viola odorata)

Even under the most trying circumstances, we've never considered turning our beloved into a cow. But that's supposedly what the Roman god Jupiter did to his side dish, Io, when wife Juno caught wind of her. As solace, he gave Io violets to munch, and her name evolved into the name for this shy spring-blooming plant. The chemical that gives violets their intense brief volley of fragrance is called ionine.

*Viola
odorata*

The Greeks thought the violet would moderate anger, while Roman naturalist Pliny suggested that a garland of violets would prevent hangovers from wine. (No word on whether this worked for wine made from violets, which was popular at the time.) The Celts soaked violets in goat's milk to create a beauty treatment. Violets have often been used as a sleep aid (one approach called for soaking one's feet in violet water before going to bed), and violet syrup was a tasty treatment for a myriad of ailments, including inflamed eyes, pleurisy, jaundice, epilepsy, and headaches.

Violets were Napoleon's annual anniversary gift to his wife Josephine. (He supposedly announced, when banished to Elba, "I will return with the violets in the spring.") Violet nosegays were all the rage early in the 20th century, when young women were warned about smelling them with too much abandon. Some people believe the scent is so strong that the nose shuts down from sensory overload after a few seconds.

You can toss violet flowers into salads and fruity drinks, candy them for desserts, or freeze them in ice cubes. Violet water, like rose water, adds subtle flavor to fruit salads and baked goods. Herb expert Jim Duke maintains that violet tea may help prevent varicose veins, since it contains a compound called rutin that helps strengthen the walls of blood vessels.

Description

A perennial from southern and western Europe, the sweet violet (also known as the English violet, garden violet, and common violet) grows to 6 or 7 inches tall and a foot wide in a mound of kidney- or heart-shaped leaves that rise out of a tuft of roots. The ¾-inch flowers have five petals and are usually purple but occasionally pink or white. The plant's runners root at their tips.

How to grow

You can start violets from seeds gathered in fall — if you can catch them. The fall flowers, which are nearly petal-less, can spit seeds several feet (the familiar spring flowers are sterile). Violet seeds need exposure to cold, so leave where they land or stratify them before sowing.

It's far easier to begin with divisions, either in fall or early spring. Space plants 18 inches apart, and give them organically rich soil and partial shade, especially in warm regions. Violets grow best in cool weather; plants often are plagued by red spider mite where conditions are hot and dry.

Cultivars and related plants

There are some 500 species of violet, many of them charming North American natives such as the birds-foot-violet *(Viola pedata)* but not widely available for sale to gardeners. In the 19th century, a highly fragrant double form called parma violets was sold for nosegays, but it, too, is difficult to find.

V. odorata 'Alba', which has white flower, is the violet you're most likely to find at the garden center. 'Queen Charlotte' has dark blue flowers; the blooms of 'Royal Robe' are deep violet and wonderfully fragrant. However, most of today's "violets" are rigorously cultivated pansies.

Heartsease or Johnny-jump-up *(V. tricolor)* is an annual or short-lived perennial (hardy through Zone 3) beloved for its little "face" of dark purple, lavender, and yellow. It's used medicinally, like the common violet, as an expectorant, and as a wash for itching, acne, and other skin problems.

Watercress (Nasturtium officinale)

There's not nearly enough overlap between herb gardening and water gardening. Those who like to do both should be grateful for watercress, which also happens to be tasty and nutritious. It has been used since ancient times to prevent scurvy, and as early as the 5th century B.C., watercress was thought to make children stronger. The Greeks considered it brain food, which meant it was something of an insult to be told to "eat cress."

Nasturtium officinale

According to the Roman Pliny, the genus name comes from the Latin *nasus tortus,* which means "writhing nose,' an allusion to the plant's peppery quali-ties. We don't know whether or not watercress's slightly shocking flavor has anything to do with the plant's being recommended for stimulating hair to grow, but we prefer to tuck it in salads, soups, sandwiches, and stir fries, where we can take advantage of its nip and the vitamin C it contains.

Description

A perennial member of the mustard family, watercress is native from Europe and southwest Asia, where it is found growing wild in slow-moving water. Plants creep along for a way, then stick up 12-inch stems. The dark glossy leaves are compound, with oval or heart-shaped leaflets; the small, white, four-petalled flowers, which are borne in flat-topped clusters, bloom from late spring through summer.

How to grow

Watercress, which is hardy through Zone 4, is unusual even among water plants for preferring moving rather than still water. It will be at home in a cleared area along a natural streambank (be sure the water isn't polluted). If you've built your own back-yard pond, grow it in a container placed where the pond's waterfall or fountain creates some gentle turbulence. You can start seeds indoors in flats. Easier and quicker, buy watercress at the super-market, take cuttings, and root them in wet soil.

No river running through it? You can also grow watercress by submerging clay pots in large tubs of water. To make the plants believe they're in running water, run a hose into the tub for several hours at least four times a week.

Cultivars and related plants

In England, gardeners can choose among all sorts of named watercresses (usually named for towns), but American gardeners must make do with the species or with 'Broad Leaf', an improved cultivar with larger leaves.

Cresses grown on dry land are also members of the mustard family and taste like watercress, but they're members of other genera. They include garden cress *(Lepidium sativum);* curly cress, or cresson *(L. sativum* 'Crispum'); and upland, or winter cress *(Barbarea verna).* You can have cress continuously from spring to fall by sowing a crop every two weeks, and through the winter by sprouting seeds indoors.

Wormwood (Artemisia absinthium)

Wormwood is sometimes called absinthe. It was the primary ingredient in the addictive liqueur by that name that became notorious in 19th-century France. Immortalized in a painting by Edgar Degas, it was banned in 1915 after being linked to convulsions, madness, and death. Drinking absinthe reputedly caused the deaths of both painter Toulouse Lautrec and the poet Verlaine.

Artemisia absinthium

Also an ingredient in vermouth, wormwood was called "wermuth" — ironically, "preserver of the mind" — since it was thought to stimulate the brain. *Absinthium*, meaning "without sweetness," was a more appropriate name for this bitter herb. Its strong scent made it popular as a strewing herb and insect repellent, and it sometimes was used a substitute for hops in beer making.

Wormwood contains large amounts of thujone (also found in sage and tansy), which may work in the brain in the same manner as THC, the active substance in marijuana. Use it only externally, in a compress to relieve pain and kill germs. It contains antiseptics and also seems to act as an anesthetic and anti-inflammatory. The camphorous scent may help drive moths from your closet.

Description

A hardy Mediterranean perennial averaging 3 feet tall and 2 wide, wormwood has with a woody base and forms a sprawling mound of silver-green. Its pungent leaves are deeply divided and covered with silky hairs. In summer, plants produce upright panicles of small yellow and gray flowers.

How to grow

Like other artemisias, wormwood looks delicate but grows tough (it's hardy through Zone 3). You can start the seeds indoors and then transplant them, keeping in mind their slow but inevitable spread. Or propagate new plants from divisions or cuttings.

You may want to site wormwood away from other plants, especially expensive specimens. Absinthin, one of the compounds that gives the herb its bitter taste, is toxic to some other plants, stunting them or killing them outright.

Cultivars and related plants

A popular cultivar is 'Lambrook Silver', whose foliage is both more gray-green and more deeply divided. It is less hardy than the species, however, thriving only through Zone 5. For information about other artemisias, see the entries for southernwood, sweet Annie, and tarragon.

Yarrow (Achillea millefolium)

Names like devil's nettle, devil's plaything, and bad man's plaything (which sounds like the name of an X-rated movie) might scare anyone away from this herb, which was favored for incantations in days of yore. But yarrow was actually more famous as an herbal Band-Aid, earning it the sobriquets soldier's woundwort, knight's milfoil, and carpenter's weed (which you understand if your do-it-yourself skills are as lacking as ours).

The most famous story about yarrow holds that Achilles used it to treat the wounds of his soldiers in the Trojan War. (Apparently, it was no good for his famously flawed heel.) Popular for stopping nose bleeds, it was also used to trigger nosebleeds as a means of relieving headache pressure. If a young maiden's nose bled when she stuffed yarrow in her nostril, it meant she was beloved (at least until her sweetie caught a glimpse of this behavior). Seems much more seemly to slip yarrow under your pillow (another tradition) for a vision of your dreamboat.

Modern researchers can't decide if Achilles was right. The chemistry of yarrow plants varies immensely. But some scientific evidence that the herb contains blood-clotting and anti-inflammatory compounds — plus anecdotal accounts from friends— would prompt us to try a yarrow poultice if we had an accident in the garden.

Description

A perennial in the daisy family, yarrow is native to Europe and western Asia. It grows upright to 3 feet tall, and bears leaves up to 6 inches long that are so feathery they look like they belong in a hatband. The white flowers — occasionally pink — appear in 3-inch flat clusters in late summer.

How to grow

How to control may be a better question than how to grow. Yarrow has natu-ralized throughout North America — in old farm fields and along roadsides — and it may romp all over your garden if not there already. Impressively drought tolerant and hardy through Zone 3, yarrow will be happy and healthy if it has sun and enough soil in which to sink its roots. Seeds germinate quickly, or you can begin with divisions or purchased plants.

To keep the flowers coming, deadhead your plants And if you *really* need more yarrow, divide. Dividing, which is the only way to propagate yarrow cul-tivars, will also make your plants more vigorous.

Cultivars and related plants

There's a whole world of yarrows beyond the somewhat muddy white flower color of the species. Better yet, many cultivars are also less invasive than the species. Possibilities include the pink-to-cherry 'Cerise Queen', bigger and whiter 'White Beauty', and mixes such as 'Summer Pastel Beauty'. You can also find lavender, red, cream, rose, salmon, and purple cultivars.

Popular evergreen yarrows that form clumps instead of mats (so they tend to be less invasive) are the huge *A. filipendula* 'Cloth of Gold', 5 feet tall with golden yellow flowers, and *A.* 'Moonshine', 2 feet tall with pale yellow flowers. Most cultivars are hardy through Zone 3.

Woolly yarrow *(Achillea tomentosa)* has fuzzy leaves; try the bright yellow-flowering dwarf cultivar 'Aurea'. Avid cooks might want to experiment with mace yarrow *(A. ageratum),* which grows only 6 or 8 inches tall. It has silvery leaves that smell like the spice called mace, which comes from the membrane of nutmeg seeds. Both of these yarrows are hardy through Zone 3.

For cut flowers you'll want sneezewort *(A. ptarmica),* once used for headaches and toothaches, as well as sneezes. Its popular cultivar 'Pearl', grown for its double white flowers, is hardy through Zone 3.

Part V

Weed 'Em and Reap

The 5th Wave　　　　　By Rich Tennant

IT WAS WORSE THAN SARAH THOUGHT – HER GARDEN HAD BECOME INFESTED WITH WORMS, MAGGOTS, AND PERSONAL INJURY ATTORNEYS.

In this part . . .

Pull on your gloves — or prepare to get dirt under your fingernails! Part V is strictly hands-on, with advice about clearing a garden site and preparing the soil for planting, buying and sowing seeds, raising seedlings, transplanting, and more. We'll show you how to make compost and how to avoid pest and disease problems in the herb garden.

Here, too, are our suggestions for keeping up with your herb garden — routines that will keep maintenance low and give you more time to enjoy and use the herbs you grow. Part V also contains directions for harvesting your herb garden and for getting a head start on next year.

Chapter 7

Getting Down to Earth

. . . .

In This Chapter

▶ Clearing your site

▶ Enriching the soil

▶ Making compost

▶ Breaking ground

. . . .

*A*ll right, enough dreaming about creating an herb garden exactly like the one you saw in England or sitting on a chamomile bench with a cup of lemon balm tea. You have to knock off a couple of jobs before you can sow the first seed or set out the first plant. You must clear the garden site — if you're starting from scratch — and prepare the soil.

Don't be discouraged if the future home of your herb garden looks as neglected as the grounds of Sleeping Beauty's castle. Clearing and improving soil are straightforward jobs, tasks that demand the intellectual acumen of a turnip. True, you need to use a little elbow grease, but not nearly as much as you might expect. What's important is doing these chores right the *first* time. Trust us, it will mean a lot less work in the future. Your goals are to remove all vegetation and to improve the soil, making it rich in organic matter and nutrients. This process may sound hard, but it's not.

A Clean Sweep

After you decide where to put your new herb garden and have developed a plan (see Chapters 3 and 5), you'll need to clear the site if it's never been a garden or if it hasn't been a garden in a long time. Clearing means removing everything, every last plant. Think scorched earth.

If you face a plot of weeds, you may be tempted to reach for an *herbicide,* one of those skull-and-crossbones chemicals that kills vegetation as quickly as bad breath kills romance. Stop! All herbicides are toxic, and most are persistent, which means they stay around to do damage long after the weeds are history.

Laying down black plastic kills even woody plants eventually. (Guidelines on how to do it appear in the section titled "Shade power: Clearing sod with covers" in this chapter.) If you have a thick stand of poison ivy that isn't fazed by being cut back repeatedly, then an herbicide may be necessary. No poison is safe, even if it's organic. Herbicides, however, should be a last resort. Handle them carefully and read the directions: Not only are they dangerous to you, it's awfully easy to liquidate plants (and wildlife) you don't want harmed. Choose a windless day and always spot-spray individual plants rather than drenching an entire site.

Consider the following herbicides if you must take that route:

✔ You can find a handful of organic herbicides on the market that are derived from corn gluten, lemon juice, vinegar, and other natural substances (the best-known is Sharpshooter, a soap-based product). Most organic herbicides are slow-acting and less effective than synthetic killers but work moderately well on emerging annual weeds. An even safer bombs-away approach is to pour boiling water on annual weeds.

✔ Many gardeners consider Roundup, a glyphosate-based weed killer, to be the least harmful of the synthetic herbicides. Its persistence is brief yet it's an effective assassin. Roundup is also *nonselective,* which means it will kill anything you spray. Aim carefully.

Try to clear your garden site well ahead of time. Autumn is the best time to do this, but if you're someone who fills out income tax returns on April 14, don't close this book and decide to take up needlepoint. You can clear a garden site in spring, even on the same day you plant. Waiting until the last minute, however, means hand-digging and other hard labor instead of using some of the labor-saving methods we show you in this chapter.

Whether you're an early bird or a procrastinator, begin by marking your garden's boundaries. If the garden has straight sides, outline it with strings stretched between small stakes. Either leave the strings in place or remove them after marking the boundaries with ground limestone, flour, or sand. For free-form designs, use rope or garden hose to lay out the boundaries and then mark them. Now remove all the large debris and woody plants (be sure to grub out the roots), mow the site, and remove the sod.

Sod, or *turf,* consists of all those ground-hugging plants, mostly matted grasses. You need to strip off the sod before you cultivate the soil. Getting rid of every plant *and* all its roots is essential. Leaving behind even a small piece of leaf, stem, or root tip — which is inevitable when you pull weeds by hand — usually means you've left enough to sprout the minute your back is turned.

Spade power: Clearing sod by hand

A spade (see Chapter 15) is the tool of choice for stripping sod by hand, but a shovel works, too. The goal is to remove all the vegetation but to take away as little soil as possible. Before beginning, water the site thoroughly. Start on one side of the plot. Slice into the sod, about 1 or 2 inches deep, and then lower the handle of the spade so that its blade is nearly parallel to the soil surface. Now push forward until the spade face is completely buried and then lift the piece of sod and set it aside. When you're done, add the sod (upside down) to your compost pile or use it to fill in low spots in your landscape. (If you want a giant-sized herb garden, check into renting a gasoline-powered sod stripper.)

Shade power: Clearing sod with covers

Hands down, the easiest and most effective way to kill weeds is to turn off the sun. Plants, if you don't count mushrooms and a few other things that grow plump in the night, can't live without bright light. Flip the solar switch by covering your site with black plastic or dark landscape fabric to stymie the sun; use bricks, boards, or U-shaped pins made from clothes hangers to secure the edges of the cover. And don't dilly-dally: You need to cover the site for eight months to a year before planting time. Rolls of black plastic are sold at garden centers and by mail-order firms.

Making Your Soil Richer

We hope you already know what kind of *terra firma* you're standing on — whether the soil in your embryonic herb garden is heavy or light, sweet or sour, whether it's fertile or can barely keep a dandelion alive. If you're not sure, head over to Chapter 4 before you make any of the unnecessary and time-consuming mistakes that your authors have chalked up.

Congratulations if you already have perfect soil for growing herbs: near-neutral loam that is rich in nutrients and organic matter and retains moisture but never is soggy. Everyone else — and that's 99.9 percent of gardeners — needs to improve the soil that came with the mortgage.

In fact, enriching, or *amending,* the soil is like a mortgage, a long-term proposition. Like monthly payments to the bank, everything you deposit in the soil helps. If you don't make your payments, you regret it. You can't change clay or sand into fertile loam overnight, but over time you can turn your soil into an inviting home for herbs.

Organic matter is the miracle cure for all soil ailments. Adding it is the single best thing you can do for your garden and plants. It helps wet, clay soils drain and sandy soils retain moisture. It makes soil fertile. The *crème de la crème* of organic matter is *compost,* a dark, crumbly mix that you can cook up yourself.

Compost happens

You may have seen the bumper sticker that reads "Compost Happens." It really does! Making compost is like making a good stew. Add the right amounts of the right ingredients, let them simmer, and it just happens. (In fact, millions of microorganisms actually do the work, but take the credit yourself. We do.)

The easiest approach to composting is to throw all the organic matter you can get your hands on into a pile and wait.

Raw ingredients

Good ingredients for compost include animal manure, coffee grounds, conifer needles, eggshells, grass clippings, hair, hay, leaves, sawdust, seaweed, shredded newsprint, soil, straw, vegetable and fruit scraps, and weeds — almost any plant matter. Remember to aim for a 3:1 ratio, three parts brown and dry matter to one part green and gooey.

Not everything organic belongs in a compost pile. Don't add bones or meat scraps; diseased plants; pet feces; any vegetation that has been sprayed with a pesticide or herbicide; or allelopathic plants, such as eucalyptus. (An *allelopathic* plant is one that contains chemicals that stunt the growth of other plants.)

Remember: Everything decomposes much faster if you shred or chop it before you add it to the pile.

This *laissez-faire* method works — it's called *cold composting* — but it's darned slow. (On the other hand, ignore ads promising "Great Compost in Three Days.") You can speed up decomposition by providing the perfect working conditions for the herd of microorganisms living in your pile. When they're working flat-out, your pile's temperature will reach an ideal 160°F.

Keeping the pile well-aerated is basic to speeding up the composting process. Aerating means more work — you have to stir or turn the pile — so decide how much of a hurry you're in.

If you're in a rush to have finished compost, try this:

1. **Make sure your pile contains a mix of brown (high-carbon) and green (high-nitrogen) stuff.**

   The rule of thumb is three parts brown (dry matter, such as leaves, sawdust, or hay) to one part green (wetter items like apple peels, overripe tomatoes, manure, and fresh grass clippings).

2. **Chop or shred organic matter before adding it to the compost pile. (If you don't have a shredder, try running your lawn mower over the material.)**

3. **Mingle green and brown ingredients.**

   Know thyself! If you know you won't have the time to stir the compost pile, then layer green and brown materials (see the sidebar "Raw Ingredients") when you put them in. If you have way more of one kind than the other (a ton of maple leaves in the fall, for example), then chopping and aerating is even more important than usual.

4. **Add an occasional handful of soil, which is full of the same bacteria, fungi, and enzymes that commercial "compost starters" contain.**

5. **Keep the pile small, no more than 4 feet tall, 4 feet on each side (but not less than 3 x 3 x 3 feet).**

6. **Aerate your compost pile by turning it — every few days if you can.**

7. **Keep your pile damp but not soggy — the usual description is "damp as a wrung-out sponge."**

The simplest compost pile is just that, a freestanding pile. Rake up leaves, shred them, and toss them on. If you produce only dabs of organic waste, you can use a trash can as a composter (cut the bottom out first or make large holes in the bottom for drainage). For larger amounts of waste, fashion an organic compost bin out of bales of straw or hay: Place the bales to form three sides of a square, the sides stacked two or three bales high. When the bin itself begins to decay, compost it!

Our favorite compost bin — easy, cheap, and reasonably attractive — is nothing more than three wood pallets, which you should be able to scrounge from local businesses (see Figure 7-1). Turn each on its end and wire (coat hangers work nicely) or nail them together to form a three-sided container. Leave the top, bottom, and front open. Or you can cover the front with a fourth pallet or wire mesh to keep the compost in and dogs out. To build double or triple side-by-side bins, add more pallets.

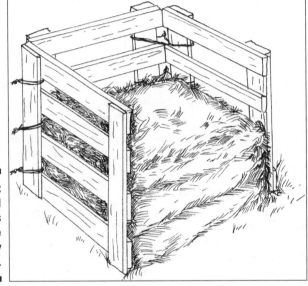

Figure 7-1:
Use wood
pallets
to make
an easy
compost bin.

An array of barrel and drum composters is available from garden centers and mail-order companies. These composters are expensive and their capacity is small, but they produce compost quickly and are handy for gardeners in small quarters.

Fertilizer: Where the next meal comes from

Fertilizing plants is just a variation on the nursery rhyme about the house that Jack built: This is the organic matter that feeds the microorganisms that feed the soil that feeds the herbs that you plant. Regularly enrich your soil with compost and other organic matter, and your plants are unlikely to need any additional fertilizer. Healthy soil grows healthy plants. It's as simple as that.

Plants get some of the elements they need to live from air, sunlight, and water, but most of their needs — 13 crucial mineral elements — must come from the soil. A soil test, in addition to giving pH readings, can tell you if any of these nutrients are missing in your garden.

- ✔ **Macronutrients.** Nitrogen, phosphorus, and potassium. Herbs need a generous helping of the big three.

- ✔ **Secondary macronutrients.** Calcium, magnesium, and sulfur. Herbs need lesser amounts of these elements.

- ✔ **Micronutrients.** Boron, chloride, copper, iron, manganese, molybdenum, and zinc. Herbs need tiny amounts of these seven.

Nitrogen (N), phosphorus (P), and potassium (K) are the most important plant foods. The three numbers on the bags of commercial fertilizer refer to the percentage of each element that is immediately available to plants. A bag of 5-10-5, for example, contains 5 percent nitrogen, 10 percent phosphorus, and 5 percent potassium. The remaining 80 percent may contain some usable nutrients but consists mainly of *carrier* (scientific lingo for the inactive agents that the usable nutrients attach to).

Each macronutrient plays a vital role in plant growth:

- ✔ **Nitrogen.** Produces good growth and healthy green leaves.

- ✔ **Phosphorus.** Encourages plant growth, strong root development, and the production of flowers, fruits, and seeds.

- ✔ **Potassium.** Aids photosynthesis and flowering, increases resistance to cold and diseases, and improves overall plant vigor.

Synthetic fertilizer

Almost nothing is easier than using synthetic, or inorganic, fertilizers: Open the bag and pour. Your plants won't care if their meal came from a bag. To them, nitrogen is nitrogen, inorganic or organic. Synthetic fertilizers, however, are a second-best way to feed your herbs. These fertilizers work fast and give plants a nutritional lift, but they don't help the soil. Synthetics lack the organic matter that microorganisms eat. If you use only synthetics, then you inadvertently starve the billions of inhabitants that live and work in your soil. Having the microorganisms die off affects the fertility, structure, and pH of the soil. You're back to square one!

Organic fertilizer

Organic matter doesn't work overnight like a bag of synthetic fertilizer. Releasing half its nutrients could take a year, so its immediate nutritional boost is less. In this case, less really is more, and your garden will be ahead in the end. The traditional saying is worth remembering, "Feed the soil, not the plant." If you keep your soil healthy, the soil will provide the nutrients that your herbs need. Nothing feeds the soil better than organic matter does, especially compost. (Do you see a theme emerging?)

Spreading a thin layer of grass clippings or a few cow patties around your herbs once each summer won't do the job, however. No single kind of organic matter is a *complete fertilizer,* which means it doesn't contain all 13 elements that plants need. Manure and blood meal, for example, are high in nitrogen; wood ashes provide potassium; bonemeal is rich in phosphorus, egg shells in calcium. That's why compost, which is made from many organic materials, is such a good fertilizer — it's complete.

Lay on the compost

Don't stay up nights worrying whether your marjoram and mullein are getting all the molybdenum they need. Just add compost to your soil. Then add more compost to your soil. If you're not making compost, be sure to add different organic materials into your soil so it gets a balanced diet of nutrients. Adding too much is almost impossible.

If you don't have access to grass clippings, sawdust, leaves, chicken manure, and buckets of seaweed, you can buy commercial compost or organic fertilizers, which are available by the bag. All bear labels that indicate the nutrients they contain. Choose a fertilizer that comes near to being *complete* (having near equal amounts of N, P, and K), rather than one that is high in a single element. You may have to buy more than one product.

Of course you'll add scads of organic matter when you first prepare your soil for planting. (See the section "Breaking Ground" in this chapter). But also add organic matter any chance you get — any amount, any time of year. That process of digging organic matter (or any fertilizer) into the soil is called *incorporating.* If you spread compost or other fertilizers on top of the soil but don't dig them in, you're *top-dressing. Side-dressing* is spreading fertilizer alongside or around plants.

Make it manure

If you have access to manure — horse, cow, sheep, chicken, rabbit, gerbil, whatever — count yourself lucky. Animal manures are nitrogen gold mines, a sure way to enrich the soil, but they're also dangerous. Fresh manure can burn leaves and stems, even kill young plants. Because it is high in nitrogen (as is green plant matter), manure sends the soil's microorganisms into over-drive, temporarily reducing the nitrogen available to your herbs.

You're better off if you add fresh manure to the compost pile where it can age or spread it on gardens in late autumn when the growing season is over. (Well-rotted manure can be added anytime.) In addition to supplying nitrogen, manure supplies smaller amounts of phosphorus, potassium, calcium, sulfur, and other micronutrients. Manure also adds organic matter to the soil.

TIP

Time for tea

Watering with *compost tea* gives growing plants a nutritional boost. To brew, fill any large container half full of compost, half warm water (or fill a cloth bag with compost and immerse it in water). Let the mixture steep for several days, and then strain it through a cloth or window-screen wire. If you use the bag method, straining is unnecessary. Dilute the liquid until it is the color of weak tea before using it on plant leaves.

Breaking Ground

After you clear your site, it's time to ready the soil for planting. You'll be doing two things at once: loosening, or aerating, the soil and improving the soil by adding all that organic matter you've collected and composted. Fall is the best time to tackle this job — so you can let frost break up clumps and clods for you during the winter — but you can take it on any time that the soil's not frozen or soppy wet.

Begin by covering your garden with a generous layer — 3 inches or more — of organic material. (Not only do you want to enrich your soil, you want to raise the soil level, because you lowered it an inch or two when you removed the sod.) If your garden is both new and large and your time is limited, consider renting a rototiller to turn the soil. (Ask for a model with rear-mounted tines, which is much easier to manage than a front-tine tiller.)

Rototillers, or just plain tillers, are real back- and time-savers, but they are too good at their job. Run one over a garden three or four times and the soil looks terrific. Well, it looks terrific, but it isn't really terrific. Overtilling pulverizes soil, destroying the pore spaces that air, water, and nutrients use to travel to the roots of plants. The goal is soil with the consistency of bread stuffing, not flour. Don't overdo.

Going overboard is all too tempting, so follow the rules of rational rototilling:

- ✔ **Don't till when the soil is wet.** (Squeeze a handful of soil. If it doesn't crumble when you open your hand, it's too wet to be tilled.)

- ✔ **Don't till when the soil is bone dry.** (If you can't squeeze a handful of soil into a ball, it's too dry to be tilled. Water the plot thoroughly, wait a day, and then till.)

- ✔ **Don't overtill the soil.** One pass is usually enough. (If you do overtill, add organic matter to correct your mistake.)

- ✔ **Don't use a rototiller for routine weeding or cultivation.**

Single digging

Digging a small garden by hand is altogether manageable, even for rookies, the out-of-shape, and the over-50 crowd. A spading fork is the best tool for this work, but a shovel or spade is nearly as good. Unless your soil is extremely heavy (clay) or extremely light (sand), you need to cultivate only one spit deep to grow herbs. (A *spit* is gardenese for the length of your fork or shovel's blade, about 1 foot.)

Most garden plots can be prepared by *single digging:* digging one spit deep and turning the soil. After covering your garden with a thick layer of organic matter, begin on one side. Lift a forkful of soil and flip it over. Use the fork to break up large clods and mix in the organic matter. Work facing out so that when you move backward you don't tramp on the soil that you've just turned.

If you're adding herbs to an existing bed or border, then single-digging a small area or just making a hole to slip in a clump of lavender or parsley may be all you need to do. Every time you dig, you also have an opportunity to add more organic matter to your soil. Don't pass it up!

Double digging deluxe

If the soil in your garden lies at either end of the sand-clay soil continuum (see Chapter 4), if it drains poorly, or if it's badly compacted (that otherwise perfect site where your kids used to play basketball or your overweight St. Bernard once paced), then single digging won't be enough. You need to double dig.

Oh, my aching back

To avoid a date with a chiropractor, dig *ergonomically*, a fancy term that refers to a design or method to reduce "operator fatigue and discomfort." If you already have big-league back problems, consider buying ergonomic tools and follow this advice for all gardeners on the working end of a fork, shovel, or spade. Here's how to dig properly:

1. **Keep the handle of your tool straight up and down.**

2. **Put your foot on the tread, or footrest, and use your weight to drive the tines or blade into the soil.**

3. **Bend at the waist and knees to push the handle down and forward.**

4. **Straighten your waist and knees to lift and turn the dirt.**

Double digging is a time-honored tradition, *de rigueur* on the other side of the Atlantic, where it's called *French intensive digging*. The process involves a fair amount of work, because you need to dig deep (about 2 feet) and move soil from one spot to another. The bright spot is that it's a once-in-a-lifetime event, like getting chicken pox.

In addition to working off a pound or two, double digging gives you yet another a chance to add organic material to your soil — which is why we call it double digging deluxe. If that sounds like a flavor of the month, it's because the method is like jamoca triple almond white fudge for your garden.

Tackle double digging with these steps:

1. **Mark off your garden and then remove the sod by hand and set the sod aside.**

   For details on removing sod by hand, see the section titled "Spade power: Clearing sod by hand" in this chapter.

2. **Start on one side and dig a trench 1 foot wide and 1 spit deep.**

   Set soil aside on a tarp or in a wheelbarrow or garden cart.

3. **Use a garden fork to loosen the subsoil another spit deep (for a total of about 2 feet).**

4. **Place a layer of sod (grass side down) in the trench.**

5. **Cover the sod with 2 or 3 inches of decomposed organic matter, such as compost.**

6. **Dig a second, adjoining trench 1 foot wide and 1 spit deep.**

   Place the soil you remove from the second trench on top of the organic matter in the first trench.

7. **Loosen the subsoil 1 spit deep and cover with sod, grass side down, and a layer of organic matter.**

8. **Dig a third, adjoining trench 1 foot wide and one spit deep.**

   Place the topsoil from the third trench on top of the organic matter in the second trench.

9. **Continue the pattern until the entire garden has been dug.**

   Fill the last trench with the turf and topsoil that you set aside from the first trench.

10. **Cover the garden with 2 or 3 inches of organic matter, work it in with a garden fork, and rake smooth.**

Once the soil is turned, put on the finishing touches. Use a garden rake to remove any debris and smooth the surface. The soil is ready to be planted. Now pat yourself on the back . . . and smile.

Basil, Sweet *(Ocimum basilicum)*

Bay *(Laurus nobilis)*

Betony *(Stachys officinalis)*

Borage *(Borago officinalis)*

Fennel *(Foeniculum vulgare)*

Feverfew *(Chrysanthemum parthenium)*

Geraniums *(Pelargonium)*

Horehound *(Marrubium vulgare)*

Horseradish *(Armoracia rusticana)*

Hyssop *(Hyssopus officinalis)*

Lavender *(Lavandula hunstead)*

Lemon Balm *(Melissa officinalis)*

Lemon Verbena *(Aloysia triphylla)*

Nasturtium *(Tropaeolum majus)*

Oregano *(Origanum vulgare)*

Rosemary *(Rosmarinus officinalis)*

Rue *(Ruta graveolens)*

Sage *(Salvia officinalis)*

Southernwood *(Artemisia abrotanum)*

Sweet Ciceley *(Myrrhis odorata)*

Sweet Woodruff *(Galium odoratum)*

Tansy *(Tanacetum vulgare)*

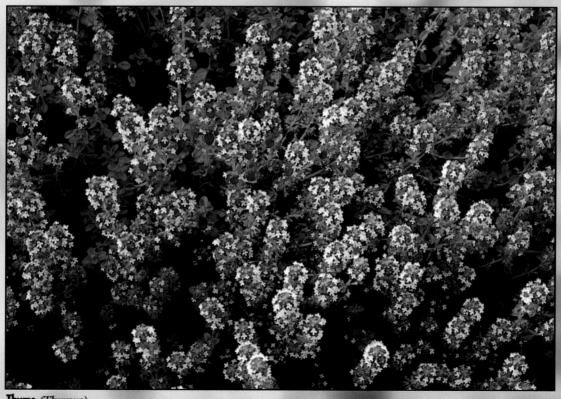

Thyme *(Thymus)*

Valerian *(Valeriana officinalis)*

Violet *(Viola odorata)*

Yarrow *(Achillea millefolium)*

Chapter 8

When We Were Young

. . . .

In This Chapter

▶ Buying seeds

▶ Planting indoors

▶ Transplanting indoor herbs

▶ Planting outdoors

▶ Keeping track of what you're growing

. . . .

*E*verything's ready. You know what herbs you want to grow and where you want to grow them. You've prepared the soil in your beds and borders, cleaned out the window boxes, and retrieved your terra-cotta pots from the garage and cleaned them. It's time to plant!

Growing from seed is one of the miracles of gardening. Every seed is a plant-in-waiting, a tiny package of roots, stems, leaves, flowers, and more seeds. Although they aren't foolproof, seeds *want* to sprout and grow: It's their destiny. As American writer Henry David Thoreau observed, you can have "great faith in a seed."

We're fans of starting plants from seed. The process is fun, interesting, and satisfying, and it's cheap — compare $1.50 for 100 basil seeds with $3 for six three-inch plants. Moreover, you can get your hands on dozens and dozens of unusual herbs and herb cultivars only if you're willing to sow seeds. For example, Canadian seed company Richters offers 30 different kinds of mint. Trust us, you won't find grapefruit mint or variegated peppermint at your local nursery. You also won't find plantain *(Plantago major)* a folk remedy for soothing stings and bites, or celandine *(Cheliodonium majus)*, the juice of which is sometimes prescribed for removing warts and corns.

Starting from seed isn't required, however. Don't feel like a second-class gardener if you decide to begin with plants grown by someone else. Most garden centers offer the basic culinary herbs — basil, thyme, cilantro, chive, oregano, parsley, dill, mint, rosemary, sage, and tarragon — and perhaps a modest selection of less popular plants. We can't debate the fact that buying plants is simpler, and it saves you time.

Whether you're ordering packets of seeds or purchasing plants, let us sow one idea now: Start small. Remember that the work doesn't stop after you plant your garden — you have to take care of these herbs! You probably don't need four 20-foot rows of cilantro or 50 horseradish plants or a 20 x 20–foot bed of fenugreek (which was one of the ingredients in Lydia Pinkham's famous cure-all tonic that was popular at the end of the 19th century). In fact, you may not need any of these herbs.

Grow only what you'll enjoy and use, and only as much as you'll use and have time to care for. A weedy, out-of-control garden is more depressing than no garden at all.

Seed Time

For us, each garden season includes the past and the future. We always purchase herbs we've grown before, herbs that we know we like and that will thrive in our gardens. 'Sweet Genovese' basil is an annual purchase, as is broad-leaf parsley. But we also try new things each year — a new cultivar, such as 'Red Rubin', a purple basil that recently came on the market, or an herb we haven't grown before.

No one has time or room to grow everything, so ask yourself the following questions in order to rein in your purchases:

✔ **Will I use it?** You can grow herbs for their own sake — with no thought of using them — but if you're the practical sort, be realistic about what herbs you'll use.

✔ **Will it grow in my garden?** Every herb has peculiar needs. Basil will be a bust if your garden is a large pot on a cool, shady patio; angelica won't survive in southern Florida's heat. Be sure to check our plant encyclopedia (Part IV) to see if you have the basic conditions necessary for the herbs you'd like to grow.

✔ **Is it too much trouble?** The majority of herbs are like good friends: cooperative, undemanding, tolerant, even forgiving. But all herbs require some care. Marsh mallow requires lots of moisture — do you have time for watering? Do you have time to start chive seeds in January so you'll have plants in June?

✔ **How much should I grow?** Seed packets usually indicate how many seeds they contain — probably 50 times more than you need. Six basils are not enough if want to freeze enough pesto to take you into spring, but six sage plants are probably more than the *hautest* gourmet cook can use.

TIP

Seed savvy

Mail-order seed catalogs are some of our favorite reading. They're also gold mines of gussied-up photographs and hyperbolic prose, designed to seduce even an experienced gardener. Every new cultivar is bigger or brighter or better, every seed guaranteed to grow faster and taller. For the record, every new cultivar isn't better, and every seed won't grow.

Having gotten that off our chests, we're still devoted mail-order shoppers. That's for two reasons. First, you must start with seeds in order to grow more than the run-of-the-mill herbs. And second, to find more than the run-of-the-mill herbs, you have to order them by mail. Seed racks at the supermarket or garden center contain only a few common herbs.

Once you start turning the catalog pages, though, you'll want one of everything. We recommend that you pretend you're Santa Claus. After you've made your list, check it twice. Maybe three times.

Be sure to start small. Beginning seeds indoors takes lots of room. If you don't plant enough, there's always next year (with some herbs, there's even time for a second crop this year). Dying, drying, and craft projects require a hefty number of plants, but culinary herbs usually can be grown in smaller numbers unless you're planning to supply all your neighbors or to preserve your harvest.

Seedy business

"I've got to get some seeds, right away." That's what Willy Loman says in *Death of a Salesman*, and that's how we feel every winter. Yes, *winter*. Starting from seed also means starting early, as many as 12 weeks before the last spring frost for perennials, four to eight weeks for biennials and hardy annuals.

Winter also is when the seed catalogs arrive (once you're on mailing lists). If you're starting plants from seed, start with a seed catalog. Most seed companies send one without charge (or will deduct the dollar-or-so cost from any order you place); some companies now post their catalogs on their Web sites.

A seed company with a broad range of wares, such as Shepherd's Garden Seeds, may be all you need for your first few orders. Before long, though, you may be looking for new forms of tri-colored sage or the 19th-century scented geranium you saw at Monticello. That's when specialist seed houses become indispensable. We list some of our favorites of each type in the Appendix.

All-Americans

A few herbs have been awarded the designation of All-America Selection (AAS), which indicates that they have been grown in more than 60 trial gardens located throughout the country and judged superior to other cultivars. The AAS program, which identifies outstanding plants for home gardens, began in 1932. Past herb winners include Thai basil 'Siam Queen', lemon basil 'Sweet Dani', lavender 'Lavender Lady', and a compact dill, 'Fernleaf'.

Nonprofit organizations are another great source of herb seeds. If you belong to the Flower and Herb Exchange, a laudable nonprofit group that works to preserve *heirloom,* or older, cultivars of flowers and herbs, you'll also have access to hundreds of herb seeds, many available nowhere else. Some regional garden organizations and local garden clubs sponsor annual seed exchanges, as do plant societies. See the Appendix for our list of horticultural organizations.

Conquering the catalogs

With all their purple prose, it's not entirely easy to read a seed catalog. And invariably, there are too many herb choices. Don't be intimidated by the wealth of information and possibilities, though. Think of seed catalogs as resources. If you need an explanation or more information, phone the company and ask. As a rule, seed sellers are generous with their time and advice.

Planting Indoors

All that most seeds need to *germinate,* or sprout, are oxygen, water, and heat. Sounds easy, and usually it is. Whether you sow seeds indoors or outdoors depends on what you're growing and where you live. Gardeners who live where the mercury falls well below freezing in winter — and especially those whose summers are short — start many herbs indoors. If your winters are mild and summer stretches on forever, you can *direct seed* many herbs — that is, sow them directly in the garden.

If you sow even part of your herb garden indoors, you will have *seedlings,* or young plants, to set outdoors when the soil and air warm up in spring. Starting your plants inside gives you a head start on the growing season: Instead of planting seeds on May 15 — or whenever your soil warms — you will be setting out young plants.

Sow annual herbs from four to eight weeks before your frost-free date. Most perennial herbs grow more slowly than annuals, so you may need to sow them as many as 12 weeks before the last frost. (You can also find planting recommendation on the back of seed packets.)

What you need and what to do

You don't need a greenhouse to begin your herb garden indoors, but you do need the following items:

Containers

You can sow seeds in almost any container *if* it has drainage holes in the bottom. Plastic seed trays, or *flats,* are inexpensive and reusable (see Figure 8-1.) If you use terra-cotta pots, choose shallow ones, commonly called *azalea pots. Cell trays* (or *plug trays*) have the advantage of keeping the roots from several plants from tangling because each seedling grows in its own space.

Want to use homegrown seed-sowing containers? Paper cups and yogurt and cottage cheese containers work fine. So do cardboard milk cartons and 1-gallon milk jugs (cut jugs off three inches from the bottom; staple the top of cartons and remove one side to form a rectangular container). With all of these, don't forget to make drainage holes.

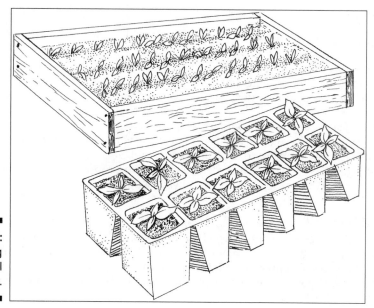

Figure 8-1:
Seedling flat and cell tray.

A few seed-container don'ts:

- ✔ **Don't pick huge, deep containers.** Seeds germinate better in shallow quarters — no more than 3 inches deep.

- ✔ **Don't be tempted to half-fill a deep container.** Seedlings need fresh air, and they won't get it if the sides of a container surround them.

- ✔ **Don't use a dirty container.** Especially if you're reusing a container, wash it with soap and water, dip in a 10 percent bleach solution, and rinse in clear water.

- ✔ **Don't sow different herbs in the same container.** Each herb has its own needs and timetable. Having all the lemongrass seedlings in one flat or pot makes care easier.

Planting medium

Don't use soil from your garden — it contains weed seeds and diseases. Instead, use a soil-free commercial mix, one made especially for starting seeds. Seeds don't need fertilizer to germinate, so commercial mixes usually are nutrient-free, as well as sterile, water-retentive, and light.

If you want to make your own soilless seed-starting mix, combine 1 quart each of peat and *vermiculite* (the exploded granules of mica) or *perlite* (the exploded granules of volcanic rock) and a scant tablespoon of ground limestone. All these ingredients are available at garden centers.

Heat

Seeds need even warmth (70°F–80°F) to sprout quickly. (Seeds can sprout at lower temperatures but do so more slowly.) If your house isn't that warm both day and night, put your containers on top of a radiator or refrigerator or on an *electric heating mat* (a hot pad for sprouting seeds, available from garden supply companies) to speed germination.

Seeds sown indoors sprout more quickly than those sown outdoors, so don't start too early. Seedlings that have been grown too long indoors, especially without enough light, tend to be spindly and weak. Be patient. Clean the garage, sharpen your garden tools, varnish the canoe paddles. Do anything! Beginning the garden too soon is always a mistake.

Special care

A few herb seeds need special handling before they can germinate. Those of some species, such as sweet Cicely, must be *stratified,* or chilled for a period of time. (See Chapter 11 for information about stratifying seeds.) If you've purchased your seeds, any special treatments have been done for you. All that's left is the sowing.

Sowing the seeds

Now you're ready to make the seeds meet the soil. Here's how:

1. **Wet the soilless seed-starting mix in a bucket.**

   The mix should be completely moist but not soppy wet. Moisten only as much as you can use at one time; in storage, damp mix attracts disease organisms.

2. **Fill your containers to the top and then tap the container on a solid surface to settle and even out the mix.**

   Don't compact the mix by pressing down on it. Leave about ½ inch of headroom in the pot.

3. **Sprinkle seeds on top of the mix.**

   Most herbs have a high *germ rate* (the percentage of seeds that sprout — the number appears on the seed packet), so sow sparingly. It doesn't take 50 seeds to get 15 plants. If you're using cell trays, three seeds per cell is plenty.

4. **Cover the seeds with vermiculite and firm gently.**

   The general rule is to cover seeds two or three times as deep as their diameter. Some herbs, including angelica, anise hyssop, chamomile, chervil, dill, echinacea, feverfew, lemon balm, savory, wormwood, and yarrow, prefer to have their seeds only partially covered. These seeds need some light to sprout: Lightly press them into the soilless mix with your finger and mist them with water.

5. **Label each container with the name of what you've sown and the date you sowed it.**

   You may think you'll remember what it is. You won't. For more advice on labeling, see the section titled, "Senior (and Junior) Moments" in this chapter.

6. **Mist the container and then cover it with plastic wrap to retain moisture.**

   Remove the wrap for a few hours every day to ensure good air circulation and to avoid a seedling disease known as damping-off.

7. **Set your containers in a warm location out of direct sunlight.**

   Watch the containers carefully so that they don't become too damp (remove the cover if they do) or dry out. Water carefully so that you don't disturb the seeds. Pour off any water that accumulates beneath the containers.

Don't panic when all your seeds don't sprout in three days or at the same time. Germination for each herb is different: Lavender seeds can take a month, while German chamomile seeds sprout in less than one week.

Germination, *not*...

So you planted according to our directions and nothing came up. First, go back and test your seeds to make sure they're *viable*, that they're capable of sprouting. Spread 10 seeds on half of a damp, white, nonscented paper towel, fold the towel over to cover the seeds, and place in an open plastic bag in a warm location (75°F). Keep the towels moist (not soppy wet) and keep your eye out for signs of sprouting. If only a couple of seeds germinate, or none at all do, you'll know the fault isn't yours.

If you used *viable* seeds and nothing came up, the most likely explanation is that you've over-watered and the seeds have rotted or that you haven't given the seeds enough moisture to trigger germination. Other possibilities:

- Soil is too cold or too warm
- Seeds were set too deep or soil wasn't firmed around seeds
- Soil is contaminated

Whatever the reason, start afresh by using clean, sterile containers, sterile soil, and seeds you know are viable. Don't despair. As Big Bird from *Sesame Street* says, "Everyone makes mistakes." We know we have.

Up and at 'em (What to do as the herbs grow)

When green sprouts shove their way through the soil's surface, you must be ready to give them the new conditions they require. A warning: If you can't provide seedlings with at least 14 hours of sun daily — or don't have artificial lights — you're better off buying plants at a local garden center or direct seeding.

The following sections show you what you need to set up an indoor nursery for your herb seedlings.

Good light

Young plants need light — bright light, and lots of it. Growing seedlings on a windowsill is possible, but windowsills usually get too hot during the day and too cold at night. Even a south-facing window rarely gets as much sun as your new plants need.

You'll be forever glad if you purchase two inexpensive items from the local hardware store: a fluorescent light fixture, one of the simple industrial types designed for illuminating a workbench, and a timer. Pick a fixture that holds at least two bulbs (use both "cool white" and "warm white" bulbs) and is suspended on chains. (A 4-foot model with two bulbs will light a 12 x 40–inch area.) Set the lights between 2 and 4 inches above the seedlings — raise them as your seedlings grow — and keep the bulbs running 16 hours a day.

Cooler temperature

Seedlings are young, tender, and vulnerable, but they don't need the heat that germination required. Seedlings prefer cooler conditions — temperatures ranging between 65° and 75°F and 5 degrees colder at night. Too much heat not only promotes spindly growth, it encourages bugs and diseases.

Good air circulation

Stagnant air invites pest and disease problems. Set your seedlings where they can get plenty of fresh, circulating air, but keep them out of strong drafts. A small fan set on low aimed near, but not at, the plants can do the trick.

Don't crowd seedlings. Give each plant enough room to grow without bumping into its neighbors. Doing so helps ensure good air circulation. If you have more seedlings than you want, thin your crop by snipping off the extra plants at the soil surface with a pair of scissors. (For the full skinny on thinning seedlings, see the section "Getting thin" in this chapter.)

Room to grow

Seedlings need room to grow below, as well as above, the soil surface. As soon as your plants start to develop their second set of *true leaves* — which look different from their original *seed leaves,* or *cotyledons* — they're ready to be moved to larger containers, one plant per container. Gardeners call this task *potting on,* or *potting up.*

Be sure to hold seedlings by the leaves, not the stems, and never pull them from the soil — seedling roots are small and easily damaged. Either prick seedlings out with the tip of a knife or turn the container upside down to dislodge the *root ball* (the roots and the soil that surrounds them). If the roots of several seedlings are hopelessly tangled, sacrifice a few plants by cutting them off rather than killing all the plants in an effort to pull them apart (allowing seedlings' soil to dry out slightly makes separating easier). Inspect each seedling before you move it to larger quarters. If it's pale or sickly, toss it.

When you pot, use containers that are only a little larger than the ones your seedlings were growing in. Fill each with either a moistened commercial potting soil or a moistened homemade mix that contains the basic nutrients that plants need for healthy growth. (For information about plant nutrients, see Chapter 7.) Make a planting hole in the soil and set each seedling *slightly* deeper that it was growing before — you can cover to just above the seed leaves. Firm the soil around the roots, and water. Set the containers away from bright light for 24 hours to let the seedlings recover from being transplanted, and then move them back into bright light.

Seedling soil

Seeds not only contain new plants, they contain all the food new plants need for the first week or two — but *only* a week or two. If you've sown seeds in a soil sterile mix without nutrients — which we recommend — you must feed your seedlings shortly after their first true leaves appear. You can also pot up by using a soil medium that contains nutrients. To make potting soil, combine 4 quarts of peat or compost, 4 quarts of vermiculite or perlite, and ¼ cup balanced organic fertilizer. (This recipe makes 2 gallons of mix.)

Water

Seedlings need water, but they're not fish. Check the soil daily. When the surface is dry to the touch, water gently, pouring off any water that accumulates in the drainage trays. Wilted leaves can signal too much moisture as well as too little, so always feel the soil before you water.

Seedling leaves like moisture just as their roots do: Mist your plants every two or three days to keep humidity high.

Food

Your seedlings may not need additional fertilizer before they go outside if you've potted up with a soil mix that contains plant nutrients. If the seedlings are growing in a sterile medium, however, you should feed them every 10 days with a diluted solution of equal parts of fish and seaweed emulsion (use 1 tablespoon of each per gallon of water); compost tea (see Chapter 7 for our recipe); or other balanced liquid organic fertilizer.

You may be tempted to overfertilize: A little is good, so a lot is better, right? *Wrong!* (Leaves that curl under are one signal that you've overfed, and rapid, spindly growth is another.) Telltale signs that seedlings do need feeding include pale leaves or leaves tinged with yellow, red, purple, or brown. Seedlings that have been growing indoors for more than six weeks are likely to need extra food, even if their potting mix contains nutrients.

What about store-bought herb plants?

Purchasing young herb plants is a great idea if you don't have the space, energy, or patience to start from seed. You also may not have the time to take care of seedlings. Perennial herbs, such as monarda and scented geranium, take a year or more before they're good-sized, so many gardeners purchase plants rather than grow them from seed.

Before you cash out at the nursery, though, make sure that you haven't chosen:

- ✔ **Plants that have yellowed or wilted leaves.** Both signal that bad things have happened to a good plant.

- ✔ **Plants that are tall and spindly.** You're not picking players for an NBA franchise. Tall and spindly means a plant has received too little light and/or has been growing too long in a too-small container.

- ✔ **Plants that have lots of roots coming out the bottom of the container.** This condition means the plant is *pot-bound* — it's been in cramped quarters longer than was good for it — and it's unlikely to flourish, even after you plant it in your garden.

- ✔ **Plants that show signs of insects or diseases.** Look for bugs (especially on the undersides of leaves), leaves that are sticky or appear to have been munched on, leaves with black or white spots, or weird blotches or marks. All are warnings that you're not only buying an unhealthy plant, you're carrying problems back to your garden.

- ✔ **Plants that are already in flower.** Today, almost everything at the garden center is in flower, but if you have a choice, pick plants that haven't bloomed yet. These plants will adjust better to transplanting. If you can bear to do it, remove any blossoms before you set out your plants — removing flowers encourages root and leaf growth, giving you larger, more vigorous plants.

Youth Movement: Moving Indoor Herbs Outdoors

Seedlings — whether you've grown them yourself or bought them — must be *hardened off,* or acclimated, before they go into your garden. Transplanting young plants too suddenly from their cozy indoor quarters to the outdoors can halt their growth for weeks.

Begin hardening off your plants a week or two prior to transplanting. To harden off, set the plants outdoors in a sheltered location, one where they're protected from direct sun and strong winds. A *cold frame* is ideal for hardening off plants. The cold frame is a bottomless box made of standard 2-inch pine lumber — typically about 4 feet wide and 8 feet long, 12 to 18 inches high in the back, 8 to 12 inches high in front — with a hinged glass or clear plastic *light,* or lid.

You can build your own (cold frames are a classic way to recycle old windows) or purchase a high-tech model from a mail-order supplier, such as Gardener's Supply Co. If you use a cold frame, don't forget to raise the lid on sunny days to ensure that your herbs don't get cooked.

If you don't have a cold frame, harden off your plants by putting them in a protected outdoor location. Begin by leaving them out for only for a few hours (be sure to bring them inside if temperatures drop suddenly). Gradually move them into the sun, increasing their time outside to 24 hours daily.

When to move young plants outdoors depends on your climate — and the herb. Don't be in a rush with plants such as basil, which are frost-tender; hardy annuals and perennials, such as caraway and yarrow, can withstand colder temperatures and go out sooner. If you're unsure about frost-free dates in your garden, ask other gardeners for advice.

Transplanting is hard on young plants, even those you've hardened off. To make their change of address easier,

- **Soak your herbs' soil in a weak, balanced, organic fertilizer** a few hours before transplanting.

- **Transplant on a cool, overcast day;** if the sun always shines in your garden, transplant in late afternoon.

- **Untangle and spread out the roots** as best you can if your plant is *root-bound* — its roots have entirely filled its container. Otherwise, transplant the entire root ball, disturbing the roots as little as possible.

- **Cut a few slits in the sides of a biodegradable pot** (if that's what you've used) before you place it in the planting hole. A *biodegradable* pot — one made of peat, newspaper, or another material — decays in the soil. Be sure to bury the entire pot; otherwise, the exposed material acts as a wick and draws moisture away from the roots.

- **Make the planting hole only a bit wider than the container the plant was growing in,** and set the plant just slightly deeper than it was previously growing. Firm the soil and water gently.

- **Use compost or other organic matter to mulch your transplants.** Mulch suppresses weeds, helps retain moisture in the soil, and keeps it cool. (In very cold regions, wait until the soil warms fully before you mulch.)

- **Protect your transplants from sun and wind** during their first few days in the garden by covering them with *floating row covers.* Or use pieces of cardboard or wood shingles to shade them. Mist plants with cool water if they wilt.

  Floating row covers, which are made from spun plastic, can be used to protect young plants against cold.

- **Label the transplanted plants.**

Planting Herbs Outdoors

There are many good reasons to *direct seed* (sowing seed directly into your garden) outdoors. Seedlings with a *taproot* (a long single root with little side growth), such as borage and fennel, resent transplanting. You can start these herbs indoors, but grow them in individual containers so you don't have to disturb their roots.

Direct seeding (or direct sowing) also makes sense if you want to grow a huge quantity of herbs — few of us have space indoors for 200 calendula seedlings. In fact, many herbs simply don't need a head start. Sow most hardy annuals outdoors in spring, and they'll mature in plenty of time to provide you with a bountiful harvest.

Direct sowing is also a lot less work *if* you heed two warnings:

✔ Don't sow seeds too early.

✔ Don't sow seeds too deep.

Ignore our warnings and you'll be replanting. Most seeds rot if buried in cold, wet soil. Be patient. Wait until the soil warms up (70°F for most herbs); soil thermometers are available from garden-supply companies. Also, don't bury your seeds so deeply that the sprouts can't make their way to the soil surface. The general rule for planting depth is to cover seeds two or three times their diameter — a little deeper if your soil is sandy and dries out quickly.

Into the ground

The *seedbed,* the place where you're going to sow your seeds, must be cleared of weeds and debris. (See Chapter 7 for details about preparing soil for planting.) After you rake the bed smooth, then sow your seeds, either in rows (use stakes and string to keep the rows straight) or by *broadcasting* (spreading the seeds over the bed rather than in rows).

Space seeds as evenly apart as you can, but sow more densely than you would if you were indoors planting in a container. (The percentage of seeds that sprout will be lower outdoors, where you can't always provide ideal conditions.) Use a hoe or rake to cover the seeds; then tamp, or press down, the soil; water gently. Label.

ECO-SMART

For peat's sake

Adding peat is a recommendation you find everywhere — books, magazines, newspaper columns, garden-center employees, and from us. It is a good way to add organic matter to your soil, but for all *practical* purposes it is a finite resource. The peat you buy is sphagnum moss and other plants that have been decaying in bogs for millennia.

Most scientists believe that peat bogs, once harvested, can be reclaimed but cannot be regenerated. Bogs that have been drained are unlikely to recover, to reestablish the conditions that produce peat. Even if they can recover, the time frame is 3,000 years and longer. As one scientist told us, "Harvesting peat is an euphemism for mining." Two *renewable* alternatives to peat are cocoa hulls and shredded coconut husks, products that are increasingly available at garden centers.

If you use peat, apply it sparingly as an additive to soil mixes or to amend planting holes when setting out individual herbs. Be aware that peat contains no nutrients and is devilishly difficult to

wet. Spreading it on the soil surface is almost like laying down a layer of plastic: Water runs off rather than sinks in.

Buying peat can be confusing; you can choose from several products for sale:

✔ **Black peat**, or peat humus (*terre noire* if it comes from Canada), looks like rich topsoil and is often sold in bulk. **Sedge peat,** like black peat, comes from sedge plants, but is less decomposed and reddish brown in color.

✔ **Sphagnum moss**, or floral moss, consists of moss plants harvested from the tops of peat bogs; it's sold in small, packaged quantities for lining hanging baskets and other decorative purposes.

✔ **Peat** — also known as sphagnum peat, brown peat, and peat moss — is the most common garden additive. Made of dried, partially decomposed sphagnum mosses, it is very acidic and can absorb 15 times its weight in water.

Getting thin

Keep soil moist to encourage germination. As soon as your seedlings are an inch or two tall and have developed at least one set of true leaves, you need to thin out the plants. You can either pinch or cut out the extra seedlings or lift them carefully — don't disturb the roots of the neighboring plants — and transplant them to another location.

HEADS UP

Thinning is a painful job, like discarding all those perfectly good items that you stored in the attic 20 years ago. Thinning seems wasteful, but it isn't. Plants grown too close together rarely reach normal size, and crowding causes poor air circulation, which makes plants more susceptible to bugs and diseases. When they're growing too near their neighbors, more plants will give you less. You may want to thin in a couple of stages, but don't wait too long to thin, and don't lose your nerve. Rip 'em out!

Senior (and Junior) Moments

Unless your memory is a lot better than ours — not filled with "senior moments" — you need plant labels to remind you what you've planted and where you planted it.

Even if you plant only basil, knowing it's basil isn't enough. Not all basils are alike. You'll want to awe your friends with your herbal prowess and tell them your basil is 'Mrs. Burns' or 'Red Rubin' or 'Fino Verde'. More important, if lemon basil isn't your cup of tea, you don't want to plant 'Mrs. Burns' again next year.

While you're at it, include the scientific name on each label. It will help you remember that French thyme is *Thymus vulgaris*. Knowing scientific names isn't required, but the more you know about plants, the more fun gardening becomes. Gardeners are a friendly bunch — even the rank beginner is welcome — but being able to spit out horticulture Latin will give you a certain cachet. It's like knowing the secret handshake or the *mot de passé*. (See Chapter 1 for an explanation of scientific names.)

Don't delay labeling, and make sure your labels are permanent enough to survive the garden season (use an indelible pen). Plastic isn't pretty, but plastic labels are inexpensive, and they last. A seed packet stuck on top of a stake is picturesque, but it doesn't last.

Dear Diary

In addition to knowing exactly what we're growing, we like to record when we planted it, how we grew it, and how successful we were — or weren't. A garden diary can hold all that information and more.

In addition to names and dates, you may want to note that catnip took 11 days to germinate or that the chervil growing in partial shade did a lot better than the plants you set in full sun. Or that using garlic chives to edge your perennial border was a mistake. Or that cilantro tastes like soap and you never want to grow it again. Or that lemongrass did a lot better in a pot on the patio than it did in the garden. Or that monarda, appropriately named bee balm, attracts so many bees that you want to move it away from the picnic table.

Record anything that seems important — or strikes your fancy. Most gardeners like to include weather information, especially frost dates and rainfall amounts, and make notes on what's blooming in the wild. Jot down yields so you'll know that six dill plants weren't enough and six rosemary plants were too many.

A garden diary can be a superb source of information for next year. It helps you repeat your successes and avoid repeating your failures. You don't have to write every day, but you'll be glad if you do.

Chapter 9

From Plagues and Pestilence, Deliver Us

* *

In This Chapter

▶ Preventing insect and disease problems

▶ Identifying problems

▶ Finding safe solutions

* *

Several ounces of prevention. That's the *best* defense against the "foul and pestilent congregation" of plant problems, to use Hamlet's phrase. Shakespeare's Prince of Denmark, who was in one of his usual low moments, was describing the Earth — not the flock of Japanese beetles that is devouring the frilly leaves of your 'Green Ruffles' basil, the damping-off that toppled the nasturtium seedlings, or even the witch grass that is overwhelming your sweet Cicely.

Several ounces of prevention is also the *safest* defense — for you and for your surroundings and its wild inhabitants. The American landscape is already up to its knees in toxins — chemicals blended to combat weeds, diseases, and pests large and small. Don't add to the problem by bombing bugs and drenching diseases with more poisons.

You may take on some small battles for control with these and other foes, but don't engage in any all-out wars. Total extermination is not your goal. In fact, killing everything except the herbs you want to grow makes it unlikely you'll be able to grow healthy herbs. Or anything else!

So don't reach for a remedy that is worse than the problem. Strive for an acceptable truce with all the things that may plague your plants, outdoors or in. *You* have to accept a few imperfections — an occasional hole in a leaf, a nibbled flower, even a dead plant or two — and *they* have to leave you plenty of herbs to use and enjoy. Tell yourself that little things don't mean a lot.

Before you anticipate the horticultural version of Murphy's Law kicking in, remind yourself that herbs are among the garden plants *least* bothered by diseases and pests. With help from you, they'll grow vigorously, untroubled by plagues or pestilence.

Avoidance Therapy

One invasion of mealybugs or one bout with crown rot is all it takes to realize that avoiding problems in the herb garden is easier than trying to cure them. Everything you do to make your plants strong and healthy increases their resistance to pests and diseases. Good gardening practices prevent troubles.

Gardeners call these preventive practices *cultural controls*. Some things that you do, such as using a sterile mix to start seeds, have an immediate effect: no damping-off. Others practices — improving your soil, for example — take time to pay off.

All of the following cultural controls should be part of your garden routine:

- ✔ **Keep your soil healthy.** We sing our anthem to the value of organically rich soil in Chapter 4.

- ✔ **Mulch plants.** Mulch (see Chapter 10 for different types of mulch) protects plants from soil-borne diseases by keeping water from splashing from the ground onto stems and leaves. Mulch also suppresses weeds.

- ✔ **Give plants what they want.** Planting basil in shade is asking for sickly, diseased plants. Be sure you give each herb the conditions it needs to succeed — the right amounts of sun, space, food, and water.

- ✔ **Know when the time is right.** Sowing seeds or transplanting seedlings at the wrong time — either too early or too late — stresses plants, making them more susceptible to pests, diseases, and weeds.

- ✔ **Move plants around.** Rather than planting parsley or any other annual herb in the same place every year, move it to a different spot. Changing the location of plants reduces pest and disease problems.

- ✔ **Choose resistant cultivars.** Herb breeders haven't spent much time developing disease- or pest-resistant cultivars, but if you grow herbs among other plants, look for vegetable and flower cultivars that have built-in protection. It doesn't make sense to spread powdery mildew from your cucumbers to the bee balm and germander when you can sow cucumbers that are resistant to powdery mildew.

- ✔ **Practice diversity.** Planting a large bed of nothing but lavender — or any one herb — makes it an easy target for marauding insects or incipient diseases. When possible, mix herbs with each other or with vegetables and flowers.

✔ **Practice restraint.** If a particular disease or pest is overwhelming your herbs, consider leaving the plants that attract it out of your garden for a year or two — at the least, move them to a new location.

✔ **Make friends with natural predators.** Insects, spiders, toads, and birds are among your allies in controlling pest problems. You can encourage beneficials to linger in your yard and garden by providing them food, water, and shelter. Details come later in this chapter.

✔ **Keep foliage dry.** You can't stop the rain, but if you water plants, don't wet their leaves (many diseases are spread by water splashing from the soil to the leaves); instead, water herbs at their roots. Similarly, *you'll* be the Typhoid Mary if you work among wet plants. Stay out of the garden until foliage is dry.

✔ **Take it easy!** You don't have to baby herbs, but be careful. Bruised and torn leaves, snapped stems, damaged roots, anything that stresses plants leaves them more open to diseases and pests.

✔ **Don't make things worse.** Be sure that *you* don't bring problems into the garden. Inspect new herbs and other plants for signs of disease and insects before you add them to your beds and borders.

✔ **Be a good housekeeper.** Diseases and pests lurk in weeds and plant refuse. Keep your garden weeded and cleaned up. Remove and destroy plants that are diseased or severely plagued with pests. Remove plant residue at the end of the garden season.

✔ **Keep your eyes open.** Catching a problem early can keep it manageable. Inspect your herbs regularly, especially leaf undersides.

ECO-SMART

Organic pest management

Many Americans have adopted the *integrated pest management (IPM)* approach to garden and landscape management. While we're great fans of IPM, we're even more keen about OPM, which stands for *organic pest management*. Both have the same goal — to maintain a diverse and safe garden ecosystem — but OPM does it without using synthetic chemical products.

Take an organic approach to gardening with these guidelines:

1. **Monitor the garden.** Watch carefully for changes or problems.

2. **Identify the problem.** Determine what's causing the trouble and learn how best to deal with it.

3. **Set tolerance levels.** Decide what sort of damage to your garden you will accept.

4. **Start with the safest controls.** Use cultural controls, physical controls, and biological controls, in that order; turn to organically certified pesticides as a last resort.

Let's Get Physical

We know, we know: You've followed our advice for growing herbs — you've implemented all the cultural controls — and you're still worried that the tarragon will develop root rot and that slugs will dine on the violets. So now what?

Now you try *physical controls,* the least-invasive method for avoiding garden problems (and sometimes dealing with existing problems). Physical controls are the garden equivalents of a chain link fence to keep the neighbor's Jack Russell terrier from doing his business on your patio. Like chain link fences, physical controls are infinitely practical but not necessarily pretty.

Disappearing act

A straightforward approach to solving garden problems is to remove the problem. It's not always 100 percent effective, but sometimes you can help your plants by simple subtraction.

- ✔ Remove weeds, which harbor insects and diseases (and steal water and nutrients from your herbs).
- ✔ Remove any plant or plant part that looks diseased or infested.
- ✔ Dislodge pests with a blast of water from the hose.
- ✔ Remove any pests large enough to grab by hand. If you're squeamish, wear gloves and drop the pests in a jar of soapy water; if you're not, squish them with glee.

Beneficial barriers

Barriers stop diseases and pests from reaching plants. The trick is to erect them *before* you discover your lemongrass is under attack. It's exactly like shutting the barn door after the cow has escaped: There's no sense putting a paper collar around an herb after the cutworm has felled it.

Floating row covers

Floating row covers are one of the great garden inventions of the last quarter century. Made from spun plastic, row covers were intended to protect plants from cold, but savvy gardeners discovered that while they were keeping the basil from freezing, they were also keeping the Japanese beetles and other flying pests at bay. Row covers are so light, you can lay them directly over seedbeds, seedlings, and plants. Remove the covers, which are available in different lengths and widths, when the threat is gone.

Plant collars and shields

Plant collars and *shields* are old-time, proven barriers (a collar goes around a plant stem to protect against cutworms; a shield covers the ground around a plant to prevent root maggots and others from laying their eggs at the base of plants). Fashion collars from paper-towel and toilet-paper tubes or cardboard; the collar should be about 5 inches tall, with 2 inches buried in the soil. You can use a 6-inch square of heavy black plastic or tar paper to make a shield. Punch a hole in the center large enough for the stem and cut a slit to one edge to slide it around your plant.

You also can cover small plants with plastic milk jugs (cut out the bottom and remove the cap) to protect them from pests. The jugs also serve as mini-greenhouses, giving tender young herbs protection against the cold; don't forget that they can heat up during the day and may need to be removed, or your herbs will be cooked.

Traps

Traps are an alternative to mashing bugs by hand or under foot. Before you empty a trap, take a look at the contents to be sure you're catching what you're after. Don't measure success by the number of victims — instead, measure it by reduced damage to your herbs. Among the arsenal of traps are

- ✔ **Pheromone traps.** *Pheromones* are chemicals secreted by females to attract males. Use these traps cautiously: Most research shows that unless all your neighbors also set out traps, you're likely to attract more pests than you capture. If you use them, locate them *well away* from the plants you want to protect.

- ✔ **Sticky traps.** The outdoor version of fly paper, you can buy sticky traps at garden centers and by mail, or you can make your own by painting a foot-square piece of hard plastic or plywood yellow and then coating it with Tanglefoot or another commercial product. Nail the square to a stake and set it in your garden; clean and recoat as necessary.

- ✔ **Food and plant traps.** Some pests are attracted by specific foods (slugs and snails to beer, for example). You also can grow trap plants to lure pests away from your herbs (a hollyhock may divert Japanese beetles from your basil). Once the trap plant is infested, either handpick the pest or remove and destroy the trap plant. (See our recommendations for trap plants in the section titled "Bad bug!" in this chapter.)

- ✔ **Shade traps.** Slugs and snails are shade lovers. To lure them, lay boards or shingles on the soil, checking under them each morning (destroy your catch by dropping it into a can of soapy water).

Repellents

Repellents are physical controls, although most are less visible than collars or sticky traps. Garden suppliers sell organic products to ward off pests and diseases, or you can mix your own. You must reapply repellents after a rainfall.

Take 1 cup of slugs . . .

A famous homemade repellent is bug juice — a form of fighting fire with fire — which requires collecting 1 cup of insect pests and adding them to 3 cups water. Puree, strain, and dilute to ¼ cup insect juice to 1 gallon water. If you're up to pureeing Japanese beetles and slugs in your blender, give it a try. Look at the bright side: If this recipe doesn't work, at least you've killed a cup of predators.

Keep the following tips in mind:

✔ Many repellents use hot peppers to discourage pests. (The heat comes from flavorless chemical compounds in the peppers and is measured in Scoville Heat Units: zero for a sweet bell pepper and up to 200,000 for a mouth-scorching habañero.) Warning: Keep your hands away from your face when you're working with hot peppers!

A standard hot pepper spray consists of 1 cup of pureed hot peppers (be sure to include the seeds and membrane — that's where the fire burns) and 4 cups water. Strain the mixture, add 1 teaspoon dishwashing liquid, and mix.

✔ Wood ashes discourage stem-attacking pests, such as root maggots. Spread them around *but not on* herb plants. Because wood ashes are alkaline and will raise your soil's pH (see Chapter 4 for more information about pH), apply them sparingly.

✔ To help repel fungal diseases, such as powdery mildew and black spot, try a baking-soda repellent: 1 tablespoon baking soda, 1 tablespoon horticultural oil, 1 gallon water. Mix and spray plants thoroughly.

✔ Evidence shows that commercial *antidesiccants,* or *antitranspirants* — products developed for helping plants retain moisture — also protect against a variety of plant diseases, including rust and powdery mildew. Follow label directions.

✔ Spraying herbs with compost tea (see Chapter 7 for brewing instructions) helps repel fungus diseases at the same time it provides nourishment.

Good Fellows

Biological controls are living organisms; using biological controls is based on the theory that every pest has a mortal enemy. It's a relatively new field of long-term pest control. The controls themselves, however, have been around forever — and many of them are already sharing your zip code.

Good bugs, or beneficial insects (even though some aren't technically bugs or insects), greatly outnumber bad bugs. Beneficials not only pollinate flowers (remember the birds-and-the-bees talk with your mother?), they seek and destroy many plant pests. And they make the supreme sacrifice, giving themselves up as dinner for bats, toads, birds, and other FOTG (Friends of the Garden).

Following is a short list, a beneficial top ten. These are flyers, creepers, and crawlers that you want to keep around. Most are native to the United States, so all you may have to do is make them feel welcome:

- ✔ **Aphid midges.** It's the midge larvae — tiny orange maggots — that commit "aphidcide."

- ✔ **Arachnids (spiders and mites).** Predatory mites prey on less-desirable relatives (spider mites and rust mites), thrips, and other pests; spiders lunch on anyone they can catch.

- ✔ **Beetles (lady beetles, rove beetles, ground beetles, and friends).** There's an army of pest-control beetles that feed on aphids, cutworms, mealybugs, root maggots, snail and slug eggs, spider mites, and more.

- ✔ **Beneficial nematodes.** These tiny worms parasitize soil-dwelling villains, such as cutworms and grubs.

- ✔ **Dragonflies.** You need water to attract these flyers, one of the garden's most beautiful do-gooders. (It turns out that praying mantids, possibly the garden's most interesting do-gooders, don't really do all that much good: Not only do they eat each other, they're as likely to eat beneficials as they are to eat pests.)

- ✔ **Flies.** These are good flies, not the household type, whose larvae scavenge aphids, cutworms, caterpillars, and other pests.

- ✔ **Lacewings.** Lacewings give twice: They feed on aphids, mites, thrips, and other soft insects and insect eggs as larvae, and then they eat again, as adults. Like humans, they're much hungrier in their youth.

- ✔ **Parasitic wasps.** Insects that lay their eggs inside other bugs, parasitic wasps control aphids, whiteflies, and some caterpillars.

- ✔ **True bugs.** Believe it or not, "true bugs" is the scientific name for a group of insects, which includes predatory members that attack aphids, beetle larvae, caterpillars, and thrips.

- ✔ **Yellow jackets.** If yellow jackets nest far enough away not to sting you, leave them alone to gather caterpillars, flies, and assorted larvae for their offspring.

Bugs for sale

Beneficial-insect companies won't ask you questions, but you should question them. Before you buy, be sure you know what it is you want to control and what the best bug is for controlling it. Know, too, when to release beneficials and what you need to do to keep them in your garden. One warning: Lady beetles, which are collected in the wild, are effective in greenhouses but rarely stay in the garden long enough to do much good. See the Appendix for suppliers of beneficials.

In addition to these small pest-control champs, some larger animals are worth having on garden patrol. We don't suggest you import these helpers — they may be inappropriate for your location or sensibilities — but don't discount the good they can do.

- ✔ **Bats.** Forget all the scare stories about rabies — scientists say the danger is remote — and remember that bats are champion insect-eaters. Maybe not the 500,000 bugs a night as some bat fans claim, but more bugs than we'd want to count.

- ✔ **Birds.** There are so many reasons to want birds in your yard that you'll forgive them a few transgressions, such as eating the cherries and blueberries. Keep in mind that they're also eating beetles, grubs, caterpillars, leafhoppers, and more. One estimate is that aphid eggs make up half a chickadee's winter diet. That's *our* little chickadee!

- ✔ **Skunks.** What's black and white and loves grubs? You guessed it, although we do admit that skunks are debatable as garden ornaments, especially if you own a dog. Moles are also great grub grubbers if you can put up with the lawn damage they cause; voles, which are vegetarians, are garden villains.

- ✔ **Snakes.** We're sympathetic if you draw the line at encouraging snakes to dwell in your herb garden. Just remember that they're after rodents and insects, not you.

- ✔ **Toads.** You didn't have to read *The Wind in the Willows* as a kid to love toads. They eat an almost exclusive diet of grubs, slugs, beetles, and other harmful insects, and no, they don't cause warts. To build your own Toad Hall, chip a doorway on the side of a terra-cotta pot and leave it, turned upside down, in a shady spot in your garden.

How to keep 'em down on the farm

Increase your garden bounty by encouraging beneficials to stay around, to be fruitful, and to multiply. Here are our suggestions for turning your property into a five-star hotel:

✔ Use as few toxic controls as possible. Using none is best.

✔ Do not install an electric bug zapper — data now show they kill far more beneficials than mosquitoes.

✔ Keep your soil rich in organic matter.

✔ Provide beneficials with food, water, and shelter.

✔ Practice diversity by growing many different herbs and other plants in your garden, rather than just one or two species.

✔ Grow plants that attract and feed beneficials. Good host plants include angelica, anise, aster *(Aster* spp.) and other daisylike flowers, baby blue-eyes *(Nemophila menziesii)*, butterfly bush *(Buddleia davidii)*, calendula, candytuft *(Iberis sempervirens)*, coriander, dill, evening primrose *(Oenothera* spp.), fennel, goldenrod *(Solidago* spp.), morning glory *(Ipomoea* spp.), Queen Anne's lace *(Daucus carota)*, sunflower, yarrow, and zinnia *(Zinnia elegans)*.

The Usual Suspects

See some holes in the marsh mallow's leaves? Did your cilantro seedlings keel over just five days after they sprouted? Before you can remedy the problem, you need to know what's causing it.

You could be facing a slew of possible causes. If you can't figure out what's after your borage or elecampane, contact the experts at your local extension service or Master Gardener program. (Look under the state or county government listings of the phone book.) Before you start mailing off leaves marked with red spots and jagged holes, take a look at our short list of bugs and plant illnesses. These adversaries are the ones you're most likely to find in the herb garden.

Bad bug!

You can find these herb pests indoors and out. Some, such as spider mite, mealybug, scale, and whitefly, are most troublesome inside. Borers, beetles, caterpillars, leaf miner, slugs, and snails are pretty much outdoor problems, while aphids and nematodes visit both house and garden.

Many of the bad bugs mentioned in the following sections are shown in Figure 9-1.

Aphids

Tiny black, green, or pink insects the size of a pinhead, *aphids* cluster on the undersides of leaves, especially angelica, basil, caraway, chervil, chive, lovage, nasturtium, oregano, scented geranium, and southernwood. In addition to damaging leaves, they carry diseases that distort and yellow foliage.

Prevention and control: Cover herbs in spring with floating row covers; encourage or release lacewings, ladybugs, aphid midges. Plant nasturtium as a trap. To control, spray plants with a strong stream of water. Spray with an insecticidal soap every two days until aphids are under control.

Beetles

All sorts of *beetles* (insects with wings and wing covers that meet in the middle of their back) may feed on herbs. Most range between ¼ and ½ inch long. Metallic-green *Japanese beetles* are especially fond of basil, echinacea, elecampane, and sorrel. Look for foliage that have holes or have been skeletonized. *Mint flea beetles* (very small dark beetles that leap when disturbed) feed on mints. Flea beetles attack horseradish.

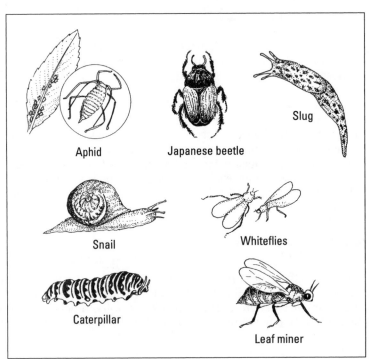

Aphid Japanese beetle Slug

Snail Whiteflies

Caterpillar Leaf miner

Figure 9-1:
Bad bugs!

Prevention and control: Cover herbs in spring with floating row covers. Weed and cultivate regularly. Plant traps include borage, grape, hollyhock, and white zinnia for Japanese beetles; flea beetles flock to Chinese cabbage and radish. To control, handpick. Apply milky spore to control beetle grubs. For crop-threatening infestations, apply pyrethrum or sabadilla.

Caterpillars and borers

The color and size of these critters vary, but you'll recognize a *caterpillar.* *Parsleyworms* (a 2-inch-long green character) and *hornworms* prefer chomping on parsley, dill, and all members of the carrot family; cabbage loopers are also fond of parsley. *Cutworms* are gray caterpillars that live in the soil, emerging in spring to feed on tender shoots of emerging plants.

Prevention and control: Surround new plants with paper collars to discourage cutworms. Carrot and Queen Anne's lace are good food plants for attracting caterpillars. To control most caterpillars, handpick.

Every caterpillar is a butterfly-in-waiting. Parsleyworms become swallowtail butterflies, so you should move rather than destroy them.

Leaf miners

Leaf miners are tiny black flies that lay their eggs on plant leaves. The maggots burrow into the foliage, leaving irregular white markings on leaf surfaces, especially on angelica, lovage, madder, oregano, and sorrel.

Prevention and control: Cover herbs in spring with floating row covers. Keep the garden weed-free. Attract parasitic wasps and other beneficials. Grow radish or beet as a trap plant. Spray with neem in spring, before adult flies lay their eggs. To control, remove and destroy infected leaves.

Mealybugs

Mealybugs are tiny, sucking insects that band together to form colonies that look like bits of cotton, usually on leaf undersides. Indoors, almost any plant is a target, but mealybugs are especially partial to rosemary.

Prevention and control: Apply horticultural oils. To control, spray plants with a strong stream of water. Dab the insect clusters with rubbing alcohol; treat with insecticidal soap or neem.

Mites

You need a 10-power hand lens to see *spider mites,* microscopic web-spinning arachnids that show up as red dots. They suck on plant leaves, especially those of angelica, germander, lavender, lemon verbena, mint, oregano, rosemary, sage, savory, and thyme. Watch for their telltale webs.

Prevention and control: Spray plants frequently with cold water. Encourage lacewings, ladybugs, and predatory mites. To control, apply an insecticidal soap or a horticultural oil.

Nematodes

Also known as *ellworms, nematodes* are soil-dwelling microscopic worms that feed on plant tissue. The root-knot nematode occasionally troubles lavender, parsley, and rosemary. (Look for stunted growth, yellow, or wilted foliage.)

Prevention and control: Practice crop rotation and amend soil with organic matter. Plant castor bean as a trap plant. To control, solarize soil.

Scale

Sucking insects fond of bay and rosemary leaves and stems, *scale* appear as brown oval bumps and are horribly difficult to get rid of. Sticky sap residue is another sign your herbs are infected with scale.

Prevention and control: Spray plants with a horticultural oil in spring and summer. Wash leaves and stems with insecticidal soap. To control, dab with rubbing alcohol. Remove and destroy infected leaves.

Slugs and snails

You'll recognize a *snail*; a *slug* is a snail without its shell, a 1- or 2-inch slimy gray-brown mollusk. Both creatures are nocturnal, so you must stay up late to handpick. Slugs and snails are fond of basil, calendula, sorrel, and violets.

Prevention and control: Encourage predatory beetles. Keep garden free of plant debris; reduce mulching. Apply diatomaceous earth around herb plants. Grow hosta as a trap plant. To control, handpick. Leave out shallow trap containers of beer or lay boards in the garden.

Whiteflies

Primarily an indoor problem, especially in greenhouses, *whiteflies* cluster on leaf undersides, where they also lay their yellow eggs. They're hard to miss — bump a leaf and they fly off *en masse*. Favorite leaves are those of lemon verbena, mint, rosemary, and sage.

Prevention and control: Use yellow sticky traps. Encourage lacewings and ladybugs. Grow flowering tobacco *(Nicotiana* spp.) as a trap plant. To control, spray herbs with insecticidal soaps or pyrethrum. Apply horticultural oils.

In sickness and in sickness

Plant diseases are sometimes tough to identify — a 10-power hand lens is indispensable for seeing signs of diseases, as well as the small pests that can spread them — and the list of *possible* herb ailments is substantial. Most can be avoided by following the "avoidance therapy" suggestions at the start of this chapter. Don't let this litany of common diseases put you off — with any luck, plenty of sunshine, and organically rich soil, your herbs won't even develop the sniffles.

Bacterial wilt

Bacterial wilts cause leaves, then entire plants to droop and die, especially coriander, nasturtium, sage, and scented geranium.

Prevention and control: Practice crop rotation to control cucumber beetles, which spread the disease; cover plants with floating row covers in spring. There is no safe control. Remove and destroy infected herbs.

Crown rot

A *fungus* that attacks the base of plants, *crown rot* turns plants yellow, followed by wilting. Angelica, parsley, and violet are likely victims.

Prevention and control: Practice crop rotation. There is no safe control. Dig and destroy infected herbs.

Damping-off

Diagnosing this fungal disease is easy. Healthy seedlings — practically all herbs are susceptible, especially those sown indoors — suddenly fall over and die.

Prevention and control: Use sterile soil and containers; don't overwater; give seedlings bright light; dust the soil surface with milled sphagnum moss; spray emerging seedlings with chamomile tea (steep 1 cup dried chamomile flowers in 1 quart water). There is no control. Discard the soil, sterilize the containers, and start over.

Downy mildew

Most common when conditions are cool and humid, *downy mildew* is a particular foe of calendula, coriander, germander, tarragon, and violet. The fungi leave yellow spots on leaf tops, gray mold on their undersides.

Prevention and control: Space plants far enough apart to have good air circulation; do not work among plants when foliage is wet; practice crop rotation. To control, use Bordeaux mixture to stop the fungus from spreading; remove and destroy infected plants.

Powdery mildew

Another fungal disease, *powdery mildew* prefers warm, humid weather and is partial to agrimony, calendula, coriander, germander, lemon balm, monarda, sunflower, tarragon, and yarrow. You'll know it by the white, powdery splotches it leaves on plant foliage.

Prevention and control: Give plants plenty of elbow room; clean up plant debris when the garden season is over. To control, remove and destroy infected leaves and plants.

Root rot

Root rot occurs underground, but yellowing and slow growth are symptoms that your herb is infected with this fungal disease. Clary, fenugreek, lavender, mullein, myrtle, oregano, rosemary, sage, tarragon, thyme, and winter savory are most likely to be struck down.

Prevention and control: Aerate your soil by adding organic material, such as compost; wait until the soil has warmed before planting in spring; practice crop rotation; clean up plant refuse when the garden season has ended. There is no safe control. Remove and destroy infected plants.

Rusts

There are many *rust* diseases, all spread by wind-borne fungi that leave reddish brown marks on leaves. Affected plants, such as germander, mint, monarda, sunflower, and yarrow, often drop their leaves.

Prevention and control: Space herbs so they have good air circulation; remove plant residue at the end of the garden season. To control, dust herbs with sulfur; remove and destroy infected plants.

Verticillium wilt

A fungal disease common throughout North America, *verticillium wilt* causes foliage to yellow and die; eventually it kills the plant. Coriander, mint, nasturtium, and sage are common victims.

Prevention and control: To prevent, enrich soil with organic matter; do not use high-nitrogen fertilizers; practice crop rotation; clean up plant refuse. There is no safe control. Remove and destroy diseased plants.

Taking the Cure

We hope you won't have to use this section of the book — that all the precautions we're recommended have meant that your herbs have been untroubled by pests or diseases. Using sprays and dusts in the garden, with a couple of exceptions, is never completely safe. Organic controls — the kind we're listing — kill beneficial as well as predatory insects. At the same time, they are safer than most synthetic products.

Beating bugs

This section shows you the safest, most common pest controls used by home gardeners. Many of these are *contact poisons* — they paralyze or kill pests when they encounter the substance; others are *systemic poisons,* which take effect when pests eat treated plants. All are widely available from garden centers, or see the Appendix for mail-order sources. Follow label directions *exactly.*

Try these organic controls:

- **Bacillus thuringiensis,** or Bt, is safe for gardeners and other mammals but murder on larvae. There is more than one strain of Bacillus — each has a favorite target — so be sure you get the appropriate type. Milky disease *(Bacillus popilliae,* or Bp), for example, attacks Japanese beetle grubs. Bacillus strains are widely available from garden-supply companies.

- **Diatomaceous earth,** which you spread both around and on plants, is made from fossilized shells of diatom algae. Its sharp particles abrade pests that come into contact with it, such as slugs, but it is virtually nontoxic to mammals. A homemade alternative is ground cinders.

- **Horticultural oils** are used to kill immature insects and insect eggs. The two main types are *dormant oils,* which you spray on woody plants in autumn to control eggs or overwintering pests, and *summer, or superior, oils,* which you can use during the growing season to control aphids, mealybugs, scales, spider mites, whiteflies, and some caterpillars. To make summer oil, mix 1 cup vegetable oil and 1 tablespoon liquid, non-detergent soap, such as Murphy's Oil Soap. To use, dilute with water: 2 teaspoons oil mixture to 1 cup water. Use a sprayer to cover the entire plant.

    Summer oils can damage fuzzy-leaved plants, such as betony, borage, and sunflower; use them only on herbs with shiny foliage and when the temperature is below 85°F.

- **Insecticidal soaps** contain fatty acids that paralyze soft-bodied pests, such as aphids, mites, and whiteflies. You must spray insects directly for insecticidal soaps to work, but don't overdo it: Too many applications can harm plants. To make insecticidal soap, mix 3 teaspoons of liquid, nondetergent soap with 1 gallon distilled water (soap mixed with hard water is ineffective).

- **Garlic sprays.** A common recipe is to combine 8–10 cloves of garlic and 2 cups water in a blender. Blend well, strain, and spray. Although safe for the gardener, garlic sprays are now recommended with reservations because scientists have discovered that they are toxic to many beneficials as well as to pests.

- **Neem oil,** a spray made from azadirachtin compounds extracted from neem trees, is both a contact and systemic poison. It controls a wide range of pests, including beetles, flies, and caterpillars, and it is most effective against immature insects. It appears not to be harmful to bees or most beneficials and breaks down quickly after it's applied.

- **Pyrethrins** are compounds extracted from the blooms of pyrethrum daisies. A nonselective insecticide, pyrethrin sprays are lethal to beneficials as well as pest insects, such as aphids, beetles, fleas, and whiteflies. Pyrethrins are also toxic to fish, so don't spray near water. Because they break down quickly, pyrethrins are often combined with longer-lasting pesticides.

- **Quassia** is a newer botanic pesticide and one of the safest. It is toxic to a broad range of insect larvae but poses no danger to bees or adult beneficials.

- **Rotenone** is a widely used, *nonspecific poison* — it is toxic to humans, birds, fish, and bugs. It's organic — made from the roots of several plants — but don't use it.

- **Sabadilla,** a contact pesticide and repellent, is effective against a wide range of garden insects. It loses its effect quickly in sunlight but is toxic to bees, so apply it in the evening after bees have hived. Unlike most organic controls, sabadilla dusts and sprays become stronger over time, so follow label directions for discarding.

Playing it safe

You won't find any pesticide that is completely safe, even if it's organic. If you purchase or make any products to kill diseases, pests, or weeds, follow these guidelines.

- Keep pesticides away from children.

- Read the label and follow its instructions exactly.

- Never mix different pesticides together.

- Use pesticides in the early evening, when beneficials are less active.

- Wear protective clothing and equipment to keep pesticides from reaching skin, eyes, nose, and mouth.

- Wash hands and face after handling pesticides.

- Don't use pesticides near water or in windy conditions.

- Always treat specific plants, not the entire garden.

- Store pesticides in their original container and dispose of them according to label recommendations and local ordinances.

Downing diseases

Curing plant diseases isn't easy for environmentally sensitive gardeners, because there are only a few organic products to control diseases. Many fungal diseases — powdery mildew is one — spread so slowly that frost is more likely to end your plant's career than the disease is. Bacterial and viral diseases are more serious. Once plants are infected, there is little to do except remove and destroy them.

Before you reach for disease-curing sprays and dusts, remember that the antibiotics produced in organically rich soil help your herbs ward off disease organisms; compost tea also appears to have some disease-fighting properties.

The most common organic controls for plant disease that appear in this list are in the order from least to most potent. Again, organic doesn't mean non-toxic. We hope you never use any of them.

- ✔ **Baking soda mixtures.** Baking soda solutions (a recipe appears earlier in the chapter, under "Repellents") seem to slow fungal infections as well as discourage them from taking hold in the first place.

- ✔ **Garlic mixtures.** Garlic sprays are still recommended to combat fungal diseases. A recipe for making your own appears earlier in this chapter, under "Beating bugs."

- ✔ **Sulfur-based fungicides.** These are the safest of the fungal controls, but they're still toxic to many beneficial organisms. Don't use sulfur in temperatures over 85°F or you'll burn the leaves of your herbs.

- ✔ **Copper and Bordeaux mixtures.** *Copper fungicides* are effective but non-specific — they kill the good with the bad. Used repeatedly, copper fungicides will stunt plants' growth. They could stunt yours, too, if not used cautiously.

A mixture of copper sulfate and hydrated lime, *Bordeaux mixture* has been used by gardeners since the 1870s. (Its fungicidal powers were serendipitously discovered by French viticulturists who reputedly sprayed their vines to keep people from stealing their grapes.) Timing is important to keep from damaging your plants, so read instructions carefully. Use at half the recommended rate on culinary herbs.

Outwitting Wildlife

What to do about Bambi, Thumper, and their friends? As usual with garden pests, there are no easy solutions for keeping them out of the garden. Stores are well stocked with repellents against deer and other wildlife. We've tried them all, as well as sacks of human hair, bars of soap, homemade hot pepper and garlic sprays, dried blood, moth balls, castor oil, even urine (thanks to family members who prefer to remain anonymous). Nothing seems to work longer than a day or two, if that.

If wildlife damage is a sometimes thing in your garden, grin and bear it. Or frown and bear it. But if marauding animals trample or munch your entire basil crop three years in a row, here are some suggestions. Good luck!

- ✔ **Scare tactics.** Birds and some other animals are frightened by unexpected sights and sounds. Scarecrows are worth trying (even if they don't work, they are ornamental and a good way to recycle your spouse's wardrobe), as are Mylar scare tapes, inflatable scare-owls, mirrors, whirligigs, aluminum pie tins hanging from strings, and a radio tuned to a heavy metal station. Animals *habituate,* or become accustomed, quickly, so move these items every few days.

- ✔ **Fences.** Gardeners who have big-league problems with deer or other four-legged wildlife usually conclude that a fence is the only effective and permanent deterrent. A fence plus electricity is even better. There are now "low impedance" controllers that make electric fences safer.

- ✔ **Traps.** Trapping wildlife — and we're talking about live trapping — is a mixed blessing for you and the trapee. The fact is that many animals are unable to adapt when dropped off in a new environment, so live trapping may not save a life. Still, trapping is more humane than guns and poisons, and much safer. Frankly, it's the only break a hungry woodchuck deserves.

Be careful when using live traps: wear heavy gloves, don't handle the animal, and choose a release site that is both appropriate and legal. Mammals and rodents are good travelers. Relocate rabbits, woodchucks, and other small animals at least three miles away, skunks and squirrels five miles, and raccoons at least ten miles.

Chapter 10

Everyday Cares

. . . .

In This Chapter

▶ Gardening every day

▶ Nourishing your herbs

▶ Solving the weed problem

▶ Figuring out how to mulch

▶ Maintaining a tidy garden

. . . .

North Carolina garden writer Elizabeth Lawrence observed that a garden "demands as much of its maker as he has to give." Or she. Those words may sound ominous, creating a vision of hours on your knees grubbing out quack grass and weekends spent on the working end of a hoe when you'd rather be on the reading end of the latest P.D. James mystery. But, Lawrence continued: "No other undertaking will give as great a return for the amount of effort put into it."

Occasionally, when the sun is directly overhead and it's hot enough to fry eggs on your patio, or when poison ivy is overtaking the chives, you may feel that you will never get an adequate return for your labor in the garden. But those moments are few, far outnumbered by the times you stand back and admire your work or by the times you race out 20 minutes before dinner to snip two cups of parsley to make parsley-lemon pesto.

We don't have time to spend all day in the garden, and we suspect you don't either. That's okay, because unless you've farmed several acres or set out 2,000 lavender plants, caring for herbs doesn't require hours and hours of daily labor. A garden does require some attention, though.

New gardeners may be surprised to discover that they can derive great pleasure from garden work — from the process of clearing, digging, planting, and the taking-care-of. Beautiful, healthy herbs are another reward. We're pretty sure that like us, you'll come to relish every moment you spend in your garden.

One of the great things about herbs is that most of them need only a few things from you as they grow to maturity. That doesn't mean herbs are no-care plants. But herbs (and herb gardens) are certainly low-care, especially if you keep on top of the basic, routine jobs. That's what this chapter is all about.

Thyme Waits for No Gardener

Gardening tasks, unlike hanging wallpaper in the guest bedroom or painting the fence, can't be postponed. You can't walk away from gardening for six or eight weeks. A few thistles are easy to deal with — a five-minute job — but an herb bed overrun by thistles may be a lost cause. At the very least, it's many hours of work that can leave you prickly in more ways than one.

If things you didn't plant are shading the herbs you did plant, you have problems. But weeds are only one challenge for the gardener. Fortunately, herbs, like other plants, are good communicators. Herbs show you if they're not happy by wilting, turning odd colors, crunching up their leaves, or giving a dozen other signs. All you need to do is watch and react sooner rather than later.

Following are some thoughts on how to keep the time you spend in the garden under control to keep garden work fun rather than burdensome.

- ✔ **Check your plants every day or two.** Establish a routine, a regular garden tour. Watch for insect and disease damage, such as chewed or curled leaves. Make sure your herbs aren't crowded or too wet or dry — that they look healthy.

- ✔ **Grow plants that do well in your region.** We don't mean that you must cultivate only native Southwest plants or indigenous New Englanders — after all, most herbs aren't North American natives. But choose plants that don't need lots of extras: lots of extra water, lots of extra heat, lots of extra whatever. Herbs that don't need all those extras usually are species that originated in conditions similar to yours.

- ✔ **Don't wait until things get out of control.** Spend five minutes *now* hoeing a few small weeds. Cut back the mint *before* it overwhelms the sweet woodruff. Deadhead the garlic chives *before* their seeds mature and start sprouting throughout the garden. Hand-pick earwigs *the first time* you encounter them munching the angelica.

- ✔ **Don't create problems.** Wait until plant leaves are dry to work in the garden so you don't spread diseases. Scrutinize new plants for bugs and disease before you add them to your plot. Don't overwater or overfertilize.

- ✔ **Use time- and energy-saving techniques.** We show you how in this chapter.

The H (How) of H₂O

You can't make the sun shine, but you can make it rain. If your herbs sag during summer's dog days, they're telling you, "A little water, please." Plants, after all, are about 90 percent water, and even moderate wilting can damage them.

Wilting is an obvious red flag; curled or dull-colored leaves are two other signs that your herbs are thirsty. Since too much moisture also causes plants to wilt, check the soil before you water. If it's dry to a depth of 3 inches, you probably need to water. (Keep your eye on herbs growing in pots: You may need to water them every day.)

Say when

Going out at noon to splash your herbs with a little cool water is a wonderfully mindless activity, one that refreshes the gardener but doesn't do diddly-squat for plants. The water may wet the soil surface, but little or no moisture reaches the plants' roots. Indiscriminate watering just wastes water.

If the rain gods aren't kind, the general rule for flowers and vegetables is to provide 1 inch of water per week, plus another ½ inch for every 10 degrees above 60°F. No rain during a week in the 90s? You need to supply about 2½ inches.

Many herbs do fine with less water than garden flowers and vegetables require — 1 inch a week is usually plenty. In fact, most culinary herbs have better flavor when they grow in moderately dry conditions. Annual herbs tend to need more water than perennial species, which have larger, deeper root systems.

Water by the numbers

To calculate how many gallons equals 1 inch of water, multiply the area of your garden by 0.083. Then multiply that product by 7.5. For example, if your garden is 10 feet by 10 feet, then its area is 100 square feet.

$$100 \times 0.083 \times 7.5 = 62.25 \text{ gallons}$$

To know how long you need to water with your hose, first measure how long it takes to fill a 5-gallon bucket. Then divide the number of minutes by 5 to determine the gallon-per-minute rate. For example, if your hose filled the bucket in 1 minute, it runs at 5 gallons per minute, and you'll have to water for about 12 minutes to apply 1 inch of water (or 4 minutes of watering three times a week).

Some herbs practically qualify as *xeriscape* plants (the word comes from the Greek word *xeros,* for dry), camel-like species that can survive in an arid landscape. Among the herbs that get by on very little water are American pennyroyal, burdock, catnip, chicory, costmary, elecampane, hyssop, marjoram, oregano, rue, safflower, santolina, southernwood, thyme, winter savory, and wormwood.

Just as you need to water more in hot climates and less in cool ones, you need to water differently depending on the texture of your soil. (See Chapter 4 for details on the different types of soil.) Whether your soil is primarily sand, loam, or clay not only affects how plants grow, it affects how and how much you should water. You may have added giant amounts of organic matter when you prepared your garden, but even amended soils fall somewhere on the sand-loam-clay continuum. (Don't know what kind of soil you have? Do the "jar" test in Chapter 4 to find out.)

When you water, keep in mind that

- ✔ **Sandy soil** drains quickly, retaining water poorly. Instead of watering all at one time, water three or four times for shorter periods. Plants growing in sandy soil usually require more water than those in clay soil and need to be watered more often.

- ✔ **Loam soil** retains water better than sand, but less well than clay. Water moderately, perhaps twice rather than all at once.

- ✔ **Clay soil**, which holds moisture well, also takes longer to move the water down to plant roots. Water slowly for long periods of time. Plants growing in clay soil need to be watered less often.

Garden flowers, vegetables, and fruits require extra water when they are forming flowers or fruits. In contrast, herbs, most of which have small flowers and are grown primarily for their leaves, need even moisture throughout the garden season.

Install a rain gauge and keep track of rainfall, but don't be a slave to numbers: If there was an inch of rain in the past week but your plants clearly show that they're thirsty, water them. If there's been no rain but your herbs look great, don't do a thing except feel grateful.

Water smart

If your herbs are begging for water, you need to respond quickly. When you do water, do it as efficiently and effectively — and be as environmentally smart — as you can.

Keep the following tips in mind:

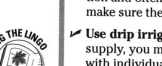

- ✔ **Water the plant, not the plot.** Rather than spraying a large area with a hose or setting up an overhead sprinkler — both lose water to evaporation and often wet some areas, such as paths, that don't need moisture — make sure the water goes where it's needed: the soil around your plants.

- ✔ **Use drip irrigation.** If you live in a region where water is always in short supply, you may want to invest in a permanent drip irrigation system with individual emitters for each plant and a computerized timer. For most gardeners, an adequate and far less expensive but efficient way to get water to your plants is to use a *soaker hose* (or *drip hose*), which has tiny holes from one end to the other. Lay it around your herbs or between rows; water oozes out, slowly and gently. In addition to conserving water — through reduced evaporation and runoff — a soaker hose waters without wetting foliage.

  You can make your own soaker hose by capping one end of an old hose (parts are available at hardware and garden stores) and punching small holes in it with an awl. To water a small area, punch a few small holes in the bottom of a 1-gallon milk jug and place it next to the herbs that need water. And don't forget about hand watering. In this age of high-tech equipment, it's easy to overlook the watering can.

- ✔ **Water during the morning or evening hours.** Water evaporates less during these times.

- ✔ **Water deeply.** Plants take in water through their roots, so the soil needs to be wet to a depth of at least 6 inches. Some herbs with shallow roots may need to be watered more frequently but less deeply.

- ✔ **Add humus.** Organically rich soil retains mositure well. It's never too late to add more humus to your garden.

- ✔ **Keep weeding.** Weeds use water too — keep them out of your garden.

- ✔ **Don't overfertilize.** Plants that grow slowly use less water than those that grow rapidly.

- ✔ **Be aware of wind and sun patterns.** Wind and sun steal moisture from plants. Create a windbreak if your herbs are growing where summer breezes are fierce. Locate herbs that don't want to be out in the midday sun, such as angelica or sweet woodruff, in a partially shaded spot.

- ✔ **Recycle water.** Use runoff from your roof to water your garden. Some household wastewater — *graywater* from the laundry, kitchen sink, and bath — is safe to use in the ornamental garden, but is not recommended for culinary or medicinal herbs. Don't recycle water that contains borax or great amounts of chlorine bleach. Apply graywater to the soil; don't pour it directly on your herbs.

- ✔ **Mulch.** Mulch reduces the soil temperature and conserves moisture. You can find much more about this subject in the section titled "The Great Cover-Up" in this chapter.

Putting on the Feed Bag

Adding compost or other organic material to your soil makes it rich with the nutrients that will feed your herbs slowly and naturally, and nourishes the micro-organisms that help makes those nutrients available to your plants. (See Chapter 7 for the full scoop on enriching soil.) Herbs are not *heavy feeders,* the garden term for plants that need big doses of fertilizer. In fact, most herbs do best in soil of average fertility, and some even prefer *thin soil,* soil with low fertility. So don't stock up on economy-size bags of 10-10-10.

A few herbs do thrive in richer soil — angelica, basil, monarda, borage, chiles, comfrey, costmary, fenugreek, ginger, horseradish, lemon verbena, lovage, tarragon, and valerian make up a partial list — but this doesn't mean you should pour on the fertilizer. If your soil has plenty of organic matter, no extra feeding is necessary, even for herbs with bigger appetites.

We don't recommend you agonize over which nutritional element is missing and how to supply it to your herbs — blood or fish meal for nitrogen, for example, or bonemeal for phosphorus. Instead, focus on improving your soil by adding organic matter regularly.

Nutritional SOS

Plants aren't shy about telling you they're hungry, but you must understand their body language. It's not an exact language — stunted growth, for example, has several causes — but slow or stunted growth, small leaves, and yellowing are dead giveaways.

Nutrient deficiencies can stem from

✔ **Not enough nitrogen.** Small leaves; pale/yellow foliage overall; thin stems; growth stunted. Add manure, fish meal, blood meal, bonemeal.

✔ **Not enough phosphorus.** Leaves darker green with red or purple leaf undersides; red or purple leaf veins and stems; leaf mottling; weak stems; slow growth. Add bonemeal, phosphate rock, greensand.

✔ **Not enough potassium.** Yellowing leaf tips and margins; brown, curling leaves; weak stems; general lack of vigor; poor root development. Add wood ashes, manure, fish meal, greensand.

✔ **Not enough calcium.** Dieback of new growth; small, distorted leaves; pale leaf margins; wilting flower petals. Add limestone, eggshells, fish meal, wood ashes.

✔ **Not enough magnesium.** Lower leaves yellow with green veins; yellow leaf edges; stunted flowers. Add limestone, manure, greensand.

✔ **Not enough sulfur.** Slow, stunted growth; yellow leaves. Add compost.

But if you see signs that your plants need feeding, we recommend compost tea, which gives your plants an immediate and complete nutritional boost. (The recipe is in Chapter 7.) You can either pour compost tea on the soil around the plant, or spray it on the foliage. Dilute the liquid until it is the color of weak tea before using on plant leaves, and wait until evening to apply.

No compost? Fish emulsion, which is sold in liquid and powered forms, is another good balanced fertilizer, as is kelp, or seaweed, emulsion. A meal of half fish emulsion and half kelp emulsion is the most complete and effective diet you can provide. You can mix your own spray or buy this dynamic duo already formulated to be used as a foliar spray, but check the package directions before you take aim. Even natural products can burn plants if they're too strong or used incorrectly.

Side-, or *top-dressing,* which is spreading fertilizers on the soil surface around plants, also provides extra nourishment, but it doesn't provide immediate help. Compost is the best side-dressing for herbs. Use a tined hoe or trowel to work it into the top two inches of soil.

At the sake of repeating ourselves, herbs growing in organically rich soil almost never need extra fertilizer. Too much is as bad as too little. Probably worse.

Keeping Weeds Under Control

Forget all those quotations about a weed just being a plant in the wrong place. In our gardens, weeds are a pain in the you-know-what, and we suspect you'll feel the same way when bindweed, a country cousin of the morning glory, uses your borage as a trellis.

You're more likely to win the lottery than to have a weed-free garden, though. We'll be forthright: Controlling weeds, like getting your kids to clean their rooms, is a never-ending battle.

So forget about eliminating weeds altogether. Instead, concentrate on keeping them in bounds so they don't interfere with your growing herbs.

The basic approaches

Weeds can be annual, biennial, or perennial. Annual weeds live only a year; biennials live for two years. Each, in its allotted time on earth, produces enough seeds to cover your county. To control annual and biennial weeds, stop them from producing seeds. Either pull them out of your garden or cut them off at the soil surface — an oscillating hoe is the ideal tool. (Find out more about tools in Chapter 15.) Then add the weeds to your compost pile where they can do you some good.

Perennial weeds live forever, or seem to. Like annuals and biennials, they make seeds, but they also reproduce vegetatively with traveling roots and underground stems. With perennials, what you can't see *will* hurt you. It's usually fruitless to pull perennial weeds: Each bit of root left in the soil produces a new plant. So grab your hoe and slice them off at the soil surface. When they resprout, slice them off again. And again.

Chapter 7 has advice about removing weeds, but those methods are most useful *before* plants are growing in your garden.

Try these methods of weed control in an established garden:

- ✔ **Consider your design.** If you don't have time to spend with a hoe, grow herbs in containers or in raised beds rather than in a traditional vegetable garden or large ornamental border.

- ✔ **Don't help weeds.** General watering and fertilizing makes your weed situation worse. (Water and feed individual plants, not the entire garden.)

- ✔ **Mulch.** Cutting off the light is a sure way to kill weeds. If you don't care about how your garden looks, black plastic, cardboard, old carpet, and roofing paper are first-rate sunblocks. If you do care, as we do, use an organic mulch. (Check out the section titled, "The Great Cover-Up" in this chapter.)

- ✔ **Keep planting.** Bare ground is like a sign that says, "Weeds Welcome!" Keep the ground covered, either with plants or mulch. Replace dead or harvested plants with new plants

- ✔ **Move things around.** Like the rest of us, weeds have special friends, plants they prefer to hang out with and insects that love to lay eggs in the soil around their feet. By changing the location of your annual herbs each year, you break up these partnerships.

- ✔ **Mow and hoe.** In the end, the best remedy is to keep cutting down weeds and going at them with a hoe. Eventually, they die.

The big guns

Several organic herbicides are now available to gardeners. Most are made from corn gluten, plant oils, and other natural substances — product names include Superfast, Scythe, and WeedzSTOP. These herbicides don't have the clout of synthetic chemical herbicides, but they are effective on emerging and annual weeds.

Of the synthetic herbicides, most environmentalists consider Roundup to be one of the least harmful. We hope you won't need them. If you're wildly allergic to poison ivy and it's about to overrun your garden, then you have cause. But there's no excuse to use a synthetic herbicide for ridding your garden of dandelions or even an unruly crop of pigweed.

If you do use these products, apply them selectively — spray individual weeds, not the whole garden. Their persistence is relatively short, but they still pose risks to you and the environment.

The Great Cover-Up

Mulching is the process of covering bare soil in your garden with either organic matter or an inorganic material. Mulching often makes a garden more attractive, and it does mulch, mulch more.

Let us list the ways:

- Moderates soil temperature, keeping it cooler in summer and warmer in winter
- In winter, reduces *heaving* (plants uprooting because of alternating freezing and thawing of the soil) by keeping the soil at a more constant temperature
- Conserves moisture in the soil
- Keeps foliage from being splattered with mud when you water or soil when you weed; this not only makes plants look nicer, but helps prevent soilborne diseases from spreading
- Suppresses weeds
- Reduces soil erosion from wind and water
- Reduces soil compaction

And if your mulch is an organic one, such as compost, it also

- Adds nutrients to the soil
- Feeds soil organisms
- Improves soil structure
- Moderates soil pH

Mulch saves time and labor. *Your* time and labor. As one busy Vermont friend always says when he shows off his lush gardens, "Brought to you by the miracle of mulch."

In spring, especially in cold regions, wait until the soil warms before you mulch; in arid climates, mulch as soon as you plant. Don't mulch seedbeds until your herbs germinate, however, and be careful not to smother small plants.

You get better results from mulching if you follow these steps:

1. **Remove all weeds — or as many as you can.**

2. **Loosen the top inch or two of soil with a hoe or rake.**

3. **Water thoroughly (until the top three inches of soil are wet).**

4. **Apply the mulch — anywhere from 1 to 8 inches deep.**

   The depth depends on the time of year, your location, your soil, your herbs, and which mulch or mulches you're using.

If you're growing annual herbs in a vegetable garden or separate bed, dig the mulch into your soil in autumn, then mulch anew in spring, after your herbs are up and growing. In perennial beds and borders, rake the mulch away from the base of perennial herbs in fall to discourage insects and other wildlife; after the ground freezes, remulch plants to keep the ground frozen and to reduce heaving.

Other general mulching rules? Shady locations, which tend to be damp, need a thinner cover than sunny ones; if your garden soil is perpetually wet, mulch very lightly or you'll be overrun with slugs and snails. Keep mulch away from plant stems, and don't pile it too high.

Fine-particled mulches break down more quickly than coarse mulches, such as bark chips. You can apply coarse mulches thickly. Grass clippings and other mulches with fine particles tend to mat, preventing water from reaching the soil, so apply them in thin layers, then reapply after they break down.

A light-colored mulch, such as straw, reflects light and helps keep the soil cool; dark mulches, including black plastic, absorb light, which raises the soil temperature. You can combine mulches, too: shredded bark spread on top of newsprint, for example, or pine needles over a thin layer of grass clippings.

Most mulches work well in any garden, so the materials you choose may depend most on where you live, how you want your garden to look, and your pocketbook. For example, straw is valuable in a vegetable or cutting garden but won't give your ornamental border much class. Use shredded bark and you'll spend more initially, but you won't have to mulch again for a couple of years.

Any mulch is better than no mulch. To borrow a slogan from the athletic shoe company, "Just do it!"

The gardener is out

Use a heavy layer of organic mulch to "baby-sit" your garden if you need to be away for a few days or weeks. While you're gone, the mulch helps keep the soil moist and the weeds down. Things won't be picture-perfect when you get home, but mulch may be better than relying on your neighbor's teenage son or daughter. We haven't anything against teenagers, but we could tell you about the kid who weeded Karan's chives, leaving her 12 healthy clumps of crab grass. . . .

Organic mulches

You have lots of choices when it comes to organic mulch: salt hay, oyster shells, rice hulls, ground corncobs, and peanut shells are five of the more unusual choices — but here is a baker's dozen of common organic mulches and some of their characteristics:

✔ **Bark.** Shredded or chipped bark is widely available, easy to apply, and contains no weed seeds. Extremely slow to break down (the larger the pieces, the longer it lasts), bark can take nitrogen from the soil as it decomposes. Moderately expensive.

✔ **Cocoa hulls.** Not available everywhere, cocoa hulls are attractive and slow to decompose (and smell like Hershey bars when first applied). They have a tendency to mat if applied too heavily (but wet them if your location is a windy one); spread them no more than 1½ inches deep. Moderately expensive, but worth it.

✔ **Cardboard.** Widely available for free, cardboard is a good material for suppressing weeds; wet it after laying it down, and cover it with some other organic matter so your garden doesn't look like an unofficial dump site. (Cut some slits in the cardboard so rainwater can reach the soil.)

✔ **Compost.** A wonderful source of nutrients, compost is expensive unless you make your own. Compost suppresses weeds well and is easily penetrated by water while conserving moisture in the soil. It breaks down quickly, and it may contain weed seeds. Apply up to 3 inches deep.

✔ **Grass clippings.** High in nitrogen, quick to decompose, and widely available for free, grass clippings also contain weed seeds. Never use clippings that have been treated with herbicides.

Fresh grass clippings spread too thickly tend to mat and then decay *anaerobically* (which means "without oxygen"); this process produces stinky odors and chemicals that can harm your herbs. To avoid the problem, apply grass clipping only 1 inch deep or dry the clippings before using them as a mulch.

✔ **Hay and straw.** Hay is quick to decompose, inexpensive (ask for spoiled, or moldy, hay), easy to spread (4 to 8 inches deep), and available almost everywhere. The bad news is that most hay contains thousands of weed seeds.

Straw is moderately slow to break down, widely available and, relatively inexpensive. Light and easy to handle, straw consists only of the plant stalk and contains no weed seeds. Spread up to 8 inches deep. Dry straw is flammable.

✔ **Leaves.** Leaves are a terrific soil additive, as well as an attractive mulch. To prevent matting, shred leaves before using them as a mulch (you can use your lawnmower for this chore, or fill a plastic trash container with leaves and use a string trimmer to chop them). Apply shredded leaves up to 3 inches deep, less if leaves are whole. Even better than shredded leaves is *leaf mold,* leaves that are partially decayed.

✔ **Newsprint.** Available everywhere and essentially free, newsprint decomposes moderately fast. Superb at suppressing weeds, it's ugly (and will blow away) unless covered with several inches of another organic material. Use several thicknesses, up to ¼ inch (8 to 10 sheets), overlap their edges slightly, and perforate to allow water to reach the soil.

✔ **Pine needles.** Available almost everywhere for little or no cost, pine needles are easy to handle and add organic matter to the soil. They decompose slowly but lower soil pH in the process (sprinkle your soil with lime to offset their acidity). In some regions, using pine needles as a mulch creates a fire hazard. Spread from 2 to 3 inches deep.

✔ **Sawdust.** Slow to break down, sawdust is inexpensive and available from most lumber yards. It is a good source of carbon but lowers pH (add lime, to offset its acidity) and can rob the soil of nitrogen unless composted before it's used as a mulch. Spread fresh sawdust about 1 inch deep.

✔ **Seaweed.** Available for free in coastal areas, seaweed, or kelp, is slow to decompose; apply 2 to 5 inches deep. Seaweed is a good source of nitrogen, potassium, boron, and other trace elements, but it may contain more sodium that is good for your herbs: Use carefully.

✔ **Sphagnum peat moss.** Available everywhere, peat is slow to decompose; it contains no nutrients and mats easily, allowing water to run off rather than sink in. Peat is a good soil conditioner if used with moderation, but a bad choice for mulching.

✔ **Wood chips.** Wood chips, the roughly ground limbs of shrubs and trees, are another mulch possibility, particularly for perennial herbs. Water penetrates easily, and they're long-lasting and weed-seed free. Wood chips, however, can rob nitrogen from the soil as they decompose. Apply up to 3 inches deep. You sometimes can get wood chips free from utility companies or public works departments.

Inorganic mulches

With the exception of stone or pebbles, inorganic mulches are mostly made of some kind of plastic or woven fabric. Inorganic mulches don't improve the soil — as all organic mulches do — but they're superb for stopping weeds, moderating soil temperature, and retaining moisture.

Opaque plastic mulches

Sold in different-sized rolls at garden centers, these mulches are ugly, but unsurpassed at killing weeds. Lay down the plastic right after you prepare your soil for planting. You can cut long slits to sow seeds or cut holes to set in seedlings. Make a few extra slits in the plastic so that rainwater can reach the soil.

Most horticultural plastics are inexpensive but last only one season; if you cover yours with an organic mulch, you may get another year's use. Don't forget that dark plastic absorbs light, raising the soil's temperature; if you live in a hot climate, it may keep your soil too hot.

Fabric mulches

Landscape fabrics are more expensive than plastic mulches but they last longer. (Also known as *geotextiles,* landscape fabrics consist of a water-permeable, weed-suppressing material. You can find them at your local garden center.) They're normally laid around permanent plantings, such as shrubs and trees, then hidden by a layer of wood chips, shredded bark, or stone.

Stone mulches

Stone mulches (pebbles, gravel, and pavers) are uniform, attractive, and right at home with herbs. Not only do they look great together, many of the most popular culinary herbs crave the heat that stones absorb. Planting creeping thyme between pavers is a garden classic, but you can use any heat-loving herb. Use stone mulches in permanent beds and borders, not in gardens that you plan to till each year.

You may want to lay newsprint, landscape fabric or some other weed-stopping material under your stone mulch. And stones, like diamonds, are forever.

Keeping Tidy

We don't want you to be compulsive about keeping your herb garden neat — a couple of small weeds aren't going to ruin the lavender — but a little good gardenkeeping goes a long way in producing healthy, vigorous herbs.

Thinning

You can prevent weeds from taking over by keeping your soil covered with plants. At the same time, however, don't let your herbs shove up against their neighbors, like passengers in a crowded elevator. You need to thin out your plants. If they grow too close to each other, they must fight for light, moisture, nutrients, and fresh air. Crowded plants are less productive and more susceptible to insects and disease.

The first wave of thinning occurs when the plants are seedlings (see Chapter 8). You may need to thin a second or third time when your herbs begin to reach their full stature. It's hard to yank out good-sized plants. Go ahead. Transplant the extras elsewhere if you can, or use them in the kitchen or in making medicinal preparations. Pot up a few for friends. At the least, compost them.

Pruning

Keeping plants in bounds usually makes them more productive and attractive. Cut back some of the stem tips of most herbs, such as feverfew, to encourage new growth and a bushy growth. (The exception is parsley or any other herb that has a *basal* form, where all its leaves grow from the plant's base). Don't prune perennial herbs until they've lived in your garden for at least one season.

Woody plants, such as bay and rosemary, need less radical cutting back. With these herbs, your aim is more to shape the plant than to encourage lots of new growth. And if you're not after flowers, you may want to pinch them off to keep plants producing new stems and leaves.

Don't be afraid to make the first cuts. Begin modestly — a few snips here and there, always cutting just above a *node,* the spot where a leaf or stem grows. As you get to know your herbs, you'll feel more comfortable pruning them. If you can combine pruning and harvesting, all the better.

Take time also to remove spent flowers — gardeners call it *deadheading* — to keep plants growing and blooming as long as possible. Like other living things, plants strive for immortality. If you allow them to produce seeds after they flower, they sense their job is done and stop growing.

Cultivating

If the soil around your herbs is well mulched, you can skip this item. But if there is bare soil in your garden, you need to keep it loose; otherwise, a crust can form on the surface and water will run off rather than sink in.

Use a tined hoe if you have one, or a common hoe. Cultivate shallowly, only an inch or two, so that you don't damage plant roots.

Cleaning up

Remove plant debris — all those dead leaves and flowers, plucked weeds, and over-the-hill plants — from the garden. As long as this refuse isn't infested with insects or disease, you can add it to the compost pile. Anything that looks suspect, such as leaves covered with a white, powdery substance, should go in the trash.

Going on pest patrol

Preventing problems such as disease and pests is a whole lot easier than curing them. Patrol your garden each day, and be on the lookout for signs that your plants have become infected or infested. The ins and outs of keeping herbs free of diseases and insects are in Chapter 9.

Bugs especially like new growth and the undersides of leaves. Chewed foliage is a sign that someone besides you is harvesting your herbs. Other signs are stunted growth, yellowing leaves, and sticky residue or white markings on leaves.

Diseases are more difficult to identify — and usually more devastating. The most common early warning signs are yellowing foliage, white, yellow, or reddish-brown splotches on leaves, and wilting leaves and plants.

Chapter 11

Coming Full Term

- -

In This Chapter

▶ Harvesting your herb garden

▶ Propagating new plants

▶ Lengthening the garden season

▶ Putting your garden to bed

- -

We're green with envy when we think of gardeners who live in regions so mild that they go outside in January to cut sprigs of rosemary, regions where the outdoor garden season slows but never ends. Yet when fall approaches, we confess to looking forward to winter. Although we like working in our gardens, a killing frost isn't unwelcome. Winter lets us stop worrying about what we're going to do with the rest of the sweet Annie or whether the freezer can hold yet another batch of pesto. A gardener's year never ends, but winter gives most of us a chance to catch our breath.

You have lots to do before winter has its nasty way with the calendula and cilantro, however. Foremost, is harvesting. We hope you've been using your herbs since spring — the seedlings you thinned were your first crop — but fall is synonymous with reaping what you've sown. (Shine on, shine on, harvest moon!)

Fall is also the time to get ready for spring — to prepare tender plants for overwintering and propagate new ones, and to prepare the soil for next year. Hold on to your straw hat, because the garden season isn't done yet!

Bringing in the Sheaves

Just as different herbs are ready to be harvested at different times, different parts of your herbs — leaves, stems, flowers, fruits, seeds, and roots — need to be collected at different times. The timing of your harvest also depends on how you expect to use the herb: to make tea, for example, or to make a wreath or a nosegay. Annuals, biennials, and perennials (see Chapter 2 for definitions of these terms) have their own quirks, but the rules for harvesting are pretty simple and straightforward.

Leaves and stems

Don't be afraid to snap a few stems or pick a bouquet — your herbs are there for you to enjoy. Most of what you harvest is foliage, whether you're just grabbing a leaf of sorrel to flavor a salad or cutting armloads of overgrown mint to dry for tea.

As a very general rule, herbs benefit from having their tips pinched off periodically, because it makes them bushier. Fast growers, such as mint, need more frequent and enthusiastic cutting back; woody herbs need only an occasional haircut to maintain their shape and vigor. Don't forget that those pinchings and prunings are also harvests.

Collect foliage when it is still tender. If you want herb leaves to use as greens in salads, harvest as soon as the leaves are large enough to be used. You know firsthand what we mean if you've ever eaten leaf lettuce that was picked past its prime — it's tough and bitter.

Late morning is by far the best time to harvest herbs, *after* the dew has dissipated but *before* the day has started to heat up. That's because the oils that make herbs taste and smell wonderful and work medicinally are at their most powerful then. Moreover, wet leaves take far longer to dry, if drying is your aim. Morning is a pleasant time to visit your garden, anyway, and to inspect plants for problems.

Keep a wicker basket handy to when you visit the garden. (We suggest a cup of coffee in your other hand.) Invariably, you'll see or smell something you'll want to snip for the kitchen or a vase. Your fingers will be adequate to pinch off soft stems, but keep florist's shears or pruners in your basket for woody herbs.

When you harvest, don't just strip off leaves so that you leave a bare stem waving around. Think "pruning." Instead of pinching off leaves or stems willy-nilly, make all your cuts above the *node* — the point where they are attached to the stem or branch — and you'll also stimulate new growth. And of course you want to harvest only healthy green foliage, not leaves that look diseased or are discolored.

If you need large amounts of material for a family feast or a major craft project, a general rule is that you can harvest up to half of the tops of annual and biennial herbs. Once perennials are established — at least a year old — you can take a half or a bit more of their top growth in late spring and another third in mid-summer. Six weeks before your expected first frost, resist the urge to pinch more than a leaf or two. Perennials are a bit like bears and need time to collect extra "fat" in their roots to survive winter hibernation. In contrast, you can harvest annual herbs up until the moment they are killed by frost.

Deadheading goes only so far to retard the maturation of most herbs. Nature's urge to procreate is strong, and many plants will eventually send up so many flower stalks that you can't keep up. Moreover, in some cases, as with rosemary, catmint, nasturtium, and others, you'll want to enjoy or harvest the flowers. So if you plan to squirrel away enough herbs for several months of food or medicine, begin harvesting as early as you can.

If you're like us, you discover something new almost every time you harvest your plants — a shortcut, perhaps, or something not to do again. Here are some tips we've picked up in our gardens and from gardener friends.

- Don't get carried away on harvest day and pile your basket high, because tightly packed, newly cut herbs generate heat. The effect is similar to what happens in a compost pile when you add a big load of fresh grass clippings.

- If you harvest more than one herb at a time, use labeled paper bags instead of a basket. Herbs can look alike once they start to dry.

- Many herbs bruise easily, so don't handle your harvest any more than you must.

- Don't rinse your herbs. Dampness can invite mold. Dust off dirt and dust specks with a soft brush; if plant leaves are muddy, rinse them off with a garden hose *the day before* you collect them.

- To store small amounts of herbs that you'll be using within the next day or two, pop *unwashed* leaves or sprigs in a plastic bag. Leave the bag partly open to prevent mold or rot, and toss it into the refrigerator.

- If you're going to dry your herbs, keep the leaves on their stems. For tips on how to proceed with drying and other means of preserving herbs, see the next two chapters.

Other body parts

Although foliage is the big draw for growing most herbs, sometimes the seeds, flowers, or roots are more tasty or potent, or have value for dried arrangements and other uses. Just as with foliage, the rules about when and how to collect them are pretty much the same, no matter the plant.

Seeds

Seeds are the real reason to grow some herbs, such as anise and caraway. With others, such as coriander/cilantro and dill, they're a bonus for the spice rack. In either case, you don't want to let seeds get away. Seeds begin forming when pollinated flowers drop away. The seeds are ripe and ready for collecting when they turn from green to brown or black. Watch, too, for seed pods to swell or change color. Shake the ripened flower head into a paper bag, and the seeds will fall into the bag. Be sure to label the bag with the name of the plant and the date you gathered the seed.

Some seeds are in a hurry to go forth and multiply and will shoot off the plant without notice. Others are hard to see within the drying flower head. A common trick is to tie a small paper bag around the flower head before the seeds drop. (Use a twist tie or rubber band to secure the bag.)

In the case of herbs with only a few large seedheads, such as fennel, you can do this bagging while the plant is still in the garden. In other cases, you need to bag the head after you've cut and hung it upside down. The seeds of a few herbs — anise is one example — ripen over a period of time. Cut the entire head, shake the ripe seeds off, and let the rest ripen in a warm, dry, dark place.

If you've dried an entire seedhead, you may find you have nearly as many pieces of pod and other plant bits, or *chaff,* in your paper bag as you have seeds. In her infinite wisdom, Mother Nature made seeds heavier than chaff. To separate the two, pour the mixture in a shallow dish and use a hairdryer, small fan, or plain old pucker power to blow away the chaff.

Flowers

For most uses — eating fresh in salads and making medicinals, cosmetics, and potpourris — harvest herb flowers just as they start to open. As with the rest of the plant, their freshness peaks and falls off quickly. Essential oils that provide flavor, fragrance, and healing qualities are all at their acme as the bud is swelling. Cut the flower off with a bit of stem (which helps keep flowers from falling apart) above the top set of leaves.

For dry arrangements, wreaths, or crafts in which you use entire flowers, you achieve a more natural-looking result if you pick flowers at different stages — unopened, partially opened, completely opened. Harvest them with at least 6 inches of stem. Potpourri, too, has a more interesting texture if you include a few tight buds along with petals.

If you are going to press flowers, let them open a bit more before you cut them — enough that you don't have to wrestle them to lay flat. Once they've fully opened, don't leave them in the garden or where their color will fade or where they can be damaged by insects.

Adding flowers to salads and other dishes increases their appeal to the eye and the taste buds. Be sure you harvest blooms that haven't been sprayed with any toxic control.

Roots

The ideal time to harvest roots (and *rhizomes,* which are horizontal stems that travel on or just below ground) is in fall, after the foliage has died back. That's when roots are at their most potent. (If you forget, you can harvest the next spring before growth starts, but you may have a harder time finding the plant. In addition, the roots may be more full of moisture and take longer to dry.)

Some of the herbs harvested for their roots are angelica, burdock, chicory, comfrey, dandelion, elecampane, ginger, horseradish, madder, marsh mallow, orris, soapwort, sweet Cicely, and valerian. These roots have a variety of uses. Horseradish, one of the herbs most commonly grown for its roots, was an often-prescribed medicine in the 17th century to "wonderfully help" sciatica, gout, arthritis, and liver ailments. It also wonderfully helps hot dogs.

Here are a few rules for the underground harvester.

✔ Be patient with roots. Don't harvest perennials before the autumn of their second year. (A couple of exceptions among culinary roots are chicory, which you can harvest the first year before it goes to seed, and marsh mallow, which is better when harvested in the fall of its third year.) Biennials, such as angelica, begin wearing out and become woody in their second year, so harvest them in their first fall or second spring.

✔ Your job will be easier if you dig roots when the earth is damp but not soppy wet. Use a spading fork (which will be less likely to damage the roots) and delve deep. Cut off the plant tops; if you can't use them, then add them to the compost pile. Roots, unlike herb leaves, need washing after harvesting; if necessary, scrub them with a brush to remove dirt.

✔ In most cases, gardeners dig the entire plant when they harvest roots. But if you want that perennial in the same spot next year, remember to slice off a hefty section of root containing an *eye,* or bud, and replant it.

Be Fruitful and Multiply

When you have a collection of plants you also have the makings of more plants. You don't have to be a professional miser to enjoy this botanical version of getting something for nothing. Well, nothing if you don't count your time and a few supplies.

Creating plants from plants — the ones already growing in your garden — is called *propagating.* Like harvesting, propagating can take place throughout the garden season. With most plants you have two choices: sex or no sex. If you're older than 10, we know which you'll choose, but your herbs also have a say in the matter.

Reproductive success begins with knowing what kind of herb you're working with: Is it an annual, a biennial, or a perennial? (If you need to know who's who, check our plant encyclopedia in Part IV.) There are exceptions, but annuals and biennials usually are propagated sexually, from seeds; perennials, which take longer to mature, typically are propagated asexually, or vegetatively, from divisions, cuttings, and other bits and pieces.

Oh say can you seed?

Herb gardeners who want to collect seeds for next year's harvest leave several plants to do nothing but set seeds — botanical brood mares for next year's garden. Diversity is the key to a healthy gene pool, so save seeds from more than one plant. Some plants are genetically disposed to be more tolerant of drought, cold, heat, diseases, and pests, so make your your healthiest plants your "breeders."

If you're growing a named cultivar or a hybrid, its seeds are unlikely to produce plants exactly like itself. Our birds-and-bees lecture is in Chapter 2, if you need to know what hybrids and cultivars are. Also know that if you've grown several cultivars of an herb that *cross-pollinates* (where the pollen of one plant fertilizes the flower of a separate plant), the seeds you save may not come *true* (produce plants similar to the plant from which the seeds came). Basil is a good example. Grow three or four types near each other and the seeds you save will produce some surprises.

Other herbs — mints are the classic example — are nearly impossible to start from seed. Either the plants rarely flower or their seeds are sterile. Most *variegated* plants (cultivars with foliage marked with colors other than green, such as cream or white) cannot be grown from seed, which is one reason that many variegated herbs are more expensive.

We provide details on collecting seeds elsewhere in this chapter. Collecting is the same whether you're going to eat or plant your harvest. Storing is a slightly different matter. Keeping your seeds in a *dormant,* or inactive, state is essential. Those seeds may look dead, but the embryos inside are just napping. As with all babies, you want to keep them that way.

Seeds saved for sowing need to be dry and clean, and stored in a cool, nonhumid location. Too hot or too cold, too wet or too dry and the embryo that each seed contains will either die or sprout prematurely. An ideal storage place is your refrigerator. Use paper envelopes — don't forget to label and date them for each batch of seeds and then place all the envelopes in a sealed glass jar. You can add one tablespoon of dried milk (wrapped in unscented tissue) to each jar as a desiccant.

All our best ideas on growing herbs from seeds are in Chapter 8. But one addendum: If you purchase seeds, everything has been done for you. But if you've saved seeds, you may need to apply some special treatments before they will sprout — or sprout quickly:

- ✔ **Scarification.** Large seeds with very hard seedcoats germinate far faster if you *scarify,* or scratch, them. Either nick them with a knife or rub them on sandpaper.

- ✔ **Soaking.** Some seeds, such as parsley and scented geranium, germinate far faster if they are soaked overnight in water before you sow them.

TIP

Seed sampler

Many more names could be added to this list, but here are some of the common herbs that you can easily start from seed.

- ✔ Angelica
- ✔ Anise hyssop
- ✔ Basil
- ✔ Borage
- ✔ Burnet
- ✔ Calendula
- ✔ Catnip
- ✔ Caraway
- ✔ Chervil
- ✔ Coriander
- ✔ Dill
- ✔ Fennel

- ✔ Feverfew
- ✔ German chamomile
- ✔ Lady's bedstraw
- ✔ Lemon balm
- ✔ Lovage
- ✔ Marjoram
- ✔ Nasturtium
- ✔ Oregano
- ✔ Parsley
- ✔ Summer savory
- ✔ Winter savory
- ✔ Wormwood

✔ **Stratification.** The seeds of some perennial and biennial herbs, such as sweet Cicely, must be chilled, or *stratified,* in order for them to germinate. Storing seeds in the refrigerator for two months takes care of the chilling requirements of most seeds.

Multiply by dividing

LEARNING THE LINGO

Dividing an established perennial herb is a quick way to turn one plant into several plants that are exactly the same as the one you're growing. Division involves pulling or cutting a plant's root system into two or more pieces. *Herbaceous perennials* — herbs that die back in winter and resprout in spring — are the best candidates for this propagation method. (Perennials with one central stem, such as scented geraniums, are not suitable.)

In addition to producing new plants to dole out to friends, dividing can revitalize your herbs. It lets you rein in aggressive species like mint and rejuvenate a large, aging plant, especially one that has died out in the center.

Dividing a plant stresses it. We recommend you take on this job either in spring, just after the plant begins to sprout, or in late summer/early autumn. If you choose the latter, be sure to divide your plants well before the ground freezes, so the divisions have time to establish themselves.

Don't be stingy when you divide. Small divisions will survive, but they'll take *your* good time turning into decent-sized plants. Small or large, note that each division must not only have a healthy hunk of roots, it must contain part of the *crown,* the section of the plant where the roots and stems meet. You can use your fingers to tease apart fibrous crowns, but you need a knife or spade to cut up tough, fleshy crowns into divisions.

Divide your herbs by following these directions — but wait until late afternoon to begin, so the divisions will have a night of cool darkness to recover.

1. **Use a shovel, spade, or garden fork to dig all the way around the plant.**

   As you dig, angle the tip of your tool toward and under the plant — then pry the plant from the ground.

2. **Remove as much soil as you can from the roots.**

   Soak them for several hours, or spray them with a hose, so you can see if there are natural divisions.

3. **Use your hands to tease the roots apart.**

   Each division should have a generous mass of roots and portion of the crown. (In spring, you'll know the crown by its swelling buds; in fall, you'll see what remains of the stems.) If the root ball is too tangled or tough to pull apart, use a spade or knife to cut it into sections. Don't forget that each division *must* have at least one bud or shoot (three or four is even better).

4. **Add the played-out woody sections from the center of the plant to your compost pile.**

   Keep the vigorous divisions from the outside of the clump.

5. **Replant immediately, setting each division at the same depth or *very slightly* deeper than it was growing, and water thoroughly.**

   If you're dividing in late summer when the plant is in leaf, cut back the plant's stalks by two-thirds to speed recovery and regrowth.

Herbs with *bulbous roots,* such as chives and saffron, are especially easy to divide. Simply dig the clump with a fork or shovel, pull the bulbs (or corms) apart, and replant them at the same depth they were growing. Orris and other herbs with rhizomes must be cut into pieces; be sure each piece contains at least two or three buds.

Division sampler

This list shows a few of the common herbs that don't mind being divided. Be sure to get the divisions back into the ground quickly and give them plenty of moisture until they have taken hold in their new location.

✔ Aloe	✔ Horseradish	✔ Rue
✔ Artemisia	✔ Hyssop	✔ Sage
✔ Betony	✔ Lady's bedstraw	✔ Santolina
✔ Catnip	✔ Lemongrass	✔ Sorrel
✔ Chamomile	✔ Lovage	✔ Southernwood
✔ Chives	✔ Madder	✔ Sweet Cicely
✔ Comfrey	✔ Marjoram	✔ Sweet woodruff
✔ Costmary	✔ Marsh mallow	✔ Tarragon
✔ Elecampane	✔ Mint	✔ Valerian
✔ Feverfew	✔ Monarda	✔ Violet
✔ Garlic	✔ Oregano	✔ Winter savory
✔ Germander	✔ Orris	✔ Wormwood
✔ Ginger	✔ Pennyroyal	✔ Yarrow
✔ Horehound	✔ Roman chamomile	

A clip off the old block

If growing from seeds and divisions weren't miracles enough, most plants — because all their genetic information is contained in each of their cells — can reproduce from bits of themselves.

Scientists have taken this approach to its lowest common denominator: Using one small piece of plant, sometimes a single plant cell, they turn out hundreds of exact copies. Test tube babies. This process, called *micropropagation,* or *tissue culture,* is becoming standard practice among commercial plant growers.

Home gardeners still rely on rooting *cuttings* — pieces of stem or root, or leaves. Rather than yielding scores of new plants, as micropropagation does, each cutting produces one new plant. The technology may be low, but rooting cuttings is an ideal method for increasing your supply of plants, especially hybrids, cultivars whose names you lost long ago, and species that don't divide or grow from seed easily.

You can take *stem cuttings* or *tip cuttings* (the green, succulent sections from the end of non-flowering stems) anytime your plant is growing actively (so don't wait until late fall, when plants are moving into dormancy). What you want is a cutting that is still growing, is firm and healthy, and is disease- and pest-free but not woody.

If you don't root cuttings in water, then you need a sterile, lightweight rooting-medium, something that retains moisture *and* drains well. Use a commercial potting soil mixed 50-50 with perlite, which lets more air and water to reach the new roots. You also need shallow (no more than 3 inches deep), sterile containers and plastic bags to enclose them. (Garden-supply companies sell inexpensive plastic flats with clear dome lids designed for rooting cuttings.) Also, buy a small jar of powdered *rooting hormone,* horticultural fairy dust that stimulates root production.

To sound like a *real* gardener, be sure to use the word *stick* when you talk about potting up your cuttings, as in "I have to stick at least 200 geraniums today." And after you stick your cuttings, give them the proper environment: bright light, high humidity, and temperatures in the 60s. If you can, set your containers on a heating mat or some other heat source: Cuttings like their feet warmer than their heads, about 75°F.

Waterworks

Discovering that zonal geraniums — the popular big-flowered geraniums that fill garden centers in spring — will root in water has been one of the great money-saving discoveries of our horticultural lives. Many herbs, including basil, lavender, lemon verbena, pineapple sage, and scented geraniums, also can root in water.

Because rooting in water is such an easy process, it's always worth trying. Just follow the simple rules:

1. **Take cuttings, 3–5 inches long, from the tips only of actively growing plants.**

   Use a sharp knife to make the cut.

2. **Remove the lower leaves so that no foliage is submerged; at least one or two nodes should be under water.**

3. **Place the cuttings in a glass jar filled with water and set it in bright light (but not direct sun).**

4. **Change the water every day so that bacteria doesn't form.**

5. **When roots are about ½ inch long, transplant the cutting just as you would a seedling (see Chapter 8).**

A cutting is helpless and vulnerable once you separate it from the parent plant, so work quickly.

Here's the routine for rooting cuttings in a sterile rooting medium (take a look at Figure 11-1):

1. **Fill your containers with the rooting mixture; use a pointed stick — gardeners call it a *dibble* — or pencil to make holes for the cuttings.**

   Space the holes so that the leaves of each cutting don't bump into its neighbor.

2. **Use a sharp, clean knife to make the cuttings.**

   Take a stem tip 3–5 inches long, severing it just below a node.

3. **Carefully remove the leaves from the bottom half of the cutting.**

4. **Dip the bottom portion of the stem into water and then into rooting hormone.**

5. **Stick the cuttings into the holes you made in the rooting medium and firm them in with your fingers; water gently but thoroughly.**

6. **Create a small greenhouse by enclosing the container in a plastic bag.**

   Use sticks or bent coat hangers to support the plastic and to keep it from touching the cuttings.

7. **Set the container in bright light but *not* in direct sun; or set under florescent lights, 14 hours on, 10 hours off.**

8. **Mist your cuttings daily.**

9. **Keep the bag closed during the day, but leave it open at night.**

   If it becomes excessively wet inside the bag, leave it open for a couple of days. Check the soil daily, and water only if it is dry to the touch.

10. **Remove any cuttings with blackened leaves.**

    Unlike Lazarus, cuttings will not rise from the dead.

11. **After about two weeks, pull gently on a couple of the cuttings. If roots are forming, the cuttings will resist your tugging.**

    When its roots are ½-inch long — uproot one to check — move the cutting from under the plastic, and transplant as you would any seedling. (See Chapter 8 for transplanting directions.)

Cutting sampler

All these common herbs are easily propagated from stem cuttings.

- Bay
- Betony
- Catnip
- Comfrey
- Costmary
- Feverfew
- Germander
- Hop
- Horehound
- Hyssop
- Lavender

- Lemon balm
- Lemon verbena
- Marjoram
- Marsh mallow
- Monarda
- Mint
- Oregano
- Pennyroyal
- Rosemary
- Roman chamomile
- Rue

- Sage
- Santolina
- Scented geranium
- Southernwood
- Sweet woodruff
- Tarragon
- Thyme
- Winter savory
- Wormwood

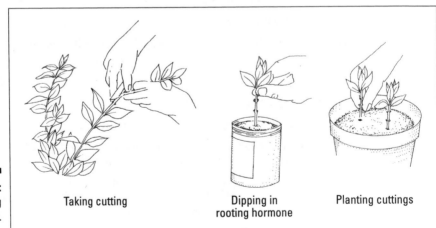

Figure 11-1: Planting cuttings.

Taking cutting

Dipping in rooting hormone

Planting cuttings

Pin your hopes on layering

Layering is rooting a cutting before you make the cut — it's rooting a stem *before* you remove it from its parent plant. (See Figure 11-2.) Not all herbs are suitable for layering. The best candidates are ground-hugging species, such as thyme, or plants like rosemary that branch close to the ground; the best time to layer is in late spring, after the soil warms.

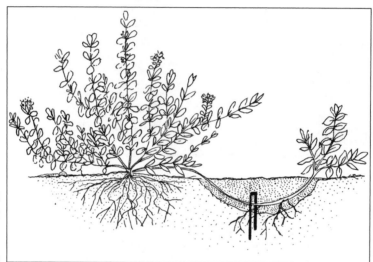

Figure 11-2:
Layering a
plant.

Try your hand at layering:

1. **Choose a long, healthy, flexible stem near the base of the plant, but don't detach it.**

2. **Starting from about 4 inches from the tip of the stem, strip the leaves from a 4- or 5-inch section of the stem.**

   It is this midportion that will be buried.

3. **If the diameter of the stem is greater than a straw's, use a knife to *just barely* scrape the bottom side of a 3-inch section.**

4. **Make a shallow trench (about 2 inches deep), lay the stripped midportion of the stem in the trench, and cover that section only with soil that is rich in organic matter.**

   If necessary, use U-shaped pins fashioned from coat hangers to keep the stem parallel to the ground.

5. **Keep the soil moist (mulch, if necessary).**

Layering sampler

These are a few of the herbs that easily can be propagated by layering.

- Chamomile
- Germander
- Lavender
- Lemon verbena
- Mint
- Monarda
- Oregano
- Roman chamomile

- Rosemary
- Rue
- Sage
- Santolina
- Southernwood
- Tarragon
- Thyme
- Winter savory

6. **After the roots form — usually in five or six weeks — sever the stem from the parent plant.**

   You can tell if the stem has rooted by gently pulling on it — a rooted stem will resist your tugging.

7. **Let the plant grow where it is for an additional two or three weeks, and then move it to its new home.**

Mound layering is another way to increase the herbs in your garden. Choose species that have sprawling stems, such as santolina and winter savory. Mound soil over and around the base of the plant; after one or two months, the covered stems should have rooted. Use a sharp knife to detach them from the parent plant.

Some herbs, those with *runners* or *rhizomes,* are do-it-themselfers when it comes to layering. (Similar to a rhizome, a runner, or *stolon,* is a horizontal stem that snakes along the soil's surface.) When the nodes on the stem make good contact with the soil (especially if it's moist, organically rich soil), they root. All you have to do is to detach the new plants from the old.

Stretching It Out

We confess we find our outdoor garden seasons quite long enough, and that we're ready to toss in the trowel by October or November. But if you want to extend your garden year, we have some ideas to help. Nothing can postpone winter forever, but you may get several more weeks' harvest from your herb garden.

Lengthen your growing season with these techniques:

- ✔ **Pruning and deadheading.** Harvesting is one way to keep plants healthy and vigorous. Pruning plants periodically and removing spent flowers are also methods for keeping plants growing actively, especially annuals.

- ✔ **Mulches.** Something as simple as putting a little extra mulch around a plant can protect it from the cold. With light mulches, such as straw or pine needles, you can cover plants on cold nights, and then uncover them in the morning when the air has warmed.

- ✔ **Cloches.** You can find a truckload of *cloches,* or covers, available from garden-supply companies. The word *cloche* is French for "dish cover," and refers to the glass, bell-shaped jars that were used to protect plants in the Victorian era. Most modern cloches are made from polyethylene, and range from individual water-filled teepees and square hot caps to both flexible and rigid polyethylene sheets that are used with metal frames or hoops to protect entire rows of plants.

  You have homemade versions of the cloche at your elbow: paper bags, clay and plastic pots, baskets, buckets, newspaper hats, gallon milk jugs (cut out the bottom), cardboard boxes, tomato cages wrapped with plastic or burlap, and more. Don't forget that you need to remove these covers after the sun comes up so that you don't fry your herbs.

- ✔ **Floating row covers.** Made from spun plastic and available in different lengths and widths, row covers give your herbs some frost protection — the usual number manufacturers give is protection to 28°F — while allowing sun and rain to reach the plants. They're so light that you can lay them on top of your plants, or you can use hoops to support them. For additional protection, spread two or three layers over your herbs.

  Even more effective against the cold than floating row covers is an array of products known as *thermocloths* or *garden quilts.* Although they are thicker than floating covers — the sellers claim protection from temperatures down to 24°F — you can still lay them directly on top of your plants, or use metal hoops or other supports to provide your plants with better air circulation.

  Don't forget the homespun versions of floating row covers: old sheets and blankets. Remove them in the morning, when temperatures rise.

- ✔ **Water.** If you have an abundant supply of water, you can try a method that commercial growers use: Spray your plants with water as soon as the mercury falls below 33°F. Keep the spray going — use an oscillating sprinkler — until the sun rises and the air warms to 33°F.

- ✔ **Cold frames.** We describe using a cold frame for hardening-off herbs in Chapter 8. You can also keep semi-hardy herbs going for an additional month or two by moving them into a cold frame. Cold frames can become hothouses when the sun comes out: Be sure to open the lid during sunny days.

- ✔ **Forcing.** Forcing, or manipulating a plant to sprout or bloom at an unnatural time, is standard practice in the bulb industry. You can use their trick with a few perennial herbs, including mint, tarragon, and chives. Dig a small clump in autumn, cut it back to 1 or 2 inches, plant it in a container filled with a potting medium that drains well, water thoroughly, and set in a cool location that gets good light. Use new shoots as they appear.

- ✔ **Overwintering.** We're not enthusiastic about growing herbs indoors — our success rate is darn low — but you may be able to extend your garden season by bringing some of your garden indoors. To overwinter, dig entire plants (smaller is better) and pot them up well before the first frost.

Our focus here is on the end of the garden season, but cold frames, plant covers, and other heat-enhancing equipment can be used in spring as well as autumn. Encourage the ground to warm by covering it with clear plastic, give your plants some protection from the chilly air, and you can get outdoors as much as a month sooner than Mother Nature planned. (The first and last word on extending your garden season is *The New Organic Grower's Four-Season Harvest,* by Maine gardener Eliot Coleman; the book focuses on vegetables, but the techniques are the same for herbs.)

Bedtime for Borage

We wouldn't push this metaphor too far, but a garden is a lot like a sailboat: When the warm weather ends, you can't just walk away and leave it. Well, you can, but to keep it in good shape, you have to do some winterizing. Old timers call this process, "putting the garden to bed."

Before you winterize, gather what's left in your garden. Cut back annual herbs to the ground — the cold is going to kill them if you don't — but don't harvest more than a few sprigs of perennials, such as rosemary, sage, and thyme. Heavy cutting triggers new growth, tender shoots that don't have time to harden off before the first frost.

It's not too late to take a few cuttings for rooting — although cuttings taken late in fall are less likely to root — or to dig and pot up tender herbs, such as rosemary, that have been growing in your garden. Growing herbs in your house is tricky at best, but bringing things indoors may give you another month of fresh herbs.

When the harvest season is over, turn your attention to your garden plot:

- ✔ **Clean up.** Remove all the dead plants and weeds — they'll attract diseases and pests over the winter — and add them to the compost pile. If plants look diseased or are loaded with insects, put them in the trash. Once their foliage has died and the soil has frozen, cut perennial herbs back to a couple of inches above the soil surface and compost the refuse.

✔ **Test your soil.** If your first herb garden has been more disaster than success, fall is a good time discover if the problem isn't in your stars or yourself, but in your soil. See Chapter 4 for details about testing your soil.

✔ **Adjust your soil's pH.** If you have reason to think — or a soil test proves — that your soil is extremely acid or too alkaline, fall is the time to make corrections. Ground limestone, which raises pH, works slowly and should be applied in autumn. (If you're using wood ashes, which are fast-acting, wait until spring.) To lower pH, amend your soil with peat in the fall or use elemental sulfur, which leaches quickly, in spring.

✔ **Improve your soil.** Don't leave bare ground to be invaded by weeds and eroded by winter winds and rains. Dig or rototill your soil, incorporating organic matter as you work, then cover your plot with more organic matter, such as chopped leaves or manure.

If there's still time, plant a *cover crop.* Also called *green manures,* cover crops are fast-growing plants that are sown with the intention of turning them into the soil. All cover crops aren't created equal — crimson clover and other legumes are especially good at improving soil fertility — but all help choke out weeds, and protect, improve, and enrich the soil.

Annual ryegrass is an especially good choice for northern gardens (Zones 3–6); you can sow it in late autumn and it will make enough growth to curb weeds and create a dense cover. Gardeners in warmer regions have more choices for late summer or fall plantings, including barley, crimson clover, fava beans, field pea, hairy vetch, oats, winter rye, and winter wheat.

✔ **Enlarge your garden.** One season of growing herbs is usually enough to make you want to grow even more herbs. Fall is the best time to dig a new bed or enlarge the one you have. Step-by-step instructions are in Chapter 7.

✔ **Mulch.** If your garden bed is empty, you can mulch it with organic matter as soon as you clean up the plant refuse. If it contains perennial herbs, wait until the soil freezes before you mulch. (The mulch will keep the ground frozen, insulating your plants from freeze-thaw-freeze cycles that can heave them out of the ground.) Loosen the soil and then mulch *around* your plants; covering plant crowns with a heavy layer of mulch encourages crown rot and other problems. In spring, dig or rototill the mulch into your soil.

✔ **Plant.** Planting isn't exactly putting a garden to bed, but fall is a good time to sow some herbs, such as caraway, cilantro, fennel, and garlic. If you live in a very warm region, the list of fall-sown herbs is a hefty one.

Autumn is also the time to clean and sharpen hand tools — and don't forget to winterize your power equipment. Nothing is more frustrating in spring than a rototiller that doesn't start.

Part VI
Cut and Dried: Handling the Herbal Bounty

The 5th Wave   By Rich Tennant

"I never meant it to be a planter. It just hadn't been washed in so long that stuff started growing out of it."

In this part . . .

You may very well decide that all you want to do with your herbs is grow them and leave them in the garden, where you can delight in their textures and fragrances and tidy up around their tired feet when autumn comes. But most of us eventually want to make the party last longer by creating culinary treats for family and friends, medicinal concoctions for winter sniffles, or aromatic candles and wreaths for Yuletide gifts and decorations.

In Chapter 12, we cover the basics of harvesting herbs — no matter what your intent — and some of the time-honored means of preserving herbs for mealtime. In Chapter 13, we whip out a plethora of techniques and recipes for other ways to use herbs. Even if you end up using only one or two of these products, we guarantee that the "doing" alone will make your house smell great.

Chapter 12

Preservation Hall

● ●

In This Chapter
▶ Drying and freezing herbs
▶ Preserving herbs and flowers for crafts
▶ Mixing and mingling herbs in foods

● ●

*W*hen you buy your first tiny herb seedlings or see them sprout from seed, it may seem inconceivable that you will ever have enough chamomile flowers for a single cup of tea or enough cilantro for a south-of-the-border fiesta. But if the fates are kind (and you faithfully follow all of our helpful tips), your beds will runneth over, and your heart may seem to shrivel at the thought of leaving any of those beautiful leaves and seeds for Jack Frost.

Overwhelmed by the bountiful harvest? As they say in Australia, "No worries." In this chapter we describe many methods for preserving your harvest, including drying herbs for foods, beverages, and crafts. We show you how to add herbs to other foodstuffs to spice up your cooking and impress your friends. And we also suggest ways to mix and match your herbs to keep things lively. ***Note:*** Always use untreated (chemical- and pesticide-free) blossoms and herbs for anything that is meant to be swallowed.

Cut and Dried

For short-term storage, a week or less, place herbs in a glass of water as you would a flower bouquet; cover with a plastic bag and refrigerate. If you aren't sure how you would like to use your herbs — as seasonings, as medicines, or to keep ants out of the cupboard and fleas off Rover's belly — drying them allows you to decide at a later date. If you love to cook, you'll probably want to try more than one approach to herbal drying to find one that best suits your taste buds. Just make sure to store the herbs properly and label them.

Most dried herbs (with the exception of a few oddballs like bay leaves) lack the flavor of fresh ones. But if you dry them carefully, they far surpass the bottled ones you buy from your grocer. And you can feel comfortable about their quality, because you know they weren't doused with chemicals or left lying in some godforsaken, vermin-infested, open bin for months. (Okay, we've lapsed into hyperbole, but you get the idea.)

The rest of this section offers guidelines for drying herbs by using the classic hanging-from-the-rafters approach, by using more technologically sophisticated methods, or by using one of several in-between options.

Just hanging around

You've seen country shops or photographs in which bundles of herbs hang from the ceiling on tidy twists of twine. They always look quaint and homey. Better yet, hanging is a good and relatively easy way to dry herbs — as long as you remember a few basics. The goal is to dry your herbs quickly in order to retain as much of their fresh flavor as possible. Fast drying keeps medicinal properties intact, as well.

A warm, dry place

The key to drying herbs this way is *location*. The perfect place to hang your herbs must be

- **Dark.** The sun bleaches and discolors herbs, stealing their precious oils and making them ugly, to boot. This pretty much rules out outdoor locations, except perhaps a roofed porch on the north side of your house. Even indoors, you may need to block sun coming in windows.

- **Dry.** It seems silly to say that a place for drying herbs should be dry, but some gardeners think a kitchen is a logical place to dry culinary herbs, forgetting how humid that room is. Ditto the bathroom. This is another reason most outdoor sites don't work, except perhaps in the western United States during a drought. Even overnight dew can retard the process. Attics are often good, but if you live in a humid climate, you need to hook up a dehumidifier there as well.

- **Warm.** Herbs dry best where the temperature stays between 80°F and 85°F. Near the end of the process, which averages about two weeks, 90°F is okay. This high heat is another reason why many people choose attics to dry their herbs.

- **Clean.** Steer clear of any sheds or rooms where you fill your lawnmower or use other chemicals, or any open areas where mice may play periodically. And that attic that was looking so good — how often do you vacuum or dust it? To keep culinary herbs sanitary, many herb gardeners envelop them loosely in cheesecloth or in paper bags punched full of holes.

Hang down your head . . .

The best herbs for hanging in bundles are those that have long stems, such as lavender and yarrow. Other good candidates to suspend, bat-like, in a cool, dark, dry location are anise, artemisia, borage, caraway, chamomile, cost-mary, feverfew, hyssop, and lady's bedstraw. You can also hang marjoram, mint, oregano, parsley, rosemary, rue, sage, santolina, savory, sweet Cicely, sweet woodruff, tansy, tarragon, and thyme.

For the record, many flowers also air-dry well. Flowers for hanging in bundles include alliums (garlic, onion, chive), artemesias, calendula, clary sage, goldenrod, hop, lavender, sage, tansy, and yarrow.

✔ **Well ventilated.** Moisture is the biggest enemy of herbs that are doing their darnedest to dry. Cross ventilation from open doors and windows is the most natural solution. If all else fails, a fan set on low helps to stir the air.

Room to breathe

Keep ventilation in mind as you hang herbs to dry. Don't hang bunches against a wall or too close to each other — six inches apart is a minimal distance. You can bunch together as many as 10 stems of a single herb if it has small leaves, as thyme does, but if you're drying succulent herbs, such as basil, borage, or comfrey, keep the bundle to six stems or fewer.

Although hemp twine looks charming, rubber bands are a more practical way to tie herbs together. They contract as the drying herbs do, and the bounty is less likely to drop to the ground. Twist ties are another option.

You can hang the bundles from individual hooks in the ceiling, but it's more efficient to set two hooks several feet or yards apart, string a clothesline between them, and suspend the bundles of herbs from the line. To expand that space even more, use clothes hangers and clip three or four bundles of herbs to the hanger with clothespins. You can also clothespin bundles of herbs to a portable drying rack.

Now wait and watch. Check your harvest often, because herbs can take anywhere from a couple of days to several weeks to dry — it all depends on the plant and the weather. Leaves are dry when they feel stiff and crumbly, like a corn flake.

Plant leaves are quick to reabsorb moisture from the air, so the minute they're completely dry, put them into airtight containers and store them in a cool, dark place. (Most experts agree that flavors last longer if you store entire leaves rather than crushing them.) Opaque glass containers are best, but clear glass is fine as long as your storage cabinet is a certified black hole.

Light and moisture erode herbs' freshness. As a last safeguard against any undetected moisture, wrap a tablespoon of dried milk in an unscented facial tissue to act as a desiccant and place it in the container.

Even when stored properly, herbs lose much of their oomph after six months. But by then, of course, you'll be started on next year's seedlings!

Rack 'em up

For some herbs, hanging isn't good enough. Their stems are too short, too soft, or too skinny and wiry to make bunching them an easy process. For these — as well as for individual leaves, flowers, seeds, and roots — you need a drying rack.

You can buy a rack, but they're easy to make, as shown in Figure 12-1. Just staple some window screening or cheesecloth to a wooden frame made by screwing together the corners of four pieces of 1 x 2 lumber. Be sure to set the frame on bricks so air circulates beneath it. (For a bountiful harvest, make several racks the same size, then stack them by setting wooden blocks on each corner.) You can also recycle an old window screen. Or, if you have only a few leaves or petals to dry, spread them in the bottom of a basket or on a paper towel laid on a cake rack or wooden dish rack.

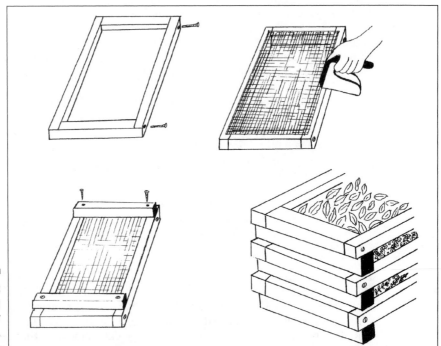

Figure 12-1:
Making racks for your herbs.

Spread out your herbs on the drying surface to make a single layer. You should stir or turn them every day or two in order to stop excessive curling and to discourage mold from developing. How long does drying this way take? As always, it depends on what you're drying and where you live, but plan on five days to two weeks.

Because roots are thick and must be washed after they're harvested, they can take weeks to dry. To speed drying, slice them into 2-inch lengths, or peel long taproots and cut them lengthwise. You know roots are ready for storing when you bend them and they snap the way a crisp stalk of celery does.

To dry seeds, lay cheesecloth over a drying rack (in a dry, well-ventilated location) and cover it with a single layer of seeds or ripe flower heads. Once your seeds are dry and you've blown off any chaff, store them in airtight containers in a cool, dark place.

Modern methods

All right, they're not faster than a speeding bullet, but some devices do help speed herb drying. Some serious herbalists create *drying cabinets* by grouping racks around an electric heater. Others purchase commercial food dryers (see the Appendix for sources). You can speed the process of drying herbs by using equipment that you probably already own.

Conventional ovens

Some experts are adamantly opposed to using a conventional oven to dry herbs because it's so difficult to set an oven to the 80°F to 90°F range that's ideal for drying foliage and flowers. Gardeners with gas stoves say the pilot light emits just enough heat. A mercury oven thermometer can tell you if your oven can heat in the right range.

To dry herbs in the oven, spread them in a single layer on a baking sheet and place them in an oven set to 80°F to 90°F. Leave the oven door open to let moisture escape and help keep the temperature below 90°F. Drying can take from 10 minutes to several hours. Check the herbs often, especially if they have delicate leaves, and turn them periodically.

Most people agree that ovens are a good option for roots, which can take several weeks to air-dry. Many gardeners like to start drying roots in the oven — a single layer spread on a baking sheet at 90°F — and then transfer them to a drying rack so the oven's free for Sunday's pot roast.

Be sure to allow herbs to cool before you bottle them; store them as you would herbs that have been air-dried.

Microwave ovens

Most culinary herbs dry in a microwave in a minute or less. The downside to this convenience is you have to watch like a hawk to make sure your herbs don't become too hot, which gives them a burned flavor.

Begin by spreading a single layer of herbs on a paper towel, then cover them with a second towel. Set the temperature to high and microwave the herbs for 45 seconds. If the herbs haven't dried completely, give them another microblast of 10 or 20 seconds. Continue blasting away until all moisture is gone. Allow the herbs to cool, and then store them as you would if they had been air-dried, in airtight containers set in a cool, dark place.

Refrigerators

This "cool" approach to preservation is becoming increasingly popular, since drying herbs this way retains both their flavor and color. Spread a single layer of individual leaves or flower petals on a baking sheet covered with paper towels and place it in the main section of the refrigerator (not the crisper). Drying usually takes two to four days, depending on the herb and the refrigerator.

Dehydrators

These gizmos are sold primarily for drying fruit and making beef jerky. They're also good for drying herbs; they operate like low-level toaster ovens that rotate their contents on racks. In terms of drying speed, dehydrators fall between the microwave and air drying. Herb foliage dries in three to ten hours, but roots can take several days. Most machines come with specific instructions for drying a variety of herbs.

The Big Chill

Freezing is an option for preserving delicate culinary and medicinal herbs that tend to go all to pieces when they are dried. Some herbs seem to retain their fresh flavor better with this method, but your experience may differ. Depending on who's talking, freezing may be as good as or better than drying for basil, chervil, chives, cilantro, dill weed, fennel, garlic greens, lovage, marjoram, mint, oregano, parsley, sage, sorrel, sweet Cicely, tarragon, and thyme.

Just as people disagree about the wisdom of freezing herbs at all, people also disagree about whether to *blanch* herbs before freezing them. Blanching means to plunge the herb into boiling water for no more than a second or two. (Gardeners who freeze vegetables usually blanch them to keep them firm, colorful, and fresh tasting.) Kathy sides with Gwen Barclay, coauthor of *Southern Herb Growing,* who observes, "Any instructions you have that say to blanch herbs are heresy. You might as well throw the herbs away and keep the blanching water." (Anti-blanchers often make an exception for basil, which blackens if frozen unblanched.)

A large blob of herbs stuffed into a bag can freeze unevenly, retaining moisture that changes the flavor and makes pieces stick together. To freeze quantities, spread herbs in a single layer on a baking sheet. Place the baking sheet in the freezer for a couple of hours, or until the herbs are frozen, then transfer the herbs to freezer bags and return them to the freezer.

Frozen herbs should keep for six to eight months. Don't refreeze them, and when you use frozen herbs in recipes, measure as though they were fresh.

If you use herbs to flavor soups and stews, try freezing them in ice cube trays, as shown in Figure 12-2. Pack chopped fresh herbs in the tray divisions and top with boiling water. (Remember to use slightly less liquid in your recipes.) For sauces, puree the herb in a blender or food processor with enough oil or water to make a paste and fill your tray with the mixture. If there's an herb combination, such as basil and oregano, that you use often, freeze the premeasured herbs together in cubes or freezer bags.

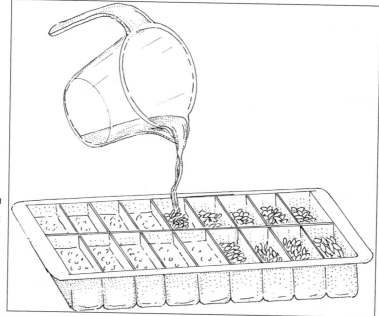

Figure 12-2:
Ice cube trays: They're not just for ice anymore.

The old salt

In the days when folks' home freezers were smaller than their radios, grandma would *salt down* her tender herbs. If you have some space in your own pantry or root cellar, you might want to experiment with this method, which leaves herbs tasting surprisingly fresh.

Cover the bottom of a glass or ceramic container (which has an airtight lid) with a layer of uniodized or kosher salt, then add a single layer of herbs. Barely cover the herbs with salt and add another layer of herbs. Continue alternate layering, ending with a salt layer. You can leave dill or parsley on their stems, but strip the leaves of other herbs to make sure they lie flat. Seal and store in a cool, dark place. Rinse the salt off the herbs as you use them.

Getting Crafty

If you want to use herb leaves, flowers, and fruits for crafts, you have even more preservation options. Herbs for potpourris, which don't require perfect flowers or leaves, can be air-dried as culinary herbs are. A few varieties of flowers can be left outdoors on their stalks until they dry — tansy and yarrow are two examples — but most flowers must be picked and dried.

To keep herbs shapely, or to keep stems, flowers, and foliage all in one piece — which is important in making dried wreaths and arrangements — you need to use special techniques. To air dry flowers, for instance, use a mesh wire rack and slide the stems down through the holes so the flowers dry upright. Following are several additional solutions for preserving herbs for bouquets, baskets, and more.

Desiccants for decorations

Desiccants are moisture-absorbing substances, such as borax, kitty litter, and cornmeal, that are used to dry plants, especially delicate flowers that don't air-dry well. Silica gel is far superior to other desiccant substances because it's lightweight, won't crush delicate plant parts, and works quickly. Available at craft and florist shops, it's fairly expensive but reusable. The powder turns blue when it's full of moisture; dry it by putting it in a covered pan in a 200°F oven for about 20 minutes. Store in an airtight container.

Until you discover how long it takes a desiccant to dry different species, work with flowers and foliage of the same kind and size so they dry at the same rate. If you're using silica gel, drying should only a few days; other desiccants may take a month or more. Whichever desiccant you use, the technique is similar. Use flowers that are not completely open. (If a wire stem is necessary, attach it *before* you dry the blossom). Then follow these steps:

1. **Sprinkle about an inch of desiccant in the bottom of a glass or plastic container.**

2. **Arrange your blooms on top so they don't touch.**

   Make sure the flowers are relatively flat. You might want to push some extra crystals between the petals of double blossoms, such as calendula.

3. **Top the blooms with enough desiccant to cover the flowers or leaves completely.**

   If you're using silica gel, seal the container; otherwise, leave it open. Be careful not to breathe the silica gel fumes, which can irritate mucus membranes. Never eat herbs or flowers that have been dried using silica gel.

4. **Place the container in a warm, dry place, checking it frequently so that blossoms don't overdry.**

Leaves and flowers dried in most desiccants have a tendency to reabsorb moisture. A spot over the living room fireplace is a better home than a humid kitchen for that dried wreath you spent hours making.

Microwave blossoms

A microwave oven can be used to preserve foliage and flowers for crafts. (See the guidelines for microwave drying that appear in the section titled "Modern methods" in this chapter.) Better still, especially for preserving flowers or any plant parts that you do not ingest, you can use the microwave oven *and* silica gel. Be sure to dry similar flowers together so that everything is done at the same time.

Fill a microwaveable container with 1 inch of silica gel. Spread the flowers or leaves in a single layer and cover them with more gel. Microwave the *open* container for one minute on high. If drying isn't complete, continue microwaving in 15-second intervals until all moisture is gone. Let the flowers or leaves sit in the oven to cool for about 10 minutes, then carefully empty the container onto paper towels.

Remember, anything that has been dried with silica gel cannot be consumed.

Pressing business

You can use pressed flowers, foliage, and seedheads to make wall hangings and greeting cards. Commercially made presses are inexpensive and easy to use. Simply arrange the material in a single layer in the press between two sheets of blotting paper, and turn the thumb screws. You can also press flowers in a city phone book or between the pages of newspapers, weighted with a couple of dictionaries or a copy of *War and Peace*.

Good candidates for pressing include single-flowered roses and the flowers of calendula, chives, lavender, bee balm, and nasturtium. Incorporate the foliage of chervil, chamomile, dill, feverfew, sweet Annie, rue, and violets, or the seed heads of dill, parsley, or rue. Most flowers dry in a week or two, but if it's warm and humid, drying can take more than a month.

Culinary Concoctions

Halfway between simply drying your herbs and whipping up *boeuf bourguignon* lie herbal vinegars, oils, and spreads. The end product not only helps preserve the herbs — albeit briefly — but can be used in more elaborate recipes.

A sour note

With vinegar, you can store your herbs for use in salad dressings, marinades, and a hundred other items that call for unflavored vinegar. You can combine any vinegar with pretty much any culinary herb or herb combination. Rice and white wine vinegars are the usual choices for more reticent herbs, while bold ones, like rosemary and sage, can stand up to cider or red wine vinegar.

Some other favorite herbs for vinegars include basil, bay, cilantro, fennel, garlic, lavender, and thyme. Chive flowers or red basil give pale vinegars a pink tint. Spices such as chilies, cloves, and peppercorns add zip to meat dishes. A few more good combinations are

- Bay, garlic, rosemary, and thyme — for marinating beef
- Cilantro, garlic, and hot peppers — for marinating Tex-Mex meats
- Lemon-flavored herbs, mint, and rose geranium petals — for dressing spring greens
- Basil, cilantro, ginger, and lemongrass — for a Thai stir-fry
- Chives, fennel, and marjoram — for dressing cooked vegetables

To make an herb vinegar, start with a squeaky-clean glass container (wide-mouthed jars are the easiest to fill) that has a non-metal cover. Don't be stingy: Cram it full of herbs before adding vinegar. Use about one cup of fresh herbs (½ cup dried herbs) for each 2 cups of unheated vinegar — our first choice is rice vinegar.

When the container is filled and sealed, set it in a cool dark place for two to three weeks; then strain off the vinegar into a clean storage bottle and discard the herbs. We love imported beer bottles with lids held on by wires for storage containers, but you can use any bottle for which you can find a cork. You can add a few herb leaves and flowers for decoration. Use any herb vinegar within one year.

Oil's well

Now that so many people are trying to cut back on animal fats, spout-topped bottles of herbal oils are replacing "the other spread" on restaurant tables. In addition to being drizzled on breads, these oils are great for sautéing meats and vegetables or mixing salad dressings. Any high quality oil makes a good base. Olive oil is the usual choice, but some herbs and oils, such as lemon herbs and walnut oil, make particularly harmonious marriages.

Many people have had a change of heart about herb oils since several botulism deaths were traced to garlic stored in oil. And garlic is not the only suspect. All herb oils are easily contaminated and must be prepared, handled, and stored carefully. Blanching herbs before adding them to the oil is not an adequate protection against toxic bacteria forming.

Always add acid, either vinegar or lemon juice, to an herbal oil, and *always* keep herbal oils refrigerated. Use them within one week. *Always* play it safe. Many toxins can't be detected by sight, so if the oil clouds or just looks funny, heed the adage — when in doubt, toss it out.

If our warning hasn't scared you off, fill a sterile, wide-mouthed jar loosely with fresh herbs that have been thoroughly washed. Aim for a 1:2 herb-to-oil proportion (1:4 for dried herbs).

Add the oil and 1 tablespoon of vinegar or lemon juice for *each* cup of oil. Seal the bottle, give it a shake, and refrigerate. After one week, remove the bottle from the refrigerator (if necessary, let it sit briefly at room temperature for the oil to reliquify), and strain the oil through a coffee filter or cheesecloth. Return it to a sterile container, seal, label and date it, and refrigerate. Use the oil within one week.

Better butter

Now that we've mentioned butter being unhealthy, we'll 'fess up — we love the stuff. Not slathered willy-nilly on instant mashed potatoes, but saved for fresh-baked muffins at Sunday brunch or garlic bread with Friday night's spaghetti. Ahhh!

Adding herbs to butter is another old-fashioned preservation method. Some of the herbs commonly treated this way are basil, marjoram, rosemary, thyme, and sage. For each quarter pound of unsalted butter (one stick, at room temperature), add two or three teaspoons of minced fresh herbs. Using a fork, incorporate the herbs and a scant teaspoon of lemon juice, which brings out the herb flavor, into the butter.

You can give soft cheeses a similar treatment. Cream cheese with chives is the classic combination, but try your bagels with dill, oregano, or even minced horseradish in your spread.

Herb butters should be stored in the refrigerator and used within three days. You can also freeze them for use within three months; herb butters freeze wonderfully — use your hands to form the softened butter into cylinders. Once the butter is frozen, you can slice it off as needed. Soft cheeses don't freeze well; store them in the refrigerator and use them within three days, tops. (Unlike commercial products, yours don't contain preservatives.)

How sweet it is

Most people associate herbs with savory (in the sense of piquant, or non-sweet) food. But herbs also offer something for those with an insatiable sweet tooth. The possibilities include sugars, honeys, syrups, cordials, jellies, jams, cakes, tarts, ice cream, and sorbets, for starters. Combining herbs with sugar and honey is really just another way to preserve, but if you're the kind who finished all the Valentine candy before Presidents' Day, you may find yourself consuming more herbal confections than you put by.

Jolly jellies

Herbs lack the pectin that is found naturally in many fruits and which causes them to gel after a period of heating. Therefore most herbal jelly recipes call for adding pectin, although some cooks substitute fresh apples or apple juice. Pectin won't work unless it is combined with the right amount of sugar and acid (usually provided by vinegar, but lemon juice also does the trick). Although some recipes call for making a *conserve* of flowering herb tops, macerated and cooked down only with sugar, most jellies begin with a strong *infusion* of fresh or dried herbs. (An infusion is really just a tea; we talk about it more in Chapter 13.)

Mint is probably the most popular herb for jelly, but you can also use basil, lemon verbena, rosemary, sage, tarragon, thyme, or even garlic. This master recipe uses pectin and is a good place to begin if you haven't made jelly before. Vary the amount of fresh herbs according to the strength of the herb and your taste.

Because this recipe does not require processing in a water bath or pressure cooker, the jelly *must* be stored in the refrigerator. Once opened, refrigerated jelly should be discarded after two months.

Herb Jelly

1 cup chopped fresh herbs

1 cup cider vinegar

3 cups sugar

3 ounces (1 packet) pectin

Make an infusion by pouring 1 cup boiling water over herbs. Steep for 15 minutes. Strain, reserving the liquid.

Pour the infused liquid into a non-aluminum pan and add vinegar and sugar. Bring to a full boil, stirring constantly. Stir in the pectin all at once and continue cooking for another minute. Remove the mixture from heat, skim off any foam, and pour the liquid into clean canning jars. Wipe the jar rims clean with paper towels and seal. Let the jelly stand at room temperature until cool, and then store it in the refrigerator.

Heavenly honey

Making herbal honey is so simple a child could do it. It's marvelous spread (thickly) on hot breads, biscuits, muffins, bagels — anything that stands still, according to a couple of our children. Lemon- and mint-flavored herbs (including hyssop and bee balm), lavender, marjoram, rose geranium, rosemary, sage, rose petals, and violet blossoms complement honey wonderfully. Use these and other herbs, singly or in combination.

Herb Honey

1 tablespoon washed, chopped fresh herbs (1 teaspoon dry herbs), tied in a cheesecloth bag

2 cups honey

Place the herb bag into a heavy pan and pour the honey over it. Heat until just warm, then pour the mixture into a sterilized glass jar and seal. Store it in a dark location at room temperature for one week.

Place the herb-honey mixture into a pan and rewarm it over low heat. Remove the herb bag and pour the flavored honey into sterilized jars. Wipe the jar rims with paper towels and seal them tightly. Store the honey in the refrigerator and use it within one month.

Crystallized confections

Edible herb flowers — especially those with flat petals, like borage, rose, and violets — can be candied to decorate pastries, to drop in drinks, or to liven up fruit trays. For a complete plant package, treat the leaves of mint or lemon-flavored herbs this same way. Begin with flowers that have just opened, and be sure to leave enough stem so you have something to hold on to. The results are certain to bring ohhhhs and ahhhhs.

Crystallized herbs are traditionally made with uncooked egg white, which is no longer considered safe. An easy and safe substitute is pasteurized egg white, which is available in both liquid and dehydrated form. Just Whites is one brand name; directions and equivalents are included in the package.

In a small bowl, beat the pasteurized equivalent of 1 egg white until it's foamy. Using a soft artist's brush (the kind that comes in a child's watercolor set), paint the petals, flowers, or leaves with egg white. Sprinkle superfine granulated sugar on the herb until it's evenly covered.

Lay the coated flowers or leaves on waxed paper in an ovenproof dish and place the dish in an oven (on its *absolute* lowest setting) for 10 to 15 minutes, turning the herbs a few times. Don't let the coating turn brown. Cool. You can store candied herb flowers and foliage between layers of waxed paper in sealed, airtight containers for up to one month.

Mixing It Up

Combining herbs with foods and each other is obviously a matter of personal taste, as are the proportions to use. Just like some people, some herbs — such as basil and parsley — get along famously in almost any situation. And some foods, such as beef and potatoes, are amiable companions for most herbs. Other herbs, like cilantro or sage, can be a bit more persnickety. Here are some of our favorite herb-food pairings.

- **Asparagus:** Chervil, lemon balm, savory, tarragon
- **Beans (dried):** Basil, cilantro, fennel, garlic, marjoram, oregano, rosemary, sage
- **Beans (fresh green):** Garlic, rosemary, thyme
- **Beef:** Bay, cayenne, fennel, garlic, marjoram, oregano, rosemary, thyme
- **Cabbage:** Caraway, dill, fennel, oregano, savory
- **Carrots:** Caraway, chervil, coriander, poppy seed, savory
- **Cauliflower:** Coriander, rosemary

- **Chicken:** Chervil, lemon herbs, marjoram, oregano, tarragon, thyme

- **Eggplant:** Garlic, marjoram, oregano, sage

- **Eggs:** Basil, chervil, tarragon

- **Fish:** Chervil, chives, dill, lemon herbs, lovage, parsley, savory, tarragon

- **Lamb:** Coriander, mint, rosemary

- **Pork:** Basil, caraway, chervil, coriander, fennel

- **Potatoes:** Caraway, chervil, dill, marjoram, oregano, savory

- **Rice:** Dill, fennel, marjoram, mint, parsley, rosemary, sage

- **Turkey:** Tarragon, thyme, sage

Classic combos

Just as certain foods go with certain herbs, some herbs mingle well. Choosing which ones to combine, to use immediately or later, is "quite a matter of fancy," to borrow from Carol Campbell, an Ohio herbalist friend.

If you're unsure about where to start when mixing and matching herbs, we suggest that you begin with some of these traditional herb combinations.

- **Bouquet garni.** A bunch of fresh herbs tied together with string in a cheesecloth bag is a *bouquet garni.* It's also a culinary classic, used to flavor broths, soups, and stews. It usually includes bay leaf, parsley, and thyme and is removed from the dish before it's served.

- **Fines herbes.** This famous combination of chopped fresh herbs calls for equal amounts of chervil, chives, parsley, and tarragon. Some cooks include marjoram or savory. It's especially good with eggs, fish, and poultry and should be added near the end of cooking so that the herbs retain their color as well as flavor.

- **Herbes de Provence.** This is a mix of dried herbs that works for almost everything, from pot roasts to potatoes, from beans to cheese spreads. Dozens of recipes don this name, but even the most egocentric chefs pretty much agree that *herbes de Provence* should contain equal parts of basil, fennel seed, lavender, marjoram, rosemary, sage, summer savory, and thyme.

- **Shaker blends.** Shakers were among the early American seed-sellers, and herbs were their specialty. Their master herb-blend recipe, a substitute for salt, was to combine two parts dried mild herb, such as basil, dill, marjoram, parsley, or summer savory, with one part dried strong-flavored herb, such as rosemary or sage.

Although herbs are often used instead of salt, we like to keep herb salt on the table. Combine 1 cup of noniodized salt with 2 tablespoons of mixed dried herbs (perhaps marjoram, oregano, sage, and thyme). Grind the salt and herbs together in a blender or food processor and place in a shaker.

An herbal cuppa

Herbs are sometimes combined for teas based on medicinal effects, such as chamomile and mint for indigestion. More likely, or perhaps simultaneously, you'll want to mix your herbs based on flavor.

If your tea is exclusively herbal (you also can add herbs to packaged black teas, such as English Breakfast), the usual formula is 2 tablespoons chopped fresh herbs or 1 tablespoon dry herbs for each cup of water. Of course you know how to make tea, but just in case:

1. **Warm your teapot with hot water and then pour the water out.**

2. **Add the herbs to the empty pot.**

3. **Pour hot water that has been brought to a boil over the herbs and cover the pot.**

4. **Let the tea steep for 5 to 10 minutes, depending on desired strength.**

5. **Strain the tea, pour a cuppa, stick up your pinkie, and sip.**

Some herbal tea blends we like: chamomile and mint; borage flowers and lemon balm; rose-scented geranium and lemongrass; fennel and savory; dill, cardamom, and mint; and tansy, sage, and rose hips.

Chapter 13

Herbs for Aches and Aesthetics

. . . .

In This Chapter

▶ Concocting herbal medicines

▶ Pampering yourself with herbs

▶ Keeping the house fresh

▶ Decorating ideas

. . . .

*I*f you tried just a few of our ideas from Chapter 12, you know that herbs can make a world of difference in cooking. But we're sure you followed all our gardening tips and still have bushels of herbs left over. That's why we now explore ways to use those herbs to improve your health and your environment.

It's true that if you've got your health you've got everything, but sometimes everything can be even nicer when you spruce up your surroundings. The quality of life goes *way* up when the house is clean and filled with beautiful things you've made yourself and when you take time to pamper yourself with long, luxurious baths and little catnaps, surrounded by fresh natural smells.

In this chapter, we show you how to make teas to relax and refresh as well as creams and compresses to soothe aches, pains, and strains. We also share ideas for using herbs to beautify yourself and your home.

The Herbal Pharmacy

Today you can buy capsules of the most popular herbs from the local supermarket and various forms of even the weirdest ones from health food stores and organic grocers. But you get a special kind of satisfaction when you whip up your own herbal sedatives and salves; the process alone can make you feel better.

Making herbal remedies isn't an exact science, and even experts disagree over precise measurements. But everyone agrees that your equipment should be clean (glass storage containers and their lids should be sterilized) and that you should label any remedy, noting its ingredients and the date it was prepared.

Before you're tempted to do all your own doctoring — which we don't recommend — we offer a few general cautions. Never take large doses of any herbal preparation, and stop taking any preparation if you experience side effects, such as dizziness or nausea. Seek a physician's advice before you combine herbal remedies and medical prescriptions, or if you're experiencing more than minor pain, or if your problem is chronic.

Dazed and infused: Herbal remedies to drink

Infusions, decoctions, tisanes — you would think there was some kind of conspiracy to make herbal remedies mysterious and baffling. Psssst, c'mere: They all mean "tea," and they're all made with hot water.

You make an *infusion* by steeping the soft parts of the plant — leaves and flowers. You make a *decoction* by boiling the hard parts — seeds and roots. That's it. What's a *tisane?* It's a synonym for infusion, but mainly, it's pretentious.

A *tincture* is also tealike, but it's made with alcohol instead of water. A *syrup,* often given to children, combines sugar or honey with herbs and disguises their flavor.

In Table 13-1, we list many medicinal herbs and indicate which ailments they relieve. First, we show you just how easy it is to make these various remedies.

A word for moms (and moms-to-be)

The list of herbs to avoid when you are pregnant or nursing is so long that we suggest avoiding all herbs at that time unless you discuss them with a doctor who is herb savvy. Even herbs as common as basil contain some substances that can cause uterine contractions and miscarriage.

A couple of exceptions might be raspberry leaf tea — said to be *the* pregnancy herb for both morning sickness and preventing miscarriage — and ginger, which allays motion sickness and might help morning sickness.

Also, do not give any herbs to children younger than 3 years old. Even chamomile, which is extremely mild, can cause an allergic reaction in someone disposed to hay fever.

Infusions

Okay, if you want to get picky, an infusion taken as medicine is measured a bit more precisely than a tea to sip with scones. But not much more. Most herbs taken for common woes like indigestion and insomnia are so mild and safe that your main worry is not getting enough of them.

The usual proportions are 2 to 6 teaspoons of fresh herbs (1 to 3 teaspoons of dried herbs) per cup of water. Boil the water, remove it from the heat, and pour it over the herbs in a warm teapot or a non-aluminum container. (Some evidence exists that aluminum releases toxins that herbs and other foods can absorb). Cover, let steep 10 to 20 minutes, and strain.

If you make more than one dose (normally you drink a cup or less at a time), put the rest in the refrigerator in a sealed glass container, where it keeps for up to two days. You can take up to about three cups a day of most herbal infusions.

Decoctions

For a decoction — the liquid made with tough parts of herbs, such as roots, seeds, and bark — the usual proportions are 1 tablespoon of dried plant material per cup of water. In a non-aluminum pan, combine the herbs and water and bring to a boil. Cover, reduce heat, and simmer for 20 to 30 minutes. (If you're making a small amount, check the pan frequently to make sure all the liquid hasn't evaporated.) Remove from heat and strain into a cup to drink immediately or strain into a sterilized glass container, which you can seal and store in the refrigerator for up to two days.

Tinctures

A *tincture* is an herbal medicine made with alcohol and taken by the teaspoon rather than by the cupful. It's more convenient to take than a tea-like remedy (on trips, for instance), and it stays potent for up to two years. You can make it with vodka or stronger grain alcohol. If you find certain herbs unpalatable, brandy or rum covers the taste. The usual proportion is 1 ounce of dried herbs to 5 ounces of alcohol.

To make a tincture, combine herbs and alcohol in a large glass jar. Seal the jar and set it in a cool, dark place for two to six weeks. (Shake the jar occasionally.) Strain the liquid into a dark glass container and seal. The usual dose is ½ to 1 teaspoon of tincture up to three times a day.

Through a glass darkly

It's traditional to store herbal preparations in dark glass containers, because light robs them of their medicinal "oomph." You can buy colored glass bottles intended for herbal vinegars, but we like recycling beer and medicine bottles.

They *must* be scrubbed thoroughly and then immersed in boiling water to sterilize them. Some experts say dark glass isn't necessary as long as the preparation is stored in the dark.

Syrups

You won't want to give alcohol-based tinctures to children, so make a syrup instead by combining one part herbal infusion or decoction with an equal measure of honey or sugar. Simmer over low heat, stirring gently, until the sugar or honey dissolves and the mixture has a syrupy consistency. Cool. Pour into dark glass bottles sealed with cork stoppers (syrups occasionally ferment — using a cork prevents the container from exploding) and store in the refrigerator for up to three months.

The standard dose is 1 to 2 teaspoons up to three times per day.

Table 13-1	Common Medicinal Herbs Taken Internally	
Herb	**Parts Used**	**Ailment**
Angelica	All parts	Indigestion
Anise	Seeds	Bad breath, respiratory ailments
Catnip	Aerial parts	Insomnia, indigestion
Chamomile	Flowers	Insomnia, indigestion
Dandelion	Roots	Healthy liver, diuretic
Fennel	Seeds	Heartburn, indigestion, flatulence
Feverfew	Leaves	Migraine
Garlic	Bulb	Healthy heart, allergies, respiratory ailments
Ginger	Roots	Motion sickness
Lemon balm	Leaves	Insomnia, headache
Marsh mallow	Roots	Sore throat, cough, indigestion

Herb	Parts Used	Ailment
Mint	Aerial parts	Heartburn, indigestion
Mullein	All parts	Respiratory ailments
Parsley	Leaves, seeds	Bad breath, diuretic
Valerian	Roots	Insomnia, headache

Salved by the bell: External herbal medicines

Many herbs in your garden, such as rosemary and thyme, have *antiseptic* properties, meaning they help to prevent infection of cuts and scrapes. Other herbs with at least some antiseptic properties are angelica, calendula, chamomile, and garlic. Some, like calendula, comfrey, ginger, monarda, and yarrow, are *anti-inflammatory* — they reduce redness and swelling. Aloe, basil, chamomile, fennel, oregano, tarragon, thyme, and yarrow contain natural *antihistamines,* which work against the allergic reaction that makes insect bites itch.

Some herbs contain tannins and other substances that have an *astringent* effect (tightening and contracting the skin). Witch hazel is the best known; aloe is another. Other herbs, such as marsh mallow and mullein, are *emollient.* They contain mucilage that expands like a sponge when it gets wet, soothing conditions as varied as chapped skin and hemorrhoids.

Hot peppers, or chilies, may be the most surprising stuff in our gardens. Herbalists usually refer to them as *cayenne,* although the term in cooking and horticulture indicates one particular type of hot pepper or the powder that is made from that pepper.

As much as they burn your mouth (or your eyes, if you're not careful), hot peppers also work against pain in several ways. Hot peppers contain *salicylates,* which are similar to the pain-relieving chemical in aspirin. The *capsaicin* that makes the peppers hot stimulates the body's own pain-quelling endorphins. And finally, hot peppers are one of the herbs known as *rubefacients,* which speed healing by drawing blood to the skin where they're applied.

In Table 13-2, we list these and many other healing substances that can be used externally. You can put any of these substances to work by applying them in one of the following ways.

Poultices

The easiest way to use herbs externally to treat bruises, sprains, cuts, and scrapes — especially in an emergency — is as a *poultice*. Just crush the herb (diehard herbalists would tell you to *macerate* it), moisten it, and apply it to the skin. If your situation is not an emergency, whirl the herb in a blender with a little water or chop it. Simmer it over low heat — with just enough water to cover — for about five minutes and apply. And if you want to go about your business with the poultice in place, cover and tie it with a strip of gauze or other cloth.

Compresses

To make a compress, start with an infusion or decoction. Dip a strip of absorbent cloth in the liquid and apply it to the affected area. For aches and pains, a hot compress feels good. Keep it cold for swelling or a headache. Compresses also feel wonderful on poison ivy and tired eyes.

Oils

Steeping or simmering herbs in oil lets you use them to massage sore muscles or arthritic joints. Because the quantities of herbs used are much larger than with infusions or decoctions, recipes are usually given in terms of weight instead of measuring spoons or cups, so it's handy to have a kitchen scale. The standard proportion is 4-6 ounces of chopped fresh herbs (2 to 3 ounces of dried herbs) for each cup of cooking oil.

Aloe out there

If aloe could be interviewed, it might say it wants to be a doctor and heal the world. Indeed, it could enter the medicinal talent competition in several categories. You've seen it in all kinds of skin-care products, and this is no mere marketing gimmick. Aloe contains an enzyme that reduces swelling and an antihistamine that relieves itching. As an antiseptic, it seems to work against both bacteria and fungi. And it also contains an immune-stimulating substance powerful enough to be studied for use against the HIV virus.

Although aloe is best known for healing burns (including radiation burns from cancer treatment, as well as sunburn and frostbite), scientists aren't sure how it works in this regard. One theory is that it speeds oxygen to the injured area, helping to heal connective tissue.

The greatest thing about aloe is that it's a ready-made poultice: Just pull off a leaf, strip the outer covering, and apply the moist inner gel to your boo-boo. One word of caution: You may see aloe products sold as laxatives, but don't take it internally. Even the commercial preparations can cause painful cramps.

To create a soothing oil, use one of the following methods.

- **Slow 'n' easy method.** This is the best approach if you are using flowers or delicate-leaved plants. Put the herbs and oil in a covered glass container and leave them where they receive as much sun as possible. Try to give them a good shake or vigorous stir at least once a day. At the end of two weeks, strain, reserving the oil; store in a sealed glass jar in the refrigerator for up to six months.

- **Quick ('n' also easy) method.** Combine the oil and herbs in the top of a double boiler and simmer on low heat for two to three hours. Even easier, simmer them in a crock pot — use a candy thermometer to make sure that it's about 100°F — for 12 hours. Cool; strain into a glass jar and store in the refrigerator for up to six months.

Salves

Making herbal salves is more fuss than making oils, but you may like using them better because they're easier to apply. Most recipes call for beeswax, which you can buy in one-ounce, honey-scented cubes at health food stores.

Begin with 1 cup of infusion or decoction (described earlier in this chapter), made double strength, and 1 cup of cooking oil. Combine them in a saucepan over low heat and simmer, stirring constantly, until the water evaporates. You should have about 1 cup of liquid. Melt 1 ounce of beeswax in a double boiler, pour it into the herbal oil, and stir thoroughly. If you want, you can add a drop of oil of benzoin as a preservative and/or a couple drops of essential oil for fragrance (see the "Non-essentials" sidebar). Store in a glass container in the refrigerator for up to six months.

Non-essentials

If you read other books on herbal crafts, cosmetics, and medicines — particularly aromatherapy — you know that many recipes call for *essential oils*. These oils are made in a laboratory through distilling or expressing various parts of the herb plant.

Scented oils vary in quality, and some are made synthetically. If you see a display of different scented oils and all are the same price, it's a clue that they are synthetic. (Some oils are much more difficult to make and, therefore, more expensive.) Synthetic oils are called *fragrance oils*.

Warning: Never use any essential oil internally. A few are extremely toxic, and all of them are highly concentrated and can burn skin. Keep them away from your eyes, nose, mouth, and genitals, and always dilute them before using.

Table 13-2	Common Medicinal Herbs Used Externally	
Herb	**Parts Used**	**Ailment**
Calendula	Flowers	Skin problems
Cayenne	Fruits	Pain
Chamomile	Flowers	Wounds
Garlic	Bulb	Insect bites
Lavender	Aerial parts	Insomnia, burns, pain
Lemon grass	Leaves	Preventing insect bites, treating fungal infections
Marsh mallow	Roots	Wounds
Mustard	Seeds	Pain
Pennyroyal	All parts	Preventing insect bites
Sage	Aerial parts	Body odor
Yarrow	Aerial parts	Wounds

Who ya gonna call? Stress busters!

When Kathy was a cub reporter about a million years ago, she got one of those stock assignments to interview a man on his 100th birthday. She asked the stock question: To what did he owe his longevity? It wasn't his diet, he said, and he had smoked since he was 12. "I don't let anything worry me for long," he said. "Worry'll kill ya, girl."

Today, we all know the toll that stress takes on our health, yet modern life makes it inescapable. So use some of those wonderful herbs you've grown to help alleviate stress. Apply them during the moments of relaxation you owe yourself: during a long bath or while you sleep. Or just breathe in their fragrances when you need a pick-me-up after a long, hectic day.

Stop and smell the roses

Teas made from chamomile, hops, lemon balm, passionflower, and valerian are well known as herbal tranquilizers. But a whole school of thought exists that says herbs can affect our moods just by our smelling them — an approach called *aromatherapy*. While the body of scientific research supporting herbal medicines is still sparse, even less information is available on aromatherapy.

Advocates of aromatherapy explain the phenomenon by observing that odors stimulate olfactory nerves (pathways for our sense of smell), which in turn trigger the release of different chemicals in our brains. We also have what are called *learned odor responses,* which cause us to have emotional reactions to the aroma of lilacs or cinnamon buns. Whatever the explanation, most of us would agree that the scent of certain herbs is relaxing (lavender) or exhilarating (rosemary).

Essential oils (see the sidebar "Non-essentials" earlier in this chapter), which you can't make at home with your garden-grown herbs, have the most concentrated fragrances. But you can still get a therapeutic kick from the fragrance of fresh and dried herbs and from your own herbal preparations.

Aromatherapists put most herbs into broad categories of being either calming (for when you're jittery or worried), uplifting (for when you're blue), or stimulating (for when you're tired or facing a challenge). Some practitioners go so far as to make much more specific recommendations, such as sniffing rose oil when you're in a funk over lost love. If the nose truly knows, here are some of its secrets:

- Basil clears the mind and lessens mental weariness.
- Chamomile calms anxiety.
- Clary sage induces euphoria.
- Bee balm lifts depression.
- Lemon balm lifts depression.
- Peppermint stimulates.
- Rose stimulates sexual appetites.

Down the primrose bath

Gardeners know that nothing beats a long, hot soak in the tub after a day of pushing around cartloads of mulch, digging planting holes, or weeding among bugs and briars. You can compound the pleasure by adding the fragrance of herbs. Just put fresh or dried herbs in a muslin bag or a double wrap of cheesecloth and tie it to the bath faucet, letting the hot water flow over it as the tub fills. Good herbs to try (alone or in combination) include comfrey, lavender, lemon verbena, lemongrass, orange mint, rose, rosemary, scented geranium, and sage (which has the double benefit of reducing body odor). Marsh mallow acts as a moisturizer.

Here are a few ideas for other preparations:

- **Bath water.** Make an infusion of fragrant herbs as you would for herbal tea (see Chapter 12). You can make the infusion as strong as you like because you won't be drinking it, but allow at least ¼ cup of herbs for each pint of water. Then add the infusion to your bath water.

✔ **Herbal vinegar.** No, it won't pickle you. Vinegar offsets alkaline water and soaps, helps remove flaky skin, and balances both oily and dry skin. It helps heal acne and is even reputed to lighten freckles.

Make a vinegar infusion as you would a culinary vinegar, using about 1 cup of fresh herbs (½ cup dried herbs) for each 2 cups of vinegar. Start with 2 cups of vinegar infusion in the tub, adding more if you want.

✔ **Bath oil.** Oil is a soothing addition to your bath, especially if you suffer from dry skin. Choose a light, sweet-scented oil such as almond, jojoba, or vitamin E oil, and infuse it with herbs just as you would for culinary use (instructions for making culinary oils are in Chapter 12). Use a couple of tablespoons per bath.

Perchance to dream

Most sleep pillows are based on aromatherapy: You stuff a pillow with a mix of herbs with scents believed to induce sleep (for example, chamomile and violet) or fragrances, such as honeysuckle, jasmine, lavender, lemon balm, and rose, that are reputed to calm frazzled nerves.

Hops is another traditional ingredient in sleep pillows. Some scientific evidence exists for the soporific effect of the female flowers from this vine that is usually connected with making beer. When hops are stored, they oxidize and produce a volatile substance that depresses our central nervous systems when we inhale it. Skeptics say even the biggest pillow can't hold enough hops to deliver more than a couple of effective doses, but you might want to make hops a major ingredient in your herbal pillow mix. (Moisten the hops with some glycerin so they don't crackle and keep you awake.)

A pillow of dried herbs can't compare to goose down for comfort. We recommend making a small herbal pillow to tuck inside a bigger, softer one, or a long bolster to lie alongside.

Getting steamed

Steam is a great way to put herbs to work for respiratory or skin problems. Fill a large bowl with just-boiled water — or fill your bathroom sink with the hottest water possible, lower your face over the steam, and make a tent around it with a bath towel. To clear sinuses, use eucalyptus or peppermint. For cleansing skin — the steam opens pores for follow-up treatment with astringents or emollients — use chamomile or mint.

If you use a bowl, crush a handful of fresh or dried herbs right into the water; if you use the bathroom sink, cleanup is easier if you add a strong infusion of the herb.

I Feel Pretty

Most of us feel our best when we also look our best. For some this means expensive new clothes, a razor cut at the barber shop, or hours spent in front of the mirror with mascara and lip liner. For others it means shiny clean hair and scrubbed skin, topped with a naturally scented body wash. This section describes some natural substances you can use as the basis for all sorts of feel-good cosmetic preparations.

Bewitching hazel

Witch hazel is a wonderful little native tree — its scientific name is *Hamamelis virginiana* — worth including in your ornamental garden for its yellow flowers, which appear in fall and look like Lilliputian streamers. (You also can buy cultivars that bloom in early winter in other shades of yellow, red, or orange.)

The tree's bark and twigs are the source of the pleasant-smelling astringent witch hazel lotion. Today, however, witch hazel lotion is made by distilling the wood with steam, which removes the tannins that give it a powerfully cooling kick.

If you're lucky enough to have a large witch hazel tree, try making your own old-fashioned tincture. Never remove bark all the way around a tree, because that will kill it; instead, remove small pieces from the tree's north side, where its bark tends to be most dense. Use mostly twigs, and add some leaves if you still don't have enough material.

Use 8 tablespoons ground fresh witch hazel bark, twigs, and leaves (4 dried tablespoons) for each cup of vodka. Combine in a glass jar, and set in a cool dark place for one month, shaking the mixture frequently. Strain, discarding the herb material; store as you would any tincture, in a sealed, dark glass container, for up to two years.

Apply the tincture full strength to cuts, scrapes, and bites. To use it cosmetically as a lotion, add a drop or two to ¼ cup water. Witch hazel lotion is especially soothing applied to tired eyelids with cotton pads (you can add some infusion of borage, calendula, or chamomile) or wiped over hot, tired feet.

Comin' up roses

Rose water is another brew for which you'll find numerous uses. You can use it to sweeten herbal vinegars or splash it on your face and neck as a cleanser and coolant. (You can also use it in the kitchen with fruit salads.)

To make "real" rose water, you must first make an *attar,* a fragrant oil, of roses. (It's one of the most expensive essential oils on the market, because it takes several thousand damask roses to produce one ounce of oil.)

Here's an old-fashioned recipe for a similar product that serves as a basis for rose water. You need a glass or ceramic container that you can cover, 2 to 3 cups of rose petals (preferably damask rose petals), and some rock or kosher salt. Starting with a layer of petals, alternate thin layers of salt and petals. Cover the container and set it in a cool, dark place for about a month until you see liquid — this is the attar — in the bottom of the container. Strain the liquid through a cheesecloth and compost the petals. To make rose water, add a few drops of the rose essence to one cup of distilled water.

Scented soaps

An easy way to add the fragrance of herbs from your garden to bath and hand soap is to melt chunks of unscented castile or glycerin soap in a double boiler over low heat. Remove the double boiler from the heat and add 1 cup of an herbal infusion for each 3 ounces of soap. A waxed 1-quart paper milk carton makes a great mold, because you can slice it up for several "bars."

Herbal hair day

You can use herbs to give your tresses more shine and color, to correct oily or dry hair, and even to combat dandruff. To darken graying locks, use sage. For better color highlights, as they say in salons, these are the standard recommendations:

- ✔ **Blonde.** Use chamomile.
- ✔ **Brunette.** Use rosemary.
- ✔ **Red.** Use calendula.

Here are some common herbs to help problem hair. You can mix and match with the list above. Is your hair blonde and dry? Use both chamomile and marsh mallow.

- ✔ **Oily hair.** Use yarrow.
- ✔ **Dry hair.** Use marsh mallow.
- ✔ **Dull or limp hair.** Use rosemary.
- ✔ **Dandruff.** Use burdock or comfrey.

The easiest approach to using herbs for hair care is to add them to commercial products.

- ✔ **To make an herbal shampoo.** Fill a glass jar with the herbs of your choice and cover with baby shampoo. Infuse for a week and strain before using.

- ✔ **To make an herbal rinse.** Begin with apple cider vinegar, which is a folk treatment for dandruff. (Vinegar also works wonders with oily hair and helps remove soap.) Steep the herbs in vinegar, just as you would for culinary use (see Chapter 12), and then strain the vinegar into a bottle.

- ✔ **To make an herbal conditioner.** The Chinese believe that safflower and sesame dilate vessels in the scalp and help prevent hair loss. You can use either of these cooking oils as the base for an herbal conditioner. Prepare it as you would a culinary oil (see Chapter 12), and then strain the mixture, discarding the herbs. You can massage it into the scalp, which also stimulates blood circulation, or treat dryness and split ends by combing it through your hair and wrapping your head with hot towels for about 15 minutes — a great excuse to put your feet up and relax.

Kiss a little longer

A number of herbs are known for their prowess in sweetening breath and improving oral hygiene. Among those you can grow in your home garden are coriander, dill, and parsley, which sweeten breath because they're rich in chlorophyll — that stuff that makes them green. You can just chew on a leaf or two if you like. You can also make an herbal mouthwash by steeping 1 tablespoon each of dried peppermint and sage, plus 1 teaspoon cardamom seeds, per 1 cup of vodka. Dilute the vodka with water before you gargle.

For Hearth and Home

You can put the power of herbs to work around the house. Not only do they smell better than last night's fish and whatever the cat dragged in, but they smell better than most of the air fresheners on the market.

The *strewing herbs* that medieval housekeepers spread on their floors served to repel bugs and vermin as well as mask odors. Insects (unlike humans) find many of them absolutely repugnant. If all that weren't enough, antiseptic herbs, such as rosemary, thyme, and sage, help sanitize whatever you spread them on.

Keep it clean

Instead of buying a heavily scented, "new and improved" (synonyms for expensive) cleaning product, why not use the scent and germ-clobbering capabilities of herbs around your house? We encourage you to experiment, but here are some ideas to get you started.

- **Glass and other surfaces.** Pick your dirt poison. Vinegar is wonderful for cleaning glass. Murphy's Oil Soap is about the only stuff that cleans the fingerprints off telephone and television surfaces (not the screen!). Infuse vinegar with one of the antiseptic herbs, or mix 1 to 3 teaspoons of Murphy's Oil Soap in about four cups of a strong herb infusion. Both can be used on painted wood, ceramic and vinyl tile, and plastic.

- **Carpets.** Sprinkle crushed dried herbs under the rug, where they also deter fleas. Or dump a handful of dried herbs on the rug and sweep them into your vacuum bag, where they'll whoosh out a pleasant fragrance as you clean. (Do it again when you change your bag.)

  If your carpet is already smelling a bit, uh, funky, mix a box of baking soda with a cup each of lavender and pennyroyal and a tablespoon of crushed coriander seeds. Spread the mixture over your carpet, leave overnight, and vacuum it up in the morning.

- **Laundry.** Make an infusion of your favorite herb and add it to the last cycle of your wash. The floral scents of rose or lavender are especially nice.

TIP

Getting in a lather

Plants in the carnation family contain a substance called *saponin* that lathers when wet. None of them is more famous for this quirk than the appropriately named soapwort *(Saponaria officinalis)*. Sometimes called bouncing Bet, soapwort is a native of Europe but has made herself at home in the East and Midwest.

Still, it's a pretty thing. Two feet tall, it has pink, red, or white fragrant flowers with five notched petals. With a little pinching back, you can keep it blooming from summer through fall. It grows in USDA Zones 3 to 9; don't give it rich soil or it flops over. Nurseries usually sell the double-flowered form, *'Rosa Plena'*.

If you've inherited or planted a patch of Bet, try whipping up some suds with some crushed root or chopped stems. (If the stems are dry, soak them overnight first.) Use about ½ cup of fresh herb for each 3 cups of water. Add the stems to boiling water. Reduce heat and simmer, covered, for about 20 minutes.

The gentle cleanser that results is recommended for upholstery, carpets, clothing, and tapestries. (Test it first in an inconspicuous place.) Apply with a sponge or soft brush, and then rinse with cool water.

Getting the bugs out

Just as you can enlist herbs to fight garden pests (see Chapter 9), you can use them outdoors to keep chiggers and fleas from chomping on you and your pets and indoors to keep critters out of your pantry.

Some of the best anti-insect herbs are the artemisias, mints, pennyroyal, and tansy. As a moth repellant in the sweater drawer, lavender is the classic, in no small part because of its clean fragrance. You can also try costmary, rosemary, rue, and santolina. Wormwood is said to be an especially good addition for repelling silverfish.

Here are a few sample formulas:

- ✔ **Moths.** In the section called "Herbs to Dry For," we talk about potpourris and sachets intended only for fragrance.You can make a sachet with any combination of the herbs just mentioned for protection from moths in a closet (or silverfish in the study). Put the herbs in small muslin bags, which you can buy for making tea, or tie them in a man's handkerchief.

- ✔ **Ants.** Crush or grind dried tansy or wormwood, mix it with a little cream of tartar, and sprinkle it under your sink. Or make a spray with 2 tablespoons of dried, crushed red pepper in 6 drops of dishwashing liquid added to a gallon of water. Spritz it around drainpipes and other potential entry points.

- ✔ **Fleas.** In addition to pennyroyal and the artemisias, eucalyptus and lemon verbena may help deter fleas.

  For a pet powder, mix 2 cups of diatomaceous earth (which you may already have on hand to prevent slugs in the garden — if not, it's available at garden centers or from mail-order suppliers) with ¼ cup of any or several of the herbs just listed, dried and crumbled.

  For a post-bath flea dip, make an infusion of ¼ cup pennyroyal in 3 cups of water, and add a cup of vinegar to make Fido's coat shiny.

  To keep fleas out of your pet's bed, stuff it with a mix of cedar chips and dried, crushed pennyroyal.

- ✔ **Biting bugs.** In a pinch, you can get some protection from mosquitoes and other stinging insects by just snatching up a handful of fresh herbs and rubbing them on your skin. A native herb called mountain mint (*Pycnanthemum muticum*) is especially good. Or try some lemongrass, which is related to the plant from which we get citronella essential oil, the fragrance used in commercial bug candles and other bug-defense products. Basil, too, is said to have some repellant properties.

  Even better than rubbing fresh herbs on your arms and legs is adding an infusion of the herbs to sweet almond oil or witch hazel. You can rub on the oil or use a recycled pump spray bottle and spray the mix on your skin and clothes.

In Part IV, we go into more detail about pennyroyal, but this is a good place to say that while it may be the crown prince of insect-repelling herbs, if you buy it as an essential oil, it is one of the most toxic herbs. Just a few drops can be lethal if you should accidentally take it internally. You should also avoid using it — and mountain mint — in any form, even externally, if you are pregnant.

Herbs to Dry For

Now that you're in peak health, you're looking great, and your house is so clean you can eat off the floor, how about some projects purely for sensual pleasure? We're talking about potpourris and sachets for your nose and dried arrangements and wreaths to please the eye.

These make scents

The great thing about potpourri is that it's quick and easy to make, and you don't have to follow many rules. We aren't going to tell you what herbs are good for potpourri, because almost all of them are. Your nose knows. Mix together small portions of herbs until you get a combination you like.

In addition to herbs, here are a few other things you probably want to include in a potpourri:

✔ **Fixative.** A fixative is a substance that helps pull all the separate aromas together and keep the less robust ones from fading out.

The most commonly used fixative is orrisroot. You can find it in craft stores, but you can also grow it in your garden: It's the rhizome of the Florentine iris (*I. germanica var. florentina*). The flowers are white with touches of purple or blue. As with most roots, you harvest them in the fall of their second year.

Chop the roots immediately because they quickly turn into botanical rocks. In craft stores, you find orris in powdered form, but you can grind your harvest in a coffee grinder if you don't let it harden completely. Standard recipes call for using anywhere between a tablespoon per cup to a tablespoon per quart of dried herbs and spices. Some folks may be allergic to orrisroot and should not handle it.

✔ **Un-garden ingredients.** In addition to the herbs listed in Part IV of this book, countless potential potpourri participants can be found by raiding your spice rack, the nearest woods, or a craft store.

For fragrance, try citrus peel, cinnamon and cloves, cedar and sandalwood, frankincense and myrrh, pinecones or pine needles, and vanilla beans.

For texture and color, consider ever-lasting flowers such as gomphrena or statice, dried lichens or moss, and berries like those of juniper (blue), bittersweet and pyracantha (orange), holly or nandina (red).

✔ **Essential oils.** These oils strengthen and complement the ingredients in your potpourri without overwhelming them. As little as one drop per cup of dried materials is enough. Once you have a theme — floral, citrus, woodsy — you can find an oil to match.

Anything goes when making a potpourri. Still, most experienced potpourri producers choose herbs that have similar fragrances — for instance, sweet or citruslike. Here are a few combinations to get you started, but don't stop with these suggestions.

✔ **For a bedroom.** Sweet flowers, such as carnations, catmint, lavender, and rose. The rose is reputed to be an aphrodisiac (early Christians kept it out of churches because of its ribald reputation). You might throw in a teaspoon of another aphrodisiac, cardamom, for good measure.

✔ **For a bathroom.** Lemon herbs — such as lemon verbena, lemon geranium, lemon balm, and lemon grass — mixed with orange peel, mint, and cinnamon.

✔ **For a kitchen.** Culinary herbs, such as bay, rosemary, sage, and thyme, plus a pinch of crushed cloves.

✔ **For a study.** Woodland scents, such as pine, juniper, and bayberry. Add basil, mint, or rosemary — all believed to sharpen mental acuity.

Shakin' it up

You can make potpourri two ways: the old-fashioned wet method and the slightly lazier dry method. We offer a quick run-through on the wet method, which is said to yield a stew of dried herbs that remain fragrant for half a century. We note, however, that Kathy made some dry potpourri with her son, now a strapping high school athlete, back in his preteen years. She found it in a tin on a shelf while cleaning recently — still as fragrant as ever.

✔ **The wet way.** You need noniodized salt; a fixative, such as orris root; essential oils; and either brandy or an alcohol-based perfume. Don't let your herbs dry out completely; they should be slightly limp, not crisp.

Mix ½ cup salt with ½ cup of fragrant spices (cinnamon, bay, cloves, cardamom). In a separate bowl, mix 3 cups fragrant herbs with one tablespoon orris root. In a large crock, make a layer of herbs and top with a layer of the spiced salt. Continue layering, ending with a salt layer. Pour the brandy or perfume over the layers and weigh down with a plate. You should stir daily for a month, then transfer to permanent containers.

✔ **The dry way.** You need 2 quarts of dry, fragrant herbs; 6 to 8 table-spoons of spices (such as crushed cinnamon sticks, cardamon seeds, all-spice, or whole cloves); 2 to 4 tablespoons of orris root; and 20 drops of one or several essential oils. In a ceramic container, combine the herbs and orris root. Add the spices and toss gently, then add the essential oils. Cover tightly and give the container a shake every few days for four to six weeks, then transfer to a permanent container.

Most people keep potpourri in a container with a lid, opening it when they need an olfactory lift, the dog has an accident, or company comes. If you have an endless supply of herbs, you can leave potpourri in an open con-tainer, then pitch it onto the compost pile when it loses fragrance.

Sassy sachets

A sachet is simply potpourri in a bag. (Some people grind or crush the ingre-dients to make the sachet lay flat.) Earlier in the chapter, we describe making a sachet to repel insects. You also can make a sachet just for its pleasant aroma, although lavender — grandma's favorite — repels moths while it per-fumes the surroundings.

Your sachet can be as pretty as you please, with appliques and lace. Sachets are a great way to use antique handkerchiefs, as long as the fabric is heavy enough for the coarser herbs. Just tie the top with a ribbon. Make a loop with the ribbon and hang it in a closet or garment bag, or tuck it in a drawer.

For the eyes alone

If you're like us, you like gazing at your herbs even when you can't scratch and sniff them. You can add them to fresh arrangements throughout the growing season, of course, and you can also dry them to enjoy almost indefi-nitely in a vase, a basket, or a wreath for the wall, door, or tabletop.

You only need a container to hold herbs, fresh or dried, but making arrange-ments is a whole lot easier if you have some of the following items, all of which are widely available from florists' shops.

✔ **Foam blocks.** You can put blocks of white Styrofoam or a finer textured green foam called *oasis* in the bottom of a vase to help hold stems upright for arrangements. You can also buy circles of foam to serve as the base of a wreath.

✔ **Floral picks.** These are little wooden stakes attached to a length of wire. You wrap the wire around weak plant stems — or several very fine stems — and stick the sharp bottom end of the pick in your foam block.

✔ **Floral wire.** You can buy different thicknesses (gauges) of wire in vari-ous lengths or on a spool. Use it to strengthen stems, wire stems together, or shape wreaths.

- **Floral tape.** This tape comes in browns and greens and lets you wrap stems together or fasten stems to wires.

- **Floral pins.** These look like old-fashioned hairpins and help you fasten dry material to a wreath base.

A nice arrangement

We're not about to dictate which herbs to use in arrangements. Beauty *is* in the eye of the beholder. Still, we can't resist offering a few tips.

- **Keep stems long.** When picking flowers, seedheads, or foliage, keep stems as long as possible. You can always shorten them, but you need the extra length for a tall vase. You can also make informal wreaths for tabletops simply by braiding stems together.

- **Use wire and tape.** Spiral florist wire around weak stems to make them to stand upright or around short stems to lengthen them. You can stick wire directly into the base of dense flowers, such as calendulas and roses, and dispense with their stems. If necessary, use tape to hide the wire.

- **Hide the foam.** If you use a clear or shallow container for your arrangement — or no container at all — you can conceal the floral block or oasis with sphagnum moss.

- **Preserve your work.** Keep dried arrangements out of direct sunlight so colors don't fade. Hair spray makes the dried materials tougher.

Wreaths

You can buy wreath frames (made either of foam or wire) at craft and florist shops — they're easy to use and inexpensive — but if you want to make your own, try these ideas:

- **Chicken wire.** Make a roll of chicken wire — the same stuff you used to fence in your herb or vegetable garden. Then bend it into a circle and use the wire ends to secure the shape. Fill the wire frame with sphagnum moss, which gives you additional material in which to secure the stems of your herbs.

- **Straw.** What about a frame made of fresh straw? This isn't the straw that comes in bales, but long stalks. Gather together enough to make the wreath the thickness you want, and then form it into a circle, securing it every few inches with floral wire.

To attach herbs to the wreath, first create small bunches of herbs (securing them with floral wire). Starting with the inner part of the wreath, attach the herbs with floral pins, being careful not to cover the center hole. Once you've made your way around the inner part of the wreath, attach a circle of herbs around the outside. Last, fill in between the two rows.

Cut and dried

In Chapter 12 we offer you tips for harvesting and drying herbs, including some special instructions for drying herbs to be used in decorations. Table 13-3 shows a few of our favorite candidates for dried arrangements.

Table 13-3	Good Candidates for Dried Arrangements	
Flowering Plants	*Foliage Plants*	*Seedheads*
Artemisia	Artemisia	Dill
Basil	Bay	Epazote
Borage	Dill	Fennel
Calendula	Fennel	Rose hips
Catnip	Geranium	Rue
Chive	Germander	
Horehound	Rosemary	
Monarda	Rue	
Mullein	Santolina	
Oregano	Wormwood	
Tansy		
Yarrow		

Herbs to Dye For

Until about 150 years ago, we all would have been the man (or woman) in the gray flannel suit if it hadn't been for plants. That's when we discovered that we could dye our clothes with aniline dyes, colors made with (hey, we're only quoting Webster here) "an oily liquid poisonous amine."

If that description makes you want to run back to the pure dyes used by our ancestors, be advised that dyeing with herbs and other plants employs pre-treatment with a *mordant* that is sometimes a poisonous metal, such as chrome.

Today, the most commonly used — and far safer — mordant is alum. Wool is the easiest material for amateurs to dye, but you must scour the wool before you can dye it. It's not a one-step process, as you can see, and you need to consult a book on dying for all the ins and outs. A standard reference is *Colors from Nature: Growing, Collecting & Using Natural Dyes,* by Bobbi A. McRae.

Table 13-4 presents a short list of dye plants and the colors they render when using alum as a mordant.

Table 13-4	Plants to Dye With	
Plant	*Parts Used*	*Color Rendered (Using Alum)*
Bayberry	Leaves	Yellow
Betony	All parts	Chartreuse
Catnip	Fall leaves	Yellow
Chamomile	Flowers	Yellow
Dandelion	Flowers	Yellow
Dandelion	Roots	Orange-brown
Goldenrod	Flowers	Yellow
Lady's bedstraw	Roots	Dull red
Lady's bedstraw	Flowering tops	Yellow
Madder	Roots	Red
Marjoram	Tops	Green
Mullein	Leaves and stalks	Yellow
Parsley	All parts	Yellow-green
Rosemary	Leaves	Yellow-green
Safflower	Flowers	Yellow
Sage	Leaves and stems	Lemon yellow

(continued)

Table 13-4 *(continued)*

Plant	Parts Used	Color Rendered (Using Alum)
Sorrel	All parts	Yellow
Tansy	Young leaves	Yellow-green
Tansy	Flowers	Yellow
Thyme	Fall leaves	Gray-gold
Yarrow	Flowers	Yellow

Part VII
The Part of Tens

"That's a cross between a winter squash and a rutabaga. It's called a winnebaga."

In this part . . .

We've scattered lists throughout this book, but in "The Part of Tens," we offer still more. You'll find shorthand answers to some questions that you probably have, and we present our views on which garden tools and equipment are most useful.

Chapter 14

Ten Often-Asked Questions about Herbs

· ·

*B*etween us, we've been writing about gardening and editing the work of *real* experts for more than 25 years. Despite time served, we don't know all the answers; there's always more to learn. But we do have answers for these ten most often asked questions.

What is an herb?

Everyone has a different response to this question. Cooks say an herb is any plant used to flavor or color food and drink. Botanists define herbs as seed-bearing plants with non-woody stems that die back each year. Gardeners tend to be less technical and more inclusive. Herbs include all plants that are grown for their flavor or scent, or used as medicines or dyes or used in agriculture and industry.

Should I start with seeds or plants?

Buying plants is easier, and it makes sense for a beginning gardener. It, saves you time and gives you a head start with perennial herbs that need to grow at least a year before you can harvest them. Some herbs are extremely slow, difficult, or impossible to grow from seeds (we tell you which ones they are in Part IV). When you're just getting started and want only one or two plants, we recommend you let someone else do the sowing.

We grow a good many herbs from seeds, and we encourage you to try your hand (all the directions are in Chapter 8). Beginning with seeds is interesting and fun, and it gives you a wider group of herbs to choose from. And seeds are less expensive than plants, a consideration if you plan to be the neighborhood pickle franchise and want to set out 200 dill plants.

Are herbs hard to grow?

Absolutely not! As a group, herbs are among the easiest garden plants to grow — and the plants least troubled by diseases and pests. Give herbs the right setting and organically rich soil, keep the weeds at bay, and you won't have any trouble filling your harvest basket.

Do I need a big garden to grow herbs?

An herb garden can be as large as a farmer's field or as small as a 12-inch pot filled with chives. Herbs, in fact, are ideally suited to small yards, even no yards, since you don't need many plants for a harvest — a single aloe, for example, or a 3 x 1-foot window box planted with parsley, basil, marjoram, pot marigold, thyme, and feverfew. Large or small, place your herb garden near living areas, somewhere you can see, use, and enjoy your plants.

Do I need special soil to grow herbs?

You don't need *special* soil, but your herbs will grow better if they're planted in soil that has been amended with large amounts of organic matter, such as shredded leaves, well-rotted manure, or compost. Soil that is organically rich is easy to dig, contains all the nutrients that herbs need to thrive, and retains plenty of moisture at the same time it allows extra water to drain.

When can I plant herbs?

When to plant is an herb-by-herb decision. You can sow some species, such as dill and parsley, before the last frost in spring. Other herbs are easily damaged by the cold; they can't be planted until the ground *and* air have warmed. Don't be in a rush: Seeds are likely to rot and plants' growth to be stunted if you stick them outdoors in very cold weather.

Where can I buy herbs?

Most garden centers and nurseries carry a selection of common herbs, both seeds and plants. However, if you want to grow something a little different or unusual, such *Tanacetum vulgare* 'Silver Lace', a tansy with variegated leaves, you'll have to find a local nursery that specializes in herbs or shop by mail. There are dozens of fine companies ready to fill your order. We list some of our favorites in the Appendix.

How much should I plant?

That's a tricky one, as the answer depends on which herb you're growing and how you plan to use it. If you know you make pesto three nights a week, you'll need a 6-foot row of basil. Or if you're growing sweet Annie to make dried bouquets for all your friends, you'll need several plants. One plant may be enough for herbs you use in small amounts, such as sage or tarragon.

Seed catalogs and packets sometimes recommend how many plants the average gardener should plant. We suggest you start small — begin with one or two plants of each herb. If you need more, there's always a next year in the garden.

What's the best way to preserve herbs?

The *best* way for almost all herbs, hands down, is by drying. There are a variety of techniques — air drying, oven-drying, microwave-drying, and more. Directions are in Chapter 12.

Where can I see herb gardens?

Visiting someone else's garden is a terrific way to learn. You'll see plants you'll just *have* to have, and designs and combinations that you'll want to borrow and adapt. (You may want to take a look at *The Garden Tourist,* an annual guide to 400 North American gardens and nearly 1,000 garden "events;" written by Lois Rosenfeld, it's published by The Garden Tourist Press.)

Chapter 15

Ten (Times Two) Great Herb Gardening Tools

Faced with so much good-looking equipment, it's impossible not to be convinced that you need one of everything. Take the advice of two middle-aged gardeners who together own a barnful of tools that do nothing but gather dust: Be timid. Start slow. Begin by purchasing just the basic tools for digging, raking, cultivating, and carrying. Growing herbs and other plants quickly becomes an addiction — a lifelong passion. You're going to have plenty of time to enlarge your tool collection!

✔ **Shovels, spades, and forks.** Digging gives you three choices — shovel, spade, garden fork — and eventually you'll want one of each. A *shovel* is made for digging, scooping up and moving dirt, compost, and other materials. *Spades* have a straight bottom edge and are good for removing sod, cutting through roots, trenching, and edging; they're less useful for digging, especially in heavy or rocky soil. A *garden fork,* which is a shovel with tines, is the best tool for turning and aerating the soil. You'll also want a *trowel,* a short-handled tool for digging transplant holes in the garden and working in containers of all kinds.

✔ **Rakes.** A *garden rake* is the best tool for leveling and smoothing soil; removing stones and debris; covering seeds; and mixing in lime, compost, and other soil amendments. Stay away from rakes with extremely wide heads (also called *grading* or *contractor's* rakes); instead, pick a model with a head — fitted with 14 to 16 curved teeth — measuring between 14 and 16 inches wide.

✔ **Hoes.** The *common, or garden, hoe* is the first hoe to buy. Its broad, flat head, or blade, is attached to a long handle at an angle. It's also known as a draw hoe, because of the way it's used — by drawing it toward yourself. The *tined hoe,* which has a head consisting of four curved tines, is perfect for aerating the soil and for dislodging shallow-rooted weeds. The *oscillating hoe* is the third hoe that belongs in the well-tempered tool shed (or the corner of your garage). Its head is shaped like the stirrup on a saddle and sharpened on both sides so that it slices as you pull and push it along the soil surface. It's made for weeding, not cultivating.

✔ **Equipment for carrying.** To get things to and from the garden, you need a vehicle for carrying big loads. A kid's little red wagon will work if you're desperate and your kids are willing to share, but *garden carts* and *wheelbarrows* are better choices.

✔ **Watering equipment.** If your herb garden is tiny — or if you're growing herbs on a small patio, deck, or rooftop — a *watering can* is what you need to keep the soil moist. Polyethylene models are lighter and longer lasting than galvanized steel; make sure the sprinkling nozzle, or rose, can be removed for cleaning. For bigger and more distant jobs, buy a high-quality, reinforced vinyl *hose* (with a psi, or pounds-per-square-inch, rating of 500). Be sure the couplings, the attaching part at each end, are made of brass, and don't forget to buy a spray nozzle.

✔ **Tools for cutting.** A *pocketknife* is an essential garden tool. Any simple type will do, something with a 2- to 3-inch carbon-steel blade. A pair of *garden scissors* or lightweight *florist shears* for cutting herbs is also useful. (Believe us when we say that household scissors don't last if used outdoors.) For herbs with tough stems, such as roses, you'll need a pair of bypass *pruning shears*.

✔ **Labels.** You'll be able to tell basil from dill, but will you remember that it was 'Green Ruffles' basil or 'Hercules' dill? Answer: You won't. *Plant labels* are required reading if you're to know what you liked and what didn't pan out. Wood markers are unobtrusive but impermanent; plastic is long-lasting but eye-jarring. For either, you need an indelible garden pen or pencil. For perennial herbs, look into aluminum, zinc, or copper markers, which will probably last longer than the plant does.

✔ **Equipment for measuring.** An *outdoor thermometer* will tell you when it's okay to move your pot marigold seedlings outdoors and when it's necessary to bring the rosemary in. Maximum/minimum thermometers are worth the extra money because they let you to see (and record) each day's high and low temperatures. (Better still, purchase a small *weather station* to keep track of all the weather conditions in your garden.)

To know when it's safe to sow seeds or transplant seedlings, you need to know the soil's temperature as well as the air's. A *soil thermometer* removes the guess work. It looks like a meat thermometer: a long metal spike with a small dial at the top. For measuring rows (and keeping them straight), have a *ball of twine* and a couple of *short stakes* handy.

Buy a sturdy *notebook* and measure your successes and failures by keeping records. Write down when you planted what; what did well and what didn't; which plants you like next to each other and things that didn't combine well. Record the weather — rainfall, temperatures, frost dates — and what you learned, what you liked and what you disliked. Making garden mistakes is inevitable. Making them over and over again is unnecessary.

Appendix

Additional Resources

· ·

As if what we presented in this book wasn't enough, we dare to offer you more sources of information and products. We give you contact info for seed companies, nurseries, and garden-equipment suppliers. We also specify our favorite books, periodicals, organizations, and Web sites.

Mail-Order Seed Companies and Nurseries

These mail-order companies have large selections of either herb seeds or plants — or both (and we've also thrown in a couple of nurseries that sell old-fashioned roses). Each firm publishes a catalog or lists that you can request. (Some companies charge a small fee, which is usually refundable with an order.)

Abundant Life Seed Foundation
P.O. Box 772
Port Townsend, WA 98368
360-385-5660
Open-pollinated and heirloom seeds

Al's Farm
Box 1282
Crystal Beach, TX 77650
(fax) 409-684-8201
Seeds

Antique Rose Emporium
93000 Lueckemeyer Road
Brenham, TX 77833
409-836-9051
mishoup@phoenix.net
Roses

Bountiful Gardens
8001 Shafer Ranch Road
Willits, CA 95490-9626
707-459-6410
countrylife.net/ecoaction
Untreated seeds

Chiltern Seeds
Bortree Stile, Ulverston
Cumbria England LA12 7PB
01229 581137/586946
Seeds

The Cook's Garden
P.O. Box 535
Londonderry, VT 05148
800-457-9703
www.cooksgarden.com
Seeds for culinary herbs

Dabney Herbs
Box 22061
Louisville, KY 40252
502-893-5198
www.dabneyherbs.com
Plants

Dam, William, Seeds
Box 8400
Dundas, Ontario L9H 6M1, Canada
905-628-6641
willdam@sympatico.ca
Seeds and plants, especially for
short-season climates

DeGiorgi Seed Company
6011 'N' Street Omaha, NE 68117-1634
402-731-3901
Seeds

Edgewood Farm & Nursery
Route 2, Box 303
Stanardsville, VA 22973
804-985-3782
Plants

Elixir Farm Botanicals LLC
Brixey, MO 65618
417-261-2393
efb@aristotle.net
www.elixirfarm.com
Seeds, traditional Chinese medicinals

Filaree Farm
182 Conconully Hwy.
Okanogan WA 98840
509-422-6940
Garlic

The Flower and Herb Exchange
Seed Savers Exchange
3076 North Winn road
Decorah, IA 52101
319-382-5990
Heirloom and open-pollinated seeds,
non-profit organizations

Flowery Branch Seed Company
P.O. Box 1330
Flowery Branch, GA 30542
770-536-8380
www.flowerybranch.com
Seeds

The Fragrant Path
P.O. Box 328
Fort Calhoun, NE 68023
Seeds of fragrant flowers and herbs

Goodwin Creek Gardens
P.O. Box 83
Williams, OR 97544
541-846-7357
Seeds and plants, specializing in
everlastings

Gourmet Gardener
8650 College Blvd.
Overland Park, KS 66210-1806
913-345-0490
www.gourmetgardener.com
Seeds of culinary herbs

Heirloom Old Garden Roses
24062 NE Riverside Drive
St. Paul, OR 97137
louise@heirloomroses.com
www.heirloomroses.com
Roses

Horizon Herbs
P.O. Box 69
Williams, OR 97544
541-846-6704
Seeds of medicinals

Johnny's Selected Seeds
1 Foss Hill Road
Albion, ME 04910-9731
207-437-4395
homegarden@johnnyseeds.com
www.johnnyseeds.com
Seeds

Logee's Greenhouses
141 North St.
Danielson CT 06239-1939
860-774-8038
Plants, especially tender species

Merry Gardens
P.O. Box 595
Camden, ME 04843
207-236-9064
Plants

Native Seeds/Search
926 N. 4th Avenue
Tucson, AZ 85705
520-622-5561
nss@azstarnet.com
www.nativeseeds.org
Seeds of southwestern native plants

Nichols Garden Nursery
1190 No. Pacific Hwy.
Albany, OR 97321-4580
541-928-9280
nichols@gardennursery.com
www.gardennursery.com
Seeds and plants

The Pepper Gal
P.O. Box 23006
Fort Lauderdale, FL 33307
954-537-5540
Seeds of hot peppers

Perennial Pleasures Nursery
63 Brickhouse Road, P.O. Box 147
East Hardwick, VT 05836
802-472-5104
www.kingcon.com/hyssop/
index.htm
Seeds and plants, especially heirlooms

Pinetree Garden Seeds
Box 300
New Gloucester, ME 04260
207-926-3400
superseeds@worldnet.att.net
www.superseeds.com
Seeds (sells small packets)

Rasland Farm
N.C. 82 at U.S. 13
Godwin, NC 28344
919-567-2705
Plants

Redwood City Seeds
P.O. Box 361
Redwood City CA 94064
415-325-7333
Open-pollinated and heirloom seeds

Richters Herb Company
Goodwood, Ontario L0C 1A0, Canada
905-640-6677
orderdesk@richters.com
www.richters.com
Large invetory of seeds and plants

Royall River Roses
323 Pine Point Road
Scarborough, ME 04074
800-820-5830
Roses

Sandy Mush Herb Nursery
316 Surrett Cove Road
Leicester, NC 28748
828-683-2014
sandymushherbs@mindspring.com
Large inventory of seeds and plants

Seeds of Change
P.O. Box 15700
Santa Fe, NM 87506-5700
888-762-7333
gardener@seedsofchange.com
www.seedsofchange.com
Open-pollinated, organic seeds

Seeds Trust-High Altitude Gardens
P.O. Box 1048
Hailey, ID 83333
208-788-4363
higarden@micron.net
Seeds for cold-climate, short-season
regions

Shady Acres Herb Farm
7815 Highway 212
Chaska, MN 55318
612-466-3391
herbs@shadyacres.com
www.shadyacres.com
Large selection of plants

Shepherd's Garden Seeds
30 Irene Street
Torrington, CT 06790
860-482-3638
garden@shepherdseeds.com
www.shepherdseeds.com
Seeds of culinary herbs

Sleepy Hollow Herb Farm
568 Jack Black Road
Lancaster, KY 40444
606-792-6183
Organically grown plants

Southern Exposure Seed Exchange
P.O. Box 170
Earlysville VA 22936
804-973-4703
sese@comet.net
Heirloom and OP seeds, especially
for southern gardens

Sunnyboy Gardens Inc.
3314 Earlysville Road
Earlysville, VA 22936
804-974-7350
sunnyboy@mindspring.com
www.sunnyboygardens.com
Plants

Sunnybrook Farms
9448 Mayfield Rd., P.O. Box 6
Chesterland, OH 44026
440-729-7232
Large inventory of plants

The Thyme Garden
20546-N Alsea Hwy.
Aslea OR 97324
541-487-8671
Seeds and plants

Underwood Gardens, Ltd.
4N381 Maple Avenue
Bensenville, IL 60106
Fax 888-382-7041
www.grandmasgarden.com
Seeds, especially heirlooms

Well-Sweep Herb Farm
205 Mt. Bethel Rd.
Port Murray, NJ 07865
908-852-5390
Large inventory of seeds and plants

Wrenwood of Berkeley Springs
Route 4, Box 8055
Berkeley Springs, WV 25411
304-258-3071
wrenwood@intrepid.net
www.wrenwood.com
Large selection of plants

Garden Equipment and Supplies

If you don't live near a good garden center or if your hardware store's inventory of things horticultural is small, contact one of these mail-order firms for what you need. Most state Cooperative Extension Services do soil testing for home gardeners. (Check in the telephone directory for the number of the office closest to you.)

American Weather Enterprises
P.O. Box 1383
Media, PA 19063
800-293-2555
www.americanweather.com
Weather stations and vanes

Bozeman Biotech
Box 3146
Bozeman, MT 59772
800-289-6656
ewayne@pop.mcn.net
Organic supplies

Cook's Consulting
RD 2, Box 13
Lowville, NY 13367
315-376-3002
Soil testing

Earlee, Inc.
2002 Highway 62, P.O. Box 4480
Jeffersonville, IN 47131
812-282-9134
Organic supplies

Gardener's Supply Company
128 Intervale Road
Burlington, VT 05401
800-863-1700
info@gardeners.com
www.gardeners.com
Tools, equipment, and supplies

Gardens Alive!
5100 Schenley Place
Lawrenceburg, IN 47025
812-537-8650
gardener@gardens-alive.com
Organic pest controls and supplies

Gempler's
100 Countryside Drive, Box 270
Belleville, WI 53508
800-382-8473
www.gemplers.com
Tools and equipment

Harmony Farm Supply
P.O. Box 460
Graton, CA 95444
707-823-9125
www.harmonyfarm.com
Tools, equipment, and supplies

IPM Labs
Box 300
Locke, NY 13092
315-497-2063
Beneficial insects

A.M. Leonard, Inc.
241 Fox Drive
Piqua, OH 45356
800-543-8955
Tools and equipment

The Natural Gardening Company
217 San Anselmo Avenue
San Anselmo, CA 94960
707-456-5060
Organic garden supplies

Nature's Control
P.O. Box 35
Medford, OR 97501
541-899-8318
bugsnc@teleport.com
Natural pest controls and supplies

Peaceful Valley Farm Supply
P.O. Box 2209
Grass Valley, CA 95945
916-272-4769
www.groworganic.com
Tools and organic supplies

Smith & Hawken
2 Arbor Lane, P.O. Box 6900
Florence, KY 41022
800-776-3336
www.vgmarketplace.com
Tools, clothing, ornaments

Sources for More Information

The amount of information about growing and using herbs is staggering. Here are our favorite places to go — magazines, organizations, and other resources — to find out more about herbs.

Periodicals

General gardening periodicals often contain articles about herbs, but these are some of the titles that deal specifically with herbs.

- *Back in Thyme,* P.O. Box 963, Tonganoxie, KS 66086; backnthyme@aol.com; bimonthly newsletter (heirloom flowers and herbs)

- *The Herb Companion,* 201 East Fourth Street, Loveland, CO 80537; hc@iwp.ccmail.compuserve.com; bimonthly national magazine

- *HerbalGram* (see Herb Research Foundation under "Organizations" in this appendix; quarterly publication on medicinal herbs

- *The Herb Quarterly,* P.O. Box 689, San Anselmo, CA 94979; herbquart@aol.com; quarterly national magazine

- *Kitchen Gardener,* 63 South Main Street, P.O. Box 5507, Newtown, CT - 06470; www.taunton.com/kg; bimonthly national magazine

- *Southwest Herbs,* 200 Highline Trail, Crest, CA 92021; bimonthly newsletter for southwest gardeners

- *The Country Shepherd Herb News,* Route 1, Box 107, Comer, GA; mfzx30A@prodigy.com; bimonthly newsletter for southeastern herb gardeners

Organizations

We've listed some of the major herb organizations, but there are scores more — everything from local and state herb groups, such as the Herb Society of Central Florida, to professional and scholarly organizations. There are also groups devoted to specific plants, such as the Garlic Seed Foundation. Many publish informative newsletters and sponsor seed exchanges.

A comprehensive list of organizations is maintained by The Herb Growing & Marketing Network, whose contact information is in the following list:

- **American Herb Association,** P.O. Box 1673, Nevada City, CA 95959-1673; www.jps.net/AHherb

✔ **The Bio-Integral Resource Center,** P.O. Box 7414, Berkeley, CA 94707; `www.birc.org` (non-profit organization providing information on least-toxic pest and disease control)

✔ **Canadian Herb Society,** Audrey Ostron, VanDusen Botanical Gardens, 5251 Oak Street, Vancouver, BC V6M 4H1, Canada; `info@herbsociety.ca`

✔ **Herb Growing & Marketing Network,** Maureen Rogers, P.O. Box 245, Silver Spring, PA 17575; `www.herbnet.com`; `www.herbworld.com` (small herb growers and sellers)

✔ **Herb Research Foundation,** 1007 Pearl Street, Suite 200, Boulder, CO 80302; `info@herbs.org`; `www.herbs.org` (medicinal herbs)

✔ **The Herb Society,** Deddington Hill Farm, Warmington, Banbury, OX 171Xb, United Kingdom; `email@herbsociety.co.wk`

✔ **Herb Society of America, Inc.,** 9019 Kirtland Chardon Road, Mentor, OH 44094; `www.herbsociety.org` (major U.S. herb organization)

✔ **Hydroponic Society of America,** P.O. Box 3075, San Ramon, CA 94583; `hsa.hydroponics.org` (soilless gardening)

Web sites

The Web is quickly becoming everyone's favorite indoor garden tool, a connection with hundreds of thousands of sites that feature information about herbs, gardening, garden equpiment, seed and nursery catalogs, seed exchanges, garden associations, and more. We've listed only a handful, a few of the best and most reliable sites we know:

✔ **HerbNet:** `www.herbnet.com`. All things herbal, including scores of links to other herb sites.

✔ **OSU Plant Facts:** `www.hcs.ohio-state.edu/hcs/hcs.html`. A searchable database maintained by the Ohio State University Extension Service. Factsheets from throughout the country about plants and other garden topics.

✔ **GardenNet:** `www.gardennet.com`. One of the oldest garden sites, GardenNet includes forums, book reviews, on-line magazine, links to other sites, shopping.

✔ **The Garden Web:** `www.gardenweb.com`. Forums, articles, resources, links to other sites.

✔ **Integrated Pest Management**: `www.reeusda.gov/ipm`. Information about IPM and non-toxic pest control.

✔ **U.S. Department of Agriculture**: `www.usda.gov`. The front door to the USDA's huge resources.

✔ **National Ocean and Atmospheric Administration:** www.noaa.gov National and local weather records.

✔ **National Gardening Association:** www2.garden.org/nga. This site includes a searchable online library of garden articles.

Many garden sites, such as GardenNet, maintain forums, where you can post questions and/or talk to other gardeners.

For lots of opinions about folk remedies and some of the fascinating lore of herbs, alt.folklore.herbs offers interesting tidbits.

Further reading

Once you begin growing and using herbs, you will want to know more. These are some of the books that we've found most useful:

Brown, Deni. *The Herb Society of America Encyclopedia of Herbs & Their Uses* (Dorling Kindersley, 1995)

Buchanan, Rita. *The Dyer's Garden* (Interweave Press, 1995)

Capon, Brian. *Botany for Gardeners* (Timber Press, 1990)

Clarkson, Rosetta. *Magic Gardens of Herbs and Savory Seeds* (Collier Books, 1939, 1992)

Coleman, Eliot. *The New Organic Grower's Four-Season Harvest* (Chelsea Green Publishing Company, 1992)

DeBaggio, Thomas. *Growing Herbs from Seed, Cutting & Root* (Interweave Press, 1944)

Duke, James. *The Green Pharmacy* (Rodale Press, 1997)

Fisher, Kathleen. *Herbal Remedies* (Rodale, 1999)

Foster, Steven. *Herbal Renaissance: Growing, Using & Understanding Herbs in the Modern World* (Gibbs-Smith, 1993)

Gardner, Jo Ann. *Herbs in Bloom: A Guide to Growing Herbs as Ornamental Plants* (Timber Press, 1998)

Grieve, Mrs. M. *A Modern Herbal* (2 vols., Dover, 1931, 1971)

Hill, Madalene, Gwen Barclay, Jean Hardy. *Southern Herb Growing* (Shearer Publishing, 1987)

Lima, Patrick. *The Harrowsmith Illustrated Book of Herbs* (Camden House, 1986)

MacCaskey, Michael, Bill Marken. *Gardening For Dummies* (2ed, IDG Books, Worldwide, Inc., 1998)

Newdick, Jane. *At Home With Herbs: Inspiring Ideas for Cooking, Crafts, Decorating, and Cosmetics* (Storey Publishing, 1994)

Olkowski, William, Sheila Daar, Helga Olkowski. *The Gardener's Guide to Common-Sense Pest Control* (The Taunton Press, 1995)

Proctor, Rob, David Macke. *Herbs in the Garden: The Art of Intermingling* (Interweave Press, 1997)

Index

• C •

• *N* •

● **Q** ●

● **R** ●

• *V* •